Richard Brandt is one of the most eminent and influential of contemporary moral philosophers. His work has been concerned with how to justify what is good or right not by reliance on intuitions or theories about what moral words mean but by the explanation of moral psychology and the description of what it is to value something, or to think it immoral. His approach thus stands in marked contrast to the influential theories of John Rawls.

The essays reprinted in this collection span a period of almost thirty years and include many classic pieces in metaethical and normative ethical theory. Among the subjects covered are the rational ways to decide what is good and what is right, key topics in utilitarianism, and the extent to which character plays a part in moral blame or legal punishment. A final group of essays explore the application of these ideas to specific moral and social problems: suicide, the rules of war, the treatment of defective newborns, and welfare legislation.

This collection is aimed at both those moral philosophers familiar with Brandt's work, who will find the volume especially helpful in teaching advanced courses in ethics, and those philosophers who may be largely unfamiliar with his work. The latter group will be struck by the lucid, unpretentious style and the cumulative weight of Brandt's contributions to topics that remain at the forefront of moral philosophy.

Morality, utilitarianism, and rights

Morality, utilitarianism, and rights

RICHARD B. BRANDT
Professor of Philosophy (Emeritus), University of Michigan

CAMBRIDGE
UNIVERSITY PRESS

Published by the Press Syndicate of the University of Cambridge
The Pitt Building, Trumpington Street, Cambridge CB2 1RP
40 West 20th Street, New York, NY 10011–4211, USA
10 Stamford Road, Oakleigh, Victoria 3166, Australia

© Cambridge University Press 1992

First published 1992

Printed in the United States of America

Library of Congress Cataloging-in-Publication Data
Brandt, Richard B.
Morality, utilitarianism, and rights / Richard B. Brandt.
p.   cm.
Includes bibliographical references and index.
ISBN 0-521-41507-1. – ISBN 0-521-42527-1 (pbk.)
1. Ethics.   2. Social ethics.   3. Utilitarianism.   I. Title.
BJ1012.B625   1992
171'.5 – dc20   91–37196
                                                                CIP

A catalog record for this book is available from the British Library.

ISBN 0-521-41507-1 hardback
ISBN 0-521-42527-1 paperback

Contents

v

CONTENTS

Sources

Chapter 2, "Moral Philosophy and the Analysis of Language," originally appeared as a Lindley Lecture at the Department of Philosophy, University of Kansas. It was published in 1976 in John Bricke (ed.) *Freedom and Morality*, pp. 1–22, Lawrence, KS: University of Kansas Press. Chapter 3, "Rational Desires," was Presidential Address to the 68th Annual Meeting of the Western Division, American Philosophical Association, St. Louis, MO, on May 8, 1970, pp. 43–64. Chapter 4, "The Explanation of Moral Language," and Chapter 19, "Utilitarianism and Welfare Legislation," were both originally published by Rowman and Littlefield. Chapter 5, "Morality and Its Critics," and Chapter 14, "Traits of Character: A Conceptual Analysis," both originally appeared in the *American Philosophical Quarterly*. Chapter 6, "Rationality, Egoism, and Morality," and Chapter 10, "The Concept of a Moral Right and Its Function," both originally appeared in the *Journal of Philosophy*.

Chapter 7, "Some Merits of One Form of Rule – Utilitarianism," is a revised version of a paper presented at the University of Colorado in October 1965 and printed in *University of Colorado Studies*, reprinted with permission of the University Press of Colorado. Chapter 8, "Fairness to Optimific Indirect Theories in Ethics," originally appeared in 1988 in *Ethics*, 98: 341–60, and is reprinted with permission of the publisher, the University of Chicago Press; copyright © 1988 by the University of Chicago. Chapter 9, "Two Concepts of Utility," originally appeared in 1982 in Harlan B. Miller and William H. Williams (eds.), *The Limits of Utilitarianism*, pp. 169–85, Minneapolis: University of Minnesota Press; copyright © 1982 by the University of Minnesota Press, reprinted from *The Limits of Utilitarianism*, by permission of the University of Minnesota Press.

Chapter 11, "Utilitarianism and Moral Rights," first appeared in 1984 in the *Canadian Journal of Philosophy* 14: 1–20. Chapter 12, "A Utilitarian Theory of Excuses," was first published in 1969 and is reprinted from *The Philosophical Review* 78: 337–61 by permission of the publisher and author. Chapter 13, "A Motivational Theory of Excuses in the Criminal Law," is reprinted by permission of New York University Press from *Criminal Justice NOMOS 27*, edited by J. Roland Pennock and John W.

1

Introductory comments

The articles on ethics collected in this volume,[1] with a few exceptions, represent views to which I subscribe today. The collection does not contain anything I have written on other topics: epistemology, metaphysics, or philosophy of mind. Various earlier pieces on ethics have also been omitted partly for lack of space and partly because I no longer like their content. But some omissions I regret are "The Concepts of Obligation and Duty" (*Mind*, 1964), "The Significance of Differences of Ethical Opinion for Ethical Rationalism" (*Philosophy and Phenomenological Research*, 1944), "The Emotive Theory of Ethics" (*Philosophical Review*, 1950), and "W.K. Frankena and Ethics of Virtue" (*Monist*, 1981), but these do not mark significant steps in the development of my mature thought. I mention some other omitted pieces below. I have not included any selections from my books; to do so would have been an enormous job and the books are readily available.

I paid little attention to the problems of ethics during my student years, at Denison University and Cambridge University; the interest began with seminars offered at Yale by W.M. Urban, with whom I thoroughly disagreed. This disagreement partly reflected some fundamental beliefs I had acquired earlier. One was that reliance on "intuitions" is no reliable basis for claims to truth of moral or value statements. I am afraid I now include in this dismissal the current view that we may find moral truth by reliance on the coherence of, or "wide reflective equilibrium" of, a person's "considered" moral/value beliefs. A second basic belief is the counterpart of this, that nonlogical truth generally is to be obtained only by the methods of the empirical sciences – reliance on observation and the "best inference" from this. But I was never a logical positivist; indeed, my first publication in philosophy (in the *Journal of Philosophy* for 1938) was a criticism of the views of Waismann, early Wittgenstein, Carnap, and others, because they banned concepts that seem necessary for atomic physics. Third, I was unconvinced by arguments, such as those by Moore and Ross, that

1 It was Brad Hooker's idea to publish this collection, and I am indebted to him. I am also indebted to Cambridge University Press for undertaking the publication and for their typically superior production performance.

ethical terms name simple objective properties. With these assumptions, where should one move in moral philosophy?

I was first led to espouse a kind of emotive theory (*Ethics*, 1941), to the effect that, just as a sense experience is the ground of a perceptual judgment, so the occurrence of an emotion determines basic moral judgments, like "That was a contemptible deed." This was somewhat like Westermarck. In support of this view I argued that such moral judgments vary with the development of major "sentiments," with physiological states such as major depressions, with states of satiety or grief, just as do emotions. In a following publication (*Ethics*, 1946) I suggested that some evaluative adjectives (for example, "contemptible," "admirable") could be defined as "is a fitting object" of the corresponding emotion (contempt, admiration) – the one I had earlier argued determines the evaluation. I conceded that questions might be raised about the meaning of "fitting."

In the early years of my teaching at Swarthmore College (beginning in 1937) I had the good fortune of close association with several distinguished psychologists including Wolfgang Koehler, Karl Duncker, and (slightly later) Solomon Asch, all of whom had a strong interest in ethics, thought that basic value/moral judgments are the same the world over, and rejected learning theories inconsistent with this. A desire to put the absolutism of these psychologists to an empirical test, and to get light on the sources of moral judgments (it having been suggested by the anthropologist Ralph Linton and others that methods of child rearing had much to do with the development of value norms), led me to wide reading in anthropology and eventually to fieldwork among the Hopi Indians, reported in *Hopi Ethics: A Theoretical Analysis* (published in 1954). This work revealed the complications in appraising the absolutism of these psychologists, since divergent ethical standards usually occur in widely varying factual circumstances and hence in the presence of diverse factual beliefs about the topic, which could be explanatory of different specific norms even if everyone actually shared basic moral principles. I argued, however, that much evidence supports the view that some ethical norms vary even when factual beliefs are the same, especially ethical appraisals of cruelty to animals. I also uncovered evidence to show the role of personal advantage to individuals in the development of social ethical norms.

Since I now held that ethical appraisals do not always vary with the factual beliefs of judges about the situation being judged, and that hence we must have a theory of the learning of morality/values which permits this, and since I held that an emotional datum determines (some) value judgments, should I not accept the "emotive theory" of ethics as it was formulated, say, by Charles Stevenson? I objected to some parts of his view, and criticized these in a symposium with him in 1950 (*Philosophical*

Review, 1950). If Stevenson had merely said that moral statements "express" attitudes in the sense that a person who heard an ethical statement would take it that the speaker had a corresponding attitude (and would be somewhat moved to conform to it, depending on the prestige of the speaker), there might not have been disagreement. But Stevenson made detailed claims about moral language. For one thing, he held that hearing a moral statement made by another tends to elicit a conforming attitude, not because the auditor takes it a certain attitude has been expressed (by a prestigeful person), but because of a *conditioned* response to the power of moral words, acquired in the process of language learning. I doubted whether there is reason to believe this. Second, he claimed that ethical disagreement must be viewed not as cognitive but as disagreement in attitude, partly because he thought facts *may* not settle *every* ethical dispute (with which I have noted that I agreed). He also argued, however, that once you have a proposal about what the cognitive meaning is, certain particular possible facts become relevant to settling a dispute, and only these, whereas we know that there is an unlimited range of reasons that may be relevant to an ethical dispute. I replied that this argument does not undermine either nonnaturalist accounts, or subjective naturalist accounts (to which Stevenson's own view was very close). Furthermore, I thought that not every "reason" that actually moves a person's view in a debate (for example, one that points to some personal advantage in preaching a certain view) is a morally relevant reason, as Stevenson thought (this debate was developed further in 1957 in *The Language of Value,* edited by Ray Lepley). I thought it somewhat cynical of him to insist, as he sometimes did, that moral disputes be viewed essentially like disputes between an employer and a labor union, each seeking an advantage for himself. Thus I did not go along with all of Stevenson.

Shortly thereafter I published a proposal (*Mind,* 1952) for how best to construe "assertion" and "cognitive meaning." I there proposed that a moral term M is best taken to designate some empirical property P for a given individual at a time if and only if it is causally impossible, at that time, that a speaker both assert "S is M" with assent or conviction and doubt that S is P. Is there any property P which meets this condition for moral predicates? Suppose it were suggested, for S is "wrong," that the property is "would be disapproved by anyone [or perhaps just by me the speaker] if he were fully informed on the relevant facts, were impartial ..." (and so on for any properties it would be plausible to include in an absolutist form of subjectivist analysis). I replied to various objections, in defense of such an analysis, defending the possibility of a cognitive account of ethical statements, such as that of Roderick Firth (another colleague at Swarthmore), or Hutcheson, Hume, and Smith before him.

In 1955, however (*Philosophy and Phenomenological Research*), I criticized Firth's proposal, partly for its details but primarily for its absolutism, because of doubts about the uniformity of responses among qualified persons.

In my *Ethical Theory* (1959) I proposed a kind of truce with the emotive theory, suggesting that one might agree that the primary function of ethical terms is to express attitudes, but that (along lines adopted by some writers at the time) the use of these special terms *implies* or *claims* that the attitude expressed has certain properties that intelligent, fully informed persons, who had thought through the problem of general policies for the endorsement of moral attitudes, would require for the appraisal of actions. I thought such persons would require that these "conditions" include full information, impartiality, and so on.

This is where I was in 1959. There ensued a rather gradual transition to the view expounded in the Locke Lectures (1974), which appeared in expanded form in 1979, in *A Theory of the Good and the Right*.

A. METAETHICAL PRELIMINARIES

The first paper in this collection, "Moral philosophy and the analysis of language" (1963), takes a major step away from the view that *normative* reflection must *start* with some theory about the *meaning* of moral terminology. Some philosophers have thought that "good" just means pleasant, and "evil" painful (Bentham), or that "right" means maximizes the good (G. E. Moore), or that "*X* is the right act in *C*" means "I hereby prescribe doing *X* in circumstances like *C* (wherever they may be), and prescribe this overridingly" (Hare); and they go on from there to decide what is good or right. Why not? Suppose your language contained only one evaluative word, "prudent." Would you be willing to base your moral philosophy on this? Suppose speakers of English use moral words in different senses, some using "wrong" to mean forbidden by God. Would we then want to develop corresponding different theories of normative ethics? Suppose you light on a given analysis (as Firth did) by observing what one does to determine one's answer to a normative question. You can then never criticize a person's normative reasoning by appeal to what his terms mean, because your conclusion about his meaning rests on observation of the form of his normative reasoning.

There must be something better than reliance on prior conclusions about the meaning of moral language. But what is there? Several writers had already suggested a somewhat different approach: Frankena, Rawls, possibly even Kant and Mill. I suggested that one possibility is to get clear about what our problems really are. For instance, it seems the

4

problem we are trying to solve when we ask what is good is about what to *desire*. If so, then we can ask what we would desire if we were fully informed about everything (the nature of the target, the etiology of the desire) that would cause a change in our desires – and this means bringing logic and facts maximally to bear on a desire. Such an inquiry might remove our doubt about what to desire. What else might we want to know? When we ask about what is *right*, perhaps what we want to know is which kinds of actions would be forbidden, or called for, by a moral system a person with criticized desires would *want* "written in the consciences of men." (Assume here, building further on my old belief about the role of emotions in moral experience, that for an individual to embody a "moral system" is for him to be motivated to avoid actions of certain types, to feel guilty if he performs a type of action he is motivated to avoid, and to disapprove others who do, and to think that these attitudes are justified in some appropriate sense.) Finding what kind of moral system a person with criticized desires would want for his society would be bringing facts and logic to bear on the wanted system. Showing this would surely be a recommendation of that moral system, although none of this would show that some moral/value statement is *true*, roughly in the sense of the empirical sciences, unless we elected to define "good" or "morally right" so that it would be, as well we might (as I explain in a paper below).

Would we be satisfied to identify the main problems of ethics in this way? These suggestions add up to a big picture of what morality and values are, and how they may be criticized. Do we really like this picture? Is there some more satisfying way to look at things? Do we want to raise questions in our old terminology, ones not wholly provided for by the new conceptual scheme? My vote was to go for the new proposal, and still is.

The second paper, Chapter 3, "Rational desires" (1970), written after a move to the University of Michigan, was intended to supplement the preceding one, by showing how full information might be utilized to determine what an informed person would desire *for itself*. It has been questioned whether knowledge can function to criticize *basic* desires. It is here argued that such a desire is in the clear if it survives repeated confrontation with facts about it or its target.

This thesis depends on a part of the psychology of motivation. (Here I was influenced by the psychologists J. W. Atkinson and Albert Bandura, among others.) There are some experiences we like (dislike) natively (nice smells, being burnt), also some we like (dislike) as a result of conditioning (scotch and water). Suppose, then, we have an image or idea like one of these experiences. By conditioning or stimulus generalization this *idea*

5

will seem attractive or have a favorable affective tone. That is what it is
to desire that of which we have the idea. Sometimes an event will be
wanted or aversive because of a relation of this sort to untypical or
abnormal cases of the thing desired or aversive. What will happen if we
face it with reflection on experiences that are typical? Answer: The desire
(aversion) will tend to be extinguished either because of nonreinforcement
or through counterconditioning (overlaying the desire/aversion with a
more powerful conflicting motive). Many conforming desires/aversions
we have learned because of scorn of parents or peers, when the relevant
experiences would support desires/aversions of an opposite kind, can be
labeled "unauthentic" and be extinguished by vivid awareness of the facts.
A somewhat similar phenomenon is misgeneralization: Acquiring a de-
sire/aversion to something of kind ABC when the initial disliked experience was to the more specific whole $ABCDE$. In more interesting cases
mere reflection on what it was that one liked/disliked about the original
situation can change the relevant desire. There are other types of situations
in which the same sort of effect will occur.

I thus argued that vivid representation of full information about a
situation can often modify desires for things for themselves. I suggested
this is a valid form of *cognitive* criticism that can recommend, but it is
not *evidence* supporting the truth of a value statement short of some
definitions that make it so.

The third paper, Chapter 4, "The explanation of moral language"
(1985), is to a considerable extent a summary and defense of my book,
A Theory of the Good and the Right (1979). It defends a conception of
"a person's morality" much like that stated above, and proposes that a
major job of moral philosophy is, not to attempt to analyze moral terms
as now ordinarily used in commonsense, but to find a pattern of sharp
concepts useful in view of what morality is: for discussion on whether
someone's wrong conduct should be excused, for giving moral advice,
for personal reflection on what is right. For this we need only one basic
concept, "fitting," since, as A. C. Ewing urged, all other moral concepts
can be defined by this concept plus empiricist language. Thus for X to
be "reprehensible" for his act A is for it to be fitting that persons disapprove of X because of A. According to Ewing, "fitting" names an
unobservable relation. It appears, however, that "fitting" can be explained in terms of the notion of a moral system being "justified." And
we can explain "justified" so that the concept is clear, does not purport
to name an unobservable property or its application require intuitions,
and it is normatively neutral (in the sense, for example, that it is not
explained as "maximizes the happiness of society"). What kind of explanation of this sort can be given? I proposed "A moral code is justified

6

for X" if X would choose to support it for his society if he were fully rational (with "rational" needing explanation). I assumed that if a moral system is justified in this sense for someone, that fact will recommend it to him. This proposal does not imply that a moral system justified for someone is justified for everyone, and the above account is designed to permit construction in a relativistic way, since "X" does not mean "just anyone." I suggested that people who understand what morality is would be satisfied with construing moral questions in this way. This set of definitions, if widely accepted, would prevent confusion in moral thinking and would make clear that morality is a rational phenomenon.

The fourth paper, Chapter 5, "Morality and its critics" (1989), in the form of a criticism of the philosophical views of Professor Bernard Williams, assembles a number of views I have wished to support. I have already suggested above that a person's morality consists of intrinsic aversions to some types of actions and corresponding dispositions to feel guilty and to disapprove of others and to think these attitudes are justified in some way. Such a system can be quite complex, perhaps nearly as complex as language (although it has to be capable of being learned). This, I suggest, is what a person's *morality* is. When there is a conflict between some aversions, the system may tell what to do by providing a "holistic" response to an individual situation. There are other standards in society, like etiquette or custom, for breach of which one can be criticized and may react by feeling shame or embarrassment, but these are not thought to be *justified* and are not part of the moral system.

Some philosophers have thought that when morality contains an aversion, for example, to harming others, it can be right to act contrary to it only when there is some stronger contrary aversion. (W. D. Ross says there is a real duty to do that, the doing of which is a prima facie duty, unless there is a stronger contrary prima facie duty.) Williams rightly denies this, but since this is not what morality as we know it demands – our morality is more complex – his objection is not a point against actual morality. What evidence is there that the Ross theory is mistaken? Morality permits telling harmless lies (even though there is a general obligation to speak the truth) when it is of personal benefit; the courts do not enforce "gratuitous" promises; morality permits pushing off a newcomer – thereby harming him – if I am clinging to a plank in a shipwreck; one is free to break one's marriage vow, thereby harming one's spouse, by getting a divorce, for no reason other than falling in love with someone else. The Ross conception of morality is thus too simple.

When is it rational to be interested in subscribing to some morality of the aversion/guilt/disapproval type? Answer: When, given we are fully informed, we *want* some such system, presumably both because of self-interest (for protection) and altruism. *Actual* moral systems often cannot make such an appeal. They may forbid harmless actions, like homosexuality or political liberalism. Reflections on the effects of a morality will make clear at which points an actual moral system needs change, and which aversions it is better to have stronger than certain others. If the moral system is of a kind we should most *want*, if fully informed, as compared with any other or none at all, it seems that its presence must be a benefit – contrary to one of Williams' claims.

Williams thinks that if an otherwise immoral (prohibited by the optimal code) action produces good, for example, contributes to art as Gauguin's actions did, then it is morally in the clear. Up to a point this is right, for an optimal moral system will presumably provide that some of its specific restrictions be set aside to avoid great harm or to produce great good. But how much harm/good? We can hardly be precise about this, but we must say "Quite a lot." Moreover, for this prospective good to suspend an otherwise stringent moral rule for a given person, the person must have good reason to think that his act is required to produce the good – not merely believe, or hope, that it will.

Williams argued that personal or aesthetic concerns also have a claim to be recognized, along with moral ones, and may be of greater weight. How should we arbitrate between them if there is a conflict? Suppose a person has very strong personal ambitions, stronger than his moral aversions and his aversion to the justified disapproval of others. Is there any reason we can offer why he should set a higher value on morality? I did not try to answer that question in this paper.

The fifth paper, Chapter 6, "Rationality, egoism, and morality" (1972), considers whether an optimal moral system – one we should want, if fully informed – might be an egoist one. A partial answer is that a person can enhance his well being more otherwise than by choosing an egoist system which requires that a person always act to maximize benefit to himself, irrespective of harm to others.

B. NORMATIVE ETHICS: UTILITARIANISM

In the papers discussed above I argued that the kind of moral system that can be recommended to thoughtful people is one they will *want* for their society, provided their wants have been criticized by facing them vividly with relevant information. What kind of moral system would this be? In the next three papers I discuss forms of utilitarianism as proposals about the moral system to be chosen.

All types of utilitarianism agree that the rightness of an act is fixed by *some* relation to the production of *benefit*. A major difference between them is on the precise kind of relation to benefit rightness involves. The first two papers below are concerned with this controversy. Another disagreement is about what counts as a benefit: some hold that the only benefit is happiness, others that it is satisfaction of desire, still others that it is the occurrence of some good different from happiness but not necessarily desired. The third paper below is concerned with this dispute.

Of the two major theories about what relation the rightness of an act has to benefits, the first, usually called "act-utilitarianism," is very simple. It affirms that the to-be-preferred (most wanted) moral system requires an act, as being obligatory, if and only if performance of that act, of all the acts open to the agent, would produce the most good for everybody affected. (There are disagreements about whether it is actual good that is to be produced, or good that, on the agent's evidence, probably would be produced.) In the first paper below, I reject this theory partly on the ground it has intuitively unacceptable consequences (an argument I later rejected). The second theory, usually called "rule-utilitarianism," is more complex. It was first clearly stated, and distinguished from the "act" view, by Bishop Berkeley in *Passive Obedience*.

The first paper defending this view (Chapter 7) is "Some merits of one form of rule-utilitarianism" (1967). Its thesis is that we should regard an act as wrong if and only if it *would be* prohibited by a moral code concerned with various act-*types*, provided the general *recognition* of these prohibitions in the society *would* do most good. It is thus an "ideal" theory. (What does "general recognition" come to? Not universal *conformity;* such a code could be act-utilitarian. I suggested 90 percent acceptance, but I think we needn't worry too much about this.) The code must contain "rules" dealing with recurrent problem situations, be simple enough to be interiorized, not leave too much to discretion, not ignore the costs of teaching or conforming, or impose unbearable demands such as requiring one always to do what will produce the most good, like act-utilitarianism. (Most decisions in life, therefore, will not raise moral questions at all.) The system of rules presumably would require keeping contracts, making restitution for injuries, helping others in distress, and perhaps bringing about a just distribution of material goods. It will hardly be a worldwide universal code, but one that does best for a given society, with its institutions.

The second paper in this group (Chapter 8), "Fairness to indirect optimific theories in ethics" (1988), was written twenty years later, and might be expected to show some progress! It is intended to add to, or amend, the foregoing theory, and to reply to various objections raised to the rule-utilitarian conception. It is pointed out that for a rational moral system to be prevalent in a society, someone must *teach* it and the teachers must have a view of the function of a moral code, and aim to teach proscriptions they think maximally beneficial to teach. We may assume that teachers will largely accept the moral code as it is in their society, and aim at only incremental changes. In the first paper I criticized act-utilitarianism partly on the ground that it is incompatible with our moral intuition; in the second I rely on more pragmatic criticisms, to the effect that if everyone were an act-utilitarian in his moral thinking it would be difficult to predict what other people might do – an obstacle to cooperation and to any planning based on expectations of the future behavior of others. Again, the problem of estimating utilities in a particular situation is such as to be a standing invitation to people to reach moral conclusions compatible with self-interest.

To objections that have been raised, I attempt to reply. It is said that it is impossible to make the utility comparisons necessary to apply the rule-utilitarian theory at a social level. A second objection is that it is irrational "rule-worship" to follow a moral rule if you happen to know which of two specific actions will have better results. Since the conception of a rule-utilitarian code does not identify what the rules will be, is there not the same difficulty in planning or cooperation that there is for the act-utilitarian? On the rule-utilitarian view, the specific rules to be followed are not decided by God, but necessarily by human agents. May they not disagree? Finally, it has been objected that it would hardly be useful to advocate following what *would* be the optimal code if everyone accepted it, when a large minority is bitterly opposed (to interracial marriage in South Africa, for example). I try to answer all these objections.

The third paper of this group (Chapter 9), "Two concepts of utility" (1982), is an attempt to adjudicate between two theories of what is intrinsically good: the happiness theory and the theory that it is desire-satisfaction in the sense of the occurrence of an event that one does (did or will) desire, irrespective of any enjoyment from it. The desire-satisfaction theory can add some conditions such as that the desire be fully informed but it is surely not clear that the satisfaction of desires is always a benefit to the agent. How about altruistic emotionally influenced desires? The concept of happiness is clear enough, and what makes one happy is often the same as what satisfies desire. Not always, however: A person may want honor or social status very strongly, when having them does not increase happiness. Moreover, I had argued in an earlier paper ("The Psychology of Benevolence and Its Implications for Philosophy," *Journal of Philosophy*, 1976), on the basis of psychological theory, that what a benevolent/sympathetic person will want for others is *experiences* like those we want in ourselves, not just fulfillment of the others' desires. I also argue that there is a larger problem for the desire theory,

10

in that desires change as we mature. How, then, shall we decide which action best satisfies an agent's desires? The happiness theory has the merit of simplicity.

There is a further defense of the happiness theory in "Fairness to Happiness," *Social Theory and Practice*, 1989.

C. UTILITARIANISM AND RIGHTS

Chapter 10, "The concept of a moral right and its function," aims to meet a widely agreed need to get a plausible definition of a "moral right." We can hardly get a useful dictionary definition, obviously synonymous with the definiendum, but must be satisfied with an "adequate replacement." I urge defining this term by employing the concept of moral obligation: "*X* has a moral right to *Y*" may be taken as "People in *X*'s society have a strong moral obligation to enable *X* to do, have, or enjoy *Y*, primarily because of the importance to people in *X*'s situation of being able to do, have, or enjoy things like *Y*." I proposed adding, "*X* morally ought to (or is permitted to) feel resentment if he is hurt or deprived because of the failure of others to discharge this obligation, and to feel unashamed to protest, and to take reasonable steps of protest, calculated to encourage others to have the motivation to enable anyone in a similar situation to do, have, or enjoy things like *Y*."

Since "ought" implies "can," it seems there can be no moral right to something that no strength of sense of moral obligation could bring about in a given society, for instance, to bring the standard of living in present-day India up to that of Sweden. What is one to say to this? We need to explain why there should be "rights-talk" at all. These queries need replies, which I try to offer.

The foregoing, however, is only a definition of the *concept* of a moral right. It does not yet tell us what are our rights, except to some extent by reference to the importance to some persons of having their rights recognized. Chapter 11, "Utilitarianism and moral rights" (1984), does discuss this issue. The above definition includes the notion of "moral obligation to . . . " The *rule-utilitarian* will say that one is obliged just in case an optimal moral code for the society would include such an obligation. It is quite consistent to be a rule-utilitarian about moral obligation and to adopt the above definition of a "moral right." We then come up with a normative rule-utilitarian theory about moral rights. One virtue of such a theory is that it enables us to identify our rights – for instance, the scope of the "right to life," and whether it is more binding than the right to free speech on political topics. I briefly criticize the views on moral rights of David Lyons and R.M. Hare.

11

D. DETERMINISM, EXCUSES, AND CHARACTER

I have argued that an act is right if a social *moral code* permitting that act would be best, do most good, and I have said that a person has a moral code forbidding a kind of action if and only if he has an aversion to doing that sort of thing, just in itself, *and* has a disposition to feel guilty if he does it, and to disapprove of others who do, and thinks these attitudes are justified in some appropriate sense. We have to recognize some qualifications in the clauses about guilt feelings and disapproval, however, as I explain in Chapter 12, "A utilitarian theory of excuses" (1969), just as, in the law, an unlawful act is not liable to punishment unless there was *mens rea*, so that an act is legally excused if it occurred owing to mistake of fact or accident. The rule-utilitarian will consider these qualifications, because which ones we allow will make a difference to the desirability of a certain moral system. A moral system works in part because people do not like to be disapproved by others, and because people do not like to feel guilty, or take a dim view of themselves as persons. Thus guilt feelings and condemnation by others motivate people to do what is socially beneficial. But marshaling these condemning attitudes will not tend to prevent certain types of behavior: injuring another person accidentally, or failing to do something impossible. These facts lead us to recognize a general principle: A person should be morally excused for some untoward act if it does not manifest some *defect of character* – at least if we take this to imply a defect in motivation. If a person's aversions to acting in certain ways are already adequate (there is no defect of character), the moral system has done its job. If this is not the case, then guilt feelings and criticism by others can help improve the level of motivation. We should note that criticism can help even if all actions are caused; this theory of excuses is not inconsistent with determinism.

The same position should be taken by the criminal law, as I argue in the twelfth paper, Chapter 13, "A motivational theory of excuses in the criminal law" (1985).

According to the criminal law, a person is liable to punishment if he performs a forbidden act (*actus reus*), unless it is *justified* (perhaps because greater social good is done than by omitting it), or is *excused* (say, by ignorance of fact or by accident), or the agent is not responsible (insane or an infant). The thesis of this paper is that an act must be excused (even if an unjustified breach of law) if it fails to show a defect of motivation. My thesis is thus two-fold: for the most part excuses recognized by the law are in fact of this kind, and such excuses are what it *ought* to recognize.

Older legal theory said an act is punishable only if it springs from an

12

"evil will," but present law seems to say an act is punishable if the agent *knowingly* or *recklessly* does a legally forbidden thing. It could as well say that it is punishable if the act shows defect of character (motivation) – *indifference* to harm, or at least to the kinds of acts forbidden, or to the fact that they are forbidden. If we follow this line, does it mean the judge must speculate about motivation? If the judge must make the decisions the Model Penal Code says he must now make, he is already speculating! In fact, we draw inferences about defective motivation from overt behavior all the time. The motivational theory implies that the following excuses should be recognized: accidents; mistake of fact; mistake of law (although here most judicial opinion clearly does not agree); involuntary intoxication; duress; provocation (as a mitigating excuse); the law of attempts; some kinds of insanity. All these permit a no-defect-of-motivation explanation.

Utilitarians will hold that the main benefit of the legal system is to reduce harmful behavior. It does this primarily by making the standards known and by deterrence (putting threats of punishment on the side of lawful behavior). If a person has broken the law but not because of defect of motivation, no benefit is gained from punishing him; there is no deterrence. His motivation may already be where it ought to be. Some people think that we should not forget deterrence of *others* whose motivations may not be perfect, and that knowledge that there is a system of excuses (that some unlawful acts are not punished) reduces respect for the law; but this remains to be shown, and a system of strict liability would make life intolerable.

The preceding articles try to show that the concept of a trait of character is important both for normative ethics and for legal philosophy. We therefore need a conception of a trait of character consistent with the reasoning about both moral and legal excuses, and fitting into common sense conceptions and contemporary psychological theory. "Traits of character: A conceptual analysis," Chapter 14, is intended to provide this. This paper argues that we must consider traits of character as dispositions, in contrast with the view of some that trait names ("sympathetic," "courageous") merely summarize past behavior, or with the view of others that they are dispositions only to manifest specific types of behavior. In fact, it is clear that traits of character like sympathy, fidelity, and truthfulness are *motivational,* wants or aversions, and enter into explanations of intentional behavior just as do other wants and aversions. We infer or deny traits on the basis of a single example of behavior, which we could not do on the specific behaviors theory.

If we define a moral "virtue" as a trait of character beneficial to society, the question arises whether *all* moral virtues are motivational, as the preceding paper implies. This is the topic of Chapter 15, "The structure of virtue" (1988). Some philosophers have agreed that traits of character like sympathy are motivational, but deny this of traits like self-control. This paper explores that topic by reflection on the kind of therapeutic treatment given for lack of control (for example, of eating, temper).

In the case of persons with problems of overeating, the treatment consists in establishing a regimen of short-term goals (no sweets just today), rewarding self for success in meeting the short-term goal, adding the motive power of appearing before a group to testify on one's success (or failure), and learning from all this that one can cope. As a result the "problem" disappears. Much the same for control of temper. These are standard ways of affecting motivation. It is true that self-control is a bit different from sympathy. Incidentally, there may not be any such thing as a *general* trait of self-control or courage; these virtues may be specific to certain types of situations (not eating versus not watching television when one should be working). A *moral* virtue seems to be one possession of which is beneficial for one's society; a nonmoral one is beneficial for self or one's small group; a virtue in general can be both.

E. IMPLICATIONS OF UTILITARIAN THEORY

The final four essays are billed as "implications" of utilitarianism, but in some cases this theory is not of central importance for the paper as a whole. This is true of Chapter 16, "The morality and rationality of suicide" (1976).

The first question is whether a person who commits suicide is subject to moral criticism, even given that his act was objectively wrong (for example, damaging his family for no good reason). We have seen that a necessary condition for condemnation is that the action show a defect of character. There need not be a defect of character if the act resulted from some mistake of fact, or when the agent was insane, or emotionally not himself.

When is an act of suicide objectively wrong? Is there any obligation not to commit suicide? We can ignore theological arguments and it is not easy to claim that suicide is an injury to society in general. It is true that an act of suicide may harm others, and that is a good moral reason for refraining, but if we ask whether it would be a beneficial thing for the moral code to contain a prohibition of suicide just as such, the question is not easy to answer.

Suicide is shortening one's life span, and the question whether it is in one's self-interest to do this is the question whether a shorter or a longer life span promises to be more beneficial. Which do we want when the

14

issue is put before us vividly? The answer seems clear if one is suffering a painful terminal illness. If a person is depressed because of loss of prestige or physical attractiveness, however, or disappointment in love, he or she must consider the options for a future life clearly and vividly; continuing to live may then seem not too aversive a prospect.

If a person is considering suicide, and that choice is manifestly right, an optimal moral code will call on his friends (and physician) to help.

The next paper, Chapter 17, "Utilitarianism and the rules of war" (1972), rather like the one on excuses in the criminal law, raises two questions: first, what is the law, and second, what ought it to be?

The U.S. Army *Manual of Land Warfare*, for officers in the U.S. Army (there is a similar manual for the Navy), lists absolute prohibitions established by conventions (for example, the Hague, Geneva) and recognized by international courts. What is their *moral* standing? Suppose, as seems true, that the prohibitions were selected by nations that were fully informed, expected to be at war at some time, and had humanitarian concerns. This seems to promise moral standing. I suggest that the rules would be – and were – chosen to maximize expectable benefit, given the nations are at war. They were chosen to benefit both people generally and military personnel of the warring parties, consistent with the aim of victory. It seems adoption of such rules is what the utilitarian would recommend.

Chapter 18 deals with an emotional topic, "Public policy and life and death decisions regarding defective newborns" (1987).

As usual, I affirm that a morally justified policy is one informed people would want for a society in which they expected to spend a lifetime, and that the policies they would want are those most beneficial for society in the long run.

This conception stands in stark contrast to the recommendations of the President's Commission (1983). These recommendations make essentially three points: (1) Decisions must ignore the impact of a defective child's life on family and society. (2) The decision should be favorable if continuation is to the net benefit of the child, from its perspective, having developed realistic goals, and not from that of adults to whom its prospective life might seem aversive. (3) Within these restrictions a decision is to be made by parents and physician if they agree; if they don't, by a hospital board or a court.

I argue against all these contentions. I also argue that, if it is decided that an infant should not receive treatment, instead of allowing the child to die after slow deterioration, it might be kinder to administer a terminating anaesthetic.

Chapter 19 deals with "Utilitarianism and welfare legislation" (1981).

Widely held nonutilitarian principles for income distribution may be (some or all) viewed as derivative from a utilitarian theory. One might think that a consistent utilitarian would favor equality of income, because of the declining marginal utility of money. This would be a mistake, however. Writers as early as Mill pointed out that the ill and handicapped need more than equal income, and that an equal distribution would have an unfavorable effect on incentive and productivity. The optimal arrangement seems, for reasons I explain, to be for (ideally informed!) economists to predict production under different wage-income-tax schedules, and identify how many will receive how much under each scheme. Congress (?) could then decide which was socially better and would maximize the total welfare. I concede this program is a bit utopian, but I think economists could shed more light on this issue than is generally thought – or than they do now. Have they shown how much production would be lost if top executives were heavily taxed?

What practical implications for the present does this conception have? *Ideally* we have universal medical service, have eliminated tax "loopholes," have one (Federal?) tax system, with identical treatment for men and women. With these things taken for granted, the scheme can provide for (1) a guaranteed job for everyone, (2) a requirement for work on everyone who expects to receive more than the minimum income, (3) a subsistence income for those who don't work, and (4) special supplements for the ill and handicapped. This would eliminate the "vertical inequities" of the present system – people who barely qualify for aid receiving more (for example, because of Medicaid) than people who work but are not quite poor enough to qualify for aid. It would also provide adequate incentives to work effectively in one's job.

In this paper, written in 1980, I speculated that the tax-welfare system in the United States was slowly but steadily moving in this direction, a speculation that, with hindsight over the last ten years, appears to have been mistaken!

A
Metaethical preliminaries

2

Moral philosophy and the analysis of language

Philosophers have sometimes divided human experiences into two major kinds: those predominantly of activity on the part of the agent, and those predominantly of passivity. As passive, man is an observer, contemplator, scientist, chronicler of events, or prophet. As active, man is an agent who directs human affairs, changes nature, formulates policies concerning people, institutions, rules, customs, courses of action, and so on. We need not inquire whether this division is very happy. The important observation is that a person can play either role with intelligence and sophistication, or on the other hand with stupidity and naiveté. Certain branches of philosophy are devoted roughly to the job of determining how a person may conduct his passive role, as contemplator, with intelligence and reason. These are epistemology, logic, and the philosophy of science, doubtless among others. In contrast to them, ethics or moral philosophy has been the philosophical discipline devoted primarily to the job of determining how to conduct the active role with intelligence and reason. At least we can say this as a first approximation.

Let us now address ourselves to a very broad question: What kind of reasoning may show how to conduct our active role with intelligence, and how far may we expect such reasoning to take us? I suppose a person's answer to this question constitutes a good part of his view about the content of moral philosophy.

I shall begin by stating what I believe to be part of the right answer to this broad question. But I shall not attempt to develop or defend this answer in detail. For the primary aim of my remarks is to criticize another answer, a much more familiar answer. According to this second answer, which I wish to criticize, reasoning aimed to conduct our active role intelligently – the substantive part of moral philosophy – must begin with a *description of ordinary moral questions, of the language of morals* (a part of what is often called "metaethics"), and only on the basis of conclusions as to the meaning of ordinary moral questions should one attempt the traditional job of answering these questions. What I wish to show is that this familiar view is mistaken in the role it gives to the examination of ordinary moral language in the activity of guiding decisions intelligently.

19

I

Let me begin by urging that moral philosophy has two main, and closely related, jobs. The first is to determine which policies, preferences, or attitudes are *rational for everybody*. "Rational" in what sense? "Rational" for a person in the sense that he *would* adopt them if he was in a normal frame of mind and was perfectly knowledgeable – that is, had at his disposal and vividly in mind all available relevant knowledge about himself and the world and was making no logical mistake. What might be an example of a policy or preference that is rational *for everybody*, in this sense of "rational"? It is not implausible to suggest that it is rational in this sense to prefer knowledge to ignorance, or pleasure to pain. I shall give attention to one particular example in a moment.

There is a second and related job. This is to give instructions to persons how they may find what is a rational policy for *them* to adopt, a rational preference for *them*, in this same sense of "rational," where it is doubtful whether it can be shown that a given policy or preference is rational for *everybody*. Such instructions hopefully would also be useful in helping a person find the rational decision in specific situations with which philosophy as a discipline can hardly be concerned.

If such jobs are the main jobs of moral philosophy, one may claim that moral philosophy is a perfectly objective discipline. It is not just a matter of proclaiming one's own precious values to the world at large, but rather of determining which attitudes or preferences would be adopted by persons who were normal and perfectly knowledgeable, and of getting clear how to determine what one's own attitude or preference would be if one were perfectly knowledgeable and in a normal frame of mind. These questions are perfectly clear, and presumably can be answered by broadly rational and scientific procedures. We may concede that it may be a difficult matter to get the answers, and that such questions perhaps cannot be answered with certainty or even, in many cases, with a high degree of probability.

Anyone who suggests that such a program is at least a large part of the proper program for moral philosophy must answer various objections. It will be worth while to consider briefly three of these, before turning to a critique of the established theory.

The first objection is that the proposal, as stated, appears not even to attempt an answer to some central questions to which moral philosophy has traditionally addressed itself, and which are urgent questions for practical life. Our proposal that moral philosophy should concern itself with finding rational preferences or attitudes, it will be said, does come close to suggesting a way to answer the traditional question of the good, or the question of a wise or prudent choice; but even if we know what is the "rational" policy for a person, we shall be no closer to knowing what is his *duty* or moral *obligation*, and this is something moral philosophy most certainly is concerned to determine. Nor, again, will we know, by knowing what is "rational" policy, what conduct is morally praiseworthy or blameworthy. It is no answer to questions about such issues, to tell us what a person would prefer, or what policy he would adopt, if he were perfectly knowledgeable and in a normal frame of mind.

This point is an important one, and the objection would be fatal if it cannot be met. But fortunately the objection rests on a misunderstanding, that of too narrow a conception of the types of situations which constitute problems for human beings, and about which they have to make choices and adopt policies. It is true that talk of rational choice or preference suggests a situation of deciding what is for one's own interest or personal advantage in a particular situation. But there are much larger issues with respect to which we must form preferences and make choices. For there are social customs and moral rules and laws; and sometimes we are called upon to decide which of these we shall support, advocate, or join with others in promoting. When this happens the question arises: Which customs, or moral rules, or laws are ones which a given person must rationally prefer – or, more important, which ones are qualified to commend themselves to *every* rational person who is living in a society? And, for persons of good will, a still narrower question will arise: What rules or laws *would* a rational person wish to see written in the consciences of men or the legal institutions of his society *if* he were also a person of a normal degree of altruism or concern for the welfare of other persons? Now these questions are at least very like the questions people raise when they ask what is obligatory or right or one's duty, in the ordinary senses of these words. Or at least it is arguable that what is *clear and important* in the questions "What is the right thing to do?" and "What is my duty in these circumstances?" and "Which action, if any, is morally obligatory in these circumstances?" could be phrased either as one of the foregoing questions about what choice would be rationally preferable, or as a minor modification of one of these. There is another kind of question. This is the question of what attitude or public policy it is rational to adopt toward persons who have disobeyed laws or rational social rules, and so on – or of what attitude or policy it would be rational for persons with a normal degree of altruism to adopt. And this question is at least very like the question people raise when they ask whether the conduct of a person was morally blameworthy in the circumstances; or at least it is arguable that it captures all that is clear and important in such a question.

It is incidentally worth notice that there is a sense in which rational

21

policies for these various types of situations may conflict. For it might be rational, in our sense, for me to prefer one course of action in a certain situation, although this course of action is forbidden by a moral rule it is rational for me to support, or at least which it would be rational for me to support if I had a normal degree of altruism. Again, it might be rational for me to perform a certain action the condemnation or even punishment of which would be decreed by social rules or laws which I must rationally support, or at any rate must rationally support if I have a normal share of altruism. Such conflicts, I think, do exist and are an important problem for moral philosophy; it is not merely, as some philosophers seem to think, that only confused philosophers think there are such problems.

My answer to the first objection, then, in sum is this. The charge is that if we construe the job of moral philosophy as that of determining which attitudes or policies are rational in the sense explained, then all the different problems of the moral life are made to collapse into one problem, that of fixing what is in the self-interest of the agent. My reply is that this charge ignores the fact that we are called upon to make many types of choices, and among them the decision whether we shall give our support to certain moral rules, or to their being written into laws and into the consciences of men. And my suggestion is that when we see that there are these various choices, we can see that the proposal after all does preserve an interest in the various problems of the moral life. I have not, of course, touched upon all the various traditional questions of moral philosophy – for instance, that of the fair or just.

There is a second charge which may be leveled against the present suggestion about the tasks of moral philosophy. It will be said that at least the first suggested job, that of determining which attitudes would be adopted by *everyone* who was knowledgeable about the world and himself, is a vain one. For, it will be said, there are *no* attitudes or preferences about which we can say that they would be adopted by *every* knowledgeable and normal person. For do we not know that any conceivable attitude or policy would be reasonable provided a person's basic values were of an appropriate kind, and do we not know that *any* basic value is possible? Surely there is no such thing as *the* rational attitude toward anything.

We must distinguish, however, between the logically possible and the causally possible. Given that there is no *contradiction* in supposing that a knowledgeable person have a certain attitude, it may still be *causally impossible* for a knowledgeable person to have that attitude, if he is in a normal frame of mind. I do not mean by this merely that we should be unwilling to say that a person was in a "normal" frame of mind if he was both knowledgeable and had a certain attitude, although in some cases this may be true. I rather have in mind, for one thing, the possibility that an analysis of what it is to choose or form a preference is such as to exclude the possibility of certain preferences. I have in mind, for another thing, the possibility that certain attitudes will be inevitable in persons whose cognitive orientations are sound, whose past lives have included normal interactions with a family and other persons, and who are free of distortions produced by fear and anxiety. To suggest this is to make a large and programmatic claim. I do not pretend that we actually have much knowledge of this sort. To make the claim stick would require, for one thing, a systematic philosophical psychology. Let me, however, for the benefit of the skeptical, present one example of what I have in mind. Some philosophers, for example Sidgwick, have argued that it would be irrational for a person to prefer what he regarded as a smaller good to what he regarded as a larger one just because the smaller one could be attained today rather than tomorrow. To be more explicit, suppose that, if the choice between having either A or B *today* were presented to a person, he would take A in preference to B. The question then is whether a *rational* person would still prefer A to B, if the choice were between having A at one time and having B at a later time. To make the question sensible, of course, we have to lay down some restrictions. A sensible person will recognize that he may be dead tomorrow; there may also be an actual disutility in waiting; and so on. So we must modify our A and B so as to compensate for these differences; or better, for purposes of simplicity, we should choose an A and B for circumstances such that these differences do not arise. Now I suggest that Sidgwick may have been correct if what he was arguing for was this: That *no* perfectly knowledgeable (etc.) human being would alter his preference for A over B (assuming these adjustments have been made or the need for them does not arise) purely because of the time at which these events would occur. Why not? When we prefer one thing to another, we prefer it as falling under some description, as something of a certain kind. Now, if a person did alter his preference solely because of the time, it must be because the description "an event A *today*" as compared with the description "an event A *next week*" elicits preference, even after the important differences, such as the possibility of death in the meantime, have been adjusted for. Is this possible for a rational person? I think it isn't. The time position of an event is something that can't make a difference to the motivating power of a conception, once it is clear to a person – as of course it is to a person who has the relevant facts vividly before him – that it is one and the same self that enjoys or undergoes the event at either time. The time at which an event occurs *ex hypothesi* does not affect the flavor or quality of the experience. The time of an event is qualityless; it is the fact of position in an order. So, if what elicits interest is the conceived quality of an event, as I incline to think it is, temporal position as such does not affect rational preference. So, if *A* is preferred to *B* now, a rational being, aware of the fact that the experiences will be the same irrespective of the times at which they occur, will still prefer *A* to *B* even if *A* is to come at a later date than *B*. The reason why some people prefer the nearer good to the further one, I suppose, is that they find it harder to imagine what it is like to get the good at a later time, or forget that it is *they* who after all will be enjoying the later experience. In so far they fall short of rationality.

If this suggestion is correct, then there is *one* kind of preference which is necessary for a rational being. I suspect there are many more like it.

To the second charge that there are no distinctively rational attitudes, then, my reply is that the charge seems formidable because attitudes are conceived in a logical vacuum, where everything is possible which is not self-contradictory. But, when we consider what human beings are, what choices and preferences are, and what it is to adopt them, we may see that many logical possibilities are not realized in fact.

Let us look at a third charge. This is simply that it requires to be made out why, of all the jobs the moral philosopher might undertake, the one described has paramount claim on him. Is there any reason to suppose that the most important thing the moral philosopher can do for practice is make clear which choices or preferences or attitudes are rational in the sense described? This is a question which will engage our attention later. But two points are worth our attention now.

The first reply to it is a hypothetical statement. It is that *if* the job of the moral philosopher is to bring facts and logic to bear in the guidance of choice to a maximal extent, then the task as outlined must be the task of the moral philosopher. For to identify a principle of action or an attitude as "rational" in our sense *is* to show which choices or attitudes are the ones required by reason and fact in the sense that a person who was perfectly knowledgeable and had the relevant facts vividly before him and made no logical mistakes and was in a normal frame of mind would adopt them. To show what is the rational act or attitude precisely *is* to bring fact and reason to bear on the practical to a maximal extent. Similarly, if we cannot identify a choice or attitude as rational for everybody, at least to show an individual how to ascertain which attitudes of his are not excluded by considerations of reason, is again to do all that can be done in the way of bringing logic and facts to bear on choice. So, granted that the job of the moral philosopher is to bring fact and logic to bear in the guidance of choices, the philosopher's job would seem to be the one stated.

A second reason why it is important for the moral philosopher to help get clear what is a rational preference in the sense explained is that a distinctive feature of knowing that a choice would be rational in this sense is that there can be no further question whether it is reasonable to make that choice. Knowing that a choice would be rational in our sense is therefore different from knowing, say, that a choice is one it is our *duty* to make; for a person can still ask whether it is reasonable to do one's duty when it conflicts, say, with self-interest. But if a man knows what he would choose if he had vividly in mind all the relevant facts about himself and the world and were in a normal frame of mind, the question whether it is rational for him to do this, at least in my sense of "rational," is devoid of all sense. Here I agree, I think, with what W. D. Falk has often argued. It is true, of course, that a person may believe some choice is rational in this sense and at the same time wonder whether it is his *duty* to make it or even if it is not his duty *not* to make it. I shall return to the question whether this fact raises a serious problem. It is also true that a man may believe some choice is reasonable in my sense but fail to make it: The alcoholic, for instance, may believe it is not a rational thing for him to take another drink, but may still go on and take it. The alcoholic's problem, however, is about motivation, not about what is reasonable; what he needs is medical advice, or sympathy, or exhortation, not argument about what it is rational for him to do.

II

The foregoing suggestion about the job of moral philosophy has to be appraised in view of another and different account. The remainder of my remarks will comprise a discussion and evaluation of this other view.

This second view is that the natural starting-point of moral philosophy is the existence in ordinary language of certain terms, and the use in ordinary discourse of these terms in certain questions, all of which may be identified as "practical" terminology. There are such questions as: "What is *desirable* in itself?" "When is a . . . a *good* . . . ?" "When is a course of action the *best* one to choose [from the point of view of a particular person]?" "When does a person have a *moral obligation* to do something?" "When is a situation or action *just*?" And so on. No one, of course, will deny that these are questions which people continually raise, or that they are important questions, or that they are questions which have occupied the center of the stage in much of the history of moral philosophy.

Many philosophers have thought that the main job of philosophy is the analysis of concepts, or of recurrent types of question – and that the main job of the moral philosopher in particular is the analysis of terms, and questions, like those just mentioned. Just as they have thought the business of the philosopher is to analyze concepts like Cause, Number, and Material Thing, so it is his business to analyze notions like Good, Right, and Responsibility.

Philosophers use the word "analyze" in more than one way. The analysis here in question is analysis in the sense of determining and describing or characterizing the *actual* meaning or use or effect of ethical words as they appear in ordinary language, not in the sense of making useful recommendations for change in meaning or use.

The purpose of such a taxonomic inquiry is often simply the satisfaction of curiosity; it is of interest to distinguish and classify all different types of terms from both semantic and pragmatic points of view – as property-ascribing, or "performative," and so on. But the purpose is often also instrumental: The analysts have hoped to pave the way for more effective moral reasoning, and have envisaged the role of the philosopher as that of the clarifying midwife who helps answer questions by helping get the questions clear. For they suppose that, once it is clear what the ordinary man's ethical questions mean, or how they should be characterized, it will already be pretty clear how one should go about answering them, what methodology one may reasonably employ in finding the answers, or how a given alleged answer may be justified. Thus they suppose that the activity of analysis of ordinary ethical language, and the results of such analysis, set the stage for and are a necessary preparation for, the activity of normative reflection, that is, proposals for the answer of these questions, with supporting reasons. Philosophers sometimes do not think it the business of the philosopher to reach or defend any answers to normative questions at all, on the ground that this activity lies outside the domain of analysis of language, which is the proper business of philosophy; but many philosophers think that, *if* one is going to try to reach and defend normative conclusions, one can proceed rationally only on the basis of conclusions about the meaning of ethical questions in ordinary discourse, and the implications for methodology laid down by these conclusions. This view I wish to question.

This view, I say, is held by many philosophers. I suppose many or most contemporary naturalists view their conclusions about the meaning of ethical terms in ordinary language as a solid base for their normative discussions. For the result of any naturalistic analysis of an ethical word

26

like "good" is that at least one proposition connecting ethical and no-nethical concepts is construed as true by definition, guaranteed by the very meaning of ethical terms in ordinary discourse. Hence the naturalist's discussion of normative questions can begin with the guarantee, say, that an act is right if it will probably maximize happiness, or would be approved by an impartial, informed, and normal judge. It is not only naturalists, however, who think that reasoning in ethics has a basis of somewhat this kind, and that ethical thinking must acknowledge the epistemological priority of analysis of meanings. Obviously nonnaturalist cognitivist philosophers, like G. E. Moore, may hold that the analysis of ethical language shows that some important ethical statements are analytic, such as "An action is right if and only if it maximizes intrinsic value." But also noncognitivist philosophers, who deny that ethical words are property-ascribing, have supposed that the analysis of ordinary ethical language can give important guidance in the identification of sound ethical reasoning. Take for instance Stephen Toulmin. He denies that ethical words are property-ascribing, but he asserts as a point about English usage that a judgment is called "moral" or "ethical" only if it is used to avoid unnecessary suffering or increase deep satisfaction, in the speaker's community, by altering behavior or attitudes. This point about language forms the logical support for his conclusion that an ethical judgment is discharging its proper function only, roughly, if it can properly be taken as the logical consequence of the application of appropriate utilitarian premises to the situation. The analysis of language, then, is made to identify broadly utilitarian reasoning as sound reasoning in ethics. Much the same is true of R. M. Hare. In his book, *Freedom and Reason*, Hare commences with the thesis that ethical statements are to be construed roughly as imperative statements, prescriptions, addressed to everyone whose situation they may fit. "It is wrong to do A in circumstances C" means "Don't anyone in circumstances C ever do $A!$" From this equivalence Hare thinks we can infer how sound ethical reasoning must proceed, and to what extent and by what devices we may hope to meet the contentions of the Nazi or the segregationist. For, by the equivalence, to know whether something is wrong is to know whether one is prepared to proscribe it for everyone including one's self. Since one hardly knows whether he wants to proscribe something until he knows what it would be like for the proscription to be accepted, it is always a point relevant to the acceptance of a moral principle, what it would be like for the principle to be lived by universally. Relevant moral thinking is thus reflection on which proscriptions one wants universally accepted in view of what life would be like if they were so accepted. A moral judgment is as well justified as it can be if, in full view of what universal acceptance

27

would be like, the speaker is willing to issue the universal imperative which is identical in meaning with the moral judgment.

This way of looking at matters is an attractive one. In any area of discourse, if we wish to assess a given thesis, we had better first find out exactly what the thesis is, and then consider what are the grounds pro and con. Surely, it may seem, this must also be true for all value judgments. And, of course, the analysis of the meaning or use of ethical statements is something about which we ought to be able to get agreement, as much as on any subtle point of empirical science. For, despite the complications, determining the meaning or use of any sentence is essentially a scientific task, and we should expect eventually to be able to reach agreement about the matter. The analysis of ethical language, at least, is "value free," so that we can expect to get solid ground on which to work out what must be the methodology of normative ethics.

I believe, however, that the expectation that the analysis of ordinary language can thus set the stage for normative ethics is unduly optimistic, and a grave oversimplification of the facts. Most of the remainder of my remarks will be aimed at supporting this assessment of the situation.

Let me begin by considering a hypothetical example. Professor John Ladd once suggested that the central moral term of the Navaho Indians is "bahadzid," which roughly is translated as "dangerous" or "imprudent." Now suppose we became convinced that this is the only term in the Navaho language which comes anywhere close to our ethical vocabulary. Would we think that the Navaho moral philosopher could properly confine himself to determining what actions are properly called "bahadzid"? I think we should answer in the negative. We should feel that, before one can think clearly about an action being dangerous or imprudent, we first need the concepts of desirable and undesirable states of affairs, indeed of the intrinsically desirable and undesirable. Again, we would think that there should be terminology available for classifying an action as beneficial or harmful from the point of view of the whole social group, and not merely from the point of view of the agent or his family group; or perhaps there should be terminology available for classifying acts as conforming to or infringing rules the acceptance of which as binding for all members of the group would be socially beneficial. If the Navaho do not have such terms, or raise such questions, we should think: "So much the worse for them!"

This hypothetical example leads to the following question: When should a moral philosopher be satisfied with a given conceptual network for ethics, including definitions or characterizations of the main terms in the system? I suggest that the answer is *not:* when the evidence is cogent that the conceptual network represents accurately the actual moral language of the community. In contrast I suggest the following alternative: A moral philosopher should be satisfied with a conceptual framework if it enables him to raise all the questions concerning conduct and choice and preference he thinks it is important to raise and distinguish, in view of his total understanding of moral discourse, human preferences, moral attitudes, of the function of all these in personal and social living; *and* if the procedure for answering questions about how to choose or act which is implied by his definitions or characterizations as being the proper procedure is all that he thinks can be or need be done to resolve questions about practice. More briefly, I suggest that a philosopher's satisfaction with a given set of conceptual tools for practical thinking should depend on his view of the distinct types of problems which life in society poses, and of ways of reasoning to resolve these problems which he thinks possible and finds satisfying.

In saying this, I am happy to find myself in fairly near agreement with various moral philosophers. R. B. Perry, with all his obscurity about procedure in ethical theory, is a notable example. Perry said that the question is not how ethical words *are* used, for they are used confusedly, but how they are *best* used. W. K. Frankena posed the issue more clearly, in advocating that the problems of metaethics demand for their solution " 'clarity and decision' about the nature and function of morality, of moral discourse, and of moral theory. . . . "[1]

A philosopher who denies that the task of moral philosophy is primarily getting clear about the actual meanings or uses of ethical terms in ordinary discourse need not advocate that philosophy abandon the job of midwife in the practical thinking of ordinary people. For there is more than one way of clarifying ethical discourse. One can do it by formulating explicitly what was implicit in a person's actual question. *Or* one can do it by showing that his actual question is better dropped in favor of another but related question, which has more point.

So far I have given no *reason* why moral philosophers should not found their normative reflections on an examination of ordinary ethical language. Why must they leave purely descriptive formulations of linguistic habits for a more reconstructive enterprise? Why must a purely descriptive account of ordinary ethical discourse fail to set the stage for ethical methodology, or normative ethics, in the way many philosophers have en-

---

1 In "Obligation and Motivation," in A. I. Melden, ed., *Essays in Moral Philosophy* (Seattle: University of Washington Press, 1958). On p. 80 he notes comments by other philosophers who have made suggestions along the same line, including C. L. Stevenson, P. H. Nowell-Smith, W. D. Falk, H. D. Aiken, and Philip Rice.

visaged? Let us look at some of the problems we face, if we choose a purely descriptive analysis of ordinary language as the basis of our ethical methodology, in one of the fashions sketched above.

First, the average person uses "good" or "obligatory," in the important contexts, without a definite intended meaning in mind. People do not have a conception of what it is to be good or obligatory in the way they have a conception of what it is to be, say, a bachelor. Hence, whereas "All bachelors are unmarried" can be supported by appeal to inspection of conscious meanings, ethical first principles (except for trivial cases) cannot be.

We may concede to naturalism that there are some exceptions to this. For instance, if several persons are on a beach and looking for stones to skip, and someone calls "Here's a good one!" his utterance perhaps just means "Here's one with the properties requisite for success in the present business." But there are many contexts, and among them the most important for practical decisions, in which the intended meanings are not so clear. Suppose a person asks whether it would be a *good thing* to make certain sacrifices in order to give himself time to develop some original ideas in philosophy. Or suppose a person asks if a system of slavery must be *wrong* because unjust, even in circumstances in which a slave system would benefit the society. In such cases, it seems the ordinary person does not have *any* intended meaning close to the surface, in the way he has it for the example above; hence the intended meaning will not support a claim for the analyticity of a corresponding ethical generalization. Perhaps the usage of some persons is an exception to this judgment. Jeremy Bentham, for instance, as a result of long preaching of his utilitarian system, may have meant exactly what he said he did; for him "is wrong" may have meant just "tends not to maximize utility." But such cases are exceptional; most persons are just puzzled if asked the meaning of their ethical terms, and look to the philosopher for light on the meaning of their own ethical questions. So when Moore says that "right action" means "action which will maximize intrinsic good" or when Hare says that "*A* is wrong" means "Don't anyone ever do *A!*" they are not proposing expressions which most persons could properly classify as synonyms on the basis of inspection of their own consciously intended meanings.

Philosophers who think that analysis of actual meanings of ethical words can set the stage for normative reasoning in one of the ways suggested may not be fazed by the above contention, even if they accept it. They may be happy to reformulate their point in terms of "implicit meanings" instead of "consciously intended meanings." They may say that what the ordinary man is doing with his ethical words is definite

30

enough; the appearance of trouble arises only from the fact that he is unable to explain or characterize his own usage. He means something definite all right, but we must dig deeper to find it – as is true in many other areas of discourse. And we can find what he means by his terms, by noticing the way in which he conducts inquiries, and by noting what he accepts as evidence or arguments pro or con. Such observations can provide a test for hypotheses about what he means by his ethical words. Hence, even when what he means by ethical words is not obvious to him on inspection of conscious meaning, we can properly talk of his "implicit" meaning, and draw inferences about the analyticity of some ethical principles, and so on, as suggested earlier. Implicit meanings are enough.

This proposal leads to my second objection. This is that, even if we do not reject the whole concept of "implicit meanings" as dubious, the implicit meanings of ethical terms cannot function as a source for criticism of a person's ethical reflection or of his ethical principles. The reason is this. The proposal in question suggests that a theory about a person's implicit meanings is to be supported by appeal to the way in which he conducts ethical reflection, and by the ethical principles he takes for granted in his thinking. But then we cannot *correct* his modes of reflection and his ethical principles by appeal to his implicit meanings, for our judgment about his meaning is based on these. If his implicit meanings, according to our conclusion, are inconsistent with his modes of reflection or his ethical principles, what is shown is simply that our views about his meanings are unfounded. For instance, suppose G. E. Moore tried to reform a man's nonutilitarian ethical principles by appeal to his own meaning of "right." Moore would be arguing that the meaning of "right" is "maximizes intrinsic value"; and it is true that if this is what one means by "right" it is inconsistent not to be a utilitarian. But Moore could hardly justify ascribing this meaning for "right" to the nonutilitarian, on the basis of the man's mode of ethical reflection, since *ex hypothesi* the man's ethical principles are nonutilitarian. It seems, then, that a man cannot be forced into accepting certain ethical principles or modes of reasoning by appeal to his "implicit meanings" and the necessity of being consistent. For this effect, if one cannot appeal to his consciously intended meanings at the outset, it looks as if one must first convince him that certain questions are the important questions, the ones he *wants* to raise; in other words, one must persuade him in effect to *accept* a certain construction of his original question. How might one convince him of this? In parallel cases in the philosophy of science, when we are considering how to use "explanation" or "cause," at least part of the reason for adopting a certain construction of these terms consists in reviewing the advantages of using the terms in a certain way, of showing how such a

31

use would fit in with the total conceptual structure. Similarly in ethics: Whether a person accepts a certain interpretation of his question will depend on considerations quite different from a review of his previous linguistic habits; it will depend on considerations like those already mentioned – those I said a philosopher will take into account before he is satisfied with a given conceptual framework for ethics.

Even if the two foregoing objections are unconvincing, however, there is a further difficulty for philosophers who wish to criticize ethical reasoning by appeal to the meanings of ordinary ethical words. For the meaning of these words, in whatever sense they have a meaning, must surely be supposed to differ from one speaker to another. Many philosophers have assumed that there is one single meaning or use of moral terms for important contexts, common to our speech-community. But this supposition ignores the extent to which a person's meanings are entwined with his total conceptual system. In general, as we learn or change our system of beliefs, our concepts change. Why should the same not be true for moral concepts? Take for instance the moral concepts of religious people. Suppose a religious person *says* that what it means for an action to be morally obligatory is for it to be required by God's will for us. He supports this testimony by his deeds: In order to find his duty he prays, or searches Scripture; and when he becomes convinced that something is God's will, that thing has supreme authority in his conduct, or if it does not he attributes the fact to his moral weakness. Why should we not take him at his word and concede the relation of his moral and theological conceptions? Philosophers have a neat dialectical device, whose use goes back perhaps to Plato, to prove that religious people are mistaken in such an explanation of their moral concepts. Philosophers refute the religious man to their satisfaction merely by raising the question whether it is or is not true *by definition* that a right action is any action that God wills. The religious man is supposed to, and almost always will, concede that this proposition is not just true by definition, not just an unimportant tautology deriving from the meaning of "right," and hence admits that his explanation of meanings was incorrect. It is not clear, however, why he must give away his case by such an answer. And if he does, the most that is proved is that he is confused, and not that his moral concepts are really identical with those of Bertrand Russell. Or to take another case, suppose an unruly school boy from the East Side tells us that for some action to be wrong is for it to be one which will get one in trouble with the law or one's father or with the school authorities. Can we really go on to prove that he has the same moral concepts as Moore and Sidgwick? It is obvious that learning the English language guarantees certain things about the use of ethical words, specifically many interrelationships of terms like "duty," "ought," and "obligation." But I suggest that on the subtler points – what it is for something to be intrinsically good or right – there may be as much disparity of concepts as there is disparity of total conceptual schemes in which moral language is embedded. By what criterion of "same concept" may we say that such diverse types of minds are expressing the same concepts by their moral words?

If I am right in this, then the moral philosopher who wishes analysis of language to set the stage for a methodology of ethics must be prepared to propose different methodologies for different people, depending on their wider conceptual schemes. It is, or may be, unwarranted to suppose that English usage commits us to one methodology for ethics.

These considerations should be enough to give pause to a philosopher who is tempted to give pride of place to the analysis of actual meanings of ethical words in his general theory of justification in ethics. But there are two other serious questions about his philosophical program.

First, these philosophers aim to use the analysis of ethical language as a device for criticizing ethical reflection, but in fact moral terms as actually used are rather blunt instruments which require to be sharpened for effective use. To be more explicit, when we reflect on the differences between various types of situations, we realize that the things which moral terms can sensibly be used to say about them are rather different. Hence, if one and the same word is to be used to make these different points, it must be capable of use in different senses in different contexts. But in fact there are no such recognized different senses of moral terms; and if one becomes clearly conscious of the different things that can sensibly be meant by them in different contexts, it is not by study of the English uses of the terms, but by the study of moral philosophy. One can master English perfectly well without learning these distinct senses at all. Moral language makes for confusion by failing to distinguish between questions that ought to be distinguished; and, as we shall see in a moment, it also sometimes confusingly labors distinctions that are without a difference. Thus moral thinking cannot be rendered more effective by appeal to the meanings of ordinary moral language; what is needed for this purpose is rather reflection about the differences between situations and noticing what can sensibly be said about the different situations.

Let me illustrate the point. Consider "wrong." Sometimes we say "It would be wrong to do that," meaning to claim that a certain possible action is forbidden by sound moral principles. Sometimes we say, "It was wrong of him to do that," meaning to condemn the agent for a past action that we think he would not have performed but for a defect of character. Now if "is wrong" is to *say* these different things, it must

33

possess corresponding different senses; but there are not recognized distinct senses of this sort in English. There is only one sense of "wrong" recognized by dictionaries, which has to do both jobs. If we see clearly that there are two different issues here, it is not simply because we have learned English. Moral language does not separate the questions for us. Immanuel Kant presumably knew German, but he repeatedly failed to distinguish these very differences. The following argument is sometimes used by ordinary persons: "One is not acting wrongly if he sincerely thinks that what he does is his duty. Therefore if a person does what he thinks is his duty he is always doing the right thing." The existence of this argument has to be charged to the discredit of English as a tool for reflection about ethical problems.

The opposite defect, which the English language also bears, is the laboring of distinctions without a significant difference. A prime example of this is the existence of the terms "duty," "obligation," and "wrong," all capable of being employed in moral contexts, in good English. These words are not exact synonyms: At least, we may say it is wrong to commit adultery or be cruel to an animal, but it sounds queer to say that we have a moral obligation not to commit adultery or be cruel to animals, or to say that this is our moral duty. But while the associations, linguistic ties, suggestions, and flavors of these words are different, it is not clear that there is a difference of substance between what one says with one and what one says with another. Yet the differences of the words are a standing temptation to suppose that there are corresponding differences of substance. C. H. Whiteley and others, for instance, have argued that something is a duty or obligation only if one has made a contract or promise; and H. L. A. Hart has suggested that a person has a duty or obligation only when there is some other person who has a right. Now, even if these writers were correct in their accounts of what English permits us to say, we could still ask if there is some important sense in which we are free to be cruel to animals, if cruelty to animals is merely wrong but there is no obligation to refrain from it? It is hard to see that the difference of terminology makes any important point, or that it does anything but obscure the moral similarity of the cases.

If one turns to such words as "just" and "justice" one hardly knows whether to say that language has added a superfluous term which confuses matters by seeming to point to differences where there are none, or to complain that there is only one set of terms for covering a great many different situations which ought to be sharply distinguished. Either way, it is doubtful whether attention to the actual use of these terms will take us far toward making the conceptual distinctions it is important to make.

Obviously, then, in many contexts the analysis of ordinary moral language can be of little help in criticizing moral principles and reasoning, because the English language itself needs reform before it is an efficient tool for clear moral thinking.

There is a final reason why it is questionable whether a philosopher should begin with an analysis of actual meanings, and then proceed to develop a corresponding methodology for ascertaining whether terms like "good" and "right" apply. This reason is simply the fact that we are not bound to accept the view that the ultimate aim of normative reasoning, or of moral philosophy, is to identify the situations in which moral terms in their ordinary senses are properly applied – in other words, to answer exactly the questions people raise in ordinary moral language. In other words, it is doubtful whether there is *any point* in knowing whether "good" or "right" in their ordinary senses apply to action or choice, *provided* these terms turn out to refer to something quite different from "rational" choice or preference in the sense described earlier. Why is this?

At an earlier stage I pointed out that a "rational" choice or preference in my sense is one that would occur if one were fully and vividly aware of all the relevant available facts about the world and one's self, and were in a normal frame of mind. A choice or preference so made, I suggested, has been guided by the facts to the full extent.

It is clear that we have a choice as moral philosophers: Whether to recommend that a person make the best choice in the ordinary sense of "best," or the rational choice in my sense of "rational"; and whether to urge, say, that a person do what is morally obligatory in the ordinary sense of that phrase, or do what conforms, say, with the rules he would want written in the consciences of men if he were rational in my sense.

Consider an example. Suppose I prefer to hear one orchestra program rather than another, in the situation that I know whatever facts might affect my preferences; my preference is then rational in my sense. But suppose someone claims that the opposite preference would be better. Perhaps this could not be shown; but since it is an empirical question how "better" is actually used as applied to such choice, it is logically possible that the opposite preference is the better one in the ordinary sense. The question then arises why one must recommend the preference that is "better." Is the fact that it is better a reason for adopting it? The fact that it would be better could not be a new empirical fact that would tend to move my preference in a certain way, for our definition of a "rational" preference requires that it already have been formed in full view of *all* the relevant empirical facts, including whatever empirical fact is meant by "the other being better." One might, of course, say that some nonnatural fact is in question; but since it is not clear what kind of fact such a nonnatural fact might be, I shall ignore this possibility. I concede that perhaps it is tautologously true that it would be better to follow the better preference rather than the rational one if there is conflict; but this, if true, only re-raises the initial question, why one should take an interest in the better rather than the more rational. It is also true that the expression "is the best thing" may have *de facto* authority over conduct in the sense that when we decide that something is "best" in the ordinary sense, our conditioned responses to the phrasing may be such that we incline to do the thing that we have judged best. It may well be that our conditioned responses are firmer and more favorable to "is the best thing" than to "is the rational thing" especially when explicitly understood in my sense. But it would be absurd for a person to guide his conduct not by the facts but by the *words* which may properly be applied to it. My conclusion is that a more rational choice, in my sense, cannot in good reason take second place to a choice which is better in the ordinary sense, if there should be a conflict between the two.

Much the same may be said for conduct which is properly called "morally obligatory" as contrasted, say, with conduct which would be required by the rules of a society which a rational person, in my sense, might want for his society.

Once such questions are raised, it is clear that there is a difficult question to be answered, before we must assume that the job of the moral philosopher is to begin with the analysis of ordinary ethical words with the aim of determining to what things these words can properly be applied in their ordinary senses.

The foregoing queries about making the analysis of the actual meaning or use of ethical terms central in the enterprise of clarifying the justification of attitudes and choices, and the methodology for ethics, are not intended to deny importance to the examination of the meanings of ethical words. Indeed, there is a sense in which the actual use of ordinary language is a test for the adequacy of any framework of concepts we might propose for ethics. For if we found, after we had become accustomed to use a set of concepts, that we still wanted to ask and answer questions framed in the terminology of ordinary language in its old sense, there would be reason to think that something was wrong with the proposed structure, and that modifications were in order. We can accept a point once made by Stevenson: If the philosopher has an adequate conceptual scheme there should be no need for relapsing into the use of ethical terms in some other and more familiar sense.

My critical remarks about the limitations of the place of analysis of actual meanings are also, very probably, more applicable to a theory of what philosophers ought to be doing than to their actual practice. Phi-

losophers hardly ever make any inquiries of an empirical sort into ordinary usage. The philosopher who says he is analyzing "ordinary
language" in ethics is usually doing something more interesting than he
describes it as being. In the first place, he is introspecting to determine
his *own* usage – and his own usage has already been fumigated by what
he knows about blind alleys in philosophy, and suffused by much general
knowledge, as well as by awareness of many problems of which the
ordinary man is ignorant. The philosopher's own usage is apt to reflect
his own conclusions about what questions can usefully be raised or answered in the realm of practice. Moreover, his definitions are likely to
present an orderly conceptual framework in which distinctions are made
which he knows to be necessary, and which reflect a salutary preoccu-
pation with philosophical psychology. So, in various ways, the practice
of metaethical inquiry is apt to incorporate many of the reforms I have
been suggesting. But it seems worth while to recognize what metaethical
inquiries should be, and to confess to ourselves that what they should
be is something less simple than just a clarifying description of what
ordinary questions mean.

3

Rational desires

One of the questions discussed by the earliest philosophers was: "What things are desirable for themselves, that is, intrinsically desirable?" Various philosophers have tried, in one way or another, to justify an answer to it. Some have claimed to demonstrate that pleasure is at least one thing that is intrinsically desirable, if not the only thing, and some have claimed to show that fame and wealth do not enjoy this status.

In the present century, philosophers have become somewhat pessimistic about the prospects for reasonable arguments to show that something is, or is not, intrinsically desirable. There have been sporadic attempts to offer such arguments, but in large works such as those produced by Ralph Barton Perry or H. J. Paton, the criticism of beliefs about the intrinsically valuable is not even broached, and the authors have contented themselves with discussing how policies for action might be recommended because they promise to satisfy inclusive sets of interests consistently or harmoniously. They have criticized basic objectives only by showing that they are not compossible with other objectives. In general, philosophers have been clear enough how to criticize beliefs about what is instrumentally valuable; obviously such criticism proceeds by investigating causes and consequences. But philosophers have been wary about showing that any alleged intrinsic value is not really a value. In general it seems to be thought that if a person thinks something is intrinsically valuable, or adopts some end as a basic objective, facts and logic cannot do very much about it; basic commitments, it is thought, may be changed by propaganda but not by anything reasonably called objective criticism.

This pessimism among philosophers is duplicated among social scientists, who mostly regard the fact-value distinction as clear and important, and think that questions of fact can be resolved by appeal to logic and observation, whereas questions of basic objectives are ones to which logic and observation are essentially irrelevant. I do not suggest that this pessimism is universal and certainly some psychotherapists have argued vigorously that some basic objectives are essentially neurotic or maladjusted.

Presidential address delivered before the Sixty-eighth Annual Meeting of the Western Division of the American Philosophical Association in St. Louis, Missouri, May 8, 1970.

38

In view of this virtual unanimity of opinion one needs some excuse for returning to the topic of the criticism of views about intrinsic values, as I intend to do. One possible excuse is that discussing this old question is at least certain not to disappoint expectations; where philosophers are sure that nothing can be shown, at least they are not disappointed when nothing is. But I think there is a better excuse. I happen to think that recent psychological theory – in the areas of motivation, social learning theory, and theory of psychotherapy – while rather speculative has made some real advances, and both suggests a new way of looking at the question and provides some conceptual tools and empirical principles which give substantial assistance in the rational criticism of basic objectives. The suggestion that something in psychology can really be relevant to our philosophical question may not seem to you a likely one, but I think it will be agreed that if anything at all can be established about intrinsic values, in an objective way, the result is well worth the effort.

What I propose to do tonight is three things. First, I shall formulate a new question which I shall propose to substitute for the old question about what is intrinsically desirable. I shall then consider some contexts in which the new question can be answered from the resources of contemporary psychological theory. I shall spend most of my time on this second objective. Finally I shall explain why I think the new question does quite well as a formulation of what people have been wanting to know when they have asked the old question.

Let me plunge in and formulate at once the question I shall use as a substitute for the old question, "Is the state of affairs S intrinsically desirable?" My substitute question is this: "Is it *rational* [in a sense to be specified] for Mr. X to desire S intrinsically, or for itself?" Or, to expand a bit in order to come to a question more likely to be significant: "Is it rational for Mr. X to desire S intrinsically, to the degree, or with the intensity, he does?" Of course, we should also bear in mind a parallel substitute for the question, "Is the state of affairs S intrinsically *unde*sirable?" And the substitute would be, "Is it rational for Mr. X to have an intrinsic *aversion* to S?"

I propose to proceed as if the notion of an "intrinsic" desire were unproblematic. In view of some recent queries about the concept of intrinsic desirability, it may be dangerous to do this. However this may be, all I am going to say about the term "intrinsic" for this context is that I mean by an "intrinsic desire or aversion at a time t for a state of affairs S," a desire or aversion for S which would persist at t if the person involved bracketed, ignored, or put out of mind at t any thoughts or rather judgments about the probable consequences of S, and indeed *any* thoughts about S not included in the concept S.

39

There is another restriction to my goal this evening: I shall not be arguing that there are specific intrinsic desires or aversions which *every* rational person would have, or be without, although I think that in fact there are such desires or aversions. What I shall be arguing for is a much more modest conclusion. All I shall try to show is that certain intrinsic desires or aversions are irrational for certain persons, constituted as they are. That is, all I shall try to show is that some persons, if they were rational but otherwise as they are, would necessarily lack certain intrinsic desires or aversions. We might call such conclusions "person-relative" conclusions. Now, you may think that person-relative conclusions are unimportant, but that evaluation does not seem obvious to me. For when a person has an important decision to make, it strikes me as important to him which of his desires it is rational for him to have, and it is not obvious why he should worry about whether these desires would be rational for someone else. So I think that even person-relative conclusions about what is rationally desired are interesting.

I have not yet explained what I mean by "rational" in the phrase "rational desire," and since the interest of my contention must depend on what I mean by this expression, let me say at once how I use this term. First, I mean by a "rational" desire, a desire that is *not irrational*. I do *not* mean by a "rational" desire a desire it would be irrational *not* to have; I mean merely that it is one it is not irrational to have. What we need to know, then, is what I mean by an "irrational" desire. Roughly, I mean by an "irrational" desire or aversion one which would *not* survive, in a given person, in the presence of vivid awareness of knowable propositions. Or, to be a bit more explicit, I mean by saying that a certain desire is irrational for a given person, that the person would not continue to have the desire if he got before his mind vividly, with firm belief, not necessarily just once but on a number of occasions, all the *relevant* propositions the truth of which can be known to him at the very same time at which he was *reflecting on the object in a desiring way*. This explanation will have to be a bit further expanded in a moment, but let me point out for now that I am not saying that an intrinsic desire is irrational if a person would cease to have it at a given moment if at that moment he had vividly before him relevant knowledge; I am taking account of the fact that, in some cases at least, intrinsic desires or aversions can be extinguished only over a period of time. What I am claiming, in essence, is that some desires or aversions can be extinguished over time by facing relevant known true propositions; it is these I call "irrational."

It may be objected that it is a bit strange to use the term "rational" for any desire that survives confrontation with vivid awareness of relevant facts. And certainly this use of the term is very different from what is meant when the term "is rational" is applied to an *action,* and where the term is often used to mean simply "maximizes expectable utility" or "is the most effective means to the objectives in view." But if it is true that intrinsic desires can be extinguished or modified by bringing knowledge – facts and logic – into contact with them, I do not think it is unhelpful to use the word "rational" to designate the status of the desires which survive this confrontation. At any rate, for better or worse, that is how I am using the term "rational" this evening, and from now on I shall use it with that understanding in mind. The term, used in this sense, may not carry as favorable connotations as it normally does for you; I shall return later to the question what if anything follows if we show that some desire is rational in this sense. It may be helpful to point out that writers who have held what is sometimes called an "ideal observer" or "qualified attitude" conception of the analysis of technical terms and methodology have generally supposed that only some desires would occur in an "ideal observer," that is a person who is omniscient or at least has a vivid awareness of relevant facts. My present conception of a rational desire has affiliations with that concept.

An objection that may be raised to the concept of a "rational desire" just outlined is that it uses without explanation the notion of beliefs *relevant* to a given desire. In response to this possible objection let me say that I think there are two features we shall want to build into our concept of "relevance" in order to make the concept of a rational desire interesting and viable. First, we want to insist on a causal property: A belief will be deemed relevant only if vivid reflection on it will tend to influence the desire or aversion, either by extinguishing or reinforcing it. Second, the belief must be about either the intrinsic nature of the state of affairs at which the desire or aversion is directed, or about the desire or aversion itself, or about the conditions or consequences of these. I am not sure that this second specification eliminates very much, and doubtless a good deal of further refinement is called for. But I shall have to leave it at that.

I TWO TYPES OF IRRATIONAL INTRINSIC DESIRES OR AVERSIONS

I shall now argue that certain types of intrinsic desires or aversions will extinguish in certain conditions of vivid belief, and hence are irrational. Before I can do this, however, I must make some further preliminary remarks.

First, I must say something of my conception of a *desire* or *aversion.* The reason for this is that my argument will be an inference from principles of psychology, principles that have to do with classical conditioning and stimulus generalization. Now, these principles are obviously applicable in the way I am going to apply them only if a certain conception of desires or aversions is correct. In particular, I am going to assume that desires and aversions must be viewed as dispositions for *conditioned responses* to occur. At first sight, this may seem a quite unreasonable supposition, although on second thought, I believe, the suggestion is natural enough. At any rate, you should be warned that you may want to reject or at least reformulate my argument if you do not accept my conception of a desire or aversion.

What then is a desire? I shall ignore aversions, assuming that obvious substitutions for key concepts will enable my explanation of "desire" to cover "aversion." To repeat, what is it, then, to have a desire for a state of affairs *S*? To desire a state of affairs *S* is, I think, primarily for two things to be true. First, a person who desires *S* is in a state such that, *were* he to think of *S*, *S* would *seem attractive* to him. The notion of "seeming attractive" may seem obscure. If it does, I can suggest the terminology of David McClelland, saying instead that the thought of *S* produces or reinstates a favorable affective tone. Or, we might follow the language of Karl Duncker, and say that the thought of *S* "becomes aglow with an empathetical feeling tone of pleasantness." I hope this will be reasonably clear and shall not explain further, but merely point out that I am supposing that the "seeming attractive" phenomenon is logically distinct from *thinking* of the object *S*, and hence that it might be viewed as a *response* to the thought of *S* and therefore conceivably as a conditioned response. But a second thing is true when one desires something. If it occurs to a person who desires a state *S* that a certain action *A* on his part will tend to bring *S* about, and that failing to do *A* will tend to prevent the occurrence of *S*, he will both have and feel some impulse to do *A*. Let me point out that a disposition to do *A* if it is thought to be a necessary or sufficient condition of having *S* may also be viewed as a response to the thought of *S*, and hence possibly a conditioned response. These two aspects of desire *appear* to be logically distinct: Seeming attractive seems to be somewhat different from being ready to do something if one sees it will produce something else. But psychologically I suppose they are connected in a lawlike way.

I have said that I hope to show that certain kinds of desires (and aversions) will extinguish under certain conditions of vivid awareness of relevant facts. To show this, I shall have to appeal to the psychological theory of the extinction of desires and aversions. But I think what I shall say about this will not make much sense without some background in the psychological theory of the acquisition of desires and aversions. This leads me to a second preliminary excursus, which will be a brief summary of some salient points from the psychological theory of the development of desires and aversions; or, in other words, I shall begin by summarizing some salient points from the theory of how it comes about that to some thoughts there are connected seeming-attractive, or seeming-repellent responses.

Incidentally, at some point I should stop and acknowledge the fact that the branch of psychology concerned with our topic is not one of the more firmly established branches of human knowledge, but rather one of the more speculative. I have now done this. But we should not be deterred by this fact. One reason for this is that we do have to act, and it seems we should make use of the best information we have, and not act as if we had none at all. A second reason is that, even if the psychological theories we can now appeal to are mistaken in various ways, the main question is how in principle psychological theories can be used in the appraisal of intrinsic desires. We can get clear what psychological theory may be expected to do in this area, even if the principles we use need correction.

Now, as to the acquisition of desires. I think it would be agreed that no desires are *native;* that is, it is not a native unlearned fact that the *thought* of some state of affairs carries the seeming-attractive quality. The attachment of this quality to the thought, or the attachment of this response to a thought, has to be *learned.* And it can be learned in either of two ways: First, *indirectly,* when a person comes to *want* a certain experience because he has had *experiences* like it in the past and has liked them; and second, *directly,* by association, in a way to be explained.

Let us begin with indirect learning of desires. Let us first observe that there are some kinds of experiences that we like or dislike natively, without prior learning; we like certain tastes or smells, and we dislike loud sounds or the feeling of being burnt. These likes or dislikes are built into our physiology. There are other things which we like or dislike, not natively, but because previous experiences with them have been drive-reducing; for instance, scotch and water seems not to be liked natively but comes to be liked because drinks are tension- or anxiety-reducing. These likes or dislikes, as we shall see shortly, are undoubtedly the sources of some desires and aversions; for instance, we want to eat at least partly because we have enjoyed eating in the past. But I shall pay little attention to such cases, because rational extinction of these desires is wholly, or at least usually, impossible. Some things, however, come to be liked in a very different way, and it is important for us to notice how. Some things come to be liked or disliked because of *association* with some other experience already liked or disliked. One may like certain melodies because of association with gifts and other excitement on Christmas Day;

43

or a student may like getting an *A* on his term papers, because in the past *A*'s have been associated with parental hugs and congratulations. Likes and dislikes gained in this way are important; indeed, many psychologists think that prestige, wealth, and power are things which have come to be liked, largely for this reason. Of course, liking these things is not native, built-in. We must remember, then, that association with other experiences already liked is a very important cause for our liking some things which we certainly do not like natively.

But now, what do likes and dislikes have to do with what we *want* or *desire*? Or in other words, what do likes and dislikes of kinds of experiences have to do with thoughts of certain possible situations having a seeming-attractive, or a seeming-repellent quality? The tie between the two is furnished by the principle of *stimulus generalization*. The principle of stimulus-generalization – and I should perhaps here remark that there is controversy over the exact nature and status of the principle – is roughly this: If a person has acquired a tendency to make a certain response to a certain stimulus *S*, then he will tend to make the same response to any stimulus situation *S'*, in the degree to which it is similar to *S*. Roughly, the more *S'* resembles *S*, the more one will tend to make the same response to it. Now suppose there is a situation or experience *S*, and the person's response to it is one of *liking* it. One might, of course, question whether *liking* something is a response to a stimulus, but I think it would be widely agreed among psychologists that it is properly so classified; after all, liking has its behavioral manifestations, such things as approach responses or responses calculated to prolong the experience in question, or favorable verbal evaluations. The experience is what it is, and the liking, which consists at least in part of a disposition to behave in these ways, is a result of it. So we may call the liking a *response*.

Assuming this, then the principle of stimulus generalization tells us that if a stimulus situation *S* elicits a liking response, then any situation *S'* will tend to elicit the liking response to the degree that it is similar to *S*. Suppose now there occurs an *image* of an *S*, or an *idea* of *S*. Now imagining an *S* or thinking of an *S* is certainly different from an experience of the kind *S*, as philosophers have often pointed out; but in some important respects they are the same. And the proposal is that if *S* elicits the liking response, then by stimulus generalization the image of *S* or the thought of *S* will also elicit the liking response. And, if we may construe the liking response, in the context of images or thoughts, in terms of the seeming-attractive quality, or the tendency to produce, then stimulus generalization tells us how an experience of *S* liked in the past can cause *S* as conceived to seem attractive now. Some psychologists use somewhat different terminology. David McClelland, for instance, describes the re-

44

lation of desire to past experiences of things like what is desired, by saying that the idea partially reinstates the affective tone which went along with corresponding experiences in the past. Again, some psychologists influenced by Clark Hull or K. W. Spence prefer to speak of the thought of S – what they call a mediating response – as getting attached to it, by generalization, a *fractional anticipatory goal response* appropriate to S. However we put it, the idea is that some desires are results through stimulus generalization, of liking an experience similar to the one which is now desired. So getting an A on a term paper may be desired, as a case of stimulus generalization from liking the getting of an A, and this liking again, we saw, might derive from association with things already liked. So much, then, for the explanation of desires learned indirectly, through relation to past experiences liked either natively or otherwise.

Let me now point out that desires are sometimes acquired directly, not by the process just described, but by *direct association* with something already liked or disliked. That is, the *idea* of some state S occurs simultaneously with an experience already liked, and as a result the liking, or seeming-attractive response, gets attached to the idea of S. Incidentally, the fact that this can occur is widely relied upon at present in the treatment of alcoholism, homosexuality, and obesity. Let me explain how this works by an example from the treatment of alcoholism. Let us suppose an alcoholic wishes to make the *idea* of a martini aversive, instead of overpoweringly attractive, as it is at present. One thing he can do is *imagine very vividly* having a delicious mouthful of martini, and arrange to have himself given an electric shock simultaneously with this image. Thus, the patient gets an idea in mind and then has produced in him, by physical means, a state which is aversive, and the aversiveness gets associated with the idea of the martini. A different procedure is cognitive: That is, a person imagines very vividly having a delicious mouthful of martini, and then imagines vividly the details of how he felt the last time he was sick from martinis, or had a bad hangover. In this procedure the patient gets an idea in mind and then produces in himself, by reflection, an idea or image which is aversive, and the aversiveness of the latter gets associated with the idea of the martini. Whether physical or cognitive means are used to produce the aversive state, after frequent repetitions of the pairing, the *idea* of a martini gets associated with the affective tone of the aversive state, and the martini seems repellent. When this has happened, we say that a person has a prospective aversion – the opposite of a desire – for martinis.

We shall see shortly that this kind of direct association, instated by cognitive means, is an important part of what happens in the extinction of desires or aversions by confrontation with available knowledge; so I shall be discussing it more in detail in a moment. Incidentally, this same process, of direct association instituted by cognitive means, is the one operative when beliefs about the consequences of some state of affairs make the state of affairs attractive, or aversive, in itself. For to think of one state as regularly followed by another state, already attractive or aversive, is to associate the idea or image of one state of affairs with something already attractive or aversive.

Stimulus generalization, by the way, operates not only to extend liking responses from stimuli which are experiences or percepts to similar ideas or images; it also operates to extend the liking response from one experience to new experiences rather like it, and from the idea or image of one thing to the idea or image of another thing rather like the first.

After these preliminary remarks about the acquisition of desires and aversions, we are now ready to consider whether certain desires and aversions would extinguish, or be reduced in intensity, in certain people if they were rational, that is, if the desires and aversions were faced by clearly and vividly made affirmations of relevant known propositions. Let me remind you again that I am talking here only of *intrinsic* desires and aversions, that is, of desires and aversions for things at least partly for themselves. In what follows I shall discuss only two types of cases.

The first case I wish to discuss I shall for convenience label the case of "unauthentic" desires or aversions. I shall define an "unauthentic" desire or aversion toward some state of affairs S as a desire or aversion which could not have been developed toward S as a result, through stimulus generalization, of direct experiences of *typical* or *normal* instances of situations of the kind S. Since they could not have been developed by experience of normal instances of that kind, they must have been developed in some other way, but I am defining an "unauthentic" desire or aversion not by reference to its *actual* genesis, but by reference to the impossibility of its having developed by contact with normal samples of the kind of thing the desire or aversion is concerned with.

What might be examples of unauthentic desires or aversions in this sense? A famous case of such an aversion, reported in the 1920s, was of a child who acquired an aversion to all kinds of furry animals because an experimenter caused a very loud noise to occur when the child was in the presence of a rabbit. Obviously this aversion, which included aversion to fur coats, could not have been acquired by direct experience of normal samples of fur coats, which ordinarily do not come with loud noises! This example is unimportant. But it is not unimportant if a person acquires a strong aversion to nonachievement, or failure, as a result of traumatic experiences of censure by parents or teachers because of failure in school. And it is not unimportant if a person acquires an aversion to a certain kind of occupation, say, as a result of empathic response to seeing another person criticized for association with that occupation. Notice that direct experience of failure – and a fortiori of mere nonachievement! – in many contexts may not be very bad. You thought you would be a programmer for a computer and found that you were not cut out to be a programmer. So what? There are lots of other things to do. Or, you heard that being a garage mechanic is a low-prestige occupation and one to be shunned. But direct experience of working as a garage mechanic may be pleasant: You enjoy taking motors apart, and the job is well paid. Failure to excel, or being a garage mechanic, is not clearly a thing that would be shunned with horror on the basis of personal experience. So, if a person has a strong aversion to it, the aversion is probably unauthentic in my sense.

Suppose, for the sake of the argument, we have an aversion before us which is unauthentic in this sense. Is there any reason to think that it is therefore also *irrational* in my sense? That is, would such an aversion extinguish, or be diminished in strength, if faced with vivid awareness of known facts?

The answer, I suggest, is affirmative. Unauthentic desires or aversions are also irrational. Some traditional psychotherapists might be inclined to say that an unauthentic aversion would extinguish once there was "insight" into its own origins. I propose, however, to support my claim by appeal to principles of learning theory. Let us consider the general principles by looking at one of our examples. Let us suppose someone has a high degree of aversion, say, to nonachievement. Now I do not wish to argue that any degree of aversion to nonachievement is unauthentic. Obviously there are satisfactions in achievement; the child who first finds it possible to turn over, or stand, or walk, obviously enjoys what he has been able to do. And, just as there are natural joys of achievement, there are natural punishments of failure to excel. So, *some* degree of desire for achievement, and *some* degree of aversion to failure to excel, are authentic enough; they can derive from direct experience of achieving, or failing. But there is aversion to nonachievement which is not, and hardly could be, produced in this way – an intense fear of failure to excel such as may come only from a traumatic experience of scorn or contempt from a parent or peer. This aversion does not and could not derive from experience with normal samples of achieving or failing to excel; it derives from an association of an accidental kind. So, by my definition, *this high degree* of aversion is unauthentic. And what I wish to argue is that this aversion must extinguish in the face of vivid awareness of knowable facts, and hence is an irrational aversion. But why say that it must extinguish in the face of knowable facts?

There is a controversy in the psychological literature about what brings about extinction of tendencies to respond. One theory, which for simplicity I shall follow although it seems not to be the whole story, is that tendencies to respond extinguish only functionally – that is, they become overlaid, superseded, by a disposition to make some different, incompatible response. This may be brought about by counterconditioning, by associating a stimulus which first produced one response with another response which is incompatible with the first one, and predominates over it and prevents the first one from recurring. For instance, suppose a person, because of a traumatic experience as a child, has a fear response at the sight of a snake. The fear response may be functionally extinguished, by associating the sight of a snake with some favorable affective response, say by producing it while the person is enjoying a hearty meal or doing something else enjoyable.

Let us consider how functional extinction of this sort might occur in cases of interest to us, in the extinction of desires and aversions. In particular, we want to know if the theory implies that unauthentic desires or aversions will extinguish when faced with vivid awareness of relevant facts. Actually it does imply this. To see this, let us consider our example of aversion to nonachievement. How will awareness of the facts extinguish this? We must recall that, in our account of direct influence of desires by association, we pointed out that desires or aversions may be produced cognitively by associating the *idea* of something directly either with recollection or thought or image already pleasant or unpleasant. Now, in the case of nonachievement, if a person reflects on the possibility of his failing to excel in some particular way, or just nonachievement in general, he can make this idea or image either more attractive or more aversive by having pleasant or unpleasant thoughts. If there are pleasant, or at least not unpleasant, *facts* about nonachievement, he can dwell on these, and alter the affective tone of the idea of nonachievement by doing so. Now, if we assume that the aversion is unauthentic, it must be possible to think of, or better remember, features of failure to excel which are either pleasant or at least not very aversive. In fact, as I pointed out earlier, direct experience even of failure, in its typical or normal forms, may by no means be bad. There can also be pleasant features about it. For instance, if one did not perform in a distinguished way in something one was not competent to do, then at least one avoided the further emotional strain of trying to do something beyond one's capacities. Moreover, there are almost certain to be some pleasures of relief in thoughts of nonachievement, because of the very fact that one is *not* normally subject to the kind of traumatic punishment that brought on the aversion in the first place. If the aversion's source was scorn or contempt on the part of one's father, one can reflect that one's father is no longer living, or that he no longer treats one as a child, or that he is not quite the infallible authority he once seemed to be. Reflection on such matters will produce a pleasant relief-response. At any rate, reflection on actual features of *normal* experiences of failure to excel will tend to bring about an association of the idea of nonachievement with *their* feeling-tone, and not with the affective tone of some traumatic experiences in the past. Hence the old traumatic aversion to the idea should at least be moderated, or even extinguished altogether. The old response will have been functionally extinguished as a result of more favorable associations based on reflection on the real nature of typical situations. Functionally and effectively the old aversion in its original strength has gone.

We should emphasize that what is effective in this process of association is vivid awareness of known relevant propositions about nonachievement; in particular it is knowledge that certain events which once accompanied failure to excel are *not* intrinsic to it, and that certain other features *are* characteristic of it.

We can generalize from this example, and say that unauthentic responses – desires or aversions – will tend to extinguish when confronted with vivid awareness of knowable facts. For, since unauthentic desires or aversions by definition would not have arisen as a result of direct experience of normal samples of the sort of situation at which the desire or aversion is directed, it must be that vivid awareness of what the normal situation is will operate to bring about their extinction. Since I am using the term "irrational" to apply to desires or aversions which cannot survive being confronted with relevant available knowledge, it follows that unauthentic desires or aversions, such as neurotic aversion to nonachievement, are irrational.

This result is of considerable importance. For it enables us to distinguish between a host of desires and aversions which merely parrot popular evaluations, which we may call *conforming* attitudes, and those we may call *authentic* attitudes to the situations as they really are. Only the authentic attitudes are rational. A great many of our evaluations are derived in one way or another from the interventions of parents or peers or teachers or from empathic responses to situations depicted in films or on television. And doubtless some of our desires or aversions are strongly influenced by accidental circumstances attending a single episode; thus a man might acquire a lifelong aversion to dancing as a result of ineptness on his part as a teenager, resulting in a disastrous end to a love affair. It is important to see that such desires and aversions would, when confronted by knowledge, extinguish in favor of the attitude the person would acquire as a result of direct experience with representative samples of the type of situation in question.

I wish now to consider a second type of case. Just as I have now affirmed that unauthentic desires or aversions are irrational, I want now to argue that desires or aversions based on *misgeneralization* are irrational.

In order to explain what I mean, I shall first make a brief background statement and then offer two examples of misgeneralization. I shall then explain more precisely what I mean by misgeneralization, and why I claim that desires or aversions involving misgeneralization are irrational.

I have already remarked that stimulus-generalization is involved in the formation of desires and aversions: the attractiveness or aversiveness of a state of affairs thought of is often a consequence of its similarity to states of affairs actually experienced in the past, and either liked or disliked. The liking response to an experienced state of affairs generalizes, as a seeming-attractive response, to the thought of the same state of affairs. But now generalization may go a step further. An actual situation liked or disliked may have the features ABCDE, whereas the state of affairs as imagined or conceived, which comes to be attractive or aversive through stimulus generalization, may differ not only in being only imagined or conceived, but also in that the thought is a thought of something just with features ABC. If this happens, there *may* be misgeneralization. Let us consider some examples of what may happen.

Suppose a woman finds herself yearning for intelligent conversation, perhaps even making capacity for intelligent conversation a criterion for an acceptable mate. Now there may be a discrepancy between her abstract goal, intelligent conversation, and the features of conversation which she has actually liked in the past. For there are intelligent conversations which have bored her because she couldn't understand them, others that made her feel inferior because the participants were just too agile for her, others that were tiring because too demanding of her attention, still others that were annoying when a bright but egocentric person talked only of his own concerns. What the woman enjoys is at most only a *species* of intelligent conversation, but owing to stimulus generalization, what she wants – the goal which strikes her as attractive and worthwhile – is just intelligent conversation as such. As a matter of fact, her concern for intelligent conversation also fails to reflect her past experiences in another way; for surely she will have enjoyed conversations in the past that were not that intellectually demanding. I suggest that here there has been misgeneralization in a sense to be explained.

Let us consider a second example, in this case an aversion. Let us realistically suppose that a child tastes codfish and enthusiastically hates it. As a result, he may refuse to touch any fish, saying that he can't stand fish. In this case his dislike for the taste of codfish has generalized into an aversion for all fish whatever.

What has gone wrong in these cases? Obviously what has happened is that a specific type of thing was liked or disliked. But the process of stimulus generalization, involved in the formation of the desire, doubtless involving language and conceptual schemes in some way, has diffused the target of the attitude, so that what is prospectively desired is something broader than what was liked. Thus something is desired in prospect, which was not liked in the fact, and presumably will not be liked in the fact again. Reflection on what has happened in these cases gives us a cue to the definition of misgeneralization. So let us define the term 'misgeneralized,' for the context of a desire or aversion, so as to say that a desire or aversion is misgeneralized if and only if its target is not a collection of features which characterized the originally liked or disliked experiences, and which was responsible for the experiences being liked or disliked. Thus, if we find ourselves with a desire for anything that is ABC, when the properties which made experiences liked in the past were ABCDE, or BCD, there has been misgeneralization.

Suppose we define misgeneralization in this way. There are desires and aversions, then, which are based on misgeneralization. But is there anything wrong with this? Is there any reason why we should say that a misgeneralized desire is irrational? That is, can we say that a desire of this kind would extinguish, or at least diminish in intensity, when faced by a vivid awareness of facts? And if we are to claim that such a desire or aversion would not survive being faced with a vivid awareness of the facts, can we specify *which* facts, and explain why we should think the desire or aversion could not survive awareness of them?

It seems obvious that if awareness of any facts is to have such an effect on desire, it must be awareness of two things. First, of the *differences* between the experiences liked in the past, and those disliked in the past. And second, awareness of the fact that the one set of these experiences *was liked,* and the other not. Thus, in the case of the woman, she would need to become aware of the fact that there are intellectual conversations of the species intellectually fatiguing, inferiority suggesting, technical, and egocentrically dominated, as well as many kinds of nonaversive intellectual conversations. Second, she would need to become aware of the fact – it is hoped through recollection – that she has enjoyed or would enjoy members of one class of experiences, but not members of the other class. Now, on a common-sense level, I think it reasonable to expect that a person who is aware of such facts would find that his actual desiring attitude was acquiring a narrower target. Not that one single thought about the matter would make a big change; our habits in wanting are not that flexible. But it seems reasonable to suppose that repeated reflections of this sort will have the effect of re-directing one's prospective desires or aversions so as to conform more closely with situations actually liked

51

or disliked in the past. Why should this be? Is there anything in psychological theory which should lead us to expect this? Here we can appeal, with some hesitation, to the theory of discrimination learning. Suppose a dog has been conditioned so that he salivates five drops when he hears a tone of 1967 cycles, and salivates two drops to a tone of 1000 cycles. And suppose we want him to stop salivating altogether to the tone of 1000 cycles. What we can do is continue to stimulate him by sounding these tones in random sequence, but feed him whenever he hears the tone of 1967 cycles, and never feed him when he hears the tone of 1000 cycles. After a short time, the salivation to the tone of 1000 cycles will altogether cease. We could formulate this type of process in terms of a general principle of discrimination learning, but I shall not do this. It is obvious, however, that a process parallel to what goes on in the dog is going on in the woman, except that the effect derives not from being fed in connection with the thought of one kind of conversation, and not fed in connection with the thought of another kind. Rather, there is a kind of cognitive self-reward. That is, when she thinks of one type of conversation she remembers an occasion of it which she liked, which strengthens the likelihood of a liking response to a thought of that type of conversation; whereas when she thinks of another type of conversation, she remembers an occasion of it which she didn't like or actually disliked, which reduces the likelihood of a liking response to a thought of that type of conversation. Thus her reflections have the effect of breaking down an association between the thought of certain kinds of conversation and the liking response, and reinforcing the association between the thought of certain other kinds of conversation and the liking response. When this process is complete, we can say that she has succeeded in discriminating, as far as her liking responses are concerned, between one kind of thought and another. Just as the dog has now stopped salivating altogether at the sound of 1000 cycles, so the thought of a certain kind of conversation now leaves her cold. The target of her desire will have been narrowed to the class of objects with features that made her experiences liked in the past.

In general, then, in a rational person, that is one who has faced his desires with relevant knowable facts on repeated occasions, the misgeneralized part of a target of his desire will be pruned away. Misgeneralizations will not survive in a rational person. So my conclusion is: a rational person will not have misgeneralized desires.

It is obvious, I assume, that we can show by similar reasoning that misgeneralized aversions will also be pruned away in a rational person. So the child who has generalized his dislike of codfish into a prospective aversion to all fish has made a kind of mistake; let us hope we can get him, by reflection on what has happened, to be more open-minded about lake trout.

I conclude, then, that there are two types of desire or aversion which are irrational in my sense. Unauthentic desires and aversions are irrational. And misgeneralized desires and aversions are irrational. Incidentally, these two types of desires or aversions are not as different as may at first appear; if we concentrated on developing in detail the theory of discrimination learning, just how similar they are would become more clear. But there is just enough difference that it is convenient to distinguish them. The main difference is that unauthentic aversions are aversions to types of things which are not inherently aversive at all; they become aversive only by accidental or deliberate association with kinds of things which are aversive. Whereas in the case of misgeneralization, some species of the genus to which the misgeneralized aversion developed really are inherently aversive; the only thing that is irrational is the development of a prospective aversion not just to *some species* of the genus but to *all* species of it.

I do not wish to suggest that these two are the only types of desire or aversion which would extinguish, or be diminished in intensity, when confronted repeatedly with vivid ideas of relevant knowable propositions. In fact, there are various other types. For instance, I suggest that a desire for a state of affairs tends to extinguish when faced with awareness that it is logically impossible, or can be described only in meaningless language. Again, I suggest that at least strong desires for a state of affairs tend to extinguish when faced with the fact that it is causally impossible. Further, I suggest that a desire or aversion which has been produced by a false belief will extinguish when faced with awareness that the belief is false. Again, I suggest that a desire that exists with abnormally high intensity because of deprivation with respect to the objects of that desire, say, during one's early years, will diminish to a normal degree of intensity when faced with the contrast between early deprivation and present security about the availability of the objects of that desire. Thus persons who are neurotically concerned about love and acceptance by other people because of deprivation when they were young will become more relaxed about it all when they get vividly before them, over a period of time, their security in the affections of other persons. And so on, doubtless for various other types of cases.

II WHAT THESE FACTS PROVE

Suppose, for the sake of the argument, we agree that unauthentic and misgeneralized desires and aversions, and perhaps desires and aversions of other types, are irrational in my sense. What follows from that fact, of any interest to philosophers? What follows from the fact that certain types of desires or aversions would extinguish, or be reduced in intensity, or modified in scope, by repeated exposure to vivid awareness of relevant facts, in the manner I have suggested? Philosophers have not, I think, given attention to this question.

Now I concede it does not *follow logically* from the fact that a desire for S would extinguish after exposure to awareness of relevant facts, that S is not intrinsically desirable. English usage does not imbed any semantic rule to the effect that "is desirable in itself in relation to the person *P*" is synonymous with "would be desired for itself by the person *P* if he were rational." So there is no clear entailment relation between "is rationally desired intrinsically" and "is intrinsically desirable." Nevertheless, there is more to be said. In fact, there are two things I wish to emphasize.

First, although English does *not* imbed the semantic rule just mentioned, it is plausible to suggest that the difference in English between the meaning of "desired" and of "desirable" is that the desirable is what *would* be desired by a person who had brought to bear on his desire all relevant facts and reasoning. If this is so, and if the account I have given is a correct account of how facts and reasoning can be brought to bear on intrinsic desires, then we can say, with some plausibility, that "S would be desired for itself by a rational person" does imply "is intrinsically desirable" after all. I do not wish to insist on this, but it is something to think about.

A second point is, to my mind, somewhat more forceful; it is different, but ultimately has the same effect. This point is that a person might, in view of facts like those I have been pointing out, decide that it is *important* to know what he would desire if he were rational in my sense, and, in order to give himself a way of raising this important question and accenting it, he might *choose* to use the expression "S is an intrinsically desirable thing from the point of view of Mr. X" in such a way that this statement is correct just in case Mr. X has an intrinsic desire for S which would not extinguish if he were rational. And if one did make this linguistic decision, then a judgment about desirability in this revised sense *would* follow from the fact that a desire extinguishes in certain situations. As a matter of fact, I should myself be inclined to make this definitional move. I am inclined to think that if something's being intrinsically desirable in the ordinary sense – if there is some definite ordinary sense – is unaffected by whether that thing would be intrinsically desired by a rational person in my sense, then so much the worse for the ordinary sense of the word "desirable." In that case I would not be very interested in knowing whether something is intrinsically desirable in the ordinary sense. In fact, if "is intrinsically desirable" is not used in some such way as this, I wonder what could be the difference between asking "Do I desire this for itself?" and "Is this intrinsically desir*able*, from my point of view?." At any rate, it seems to me that the question of what I would desire intrinsically if my desires were rational in my sense is a more important question than the question what is intrinsically desirable, in the ordinary sense, if the two questions really are different. So I am inclined to declare that, for my own part, I am happy to regard the question, "What is worthwhile in itself, in relation to me?" as the same as, "What would I want for itself, if my desires were rational [in my sense]?."

Someone might object to the suggestion that we do think, on reflection, that it is important to know what we would desire if our desires were rational in my sense. Someone might ask: *Why* is this important? To this query my reply is that knowing what we would desire if our desires were rational in my sense is precisely knowing what one's intrinsic desires would be if logic and facts were brought to bear on them in the maximal way possible, indeed in the only way in which facts and logic can affect such desires. And this reply should be moving to anyone who has been wanting, in his reflection about values, to see where his intrinsic desires would come out, if facts and logic were brought to bear on them. One could, of course, push the doubts back a further stage, and ask why anyone should attach much importance to knowing what one's intrinsic desires would be if logic and facts had been brought to bear on them to a maximal extent. If anyone did raise this question, it is true that there is not much further to say to him or her. One thing we might do is point out that at least an interest in this matter seems to be widespread, perhaps as widespread as human nature itself. And we might well wonder if the doubt is a serious one; very likely the critic himself shares the very interest about which he raises a question. What is clear to me is that I have a strong interest in this myself, and that no one has shown that this interest is irrational in my sense.

In conclusion, I should like to mention a few puzzling questions that are raised, but not answered, by what I have said. First, if a person knows that a certain desire or aversion is irrational in my sense, should he or she take steps to get rid of it? Remember that extinguishing a desire may not be an easy business; conceivably it may require psychoanalysis. Second, should one stop regretting one's failure to achieve certain goals, if one knows that the desire for them is irrational? Should one, for instance, stop fretting about one's lack of achievement, or about one's poverty or lack of prestige, if one knows that one's desires for these things are largely irrational in my sense? Third, should a person drop from her life's plan the aim to achieve things she actually wants but knows she would not want if she were rational in my sense? Remember that a person may get joy from satisfying irrational desires, and be unhappy if irrational desires are frustrated. Fourth, should we ignore the desires of other persons, say those of our children, except in so far as there is reason to think them rational? In particular, if a utilitarian is considering what definition to assign to "utility" for purposes of determining which acts are right, should he make use of the concept of a rational desire in my sense, just any desire, or what? Finally, even if we conclude that we should frame our life-plans with only rational desires in mind, and perhaps even define "utility" generally by reference to them, still there is a further question of when a practical decision is worth all the trouble of identifying a rational desire. Economists sometimes say that an uneconomical allocation of resources is economical if it economizes on decision-making time. There is a parallel problem for us. All these questions are interesting questions, and hard ones, which are still with us even if we identify the intrinsically desirable with what we would desire if our desires were rational.

4

The explanation of moral language

What follows is concerned primarily with specifically moral terms: "moral duty," "moral obligation," "morally ought," "morally reprehensible," and the like; and there are implications for expressions like "is a good thing."

It is doubtful whether every language has words with the same meaning as these, or even that these English terms are used with the same meaning among all contemporary native speakers of English. Many classical scholars think the Greeks (such as Achilles and Aristotle) did not have moral concepts like ours (mine?), and it seems hard to separate the most nearly corresponding concepts in the Judaeo-Christian tradition from the concept of God's requirements on human conduct. John Gay, in a work first published in 1731 (and typical of the major theological utilitarians), said that "obligation" is just "the necessity of doing or omitting any action in order to be happy: i.e., when there is such a relation between an Agent and an action that the Agent cannot be happy without doing or omitting that action, then the Agent is said to be obliged to do or omit that action." This passage is consistent with thinking, as he later goes on to suggest, that moral obligation is just being required, on pain of future punishment by God, to do or omit something. This concept of moral obligation seems very different from ours (mine?). But Elizabeth Anscombe[1] seems to think Gay's view of "moral obligation" is the only one that makes sense. Indeed, she holds that it and "morally wrong" make sense only in the context of belief in divine commands; in the absence of such belief, she says, these terms make no more sense than "if the notion 'criminal' were to remain when criminal law and criminal courts have been abolished and forgotten." She thinks other usages, of speakers devoid of theological convictions (probably like usages of most contemporary writers on ethics), are "fishy."[2] One suspects there is even more reason to doubt that our (my?) moral concepts appear in China,

1 "Modern Moral Philosophy," *Philosophy* 33 (1958), 1–19.
2 Professor Frankena has suggested, in lectures, that Samuel Clarke was the first philosopher to have used "obligation" in the sense she regards as fishy, when Clarke said there is an obligation to do what is fitting – an obligation independent of commands or sanctions or of relation to the agent's own interest.

Japan, and India, not to mention primitive societies. Is "morally reprehensible" the same as "losing face"? If John Ladd[3] is right, the Navaho have only one "moral" term: *bahadzid*, meaning "imprudent" or "dangerous." There is a priori reason to doubt the universality of moral concepts if we think that the meanings of these terms are affected by and bound up with the total conceptual scheme of speakers.

This (possible) absence of uniformity of concepts is consistent with there being a commonsense *morality* (with variable content) in most, if not all, societies. At least it is if we say a society "has a morality" if most adult members (1) are motivated to some extent to do or avoid *doing* some things for no further reason and particularly not for reason of self-interest; (2) tend to feel guilty (at least, uncomfortable) to some extent independently of expectations about disapproval by others, if they fail to conform their conduct accordingly (there may or may not be concepts of justification and excuse), and (3) tend to be indignant at and criticize others when their conduct shows substandard motivation in this respect. Let us call this complex "moral attitudes" with respect to some forms of conduct. It may also be that every or nearly every language contains terminology to *express* these attitudes, and to claim or imply that they are in *some appropriate way justified*.

It must be left open what kind of justification is thought appropriate. Beliefs about this clearly vary; appeal to what the gods approve is one way. My suggestion that morality in this loose sense is at least nearly universal I confess is motivated in good part by my belief that resentment of deliberate injury must be at least nearly universal, and that some sympathy also is at least nearly universal either because it contributes to the survival of either small societies or the gene-type of the altruist, or, perhaps also, through conditioning from situations universal to early childhood. Anyway, Achilles seems to have been indignant when Agamemnon took away his prisoner Briseis, and I speculate from his speech that he thought his anger was justified. If some morality in this sense is universal, it does not follow that any (much less every) precise moral *concept* is universal.

Various moral philosophers, however, have thought there is in some sense a standard ordinary meaning of moral terms and have made proposals purporting to be descriptions of what that meaning is. G. E. Moore, in *Principia Ethica*, held that "is wrong" just means "produces less good than some other act open to the agent," whereas in *Ethics* he thought that when people use "wrong" they have in mind some unanalyzable property or relation. Richard Price, Samuel Clarke, and W. D.

---

3 *The Structure of a Moral Code*, Cambridge, MA: Harvard University Press, 1957.

Ross seem to share this latter view. Roderick Firth and, I think, Hume suppose that some "ideal observer" account renders the actual meaning, in some sense or other, of these moral terms; and the same appears to be true of R. M. Hare's universal-prescription account. (At least, he thinks his account describes his own usage, and he thinks others' meanings are probably the same.) Now, *whose* meanings are these philosophers purporting to describe? Hardly John Gay and his contemporaries. St. Paul? The most convincing course for them to take is to represent their accounts as explications of the meanings of themselves and some of their *readers;* to do this successfully would be a substantial achievement.

There is another tradition in philosophy, of proposals about how moral language should be "construed," which does not purport to describe ordinary meanings. W. K. Frankena has said that the problems of meta-ethics demand "clarity and decision about the nature and functions of morality, of moral discourse, and of moral theory, and this requires not only small-scale analytic inquiries but also studies in the history of ethics and morality, in the relation of morality to society and of society to the individual, as well as in epistemology and in the psychology of human motivation."[4] Anscombe seems to recommend that the word *ought* in its "emphatic" sense be dropped by persons who do not subscribe to the notion of a divine law-giver. A somewhat similar recommendation apparently would be made by Philippa Foot. Rawls, in the passage where he discusses the status of his explanation of "morally wrong" or "just," in terms of what would be chosen in the "original position," does not claim that his account replicates what ordinary English speakers mean by these terms, but he says he is offering a *replacement* that serves the same purposes and does not suffer from the problems surrounding the original terms.[5]

Should we also perhaps include Kant in this group? Immediately after the first formulation of the categorical imperative in the *Grundlegung,* he writes:

Now if all the imperatives of duty can be derived from this one imperative as their principle, then even although we leave it unsettled whether what we call duty may not be an empty concept, we shall still be able to show at least what we understand by it and what the concept means [. . . *was wir dadurch denken und was dieser Begriff sagen wolle*].[6]

---

4 "Obligation and Motivation," in A. I. Melden (ed.), *Essays in Moral Philosophy* (Seattle: University of Washington Press, 1958), p. 80.
5 John Rawls, *A Theory of Justice* (Cambridge, MA: Harvard University Press, 1971), p. 111.
6 Immanuel Kant, *Groundwork of the Metaphysics of Morals*, translated by L. W. Beck (Indianapolis: Bobbs – Merrill, 1964), p. 88 (originally 1785).

Is it being alleged this is the meaning of the ordinary concept, or is it what Kant is alleging would be a sensible one? He might mean that morality can command respect only if its principles are binding on all rational beings, and if the content of its prescriptions for conduct is the same as the conduct that actually would take place in a purely rational being (one not guided by desires or inclinations). If he had this in mind, his theory might be construed as *recommending* a certain concept of "moral obligation," not just claiming to report what concept people already have in mind. Kant thought that the moral philosopher had best begin with the morality of common sense, but he did not think it superfluous to move on to a metaphysics of morals.

Another person who may belong in this group is J. S. Mill. In the fifth chapter of *Utilitarianism* he makes a statement important for his normative ethics:

We do not call anything wrong unless we mean to imply that a person ought to be [it is desirable that he be] punished in some way or other for doing it – if not by law, by the opinion of his fellow creatures; if not by opinion, by the reproaches of his own conscience. This seems the real turning point between morality and simple expediency.

So Mill concludes that a morally wrong act is not identical with an inexpedient act, but is one it is expedient for the legal/moral system to sanction by legal punishment, public opinion, or the pangs of conscience. Thus Mill opts not for moral rightness being fixed directly by the relative utility of an act being morally appraised, but by whether it would be punished by an optimal legal/moral system. A great deal, then, turns on this point. Does Mill think that the point is one about "our" actual concepts? Perhaps he does mean that in ordinary use the predication of "wrong" carries with it the *implication* that it is desirable that the act be punished in some way. Or perhaps he intends to report just what he thinks is a widespread *belief* – that wrong acts ought to be punished in some way. Or, perhaps, might he be moved by the thought that, if one wants to produce happiness in the world, one had better sanction act-types that tend to cause unhappiness and mark this by calling them "wrong?" That would be a *recommendation* of a use of "wrong" in view of what Mill thinks is the function of morality and of the necessary place of sanctions in making it work. He could agree with what Frankena said.

Thus there are two main traditions of philosophical thinking about how moral language should be construed. One is that everybody's or somebody's (maybe just the reader's or the writer's) moral meanings are reasonably definite, and that a description of what these are can be given precisely enough to be a helpful guide in moral thinking. The other tradition is that, irrespective of how diverse or confused the meaning or use of moral terms may be, around the world, or even at various stages of the usage of a given individual, there is a certain pattern of concepts it is useful or important for there to be, when the functions of morality in society and of moral discourse in morality, and the psychology of individual morality, are taken into account. The first of these has not achieved convincing results: The nonnaturalist philosophers have not convinced other philosophers that people do have some unanalyzable nonempirical concept in mind when they use these terms. Nor have the naturalists (or prescriptivists) been convincing that ordinary ethical usage is properly described in the ways that have been proposed – although it is always possible some naturalist may come forth with a convincing account. Possible, but unlikely.

My suggestion is that the more promising line of thinking for moral philosophers to take is to work out the details of showing that a certain pattern of concepts is important because of the clarity and other benefits it would make possible for moral discourse. Unfortunately, philosophers of this persuasion have not offered precise accounts how one is to identify the purportedly optimal or clarifying conceptual scheme. Rawls's remarks are helpful, but he lays down a restriction that the optimal set of concepts must yield as analytic moral principles, which, when taken in conjunction with observable facts, lead deductively to the person's own moral principles in 'reflective equilibrium,' a view that seems to lean heavily toward revision of moral concepts in the direction of maintaining the moral status quo. In what follows I will attempt to identify criteria for an optimal conceptual framework for moral discourse that is more open to serious revision of a person's moral commitments. I proposed such an account in a recent volume (1979), but without a connected explanation and justification of the criteria for identification of the ideal conceptual framework for moral discourse. I will try to fill this gap, to some degree, by explaining the reasons for a certain conceptual framework for moral discourse. How are we to motivate, or recommend, the selection of certain explications for moral terms when we do not provide a description of some ordinary-language meaning of these terms?

I A PARTIAL EXPLANATION OF SOME NECESSARY MORAL CONCEPTS

We may begin with what seems to be the most important thing about morality: the motivational system that comprises people's personal moral codes. Compared with this, moral discourse is relatively an epiphenomenon. What is it for a person to have a motivational moral code? First, he will have aversions to some act-types for no further reason and in particular no reason of self-interest, such as an aversion to breaking a promise. Second, when more than one of these aversions is engaged by a single contemplated action, he will incline pro or con performing the action, depending on the strength of the various aversions and something analogous to a vector sum. Third, if he thinks he acted contrary to these aversions, he will tend to feel guilty unless there was some "excusing" factor present, such as mistake of fact, inability to act otherwise, and so on. Fourth, if a judge thinks another has acted contrary to the aversions the judge has, he will tend to disapprove of this agent for what he did, unless, again, there was an "excuse." Fifth, he will tend to admire and favor certain act-types, even when he is not inclined to disapprove of their omission; and it may be he will disfavor and feel some contempt for persons because they act in certain ways (such as refusing a match when someone has requested one politely), even if he would hardly disapprove of the person in the sense of feeling indignant with him (and might not feel remorseful if he offended himself). Sixth, he will disapprove of the absence of the aversions referred to; in fact, it is precisely when he finds it necessary to attribute someone's conduct to the absence of one or more of these aversions that he thinks the action is "without excuse." Finally, he believes about all these attitudes/dispositions on his part that they are justified in some appropriate way. Doubtless there is much more to be said (e.g., about what exactly it is to feel guilty). What one would like to provide is a complete phenomenology of the "moral life."

We know a good deal about individual "moral codes" in this sense. We know that individual moral systems normally make life more tolerable in society. We know that various factors play a role in the development of individual moral codes: knowing that certain act-types tend to cause harm, sympathetic concern – native or acquired early in life by conditioning – for the welfare of others, the observation of "models," conditioning from criticism of one's conduct by others, and so on (Hoffman).[7] We also know that there are differences among the moral codes of individuals in the same society (for instance, the dispute about the morality of abortion), and much more when the individuals come from quite different types of cultures.

Not everyone would agree to the above account of what it is to have a "personal moral code." Not so very many decades ago matters would have been described (and still are in some circles) in a very different way. It would have been said that what it is for a person to have a moral code

7 Martin Hoffman, "Moral Development," in P. Mussen (ed.), *Carmichael's Manual of Child Psychology II* (New York: Wiley, 1970), pp. 261–359.

is for him to have beliefs about what kind of conduct God requires of man (either because He wants people to behave so as to contribute to the social welfare, or for some other reason), and for him to think that God will severely punish those who knowingly flout his commands, and hence that the person will, out of prudent regard for his own future welfare, be strongly motivated to conform his behavior to these requirements. Alternatively, it might be said that what it is for a person to have a personal moral code is for him to have various theoretical beliefs about which types of actions are fitting or unfitting (have a certain property or relation), and, if the person has a general desire to conform his behavior to what is fitting, he will find himself motivated to behave in what he thinks the most fitting way, in whatever circumstances. Doubtless there are other ways in which having a "personal moral code" might be described. The account I gave strikes me as most realistic and compatible with what we know at the present time, so I shall stick with this account of what it is to have a personal moral code. I do not at all deny that many persons have had a moral code in the sense described in terms of theological beliefs, or that many still do; but at present it seems more fruitful to think of a moral code as I have suggested. Actually, it seems likely that many persons have a personal moral code in the sense I explained, and also in the theological sense, at the same time.

It is useful to think of people's moral codes as, like the law, an instrument for guiding behavior so as normally to bring about a desirable end-state for society. The various aversions toward act-types are normally aversions to conduct unfavorable to the welfare of society. The guilt feelings and disapproval of others function to strengthen the basic aversions when these have been too weak to control conduct. But since it is pointless for a person to be "punished" by guilt feelings or the disapproval of others when his aversions are already of standard strength, a person's objectively objectionable behavior will be "excused" when there is not reason to think it derived from a substandard level of the moral aversions; that is, from a defect of character. This feature of moral systems again has its analogue in the law.

While it is useful to think of moral codes as instruments for bringing about desirable states of society, one *need* not think of them in this way. One may view them as just phenomena, to be understood and appraised; certainly one need not think of them as a product of a process of social evolution that favored the survival of societies that managed somehow to develop moral codes among their members, any more than one need view them as a result of biological evolution.

But what has all this about motivational moral codes to do with moral *concepts?* If there are motivational moral codes, is moral *discourse* necessary at all? Much less, need there be any particular conceptual frame-work for moral discourse? The answer, perhaps obviously, is that moral discourse *is* necessary, or at least it is highly desirable. For one thing, if the system is to work, it must be possible to express one's disapproval of what has been done, if not to the agent himself, then at least to one's friends. And if there is communication among observers about whether an agent is to be disapproved of for his behavior, or his behavior excused, it must be possible to discuss whether the behavior was compatible with a standard level of aversions in the agent; in other words, with his being virtuous. So much communication in the group is necessary. Moreover, since an agent will often find situations unclear and confusing, agents will want to ask for moral advice from others, and if advice is to be given, again there must be moral discourse and terminology that makes moral advice-giving possible.

But moral symbolism – a convenient terminology indicating the status of acts in relation to a thinker's own presumed-justified moral code – is needed not just for interpersonal communication, but for an agent's own moral reflection. Suppose an agent is averse to promise-breaking, but in a particular case he happens to know that keeping a promise will be costly to him but of no benefit to the promisee; or perhaps he knows that he gave the promise originally on the basis of a deliberate misrepresentation of fact by the promisee. Now it may be that his moral code (or "intuition") is so fine-tuned that when he calls these special circumstances to mind, his hesitation to break that promise dissipates – or perhaps better, he finds he has no standing aversion to breach of *that* kind of promise at all. But it may well be that his moral code does not provide such automatic guidance. The agent has to think. Moreover, he may have a higher-order aversion to aversions of his own that he thinks are socially counterproductive; in other words, he has attitudes about moral attitudes. For the purpose of bringing the higher-order attitude to bear on the lower-order one, he requires symbolic processes. Much the same when his moral aversions conflict in a given case. His motivational code may not be fine-tuned enough automatically to guide him, everything considered, in favor of one course of action. Again he may need to think; and again he may need to reflect on what relative weighting of moral aversions would be socially most beneficial. Thinking may thus give direction to his first-order attitudes. Still again, a person may wonder if he really should feel guilty about something he did, say, something hurtful to someone. Perhaps he had had too many drinks. Is that an excuse? Is it an excuse to lose one's temper and do something one would not otherwise have done? To answer these questions, reflection is needed about what level of moral aversion should be standard in the society – and for this it may be that reflection is needed about what level of moral aversion it is socially beneficial to bring about by criticism, and so on. None of this reflection can occur without a framework enabling one to make the various distinctions.

There is actually an effective moral system in our society, and there obviously is interpersonal discussion of moral issues and intrapersonal moral reflection. So we must anticipate that there is a set of concepts, capable of making the distinctions to which I have been referring, already in our conceptual scheme. As indeed there is. We have the terminology: "Everything considered, what he morally ought to do – or is morally bound to do – is so-and-so." Then there is "he has some (or a *prima facie*) obligation to do so-and-so." and "doing that was reprehensible." Or, "he didn't do what morally he ought to have done, but his failure has to be excused because of his misunderstanding of the situation." Or, "his behavior has no excuse; if he had been as careful of the welfare of others as he should have been, he would never have done it." And so on. Morality needs such a conceptual framework.

I have not so far proposed any complete analysis of any of these terms but have merely suggested that, for an effective moral system, there must be a certain type of motivational framework and a corresponding conceptual framework.

What have philosophers to contribute to all this? Well, it is one thing for there to be roughly a certain conceptual framework available for moral discourse, but it is another thing for the concepts to be sharp, and for speakers to understand just which distinctions they are designed to make and how they are important for the functioning of the moral system. So a philosopher may be performing a valuable service if he does something to get these distinctions and their importance recognized by speakers of the moral language of his society.

II FILLING IN THE DEFINITION: THE OPTIMAL PROCEDURE

So far I have argued that a framework of concepts is requisite for a morality: the concepts of *prima facie* obligation, obligation overall everything considered, excuse, reprehensibility everything considered, the praiseworthy or supererogatory, perhaps also moral rights and "offenses," and so on. These notions must have certain connections with one another. I have not, however, argued for any complete account of the meaning or function of any of them.

The major historical controversies among writers on metaethics have not been directed at the points I have been making so far. There is, or should be, agreement among naturalists and noncognitivists and non-naturalists that the terms we have been discussing are needed for the effective functioning of a moral system, although they might not put the matter in just these terms. All will or should agree that we need to distinguish "morally ought not to," "reprehensible," and "excuse," in roughly the way suggested. The metaethical wars have been about something else. They have been about how the above terms should be explained by an account that goes to the bottom of matters. We must now turn our attention to this. Fortunately, we do not need to worry about proposing and supporting a separate explication for each of the terms we have been discussing. For we can follow a strategy proposed some years ago by A. C. Ewing, to the effect that all these terms can be construed by means of just one fundamental ethical concept, one called "fittingness," plus commonsense nonmoral notions. We can agree, except that in place of his concept of fittingness, which Ewing conceived to name a simple unobservable relation, we can take the term "justified" as our basic concept, as it is used when we speak of a *justified* moral code. It will be recalled that I said that what it is to have a moral code is for one to have certain desires/aversions and to view them as *justified* in some appropriate sense (the sense being left a bit vague).

To see how this works, let us consider how "is reprehensible" might be explained in this way. Ewing would have said something like this: For X to be reprehensible for his act A is for it to be *fitting* that persons disapprove of X because of A. Whereas my suggestion would be that "X is reprehensible for his act A" be construed as "Anyone who subscribed to a *justified* moral system would disapprove of X for his action A." These proposals seem not to be controversial. What *is* controversial is how "justified moral system" is to be construed. A nonnaturalist like Ewing will say that a person "subscribes to a justified moral system" if and only if his approvals and disapprovals are *fitting*, where "fitting" names an unobservable but intellectually inspectable relation. A noncognitivist like Stevenson would say that a "justified moral system" is one that condemns those actions that "I hereby condemn and recommend that others condemn." And so on. The problem, then, is this. Suppose we assume as agreed that proposals about a common *actual* meaning of "justified moral system" in ordinary speech, like other moral expressions, are to be ignored as unsuccessful. We also assume there is no such thing as a nonempirical property of fittingness, such as Ewing thought he had in mind, and we may therefore just ignore nonnaturalism. How, then, are we to pick reasonably among various possible explications of "justified," presumably along naturalist lines or along prescriptivist lines or some combination thereof?

It will be reassuring and helpful to remind ourselves at this point just what we are looking for. In the first place, we are not looking for some concept, or property, to which a person's moral attitudes might be a natural response in the way fear is a natural response to what is considered dangerous. Many philosophers have thought there are such concepts: That we may apprehend the supposed fact that some action or state of affairs has some property P, and that we then naturally respond to this by a desiring, or approving, or admiring attitude. This has generally been the view of nonnaturalist writers. But my suggestion here is that we look at matters from the opposite end, that we take as our basic fact that people subscribe to moral codes in the motivation sense I have sketched – that they have aversions to certain act-types, that they have dispositions to feel guilt or to disapprove, and so on. Our question, then, is: If some such moral system were in place in a given person or society, in what sense might it be *justified?* One might then ask, What is the *importance* of knowing whether an effective moral code is *justified?* What is the function of raising such questions?

I believe the importance of the concept of justification depends on the fact that most people have practical problems about their own moral codes and those of others, partly for the reason that they are well aware of the fact of divergences among moral codes. People do ask themselves: What kind of moral code am I to teach myself, subscribe to, prefer, support for the educational system? (These questions are all closely related, and we may take them as coming to the same thing for present purposes.) So a person, along with subscribing to a moral code, may entertain practical doubts about it. Nor are such doubts restricted to a society like our own, with all its information about divergences, better- or worse-founded beliefs about how people come by their moral codes; for instance, from prestige-suggestion, modeling by parents or teachers, and so on. Such doubts were present among the Greeks and, I speculate, among primitive peoples. (One old Hopi Indian, who decided not to try to answer my own queries about his moral views, said: "Those are very hard questions you are asking, and I will never know the answers to them.") So people do want to know whether their own moral codes are subject to well founded criticism, whether there are considerations that can give them assurance rather than self-doubt.

What we want to do, then, is to spell out a conception of "justified" that will do this job – that is, will answer this practical doubt when it is shown that some moral code is justified in that sense. The request for such a conception may still seem indeterminate. But let me point out that there are several properties that such a concept of justification must have, or which an explanation giving a meaning to "justified" must have. First, the concept, or explanation, must be clear; there is no point in an explanation of "justified" that is no clearer than "justified" in ordinary use. Second, there are some epistemological restrictions. "Justified" is not to be explained so that we can know if a moral code is justified only if there is a priori intuitive knowledge of synthetic propositions in ethics. Again, "justified" is not to be construed in terms merely of *coherence* of ethical commitments. If no single commitment has a justified claim to be accepted, then neither does a set of them, however large or coherent. This requirement must be admitted to be somewhat controversial, but the most serious defenders of the coherence theory of justification of theoretical beliefs at present would agree that coherence need not lead toward truth unless the system includes reports of experience that are themselves independently credible. It is plausible to make the same demand for "justification" in the context of moral codes.

Third, our explanation for "justified" must be evaluatively neutral. We may not propose, for instance, that "a moral code is justified" is to be construed just as, "The acceptance of that code would maximize happiness" as a utilitarian might have it, and as Mill may have thought when he said that the goal of happiness must be the test of actions and morality alike. The reason for this is that the function of the concept of justification is to help us discriminate among warring moral codes and to criticize our own. It would fail in this function if everyone is free to define "justified" in terms of his own preferred moral system. Fourth, the explanation for "justified" should not simply authorize everyone to follow whatever attitudes or desires he happens to have. It may not simply say, in effect, "If you believe something is right, then it *is* right." If a person raises a practical question he presumably wants some more perspicuous, helpful answer than this. Fifth – and this is a difficult requirement to meet – it must be true of any explained meaning for "justified" that *any* person who comes to believe that a moral code is justified in that sense will find that this moral code is thereby *recommended* to her, that her ambivalences are at least partly resolved, that she is made more content or satisfied with that moral code. So, if it is shown that a utilitarian moral code is justified in the explained sense, everyone will be thereby more disposed to be a utilitarian. One trouble with some conceptions of "justified" – say those that embody talk of "a moral point of view" – is that they would not recommend the so-explained "justified" moral code to anyone with egoistic inclinations.

Of course, once we have settled on a *conception* of "justification," a lot more argument is likely to be needed in order to show that some type of moral code is justified in that sense, say a utilitarian or egoist or contractarian type.

Is there any explanation of "moral code justified for *X*" that meets those conditions? I have been able to think of only one, and it turns out not to be very simple when we try to spell it out. The proposal is that a moral code is justified for a person X if he would choose or support it for his society if he were *fully rational*. This proposal may seem a bit hollow, because the term "rational" itself does not enjoy a clear and agreed meaning, and we have to spell that out with still another explanation. I have the temerity, however, to attempt this, while conceding that my proposal possibly needs some refinements. It goes as follows. Suppose I say, "It is rational for X to support moral system S." I propose we mean by this: "*I* hereby recommend that X support S, (1) taking as my objective maximizing satisfaction of the ultimate desires of X as corrected to form a transitive system, be mood-independent, and capable of surviving repeated vivid reflection on relevant facts; and (2) having as my beliefs the ones X is justified in having on the basis of his evidence; (3) in view of the fact that support of S implements a strategy that in the long run will satisfy X's corrected desires as effectively as any other strategy and is coherent with what we know, especially the psychology of motivation."

What in effect this explanation implies for how a person is to identify a rational choice for herself is that she lay out the options available (the moral systems among which she may choose), determine the probable consequences of the support of (adoption of) each and how probable the consequence is, and invite her to consider how much she "truly" wants these several consequence-sets – the degree of wanting being written down to correspond with the improbability of the consequence given that the option is taken. A "true" preference is identified as one corrected in the ways suggested. The consequences of supporting one moral system rather than another might be changes in general welfare, in the distribution of welfare, in one's own welfare, in promises being kept, the truth spoken, and so on. We invite the individual to make up her mind which set of consequences she "truly" prefers.

I believe that an explanation of "the moral code justified for X" in terms of "the moral code X would support if she were fully rational" meets all the conditions I have listed as necessary if it is to be helpful in moral reflection. So far as I can see, the conception is value-neutral. What it does require is that a moral code be chosen so as to take account of all the facts that are known, or at least knowable to the agent; I do not see that as incompatible with value-neutrality. Most important, however, I suggest that a person coming to see that a certain moral code is the one she would support if she were fully rational will recommend it to her, that any ambivalences about it will be resolved.

One might object to this proposal on the ground that it is apt just to affirm the moral commitments the agent already has, since her *present* moral preferences will fix her desires for the outcomes of a given moral system. This objection, however, would be mistaken. For the preferences on the basis of which a moral system is justified are preferences for the *consequences* of the operation of a moral system, and not desires/aversions for certain act-types for no further reason, desires/aversions that are constitutive of an agent's moral code. Thus it is one thing to be averse to *hurting* others – and that is part of one's moral code – but it is quite another thing to want people to be well-off, healthy, happy, and so on, and it is this preference that is involved in the selection of a justified moral code. So the selection of a moral system is made by reference to a person's *nonmoral* preferences for some consequences.

There is another restriction one might want to lay on the selection of a moral system, in order to assure that one is not choosing on the basis of merely conventional desires. I think myself this restriction is already implied in my definition of "rational choice," but if one disagrees about this, something should be done to make sure one can step outside one's own tradition and appraise it somewhat afresh. One might do this by insisting that the chooser's preferences not be merely what he has acquired from his parents or TV or the newspapers, but that they be ones acquired only through sensitive interaction with the environment – finding what is satisfying and what is not – and that would not be extinguished by learning that they rest causally on false assumptions about facts. The conception that desires/aversions can be criticized in this way is controversial and difficult, and I have discussed it as fully as I can elsewhere. At any rate, the present restriction implies that we are to ask a person which moral system he would support, in view of his preferences for its expectable consequences – preferences that would survive the cognitive criticism I have elsewhere called "cognitive psychotherapy."

Some persons may feel that we should not call a moral system justified for a person unless it can be shown that the very same moral system is justified for everybody. They may feel we should not speak of "justification" unless we can say something is justified, *period.* And it does not follow from the fact that a certain moral system S is justified in the sense sketched for X, that it is so for everybody. I am inclined to think that such persons want more than probably it is possible to get, and the result of their linguistic stipulation is that the word "justified" would have use only for some parts of moral systems, but not for all that we think important.

If we introduce the term "justified" with my foregoing (relativistic) explanation, then it would be convenient to explain "X is morally obligated to do A," as uttered by *me*, to mean, "The moral system which *I* would support, if I were fully rational and expected to live in X's society, would call on X to do A," where "calls on X" would be spelled out in terms of aversions to act-types, tendencies to feel guilt, and so on. Similarly, for the other moral terms like "It was reprehensible of X to have done A" or "X has a *prima facie* obligation to do A."

It would be an important objection to this line of thinking if it turned out that thoughtful people, familiar with the science of today, and with serious acquaintance with the theory of knowledge, including the necessity of avoiding moral premises in a justification, felt that our explication would not do as a replacement for "justified moral system," if "is morally wrong" is to be construed as "would be prohibited by the justified moral system." Would some such persons find that, to determine what they would normally call "morally wrong action" or disapprove morally, they must raise questions this explication does not imply one need raise? Or contrariwise, would they find that the explication requires them to assure themselves of points that they are confident are irrelevant to whether some course of action is right or wrong, to be morally approved or disapproved of? Of course, it is not easy to know what thoughtful people would think. My speculation is that persons who understand what social moral systems are and what they accomplish, and who understand what kinds of criticisms of moral aversions are possible given what we know about human psychology, would be content with the reflection on how to determine which actions are right or wrong, of the sort that is required by my explication.

What would be the effect if people came to accept these explications in the sense that they would attach these meanings to the several moral terms much as they attach a meaning to the term "electron?" One might say, very little at all, on the ground that the important thing is the kind of motivational moral system people have, and the psychological processes that institute such systems will go on irrespective of the meanings attached to moral terms, especially "justified." But that is too simple. The acceptance of these definitions into ordinary thinking would serve to avoid aimless reflection – reflection one would discard if one thought deeply about the matter but otherwise might be time-consuming and misleading. Again, it would have the effect of channeling moral thinking so that facts and logic are used maximally to control moral commitments and decisions, and it would serve to raise doubts and stimulate more reflection when this has not been done. A third effect is that it would be clear that morality is a "rational" phenomenon, not exactly in the economists' sense (although this enters into it), but in the sense in which we think some desires/aversions are foolish and irrational; the explication makes clear in what sense this is so. (The question is not, however, an answer to the question whether it is always rational to act morally.) These facts are no mean reasons in support of influencing language to embody the explication.

If we select a conceptual scheme for moral discourse in this way, there is a parallel between it and the status of contemporary concepts in science. Let us suppose that English speakers have been using "morally wrong" in roughly the present ordinary sense since around 1700, about the same length of time as "electricity," first used in 1646. We might then say that the proposals of various naturalistic/prescriptive/nonnaturalist theories of moral terms have been proposals for understanding "morally wrong" in an optimal way – in a way that takes into account all the facts mentioned above. We might then think that philosophers who have made these proposals (Hutcheson, Hume, Smith, Moore, Firth, Hare, Rawls) have improved the conceptual scheme of educated people much as there has been improvement, among scientists, in the conception of electricity as a result of experiment and theoretical development in physics. We might then take what is referred to by the *optimal* use of "morally wrong" as the *fact* of moral wrongness and hold that, rather gropingly, this same fact has been referred to all along by users of the term "morally wrong." So we could then say that there is an optimal conceptual framework for ethics, and these earlier theories of philosophers have been gradually improving approximations to it. In a corresponding sense we might say that there are "facts" of ethics, and we might then say that one who recognizes this is a "realist" about ethics.

5

Morality and its critics

Some philosophers, notably Bernard Williams,[1] have recently attacked morality, particularly as it is understood by philosophers. (1) At the extreme, Williams says "We would be better off without morality" altogether.[2] (2) The claims of morality are not ones it is irrational to deny, and (3) they are not always even the strongest claims on us. Not only is it not always better to be morally better, but other considerations are as important as those of morality in the justification, even the moral justification, of actions:[3] personal ends and prudence, aesthetic concerns, "sheer self-assertion."[4] This is true not merely of the appraisal of acts of supererogation – it is silly to think that we should all try to become moral saints – but also of what is morally required. (4) These writers are especially hard on the philosophers' thesis that morality is primarily a matter of discharging obligations, the right act being the one which discharges all relevant obligations most fully – the view, as Williams puts it, that "Only an obligation can beat an obligation."[5] (5) Again, they are critical of the philosophers' view that moral evaluation must turn solely on an agent's motivation or intention in acting, as if the morality of his action depends solely on what is within his control; whereas results also count.[6] (6) The thought is also that philosophy at present is in no position to rectify matters.

Obviously these contentions cover a great deal of ground. What I should like to point out, however, is that these contentions rest very largely on questionable understandings of morality, of obligation, of

---

1 Bernard Williams, *Ethics and the Limits of Philosophy* (Cambridge: Harvard University Press, 1985); *Moral Luck* (Cambridge: Cambridge University Press, 1981); Susan Wolf, "Moral Saints," *Journal of Philosophy*, vol. 79 (1982), pp. 419–38; Owen Flanagan, "Admirable Immorality and Admirable Imperfection," *Journal of Philosophy*, vol. 83 (1986), see especially pp. 50 ff.; Thomas Nagel, *Mortal Questions* (Cambridge: Cambridge University Press, 1979), chaps. 3 and 9; Martha Nussbaum, *The Fragility of Goodness* (Cambridge: Cambridge University Press, 1986), pp. 312–17, 333–42.
2 *Ethics and the Limits of Philosophy*, p. 174.
3 Bernard Williams, *Moral Luck*, pp. 22 ff.
4 Bernard Williams, *Ethics and the Limits of Philosophy*, pp. 183, 188 ff. *Moral Luck*, pp. 124–5.
5 Ibid., pp. 180–87.
6 See, in addition to Williams, Thomas Nagel, *Mortal Questions*, chap. 3.

moral justification, and of justification in general. Moreover, I wish to explain how philosophy can do something in support of a certain kind of morality, one that has room for something like the "agent-centered prerogatives" which Scheffler supports,[7] can do something to unscramble the complications of the Gauguin case and make headway on meeting other objections.

I shall begin with objection (4) and review some moral views represented both in commonsense *morality* and the law which do not conform with Williams' image of the "moral system" as a system of obligations, the right action being the one which discharges the strongest one. This review will therefore support the conclusion that mortality is not the kind of institution either Ross or Williams imagines.

I SOME SELF-PREROGATIVES IN COMMON SENSE AND LAW

The conception that people have "obligations *to* themselves," an idea which has been used to show that every wrong action is somehow a failure to discharge an obligation, has been largely abandoned. For it is of the essence of an obligation-to that the one to whom the obligation is owed can at will release the obligated from his obligation, so that in the case of obligation to self there is no real obligation at all. This inference leaves open that there may be duties or obligations (and in contemporary usage the terms "duty" and "obligation" are virtual synonyms) *respecting* the agent himself which are independent of obligations to other persons. Kant thought there is a duty to improve one's self (since one cannot rationally will that no one do so), but not to enhance one's own happiness. Ross thought we have a duty to "improve our own condition in respect of virtue or of intelligence," but also our own pleasure, provided we think of it as part of the objectively good.[8] I think we would nearly all agree that there are some *duties* a person has, regarding himself, which

---

7 Somewhat surprisingly, this view appears in Butler's Twelfth Sermon, except that Butler considers this a duty, not a permission. He says that a good man "would in fact, and ought to be, much more taken up and employed about himself, and his own concerns, than about others, and their interests. . . . We are in a peculiar manner, as I may speak, intrusted with ourselves; and therefore care of our own interests, as well as of our own conduct, particularly belongs to us." This part of Butler's Sermon was called to my attention by William Frankena. See Samuel Scheffler, *The Rejection of Consequentialism* (Oxford: Clarendon Press, 1982), chap. 2.

8 W. D. Ross, *The Right and the Good* (Oxford: Clarendon Press, 1930), pp. 21, 26. James Martineau held we disapprove of "rashness and recklessness," even when the interests affected are only the agent's. *Types of Ethical Theory* (Oxford: Clarendon Press, 1901), II, p. 126.

are not a matter of obligations to others: for example, not to be servile,[9] not to be a "push-over" when others seek to take advantage of one – and that there is such a thing as proper self-respect. I do not find that the above writers want to deny such duties, beyond querying the status of morality altogether.

What they do want to say is that there are actions which impinge unfavorably on the welfare of others and which morality – or at least a rational ethics – will not condemn, irrespective of any other moral obligation which these actions might discharge. It is as if morality/ethics issued a *nihil obstat*.

If there are such actions, important consequences follow. For then, contrary to Ross, and provided that he would suppose that there is a *prima facie* obligation to avoid injuring others, one is not morally bound to discharge each *prima facie* obligation except when there is a stronger obligation to do something incompatible with it. Nor is the Hare act-utilitarian view sound, that we must always perform the act which will – perhaps as far as the agent can estimate, based on his evidence – produce the most welfare in the circumstances.

Are there actions of this sort, recognized by commonsense morality or the law? It seems that at least some of the following qualify as cases – and, if there are, it shows that commonsense moral thinking is different from the Ross-Hare type (and from the image some of these writers have of morality).

(1) Telling a *harmless* lie, when this is of benefit to the agent, perhaps by protecting his reputation or merely preserving his privacy. It seems we think there is a general obligation to speak the truth, albeit a weak one when a lie would not injure the auditor. But personal benefit or preference is sometimes an exception to the obligation to speak the truth, when no harm to others is involved. Hardly morally required, but acceptable.

(2) Ross thought that there is a *prima facie* obligation to fulfill promises. So are there permissions of the sort these writers defend, in the matter of promise-keeping? Well, in general, the courts, at least, will not bind a person to fulfill a "gratuitous" promise, one in return for which no benefit was provided (with some exceptions). However, if the promisee has relied on the promise and would be injured if it were not fulfilled, the reneging can be viewed as an injury and an order be issued directing either performance or payment of damages. But, in general, a person is

9 See Thomas E. Hill, Jr., "Servility and Self-respect" in Richard A. Wasserstrom (ed.), *Today's Moral Problems*, 2nd edition (New York: Macmillan, 1979), pp. 133–47.

free to break a gratuitous promise. My guess is that commonsense morality is a bit ambivalent on this, but clearly would condemn only slightly a breach of promise when no harm is done. One can hardly be sure of this last: some people say, "A promise is a promise."[10]

(3) In the case of shipwreck, if I have arrived first at a plank to which I am clinging and it will support only one, I am morally free to push any newcomer off, thereby harming him. I concede that if I know the other person has a family dependent on him when I do not, it is a morally good act if I sacrifice myself, but it is not morally (or legally) required. Again, a person may be thrown overboard to save others in an overcrowded lifeboat, if some reasonable method, like choice by lot, is used to identify the victim. This seems contrary to the principle, "Do not kill the innocent."

(4) Although Ross says we have obligations both to tell the truth and to promote justice, it seems we think a person morally free to lie to the police in order to protect a son. (This might be viewed as an obstruction of justice, although she would hardly be prosecuted; and if she is under oath on the witness stand, would hardly be condemned morally for convenient lapses of memory.) One might, of course, say that the person is justified because of her *prima facie* obligation to protect her son, or perhaps that she is only *excused* because of the strength of her caring for her son. However this may be, it seems commonsense morality does not condemn, but rather at least excuses, an action of this sort.

(5) A man may injure his wife by seeking a divorce (where no-fault divorces are permitted), for the sake of personal advantage or preference, thereby breaking his solemn marriage vow and perhaps subjecting her to economic peril. (It is doubtful, however, if a man is morally free to abandon his children on grounds of just any personal advantage. The case of Gauguin is different.) Obviously legally, and I would think, at the present time, also morally. Of course, it is supposed that wife-desertion will be for some reason: that the man is unhappy in his marriage or is in love with another woman or that his marriage stands in the way of some project which is important to him.

All these cases seem to support the contention that there are personal "projects" or advantages which can override (alleged) moral obligations; so a contention of some of these writers seems here to be accepted as part of commonsense morality itself (and the law). Morality here does not seem to be well described by Ross. Is it morality of *this* sort that Williams thinks we are better off without? Perhaps so, but perhaps he

10 For an interesting commentary see A. W. Pickard-Cambridge, "Two Problems about Duty," *Mind*, vol. 41 (1932), pp. 145–72, 311–40.

means to criticize morality only as some philosophers like Kant and Ross conceive of it.

II THE CONDITIONS FOR MORAL DISAPPROVAL

Before we conclude that we would be better off without morality, or make some of the other claims of the writers listed, we should get clear what morality is. I take it that the *central* feature of a morality is *not* that there are some (self-evident?) *beliefs* about obligations but that there is in an individual, or group, a system of *intrinsic aversions* to *types* of actions (with a corresponding tendency to *feel guilty* or *remorseful*, if these are infringed, and to *disapprove* others for the same reason – where "disapprove" can cover a range of emotions/attitudes, such as being horrified, appalled, shocked, disgusted, and anyway having a negative "resentful" attitude toward the person, but not being amused, pitying, or feeling superior). And, I think, participants in a morality normally think that these attitudes are justifiable in some appropriate sense. If there is an aversion to someone failing to do something for another, we can say that the former party had an *obligation* to the latter.[11] There is no reason to believe that many or most of these aversion (etc.) syndromes can be viewed just as instances of some more general syndrome – as if every obligation has to be an instance of some more general type of obligation. There is also no supposition about a uniform psychological genesis of these aversions (etc.). Some may develop from, or even just be, a native tendency to sympathetic response. Some may be an outcome of love or respect for individual persons. Many are a result of some teaching: at least it having been pointed out how certain types of action tend to be harmful – or are instances of a type of act already disapproved. Some may be a result of desire to be like a parent or other admired person. In the case of motivation by natural affection for someone – say a desire to help a friend – we should not refer to the motivation as "moral" at all. If we go to visit and cheer up a friend in the hospital, we normally do it because we care for him and not because we have one of these aversions (etc.) to failing to do so. To be moral, the motivation must be for action of a certain *type*, for itself, and not because the action is aimed at some person (whom one likes or hates). Again, some of a person's (or group's) moral aversions will be stronger than others, so there will be an ordering of strength; one ordering will normally be felt to be more proper than another. A given aversion (etc.) may in fact be weak, so that one can have an aversion but lose no sleep from guilt-feelings from having in-

---

11 Williams seems roughly to agree with this. *Moral Luck*, p. 121.

fringed it.[12] (When an aversion reaches a certain level of strength, we may say the person has a corresponding virtue, say honesty or benevolence.) The system of aversions – which includes the fact of relative strength – can be quite complex; it may be nearly as complex as the language we speak. The examples cited above show how complex actual morality can be. (Remember that although Ross identified only seven moral principles of duty as "self-evident," he allowed for a much greater number of "intuitions," which he could have claimed account for the largest part of the system of approvals/aversions, and the like, a person has interiorized in acquiring his morality.) The outcome of appraisal of a particular kind of action, however, need not be specifically taught; presumably the aversions which have been taught (of differing strengths) will produce a holistic response when a situation of a certain sort is faced. This complex interiorized system of aversions does not imply that agents are not often at a loss what to do, when conflicting aversions pull them about equally in different directions. Does morality then provide a way to resolve the conflict – for example, about the morality of abortion? I have no idea how people actually decide what they then ought to do. I suppose some people may consult the Bible; what they do will depend on their educational background. I shall suggest later what it would be reasonable for them to do. Whatever the ultimate goals justifying a moral system may be, the aversions need not concern these directly but will be aimed at certain act-types.[13]

We should note that a moral system may, as Kant suggests in his talk of "imperfect duties," require a person not necessarily to perform a specific act in given circumstances but only to do something or other of a certain sort (for example, give to charity), with some leeway about for whom or at what personal cost.

Given a system of this sort, a person's *action* is *disapproved of* (or remorse properly felt by the agent) only if, in the total circumstances, the agent's action indicates that some part of his system of moral aversions (etc.) is defective, below par. (If this is correct, much of what has recently been written about the moral significance of "agent-regret" is off-target. It is true that an agent feels bad if he inadvertently does something harmful; this is a fact of psychology, but not an experience which reflects some moral point.) As in the law, an action which by itself is *prima facie* evidence that the agent's morality is defective in some way may in the *total* situation appear *justified* (like setting a fire to a neighbor's house in

12 See Philippa Foot, *Virtues and Vices* (Berkeley: University of California Press, 1978), p. 186.
13 This seems to be contrary to the view of Michael Stocker, "The Schizophrenia of Modern Ethical Theories," *Journal of Philosophy*, vol. 73 (1976), p. 458.

order to prevent spread of a conflagration). An action which provides *prima facie* evidence that one's moral aversions are defective will fail to do so – hence be *excused* – if other features of the total situation, such as one's being nonnegligently ignorant of relevant facts or being under "duress," while not sufficient to justify the act, are sufficient to rebut the *prima facie* evidence of the act that the agent's moral aversions are defective. So an act is *morally wrong* if it would be properly disapproved of, if it provides *prima facie* evidence of a defective system of aversions, in the *absence* of an excuse or justification. An act is *morally right* if it is not morally wrong.

If this entire conception of the nature of a moral system is essentially correct, it will be clear why contention (5) above is a mistake – that the morality of an act can be influenced by the subsequent outcome. The morality of an act depends only on whether its moral motivation is up to par, whatever "par" may be.[14]

Of course, it is obvious that *whenever* a person does what is morally wrong, his motivation to perform the act is presumably stronger than his *actual* moral aversion to it. But this does not begin to show that his act is not blameworthy; in the normal case, all this shows is that the agent's actual moral aversion is weaker than it should have been. But if a person's motivation to perform a normally wrong action is such as to outweigh the *proper* level of aversion, his act will not show that his moral code is below par, and his act will not be blameworthy. Again, it will be *excused*.

Some philosophers are dubious of holding that the blameworthiness of an act is fixed by a defective level of motivation, on the ground that our moral aversions are *caused*, therefore something for which we are not responsible. Nevertheless, I suggest that the moral system, like the law, works like this. It may be that from a higher, God's eye, point of view, nothing about one's motivation is to be praised or disapproved. But if the moral system operated in this way, everything would be excused, and the moral system could not perform its function of influencing behavior in the direction of social ends. That is why morality's way of thinking is justified.[15]

---

14 Bernard Williams appears to overlook the role of character (level of moral aversions, etc.) in moral judgments, perhaps as the criminal law system does (but only to some extent). Thus he says morality sees "only that focused, particularized judgment. . . . [its conception of voluntariness] will cut through character and psychological or social determination, and allocate blame and responsibility on the ultimately fair basis of the agent's known contribution, no more and no less." *Ethics and the Limits of Philosophy*, p. 194. If my picture of the "moral system" is reasonably near the truth, his view here is manifestly mistaken. See the succeeding paragraph in the text.

15 Thomas Nagel discusses the problem at some length in *Moral Questions*, pp. 28 ff. He thinks that a solution is impossible without an "internal conception of agency and its special connection with the moral attitudes as opposed to other types of value." Evidently

So, in order to be open to disapproval because of a moral-code-contrary act, there must be reason to think that the agent's aversion was not up to par, defective. How might we know this? Normally and in obvious cases, of course, we rely on our own "intuitions" or feelings; but I shall come to the question how we may give a philosophical defense of an ordering of aversions.

There is another element which should be added to the conception of a moral system, beyond the aversion, remorse, and disapproval parts, and that is admiration of acts the motivation of which goes beyond duty, normally acts that would have been an agent's duty except for the personal cost to him of performing them. We might say that this element concerns "acts of supererogation," or "morally preferable acts." I propose not to discuss how we identify acts of this sort, on the assumption that if we know what level of moral motivation defines one's duty, we can thereby draw inferences about which actions go beyond it – in the direction of what the duty would have been except for the cost to the agent.

There are acts motivated otherwise than by one's "moral system" which may elicit either praise or criticism of the agent. It may be a decision to sell all one's stocks at once, if it appears the market is about to plunge; this is a matter of self-interest. (If one doesn't, one may be subject to criticism, as not bright or not decisive.) One might intelligibly refuse to advertise some product by displays showing a sexy woman but be subject to severe criticism (maybe loss of an account) by one's peers in the advertising business, since one has shown one does not know how to appeal to the buying public. A person might fail in "duty to king and country" perhaps by disobeying some military order (possibly on moral grounds), when not to fail is strongly motivating and failure would bring charges of lack of loyalty or patriotism. A person might be motivated to send a wedding present to an acquaintance and be felt remiss if one did not – a breach of etiquette or the act of a boor; but we would hardly say it is a matter of morality if one did not, or that it reflects on one's character. One might fail to seek out the best available school for development of one's talented children, and would be criticized by some if one did not, perhaps as showing inadequate concern for one's children's life prospects. There are all sorts of motivations we have in our complex social life, and we may be *criticized* by some for having or lacking them, as being *defective* in some way, and *feel ashamed* or *embarrassed*. But is all this a matter

he does not see a solution in the fact that both law and morality must be viewed as uneasy compromises between the goals of preventing harm and producing maximal benefit, on the other hand, and, on the other, of avoiding unnecessary suffering – remorse, humiliation, shame – on the part of those who have transgressed – whose only fault is to have faults.

of morality? Morality is a special institution, in the sense of comprising aversions to certain act-types, and feelings of guilt or remorse if one fails, the failures of the aversions to guide behavior being the subject of resentful or angry attitudes on the part of others. So there are many "institutions" in society – custom, etiquette, and so on – between which and morality there is no sharp line, but with reflection we can draw a line, albeit not sharp.

The foregoing are the central features of the working moral system, although of course there are inter-cultural and inter-personal variations in the direction of aversions (etc.) toward act-types, and variations in the strength of these (and feelings about their proper strength). This complex I think roughly corresponds to what Professor Hare calls "intuitive" morality. But it hardly corresponds even remotely with Kant's view that we are morally required not to do anything which a purely rational agent, with no inclinations (*Neigungen*), would not do. Nor does it correspond with the general import of Aristotle's ethical view that the moral virtues should be taught or cultivated because possession of them is a condition of the life best for a person, one in which are realized the good, the full powers, of people in accordance with their "function." As Williams put it, on this view, "the claims of creative genius in the arts or sciences ... must be ... included in such powers [and it] is hard to reconcile, with an ideal of the development and expression of such genius, many of the virtues and commitments which belong to morality."[16] Among the Greeks of Aristotle's time, there was probably a moral system of the sort I have tried to sketch; and perhaps Aristotle's view was an attempt to refine and recommend it as being a means to the good life, one of *eudaimonia*.

Let me now offer, as an example, some comparisons between various types of motivation, some moral, some not, making clear their relative "proper" force, in contemporary moral thought – not as generalizations that obtain worldwide, but ones which pretty clearly hold for contemporary industrialized societies.

For instance, we think there are some actions which ought to be so aversive that no motivation of personal advantage can be sufficient to outweigh them: for example, an act of a deserter who subjects many comrades to death. Somewhat the same for killing in general; a person may kill in order to save himself (or those close to him) from death or serious injury (including being kidnapped) by an aggressor; but he may not kill in order to save his reputation or his fortune or the loyalty of his wife. How about robbery? We do not condemn Robin Hood on the ground of acts manifesting defective concern for the property of others,

16 Bernard Williams, *Morality* (Cambridge: Cambridge University Press, 1972), p. 71.

or for breach of law. His type of motivation is rare, however, and it is difficult to think of realistic motivation that would justify armed robbery. (Perhaps to steal a drug of which one's wife is in urgent need?) A desire for money should be weaker than the aversion to seizing the property of others, and threatening their lives to boot. How about a banker who embezzles in order to amass a fortune? Here again the moral motivation normally falls far short of what is needed. On the other hand, if the banker embezzles in order to ransom his wife from terrorists, we shall not disapprove, provided he had no other way of raising the money – this act does not show a defective level of moral aversion. It looks, then, as if, in popular "intuitive" morality, the "proper" aversion to some deeds is so high that very few motivations are satisfactory grounds for acting contrary to it; but it is also clear that some motivations to do what is *normally* wrong can be justifiably high enough (or laudable enough) that, when they prevail, there is no thought that the agent's moral aversions (etc.) are below par, and hence an act is not blameworthy. They are *morally justified.*

III THE IMPLICATIONS OF INDIRECT UTILITARIANISM

So far, nothing has been said that would offer a clue about how a par level of moral motivation could *reasonably* (on the basis presumably of philosophical argument) be identified vis-à-vis motivation to perform a contrary action (6). Nor has much been said about whether moral considerations are supreme when there is a conflict (3), or whether an action can be assessed morally solely by reflection on its motivation (whether the moral aversions are below par) and irrespective of its outcome or success (5). Nor has anything been said about whether it is irrational to deny the claims of morality (2) or whether we would be better off without it (1).

For light on these matters I turn to rule- or motive-utilitarianism – or to an indirect "optimific theory"[17] – a theory adumbrated by Butler (in his Twelfth Sermon) and held very explicitly by Bishop Berkeley. It is worth noting that Scheffler concedes that such a theory might permit the "agent-centered prerogative" for which he argues, but he does not discuss it because he thinks his view can be given an independent rationale.[18]

But first we should get clear what is the relation of a philosophical rationale or ideal for morality to actual moral systems.

17 See my paper, "Fairness to Indirect Optimific Theories in Ethics," *Ethics*, vol. 98 (1988), pp. 341–60.
18 Samuel Scheffler, pp. 16, 52 f., 87, 90–1.

I have myself argued that rational (= fully informed) persons would support an expectable-benefit-maximizing morality (in the sense explained above) as contrasted with other types of morality, or none at all, on the ground that a fully rational person would have shaken loose from any attitudes leading to preference for a non-benefit-maximizing moral system (such as one containing a prohibition of homosexuality) and prefer a moral system on the basis just of his general benevolence and his self-interest. I have inferred that a so-preferred morality will be (expectably) benefit-maximizing – not necessarily happiness-maximizing, and we can leave open the identity of the types of "benefit" – since I think such a benefit-maximizing moral system will serve both a rational person's interests best – both his benevolent interest and his self-interest. (This is the sense in which a morality can be appropriately *justified* today.) Some recent philosophers have spelled out more specifically how a self-interested person would prefer a benefit-maximizing moral system, by adverting to the problem of the Prisoner's Dilemma.[19] The thought is that in Prisoner's Dilemma situations, it is better to cooperate for a second-best good for both parties than not to cooperate, with the result of a worst possible situation for both. So, it is desirable that everyone follow a coordinative principle and, in order to secure this, that moral principles be taught (or comparable legal requirements enforced) accordingly, with the explanation that everyone's following such moral principles is a protection for the interests of each individual.[20] There are various reasons to think a benefit-maximizing system would not be actutilitarianism, either hedonistic or "ideal." This is my answer to claim (2) that it is not irrational to deny the claims of morality.

But what is the relation of this thought to actual morality? Does this conception provide an *explanation* of actual moral systems? Obviously not; too many moral systems are obviously not benefit-maximizing, even if one is moved by the wildest claims of functionalism in anthropology. The explanation of a moral system is a causal question, one about his-

19 See, for instance, Kurt Baier, "The Conceptual Link between Morality and Rationality" in *Nous*, vol. 16 (1982), pp. 78–88; Jan Narveson, "Justifying a Morality" in Douglas Odegard, *Ethics and Justification* (Edmonton, Alberta: Academic Printing and Publishing, 1988), pp. 267–9, 272 ff.; Edna Ullman-Margalit, *The Emergence of Norms* (Oxford: Clarendon Press, 1977), pp. 116 ff.; and Russell Hardin, *Morality within the Limits of Reason* (Chicago: The University of Chicago Press, 1988), chaps. 2–4.
20 This view comes reasonably close to Professor Foot's view that moral requirements are "hypothetical imperatives." I am not quite saying, however, that moral imperatives rest on desires agents actually have, but rather on a system of desires they *would* have if they had been fully reflective, including having tested their desires by "cognitive psychotherapy." The above explanation comes as close as I can come to showing that morality is "rational" (my query number 2). See also Williams, *Moral Luck*, pp. 122–3.

torical origins. I am incompetent to provide any proof, but I do offer the suggestion that considerations of benefit have played a large role in the development of actual moralities, by way of pruning and adding. I have discussed the causal origin of some alterations of moral norms in an earlier publication[21] and have nothing to add to the evidence there about how moral norms are influenced by individuals' thinking of the benefits and costs of a given moral rule. I am, however, willing to generalize from these cases and to affirm that moralities are at least somewhat influenced by the reaction of individuals to the impact of certain kinds of behavior on them personally but also, from a wider perspective, their impact on one's "moral group."

But although a philosophical rationale for a given type of moral system may not explain all moral systems causally, it may provide a convincing way of thinking about them which will show some actual moral system in a good light (doubtless with exceptions) and provide suggestions how the system should work, or can be improved, at points where it is open to specification or modification by reflection. (This is my reply to claim (6).) We must remember that moral systems are not hard and fast, with no points of doubt or disagreement. They are also highly complicated. So persons in a moral system inevitably have some problems: Exactly when is one obligation stronger than another, when the ordering is not obvious? Are there justified exceptions to the main moral principles we have interiorized? Are some moral aversions better dropped, as no longer serving group-benefit, for example, some prohibitions about sexual behavior? Should we encourage the development of a place in the moral system for problems for which it does not provide – such as duties to underdeveloped nations, conservation of resources, equal treatment for the sexes, and so on?

How will the *conception* of a benefit-maximizing morality – what I call an "indirect optimific *theory*" – play a role of these sorts: telling us how to make some of our moral commitments more specific and how to modify our morality? Incidentally, we should note that if a given type of benefit-maximizing moral system is chosen by informed rational persons as preferable to any other moral system and *to none at all*, it is not clear how it is going to be possible to argue that "we would be better off without it" (claim (1)).

How will an indirect optimific *theory* identify the level of aversion appropriate to certain types of action? Roughly, the idea is to order the acceptable level of aversion to various act-types in accordance with the damage to (one or more persons') welfare that would likely be done if

---

21 *Hopi Ethics: A Theoretical Analysis* (Chicago: University of Chicago Press, 1954).

everyone *felt free* to indulge in the kind of behavior in question – not if everyone actually indulged. The worse the effect if everyone felt free, the higher the acceptable level of aversion to the act-type. So far, the moral system is rather like an ideal code of criminal law, with punishment graded according to the expectable damage of a type of harmful behavior not being punished. More precisely, since the teaching of a moral system is itself costly, we might say that the *teaching* of a moral system should be optimal by act-utilitarian standards: what *acts of teaching* will be most beneficial in view of their costs (including the cost of possibly causing psychological problems among the youth, and the trouble of the teaching), the likelihood that the teaching will affect conduct, and the value of the conduct secured or value of the damage avoided. A good deal of empirical information will presumably be required to estimate what should be done in at all an accurate way. The decision will be the more difficult if "welfare" is construed not solely in terms of enjoyment or preference satisfaction but also in terms of states like deep personal relations, accomplishment, and so on. All of this seems reasonable enough as a long-term strategy for maximizing welfare.

I am saying that the motivations in a benefit-maximizing moral system would rationally be selected in this way, but I am not saying that they are so in civilized societies. Moreover, I think that often this order will not be fully interiorized and that when it is not, an agent (who may not be any kind of theorist) has to do some thinking about what the proper order would be, if this criterion were used – and the teacher of morality must think this through in order to decide how an actual moral system can be improved, what a more satisfactory morality would be like. I am not saying that all this reflection will be simple; teachers of morality – as well as the average person wanting to do the moral thing – need a bit of philosophy.[22]

What this sort of reflection will accomplish is of course not the setting of a cardinally measurable level of motivation to avoid certain kinds of acts, but a rough ordering of aversions (etc.) to kinds of acts relative to the kinds of motive expected to lead to them – it being better that a selected act-type aversion should prevail, rather than some typical kind of actual motivation. I have already sketched some results of this sort, as they are represented in commonsense morality. For more complex

22 Michael Stocker seems to think that interiorizing the aversions (etc.) of an optimal morality is incompatible with the existence of motives like love, friendship, affection, and community. I fail to see why. The moral motives here will operate as a "back-up" system when direct affections fail. See Stocker, "The Schizophrenia of Modern Ethical Theories," *Journal of Philosophy*, vol. 73 (1976), pp. 461–2. He also seems to think that interiorizing certain aversions (etc.) for the sake of maximizing benefit is an indirection that is incompatible with the motives of love, etc. (p. 463).

cases, for instance where a balancing of *prima facie* obligations is involved, reflection by a prospective agent (or his or her advisers), of the kind described should ideally be relied upon for the analysis of particular situations, and presumably can reach results commanding wide agreement. Is it too much to expect that people will be able to do this reasonably well?

As writers like Sidgwick have pointed out, a system of this sort will presumably recognize special obligations to wives and children; the total welfare will be enhanced if it does.[23] Moreover, unlike the theory of act-utilitarianism, it will not require a person forever to busy himself running his life so as to maximize total welfare. It is obvious that people will be better motivated in their activities, whatever they are, if they are free to follow their own values and bents and to do less for the well-being of others than the act-utilitarian code requires – although possibly with the effect of making a larger contribution to the total well-being if we include their own. Moreover, if we view morality as a system of specific "side-constraints" which specify what may not (ordinarily) be done, but otherwise leave a person free to follow his own projects, there will be an enormous gain in sense of freedom. This is the indirect utilitarian motivation for something like Scheffler's "agent-centered prerogative," and I suggest it does very well.

I propose to discuss an example which seems to play an important role in Williams' thinking about claims (3) and (5): that of whether Gauguin was "justified" in deserting his family in order to paint in the South Pacific. This example raises two questions. One is exactly when a non-moral consideration (some motivating reason to do something contrary to one's moral aversions) can override one's (justified) moral aversions. The other is how it is possible (if it is) that it was Gauguin's *success* which morally justified his act of desertion – something which appears to be just a matter of luck, as if a moral evaluation can depend on lucky considerations which could not have been foreseen.

It would seem likely that an optimal moral system will include, for the normal case, a proscription of deserting one's family when there is not a stronger prescription to do something else. So must the indirect utili-

---

23 Williams disparages such facts, saying that if a man has a choice between saving his wife and someone else in a shipwreck, if the thought of the moral principle occurs to him at all he "has one thought too many." Williams recommends that in such a situation the "motivating thought... would be the thought that it was his wife, not that it was his wife and that in situations of this kind it is permissible to save one's wife." *Moral Luck*, p. 18. I cannot empathize with this view. Suppose his wife is a highly objectionable person, about to do some serious damage? Or that the other person is the one who knows the cure for cancer? or both? Why rule out such reflections if they are obvious, even in a situation of emergency?

tarian not say that Gauguin's behavior was quite unjustified? But I believe that is not quite the end of what the moral system will say.

We must take into account that a moral system can be quite complex. Nevertheless, it may not always issue directives for particular situations which are the best strategy for maximizing benefit in the long run. Thus an indirect optimific moral system may, like the law, regard as "justified" some action forbidden by the normal moral "rules," when following the rules would be highly dangerous or harmful. Such a view seems to have been accepted by Mill, who wrote:

> Particular cases may occur in which some other social duty is so important as to overrule any one of the general maxims of justice. Thus, to save a life, it may not only be allowable, but a duty, to steal or take by force the necessary food or medicine, or to kidnap and compel to officiate the only qualified medical practitioner.[24]

How large must be the threatened loss before this is done? Substantial: I think we may follow the courts in their interpretation, say, of the First Amendment, but this is disagreeably imprecise.[25]

An indirect utilitarian morality will presumably also hold that the *normal* moral rules binding on behavior may be suspended not only to avoid a disaster but also to secure some very great good.

There are two questions to be raised – or qualifications stated – about "suspension" of the normal rules both in order to avoid a great loss, and in order to gain a great benefit.

The first is that obviously a value-judgment is involved in deciding that some disastrous or at least very unfortunate consequence is sufficiently important to exempt the agent from the normal moral obligations. There would hardly be doubt about the blowing up of New York City. The same for the destruction of a great library. The saving of a life? The saving of political freedom? Perhaps such matters are more certain than things are when we have to estimate the importance of something good, like Gauguin's paintings. We say the gain must be great, but how great, and by what standard? Presumably the justification is to apply only to exceptional circumstances. How about something which is a "condition of [a person's] having any interest in being around in that world at all"?[26] Here we must be careful not to set the sights too low; a person can feel that way just because he or she has been jilted by a lover. Williams makes the case more plausible when he speaks of actions as "flowing from

24 About a page from the end of chap. 5 of *Utilitarianism*.
25 See Charles Black, "Mr. Justice Black, the Supreme Court, and the Bill of Rights," *Harper's Magazine*, February, 1961, pp. 63–8.
26 Williams, *Moral Luck*, p. 14.

projects and attitudes which in some cases he takes seriously at the deepest level, as what his life is about."[27] I find it a bit hard to identify with a person whose eggs are so exclusively in one basket; but I can imagine a philosopher so engrossed in his work that he takes no interest in anything else: social life, exercise, family. Is this commitment enough? We surely want the value to be very substantial. But we must bear in mind that the value which is sufficient to justify "suspending" a moral rule (aversion, etc.) will vary with the strength of the optimal level of strength of the moral rule (aversion, etc.). The weaker the normal rule, the less can be the value.

But there is another question or qualification to be noted. This is that kidnapping may be justified to save a life; but the prospective kidnapper ought to know his grounds – is this really necessary to save a life? We might say that it is acceptable to torture someone to save New York City from being blown up by an atom bomb, but it is far from obvious that it is justified to torture someone about whom there is only suspicion that he is in a position to prevent such a catastrophe. (The degree of assurance we need to have about the facts is doubtless less, the more severe the prospective damage.)

A parallel requirement seems in order when it is said that moral "rules" may be suspended in order to make possible a great good. Assurance of the outcome must be strong enough, so that not every person who aspires to bring about a great good, no matter how unrealistically, is justified in flouting moral principles.

A morality following the optimific indirect theory will presumably allow for all this. Indeed, it may be that a principle directing when "exceptions" to the normal principles may occur could itself be (and maybe already is) built into the moral system, as an application of the "theory." The exceptions, and qualifications, are necessary in order that the moral system be maximally beneficial, in the long run.

Let us turn now to Williams' case of Gauguin. Suppose we think his paintings a great addition to human well-being. Then it would seem arguable that the normal moral rule concerning desertion of family be suspended in his case. And I think most of us, on this account, initially feel less inclined to disapprove of Gauguin's behavior morally if we set a high value on his work. But there is again a serious contrary consideration which we have just noted. It would seem that if and only if Gauguin *knew*, with a reasonable degree of probability, that he would produce great art if and only if he deserted his family, would it be justified to suspend the relatively strong normal moral rule in his case. Or is it

27 J. J. C. Smart and Bernard Williams, *Utilitarianism: For and Against*, p. 116.

enough that he felt strongly *committed*, irrespective of any grounds for thinking he would succeed? If he only *hoped* that he would produce great art, or felt intuitively that he might or would, is that enough for thinking the moral rules deserved suspension, admitted we may feel disinclined to disapprove his act morally, from our knowledge after the fact? I am inclined to think, on the basis of my ignorance of his personal history, that Gauguin was not morally justified, that he properly should have felt remorse and that others should have disapproved, because of the long-range disutility of permitting suspension of a relevant moral rule on such grounds – it would be a poor strategy for maximizing long-range benefit, to regard a person as excused or justified in this mental situation of merely hoping, whatever the ultimate consequences. I think an indirect utilitarian morality would unscramble this complex issue in this way.

The same would seem to be true of the aspiring philosopher, wanting to achieve something like Hume or Aristotle. We shall be happy if he succeeds, but the side-constraints of morality seem still to hold, if he had no good reason to think he would succeed.

At the same time, it is true that we are now glad that Gauguin did what he did, provided it really was true that his production of great art was possible only if he deserted his family. But does the fact we now *feel glad* that he did what he did imply that he was really *morally* justified in doing it? We are often glad, in retrospect, that morally reprehensible things were done. Williams seems somewhat ambivalent about this. Provided that Gauguin was a moral person, he says, he was open to regrets for what he had done. And, if he fails, "these regrets are not only all that he has, but . . . he no longer even has the perspective within which something else could have been laid against them." So apparently his success *can* be "laid against them." He says that if Gauguin succeeds, he will not have "the most basic regrets," and if he succeeds that will make a difference to the moral spectator. He suggests this might amount to a "moral justification."[28]

Is Williams saying that the success of the agent and the fact that moral spectators will be glad he did what he did, mean that the agent has a *morally justifiable* reason for action?[29] If he is, then he has *not* shown that a nonmoral consideration outweighs a moral obligation – what he seems to have been most anxious to establish.

Williams concedes that these reflections may not satisfy the victims of Gauguin's action, and perhaps properly so. But still, he thinks, they may be "moral justifications" all the same. But the "luck" of the success of

28 *Moral Luck*, p. 38.
29 My diagnosis of the Gauguin behavior is rather similar to that of Thomas Nagel, *Moral Questions*, p. 28, footnote.

89

those like Gauguin "does not lie in acquiring a moral justification. It lies rather in the relation of their life, and of their justification or lack of it to morality." He concludes that "scepticism about the freedom of morality from luck cannot leave the concept of morality where it was"; it leaves us with "*a* concept of morality, but one less important, certainly, than ours is usually taken to be."[30] (One might ask if there is any need to claim for morality any importance beyond what the moral system does for the well-being of society. Morality is a *means;* the system is not a good in itself.)

But is there, and is Williams saying that there is, *justification* which is not moral? I have already mentioned that Williams speaks of considerations like personal ends, prudence, aesthetic concerns, and "sheer self-assertion" as concerns proper to justification along with moral ones. But what might Williams mean by "justification"? I suggest an act is *morally* justified if it is shown to be *right* (what an informed person might do consistently with a proper level of moral motivations) or, perhaps, to be *excused* because, in the total circumstances, his act did not show his level of moral motivations to be defective. But Williams seems sometimes to speak of "justification" simple. What does this mean? He throws light on this by saying that if lack of success was not Gauguin's failure as an artist but a result of some other accident, then "he cannot in the fullest sense identify with his decision, and so does not find himself justified; but he is not totally alienated from it either, and so does not find himself unjustified."[31] (So justification means being able to identify with one's decision or not being alienated from it?) He says the moral spectator must consider that he has reason to be glad that Gauguin succeeded; and this shows that moral values are only one value among others, not "unquestionably supreme." And this fact leaves us with a conception of morality "that will not be ours, since one thing that is particularly important about ours is how important it is taken to be."[32]

Of course there are other values than moral, and optimal morality takes them into account; it is not itself an intrinsic good. Moreover, there are qualities which are admirable in addition to moral qualities. But the talk of other kinds of "justification" and the failure of morality to be "supreme" does not show that a person need not be averse to, feel remorse about, and have others disapprove of, failure to do what his justified moral aversions require. Being glad about the total outcome is one thing; remorse and disapproval are something else. Is Williams saying that we should just learn to live with such various attitudes, in conflict with one

30 Ibid., p. 39.
31 *Moral Luck*, p. 36.
32 Ibid., pp. 37–39.

another? Then we should be recognizing that there are many values in life, having adequate moral motivations being only one. Perhaps he is.

It is not easy to see exactly what general normative theory about justifications, of these various sorts, Williams wishes to affirm, if any. I speculate that what he may mean is that a *rational* (or perhaps fully informed) person would view considerations of morality, aesthetics, personal interest,[33] and perhaps other modes of life as parallel, with none able to claim supremacy universally, in all cases. But then, at a moment of decision, what *ought* a person to do – be *well advised* to do – over all, everything considered? It is no answer to this question to say that there are other considerations than the moral. By what kind of thinking are we to adjudicate among them? I would agree that possibly it is not rational for a person to prefer doing the moral thing when it conflicts with long-range self-interest. But what form might a more public, long-range view take of these conflicts of value? I do not see that Williams gives us an answer to this question. Perhaps he wanted only to point to a problem, not to solve it.

What I think my above reflections about the advice of indirect optimific theory show is that the salient rules of popular morality are to be suspended in order to avoid a *probably* great disaster or to bring about a *probably* significant good. Allowance for this, if I am right, is part of the fabric of moral thinking itself. And this means that justified morality itself issues a *nihil obstat* in *some* cases of a person's pursuing other projects in preference to conforming to the normal basic rules of the moral system. Does this mean that, after all, there is *no* conflict between the claims of morality and those of art? Perhaps this line of thinking is all we need.

One might ask why, in cases of life-enriching experiences which justify us sometimes in injuring others, morality does not *require* such behavior. Perhaps we might recommend it and criticize failure in some cases. We might think less of a man who gave up some important project in order to stick with a wife he doesn't particularly like. At least we might criticize him in some way; we might say he is lacking in courage or vision or is a creature of habit. And, if asked, we might advise doing the thing forbidden by the popularly recognized moral principles, in view of what he can do with his life. The possibility of this is an implication of the *nihil obstat* of a theoretically defensible moral system. Still, morality is too crude to permit a paternalistic stance; like the law, it cannot strongly require a person to do what is for his own good, if he is mentally competent and prefers not to: he must be left to his own free decision. Perhaps one exception is self-respect. Morality is there, in general, to protect

33 Here he is like Sidgwick.

others, and it must leave to the individual agent what he may do for the sake of goods that seem important to him. Some decisions are best left free from coercion, even the informal coercion of morality.

The foregoing reflections are quite different from the belief that a man is always free to, or bound to, follow his "conscience." Morality recognizes the fact that people's taking their consciences seriously is of great assistance to morality; and normally they should follow them. But there is an exception: conscience may not permit or require behavior obviously at variance with morality and its purpose – so much so that it is clear that a person's "conscience" could not be as it is if his moral motivations had not been below standard. If "conscience" dictates a right to do what morality clearly prohibits, even when so doing will produce maximal good, but which does not fall in the excepted classes described, then his conscience does not have the authority to be a moral guide to life.

6

Rationality, egoism, and morality

The discussion of ethical egoism[1] necessarily leads into problems central to moral philosophy. In a short paper, one has a choice between concentrating on one of these problems and trying to clean it up thoroughly, and taking a broader look at the interconnection of the problems in the hope of illuminating some of them, but with the risk of cleaning up nothing. I prefer to take the risk.

I THE SENSE IN WHICH IT IS RATIONAL TO MAXIMIZE ONE'S LONG-RANGE UTILITY

As a first approximation, we can say that the ethical egoist holds that a person *ought* (in *some* sense) to act so as to maximize his own long-range advantage or welfare – or, more exactly, in view of the fact that the outcomes of one's acts are seldom certain, to maximize his own expectable long-range utility or welfare. This formulation leaves open the question whether it is supposed that a person ought to do this in the *moral* sense of 'ought' (whatever that may be), or in some other sense of 'ought.' It also leaves open what is meant by 'utility' or 'welfare.'

Egoists and also others have often supposed the following:

(1) $(x)(y)$ (it is *rational* for x to do y iff y maximizes x's utility in the long run)

or, in case there is only probable information about outcomes:

(1') $(x)(y)$ (it is rational for x to do y iff y maximizes x's expectable utility in the long run)

and

(2) $(x)(y)$ (x *ought* to do y iff it is rational for x to do y)

---

1 I shall not discuss theories that may be classified as forms of psychological egoism. Although psychological theories of action, motivation, and learning are important for moral philosophy, the theses generally classified as forms of psychological egoism are either false or too vague to merit discussion.

93

In what follows, I shall defend (1) and (1′) as being true, although possibly in a sense some egoists will not like; I shall attack (2), at least in one interpretation.

If (1) and (2) are both accepted, the thesis of egoism, as stated, follows. I begin with comments on (1).

Let me first explain what I mean by a "rational" action. I define a "rational" action for a certain person at a certain time as the action that person *actually would* perform at that time *if* (a) his desires and aversions at the time were what they would be if he had been fully exposed to available information, and if (b) the agent had firmly and vividly in mind, and equally at the center of attention, all those knowable facts which, if he thought about them, would make a difference to his tendency to act, given his "cleaned-up" desires [as in (a)]. Essentially, I am using 'rational action' to mean "fully informed" action; if you prefer to substitute, in what follows, 'fully informed' whenever 'rational' appears, it would make no difference.

Two initial points about this definition. First, possibly, with this definition we have less trouble than we might have otherwise with the skeptic who asks, Why should we act rationally? [There *are* problems with (a); I come back to that.] For, if we define 'rational' in this way, the doubter is placed in the position of asking: Why should I do what I would do if available knowledge were guiding my behavior in a maximal fashion? I think the skeptic will find it hard to recommend action based on ignorance, in preference to (or in indifference to) awareness of the facts. Second, if we define 'rational act' in this way, we are not guilty of introducing any ethical or value biases into the definition – unless it is an ethical or value bias to recommend choices guided by information.

The above explanation of 'rational act' is too condensed, and needs to be expanded and explained a bit.

First, (a). Most of us will probably agree that often people have desires or aversions that have something wrong with them, and that we are tempted to label as "hang-ups." For instance, a person may have an intense craving for recognition by other people, that he would not have had but for deprivation of affection in his childhood. Again, a person may have a strong aversion to being in a certain occupation, or having any close association with people in it, because parents or teachers showed contempt for that occupation. Now there is reason to think that such intense cravings and aversions would vanish if the persons were "fully exposed to available information," or rather (and this is an expansion of the above condensed statement) if they *repeatedly brought to mind, with full belief and maximal vividness,* all the knowable facts that would tend

94

either to weaken or to strengthen the desire or aversion, or, we might say, if the persons were to go through "cognitive psychotherapy." Full and vivid awareness of the facts has, over time, influence on desires and aversions. Let us say that a person's desires and aversions have been *cleaned up*, if they have been maximally influenced (either strengthened or weakened) by awareness of knowable facts in cognitive psychotherapy.

I mentioned that there is a "problem" with (a). Now I personally do not want to give an action the kind of recommendation one gives it by calling it "rational" if it is an action that would not have been taken if there had been cognitive psychotherapy, an action that was taken either because an irrational desire (aversion) had not been removed or reduced, or because a desire (aversion) the absence of which was irrational had not been introduced or strengthened. But I am prepared to admit that a person might ask *why* I say this. Why is it rational to act *as if* one did not have a certain desire when one in fact has it? And why is it rational to act as if one did have a desire that in fact one does not have, just because one knows one *would* have it if one had had cognitive psychotherapy? These queries require discussion for which there is no space here; if you agree with the objector, you should disagree with my definition of 'rational action' to the extent of dropping (a) from it.

Now for (b). I said that an action is to be called "rational" (or "fully informed") if and only if it would occur if the agent firmly believed, and had in mind with optimal or equal vividness, all those knowable facts which, if he thought about them, would make a difference to his tendency to act. Which thoughts might these be, that would make a difference to his tendency to act? Obviously thoughts about features of the action, or about probable outcomes of it, which the agent wants, or to which he has an aversion, at the time. What are examples of these? "External" events or states of affairs, like my owning and having in my hall a grandfather's clock; like the chairman of my department, who has recently insulted me, getting his comeuppance; like my daughter's getting a raise in salary or a better place to live. There are also states of my self in a narrower sense: like drinking wine, eating food, glowing because of the admiration of persons, being in the state of tension I experience when my airplane goes through a thunderstorm. And also, of course, the angry resentful feelings I shall have toward my chairman unless he either apologizes or gets his comeuppance, or the feelings of distress I have when I reflect on the shabby apartment in which my daughter lives or on the anxiety she feels because of her insecure job. It is important to be clear that we do have genuine desires or aversions for both types of events or states of affairs: for internal states of the self, like being nervous in an airplane, and for external states of affairs, like my daughter's getting a raise in salary. It is all the relevant facts of these sorts that we must have fully and equally in mind if our action is to be "rational."

It is a fact of empirical psychology that a person actually performs that act, among those he has in mind as possibilities at the time, which he most wants (not only the act itself but the associated outcomes). Such, at any rate, is the view of the most defensible psychological theory of action, such as that held in their later years by Tolman and Lewin, and by "subjective-expectable-utility" theorists, or by somewhat eclectic writers like John Atkinson. One complication we have to add, although the facts are less clear and perhaps we could skip it for our purposes. This complication is that we must think of the effect of the want/aversion associated with each anticipated outcome as scaled down by the extent to which the agent's expectation of that outcome, given the action, falls short of certainty. So, strictly, the view is that that act is performed, among the possibilities in mind, toward which there is the strongest "tendency" at the moment; and the strength of the tendency to perform any act corresponds to (if we may put it, for simplicity, in mathematical terms) the sum of a set of products one for each feature or outcome associated with a given action: the product, for each, of a number representing the intensity with which it is wanted (positively or negatively) and a number representing the probability with which it is expected if the action is performed. (There is another scaling down that has to be made, for lack of vividness of representation or centrality in attention; but we can ignore this, since we are specifying that in the case of rational actions these are maximally – or equally – present.)

I believe it follows from my definition of 'rational action' and from the just-stated principle of empirical psychology that theses (1) and (1′) are both true, *provided* we define the "utility" of the agent in terms of the intensity of his desire, at the time, for various outcomes, or features of the act itself. Incidentally, it also follows that a rational act in my sense has various properties many writers are accustomed to associating with "rational actions" (in their sense). For instance, if two courses of action will achieve the same positive (wanted) goals, then that one is rational which does so at less cost (less aversive means or outcome). Again, if two plans will have equal costs, but one will lead to all the desired goals the other will lead to, but to further desired goals as well, that is the rational act. Again, if both of two plans of action promise the same costs, but one will lead to the desired ends more probably than the other, the plan leading to the desired ends with higher probability is rational.

We had better get clear some features of this outcome which some past and doubtless some present egoists will not much relish. First, it follows from the foregoing that my act may be perfectly rational (or well informed) if it sacrifices some personal pleasure for the happiness or security of my daughter, or for the discomfort of my chairman, or, doubtless, for all sorts of causes or ideals, *provided* I really do want these things (and provided, of course, that my desires have been "cleaned up"). Thus it is just not true that it is rational for me to sacrifice a personal enjoyment *only* for the sake of some desired state of my person in the narrow sense – such as eating a good meal, having sex, or glowing from admiration. I find nothing surprising in this. If I really care about my daughter's welfare, why is it not rational for me to sacrifice some personal pleasure to that end? Any supposition to the contrary seems to me just to reflect some unsupported dogma. I am prepared to grant that some people want only the satisfaction of their so-called physical desires, and a state of euphoria for themselves; if so, then the rational act for them might not be to sacrifice personal enjoyment for the welfare of a daughter (except when an improvement of her welfare would increase personal enjoyment sufficiently to overbalance the loss from producing the greater welfare for her).

The second, and closely related, point that some egoists may not relish is the definition of 'utility' (or 'welfare') in terms of the strength of a person's desires/aversions at the time. There are some serious questions about this, such as what has to be done in case of cyclical desires, which change in intensity almost from one moment (of deprivation) to another (of satiation); or of desires that we know will have different intensities at some later time. There is not space even to begin discussion of this large topic. But I think egoists may be most bothered by the inclusion of desires for external states of affairs, and the "benevolent" desires, on an equal basis, in defining the "utility" or "welfare" of an agent. And they might have a point – if such desires are in themselves irrational, and would remain in cognitive psychotherapy. But would they? I confess to a desire to do philosophical work of some significance, and would exchange a good deal of personal enjoyment for the production by me of philosophical work as memorable as that of Aristotle or Plato. I tend to think that a philosopher who did not share my desire would be virtually insane! Now this desire is certainly not a desire for a state of euphoria of my self. It has been thought, most notably and judiciously by such writers as Henry Sidgwick and F. C. Sharp, that when we think carefully and make all the requisite distinctions, the only goal that appeals to us is pleasure or happiness. We could rephrase this by saying that "cognitive psychotherapy" would extinguish desires for other things. You might go this way; but I see no reason for accepting their conclusion. (Sidgwick also leaned the way he did because he thought that otherwise the task of comparing the values of different things would be hopeless;[2] but we need not adopt a simplistic view just because the identification of the rational act would be a more tractable problem if we did so.) Consequently, I hold that if I really desire the happiness of my daughter, or the discomfiture of my department chairman, or some cause or ideal, then getting that desire satisfied – that is, the occurrence of the event or state of affairs desired – counts as being an enhancement of my utility or welfare (assuming, of course, that the desire would not be extinguished in cognitive psychotherapy) and counts to an extent corresponding to how strongly I want that outcome.

I conclude, then, that theses (1) and (1') are true, when interpreted as I interpret them, especially with respect to the terms 'rational' and 'utility.'

You may think the above is a very circuitous way of arriving at this conclusion. You may think that we might have got to the same result much more simply: either by asserting (1) and (1') as self-evident, or by *defining* 'rational' so that both (1) and (1') turn out to be analytic. If you do, then at least we agree on the conclusion. At any rate, the above is the kind of defense that I would offer for the egoist's thesis that the rational act is that which maximizes the agent's long-range (expectable) utility.

The phrase "You ought to . . . " could helpfully be used, and I think very often is used, as a substitute for "The rational thing for you to do is to. . . . " So we say, "You ought to see a psychotherapist," or "You ought not to marry Miss *X;* she would make you very unhappy." I shall call this the "prudential" sense of 'ought,' or the "prudential ought."

It is obvious that people often perform acts that are not rational in my sense. A person's desires may be such that, if his choice were rational or informed, he would not smoke a pack of cigarettes a day; but he does. Again, a person may be excited by the honor of a certain job offer, and he may accept it, without getting vividly before his mind the day-to-day duties of the job, which he would hate performing; so he does an irrational thing. In the prudential sense, we can say that the person *ought* not to have done these things.

When we ask a person for his advice about what we "ought" to do, in a matter that raises no moral issues, what we are asking for is his sincere opinion about the identity of the rational action for us, given our desires (or cleaned-up desires). Obviously when a person tells us what he thinks we ought to do, if he is sincere he is telling us what he thinks is the

2 *The Methods of Ethics,* seventh ed. (London: Macmillan, 1922), p. 406.

rational act for us, given *our* desires, not what he would have us do, given *his* desires.

Since people's desires and aversions differ (even, I believe, the cleaned-up ones), it may be rational for one person to do something it would be irrational for another to do, even when the situations are identical except for the desires and aversions of the two parties.

II WHAT IS ETHICAL EGOISM?

Let us begin with one formulation of ethical egoism (there are others; the one I state is usually accepted and is the most interesting):[3]

(3) *(x)(y)* (x ought to do y if and only if y maximizes x's utility)

This statement will do as a formulation of the egoist's view about what one *objectively* ought to do; I prefer, because it is more realistic, to use a closely related formulation, which states his view about what should be done when there is only probable information about outcomes. This is:

(4) *(x)(y)* (x subjectively ought to do y if and only if y maximizes x's expectable utility)

How are we to take the term 'ought'? One possibility is that we are intended to take it in the *prudential* sense. If we do this, we can rewrite the above theses of the egoist as "It is rational for a person to do y if and only if ... " (We could, if we wish, distinguish 'subjectively rational' from 'objectively rational' to call attention, in the former case, to the fact that there is only probable information about outcomes.) If 'ought' is taken in the prudential sense, then (3) = (1) and (4) = (1'). I have already argued that (1) and (1') are true. Hence, if what the egoist means to assert is (3) and (4) in the prudential sense of 'ought,' I am an egoist.

Usually, however, the egoist seems to say more than this; he says his thesis is about what one ought to do in the "moral" sense; it is a thesis about moral obligation, duty, and so on. Unfortunately, this clarification of his thesis does not help much until we are told what is to count as the meaning of 'morally ought' or what is the "moral" sense of 'ought' – or what it is to be morally obligated, have a moral duty, and so on. Moreover, there seems to be a good deal of disagreement, or unclarity, about what is a "moral" sense of 'ought.' W. K. Frankena, for example, iden-

3 This is very similar to the formulation by Jesse Kalin, "In Defense of Egoism," in David Gauthier, ed., *Morality and Rational Self-Interest* (Englewood Cliffs, NJ: Prentice-Hall, 1970), p. 65.

tifies a "wider" sense of the term 'moral' (which he contrasts with a narrower sense that he accepts himself), to the effect that an action-guide (one or more ought-statements) counts as moral for a person or society X, if X takes it as prescriptive, universalizes it, and regards it as definitive, final, overriding, or supremely authoritative. This wider view, he says, appears to be held by R. M. Hare, John Ladd, W. D. Falk, "the existentialists . . . , many religious thinkers, and at least some Aristotelians."[4]

If one construes 'morally ought' in this wider sense, it is not clear that there is any inconsistency between taking the above theses of egoism so that 'ought' is understood *both* in the prudential sense *and* in the moral sense, at once. For it seems to me that, taken in the prudential sense, the thesis of egoism is prescriptive; it is so stated that it is universalized; and evidently egoist regards it as supremely authoritative. It may well be that this position is what Jesse Kalin has in mind in his defense of egoism. For he says: "The egoist's basic question is: 'What ought I to do; what is most reasonable for me to do?' This question seems to me a moral question through and through, and any coherent answer to it thereby deserves to be regarded as a moral theory" (op. cit., p. 86).

How, then, are we to understand the theses of egoism? Let us, for a start, and without any assumption that it will clarify anything, insist that the doctrine is to be *moral* affirmation in *some* sense. In order to mark this, let us rewrite the theses as follows:

$$_{\text{or}}(5) \ (x)(y) \, (x \text{ objectively morally ought to do } y \text{ iff } y \text{ maximizes } x\text{'s utility})$$

(6) *(x)(y)* (*x* subjectively morally ought to do *y* iff *y* maximizes *x*'s expectable utility)

If these theses are not construed in the way suggested above, as combining the wider sense of 'morally ought' with the prudential sense of 'ought,' they strike me as highly implausible – for, if not so construed, they are naturally taken to imply that a person is morally blameworthy if he is not busily maximizing his utility. In a different, and perhaps more natural, sense of 'morally ought,' egoists themselves, I think, do not want to affirm these propositions. Thus I (and they) find it more plausible to say not that it is morally binding but rather that it is only *morally permissible* for a person to do what advances (or what he thinks advances) his welfare to some degree, irrespective of how it affects the interest of others. I do not think (and egoists do not seem to think) that there is a moral obligation in any ordinary sense to maximize your own welfare,

---

4 "The Concept of Morality," *Journal of Philosophy* 63, 21 (Nov. 21, 1966): 688–96, esp. p. 689; reprinted in Kenneth Pahel and Marvin Schiller, eds., *Readings in Contemporary Ethical Theory* (Englewood Cliffs, NJ: Prentice-Hall, 1970).

although it might be argued that you do have a moral obligation to avoid doing things that seriously jeopardize your welfare (for instance, driving when drunk, not wearing a seat belt, etc.) – although even this may be questioned. What egoists seem sometimes to have in mind is primarily a *moral freedom* to pursue your own advantage, or putative advantage, as you like, without heed to the effects on others, however catastrophic. How might we state this? Perhaps thus:

(7) $(x)(y)$ (it is morally permissible for x to do y, iff either y will advance x's welfare to some degree or x thinks it will, absolutely irrespective of the actual or probable effects of y on any other person)

It is clear that if 'morally permissible' is taken in the sense of 'prudentially permissible' (that is, "it is not true that one prudentially ought not"), then (7) is not true; egoists must be well aware of this fact. So if and when they make this affirmation, or represent it as the fundamental thesis of egoism, they can hardly be using 'morally ought' in the prudential sense. In what sense, then? I shall not pursue this question, for I do not want to divert discussion to this formulation of egoism. It will do no harm if we concentrate on (5) and (6). My arguments will be equally effective either way, and anyone who likes (7) can easily see how these arguments bear on it.

Whether (5) or (6) is true, or even consistent, depends on how we construe 'morally ought,' that is on our metaethical views about 'morally ought' – what we think it does mean, or what we think it is best taken to mean. Some philosophers (for instance, G. E. Moore at one point) have taken it to mean, "will produce at least as much intrinsic good as any other action open to the agent." If that were what is meant, then the theses (provided we add to them, "even if it reduces the utility of others to a much greater extent") are self-contradictory. There are various ways of taking the theses if you adopt a prescriptivist or emotivist metaethics; Brian Medlin has shown some of the difficulties one gets into if one adopts certain forms of this. One might take the formulations as just expressions of one's *moral* attitudes (meaning by "moral attitudes" one's tendencies to feel guilt in one's own case and to have unfavorable attitudes to others because of their conduct, either indignation or disgust or contempt), as perhaps Kalin takes them; then I think the theses are consistent, although perhaps not defensible. One could construe the expression 'morally ought' in some "ideal observer" way; I have discussed elsewhere[5] some difficulties for the egoist thesis that one gets into if one adopts a form of this view. And, like Price and Reid, one might take the term as

5 *Ethical Theory* (Englewood Cliffs, NJ: Prentice-Hall, 1959), p. 374.

simple and indefinable, in which case the theses would not be inconsistent, but are perhaps self-evidently false.

Since I cannot hope to appraise egoism in all possible interpretations, I shall try only to appraise it when 'morally ought' is understood in what I think is one interesting way. This understanding has some affiliations with views of Kurt Baier, John Rawls, and J. S. Mill, among others;[6] I do not say they hold it.

I suggest, then, that we consider the possibility that "X morally ought to do y" be taken to mean "X would be required to do y by the moral system that all rational (in my sense) persons would, if they had the opportunity to choose, *collectively* agree in selecting as the moral system for the consciences of adults of the society in which they knew that they and/or their children would spend their lives." This formulation needs a good deal of explanation, which there is not space to give it here. For instance, 'would collectively choose' cannot mean 'would be the first preference for each person'; it has to mean some kind of compromise choice that suits everyone as well as any selection could – something to be explained at length.[7] We should note that on this view the prudential "ought" is involved in the concept of moral obligation, via the notion of what "rational persons" would choose.

If we substitute the above definition for 'x morally ought to do y' in (5) and (6) we get the following (for 6), which I shall regard as a thesis of Egoism:

(8) $(x)(y)$ (x would be required to do y by the moral system that all rational persons would, if they had the option, collectively agree in selecting as the moral system for the society in which they knew they and/or their children would spend their lives, iff y maximizes x's expectable utility)

We should notice that (5) – as well as (6) – is very similar to act-utilitarianism and, of course, so is (8) – if 'morally ought' is construed as I suggest. If we omit the 'x's' from the phrase 'maximize x's utility,' we have, in fact, a possible way of formulating act-utilitarianism. This fact reminds us that there might be some kind of rule-egoism, parallel to

---

6 See Kurt Baier, "Moral Obligation," *American Philosophical Quarterly, 3* 3 (July 1966): 210–26; John Rawls, *A Theory of Justice* (Cambridge, Mass.: Harvard, 1971); J. S. Mill, *Utilitarianism*, ch. 5. See also Russell Grice, *The Grounds of Moral Judgement* (Cambridge: University Press, 1967), and D. A. J. Richards, *A Theory of Reasons for Action* (New York: Oxford, 1971), chs. 6 and 7.

7 For our present purposes it would not make any real difference if we substituted a more Rawlsian proposal, say "which each and every rational (in his sense) person would rank as his first choice, if he were familiar with the laws of science but ignorant of facts that might enable him to advantage himself." (This is my terminology, not his.)

some kind of rule-utilitarianism, that is more plausible than either (6) or (5). For example, we might consider this:

(9) $(x)(y)$ (x morally ought to do y if and only if y would be called for by that set of resolutions, policies, or action-habits of x, the adoption of which by x would maximize x's utility)

I shall not pursue this possibility.

III THE DIFFICULTIES OF EGOISM

If the thesis of moral egoism is as I have stated it in (8), there is a definitive refutation of it – perhaps more than one.

The definitive refutation is this. It is that rational people would *not* agree to choose, as the moral system for a society in which they expected to live, one in which the dictates of conscience (motivation to avoid certain forms of behavior, to feel guilty for performing them, to disapprove of others for performing them) correspond to the principle of egoism. Why not? The answer is that they could do much better for themselves by some different system, say a form of rule-utilitarianism or a system including some of Rawls's rules of justice. Since the choosers are assumed to be rational, they will choose so as to maximize expectable utility for themselves (and this, of course, includes the welfare of others they care about, such as their children) in so far as this is compossible with the choice of others. (Remember, the decision is to be collective.) We need not speculate on what form of moral system they would choose; but it will not be egoism. For rational people will see that they will do better if the moral system prohibits assault (except in very special situations) and if it requires promise-keeping (again except for special situations). Egoism does not do this. An egoistic moral system would roughly put us, or leave us, in the "state of nature."

Some recent writers for various reasons have criticized egoism on the ground that there *could not be* any such thing as an egoist moral system in a society. (This is like Kant's proposal that some maxims *could not consistently* be universalized, whereas he claimed of others only that persons could not *choose* that they be universalized – the latter claim being like my argument above.)

For instance, it has been argued that the very conception of a system of rules of right rules out egoism. For the conception of rules of right implies that the rules *order* the competing claims of different people. Whereas, in the case of egoism, claims of different people are not ranked at all, and clashes of interest have to be resolved by force or cunning. Others have claimed that there could not be an egoist moral system for a different reason. It is said, for instance, that an egoist could not consistently teach others to be egoists, or proclaim and defend his views publicly, or show disapproval of altruistic behavior, or give sincere moral advice. But the absence of these activities makes an egoist society so different from our own, with its nonegoist moral code, that we can hardly say that the egoist society has a "moral system" at all.

I think the egoist can, however, with plausibility, refuse to be moved by such purely conceptual points. He may reply that the critic may use words as he likes, but that the substance of egoism is hardly refuted by such terminological decisions.

IV   SOME BASIC POINTS OF STRATEGY

I have just suggested that the egoist might turn aside certain attacks made on him, on the ground that they are really only terminological, not substantial. But, then, he could do the same thing against me. That is, he could say that the purported "definitive refutation" of egoism sketched above works only if one has adopted my proposed definition of 'morally ought' so that egoism gets formulated as in (8). He might agree that if 'morally ought' is defined as I suggest, his view is in difficulties; but why agree to my definition?

If he says this, however, we may very well ask him what he is after. Why does he want to make a point of claiming that people *"morally* ought" to do certain things, and what does he mean by 'morally ought'? Why does he not formulate his claim only in terms of 'prudentially ought'? If he did, then, I have argued, his thesis would have the virtue of being true. Further, I have agreed that there is a wider sense of 'morally ought' such that the egoist could both claim that one prudentially ought to maximize one's own utility and also claim that, in saying this, he is in effect saying that one morally ought in one possible sense of that phrase. So, why should he object to anything I say? In particular, why should he object to admitting that there is a possible sense of 'morally ought,' a narrower sense, such that egoism as a thesis stated in terms of that sense (8) is false, for the reason I gave? So where is the debate?

The egoist might well reply, however, by turning the tables. He might say that I have myself held that egoism in one sense is true – that a rational person would seek to maximize his own utility. So in a sense I have been recommending to people that they maximize their own utility, be egoists. On the other hand, I have proposed a definition of 'morally ought' in terms of what would be required by the moral system that rational persons would collectively choose, and have said that it is false that a person morally ought, in that sense, always so act as to maximize his own utility, or expectable utility. The egoist then may properly ask whether I am not embracing an incoherent position. Am I recommending that people maximize their expectable utility, or not?

This question that the egoist poses is a difficult one. I shall conclude by making some remarks that I hope will make clear there is no inconsistency in the view I take, and at the same time make clear why the egoist needs to come much closer to my view – the affirmation of (1) and (1′), but the rejection of (8).

In the first place, no rational person will want to live in a state of nature. Not only will he wish to live in a society governed by law; he will also want to live in a society with an internal system of control of behavior – a moral system, and indeed a nonegoist moral system. One important condition of the egoist's living well is that there be a nonegoist moral system in society. What kind of moral system will a rational person want for society? He will, of course, want a moral system that will maximize his expectable utility (including in this the utility to him of the welfare of his children and others he cares about). For this reason he will not want to continue the present system of morality, in so far as it involves restrictions to no purpose and omits restrictions with a purpose. Ideally, he would like a moral system that would especially favor him; but realistically the most he can hope to get, through discussion with others (since in so far as they are rational they will be equally concerned with their interests), is a moral system that protects and promotes the interests of everyone equally. Now, if he really wants this, as the best realistic possibility, he will be ready to participate and urge his friends to participate, in straightening out (to conform better with the ideal) and clarifying the actual moral system. For this purpose I suggest he must refer to the ideal of a moral system that rational people would want adopted for their society (or one that would serve well the interest of all). And he must refer to the requirements of that moral system for the behavior of individuals in particular situations. It seems, then, that, though he may dislike the term 'morally obligatory' in my sense, he must use substantially the concept I have explained; he will not want to restrict his discourse to the use of 'morally ought' in the purely prudential sense, in the "wider" sense of 'morally ought.' So, in consistency, he must allow *my* concept of 'morally ought' and even the importance of it. He may, then, in pursuance of his own utility, engage in giving *moral* advice (about what is a person's *moral* obligation in my sense); and he may reproach people for their conduct where it fails to meet this demand, and so on.

I say he will do these things. What I mean is that he will do these things, if he is rational, unless he is in a special position such that he can command action for his benefit without appeal to a moral code, or unless he sees these things are already being adequately done by others (in which case he can relax and enjoy the benefits). Others not so fortunately situated, however – and this means almost everybody – will, if they are rational, bestir themselves to support a system of morality along the lines suggested.

There is doubtless a good deal more to be said in development of essentially this point. The main idea is, schizophrenic as it may sound, that a person who believes that a rational person will aim to maximize his own utility will also believe that a rational person will support, preach, and teach a rational moral system, and make use of the concept of moral obligation in my sense.

Let me now pass to some further points.

(1) For reasons which there is no space to develop, I think a *rational* person will almost certainly have some degree of sympathy for other persons, some degree of concern for their welfare. (An egoist need not deny this.) Therefore, when a rational person sees that an action y would be required by the moral system on which fully informed rational persons would agree, presumably because the requiring rule is important for the benefit of the group (conduct would not be required if it were not important that it take place, from the point of view of the group), he will find himself somewhat motivated by his sympathy to perform that act. In fact, he will be increasing his own utility (given his interest in others) by so doing. Of course, some actual persons may be without interest in others, and this point does not hold for them.

(2) A person will want a moral system for his society, not merely because it provides some protection against violence and some assurance of fidelity (etc.), but because of other features of life in a "kingdom of ends," where each regulates his conduct by reference to a system of rules he knows is the system on which all rational persons would agree. Why? Because a person must see that there would be, in such a self-regulating group, a quality of life – of autonomous self-restraint and mutual respect – which is appealing, one in which there is relaxed mutual trust, openness, absence of need for being on one's guard, and friendly warmth among persons. So, again, on prudential grounds a person will want to support a nonegoist moral system in his society. He will be somewhat motivated to do his moral duty in my sense, because so doing helps usher in, or secure, such a state of affairs; whereas failing to do so helps destroy such a world – and indeed effectively does destroy it as far as his small world is concerned, including those persons whom he assaults, slanders, cheats, or takes advantage of.

(3) Let us now add to our considerations the fact that in our actual society people do have a concept of moral obligation somewhat like the

one stated, and that for the most part the actions that they think are morally obligatory are those which rational persons would agree to require by the moral system of a society in which they were to live. Moreover, people do not merely have these thoughts; despite all the rationalized wrong-doing or conscious flouting of such moral standards, by and large people do behave in a way that shows there is an effective moral code in force in our society. In this situation, the thoughtful person must see that there is a kind of system, approximating somewhere near the ideal system, which works reasonably well, and from which he has benefited or stands to benefit. Now I suggest there is a "natural" motivation to respond in kind to the self-restraint of others on one's own behalf, by a reciprocal self-restraint on their behalf. One wants not to be a "free-rider" on this system; one naturally feels shame if one has to admit to being one. Moreover, it is not comfortable to think that others know that one has offended against the rules most persons are willing to obey – or to feel that one must practice deception or secrecy in order to avoid the contempt of others. The exact psychology of all this may be complex, but I suggest the motivation is a fact.

What does all this prove? (1) A rational person will want a moral system in his society that will maximize his own expectable utility; and as a consequence he will, especially if he is sympathetic (as a rational person will be), in rationality preach and support a system that rational persons can collectively agree upon, and will make use of the concept of "moral obligation" in my sense and give his support to people doing what they morally ought in this sense. (2) There are various sources of motivation to conform to the requirements of this system, even when so doing conflicts with other interests. (3) A person is acting so as to maximize his expectable utility when he gives support to the moral system on which rational persons can collectively agree, and usually when he conforms his behavior to this system despite conflict with other interests.

It is not denied that there are occasions on which it is rational for a person not to conform with the requirements of the moral system, although in these cases it will be rational for other persons to criticize or even punish him, and in general to support the system.

Having said these things, some might say I am essentially an egoist. There is no point, however, in disputing about the labels.

At any rate, my answer to the puzzle that I suggested the egoist might pose for me is that I have now made clear that it is consistent to think both that a rational person would aim to maximize his own utility and that a rational person will advocate a moral system that is nonegoistic, and in almost all cases have very good reason to conform his behavior to it. I am saying that what the egoist ought to do is to claim only that a person prudentially ought to (that a rational person would) aim to maximize his own utility, but that it is a mistake for him not to recognize that a rational person will want, and advocate, a moral system for his society the requirement of which will be very different from simply that of maximizing one's own utility.

B

Normative ethics: Utilitarianism

7

Some merits of one form of rule – utilitarianism

1. Utilitarianism is the thesis that the moral predicates of an act – at least its objective rightness or wrongness, and sometimes also its moral praiseworthiness or blameworthiness – are functions in some way, direct or indirect, of consequences for the welfare of sentient creatures, and of nothing else. Utilitarians differ about what precise function they are; and they differ about what constitutes welfare and how it is to be measured. But they agree that all one needs to know, in order to make moral appraisals correctly, is the consequences of certain things for welfare.

Utilitarianism is thus a normative ethical thesis and not, at least not necessarily, a metaethical position – that is, a position about the meaning and justification of ethical statements. It is true that some utilitarians have declared that the truth of the normative thesis follows, given the ordinary, or proper, meaning of moral terms such as "right." I shall ignore this further, metaethical claim. More recently some writers have suggested something very similar, to the effect that our concept of "morality" is such that we could not call a system of rules a "moral system" unless it were utilitarian in some sense.

This latter suggestion is of special interest to us, since the general topic of the present conference is "the concept of morality," and I wish to comment on it very briefly. It is true that there is a connection between utilitarianism and the concept of morality; at least I believe – and shall spell out the contention later – that utilitarianism cannot be explained, at least in its most plausible form, without making use of the concept of "morality" and, furthermore, without making use of an analysis of this concept. But the reverse relationship does not hold: It is not true that the concept "morality" is such that we cannot properly call a system of rules a morality unless it is a thoroughly utilitarian system, although possibly we would not call a system of rules a "morality" if it did not regulate at all the forms of conduct that may be expected to do good or harm to sentient persons. One reason why it is implausible to hold that any morality is necessarily utilitarian is that any plausible form of utili-

A revised version of a paper presented to a conference on moral philosophy held at the University of Colorado in October, 1965.

tarianism will be a rather complex thesis, and it seems that the concept of morality is hardly subtle enough to entail anything so complex – although, of course, such reasoning does not exclude the possibility of the concept of morality entailing some simple and unconvincing form of utilitarianism. A more decisive reason, however, is that we so use the term "morality" that we can say consistently that the morality of a society contains some prohibitions which considerations of utility do not support, or are not even thought to support, for example, some restrictions on sexual behavior. (Other examples are mentioned later.) Thus there is no reason to think that only a utilitarian code could properly be called a "moral code" or a "morality," as these terms are ordinarily used.

In any case, even if "nonutilitarian morality" (or "right, but harmful") were a contradiction in terms, utilitarianism as a normative thesis would not yet be established, for it would be open to a nonutilitarian to advocate changing the meaning of "morality" (or "right") in order to allow for his normative views. There is, of course, the other face of the coin: Even if, as we actually use the term "morality" (or "right"), the above expressions are not contradictions in terms, it might be a good and justifiable thing for people to be taught to use words so that these expressions would become self-contradictory. But if there are good reasons for doing the last, presumably there are good and convincing reasons for adopting utilitarianism as a normative thesis, without undertaking such a roundabout route to the goal. I shall, therefore, discuss utilitarianism as a normative thesis, without supposing that it can be supported by arguing that a nonutilitarian morality is a contradiction in terms.

2. If an analysis of concepts like "morally wrong" and "morality" and "moral code" does not enable us to establish the truth of the utilitarian thesis, the question arises what standard a normative theory like utilitarianism has to meet in order for a reasonable presumption to be established in its favor. It is well known that the identity and justification of any such standard can be debated at length. In order to set bounds to the present discussion, I shall state briefly the standard I shall take for granted for purposes of the present discussion. Approximately this standard would be acceptable to a good many writers on normative ethics. However this may be, it would be agreed that it is worth knowing whether some form of utilitarianism meets this standard better than any other form of utilitarian theory, and it is this question which I shall discuss.

The standard that I suggest an acceptable normative moral theory has to meet is this: The theory must contain no unintelligible concepts or internal inconsistencies; it must not be inconsistent with known facts; it must be capable of precise formulation so that its implications for action can be determined; and – most important – its implications must be acceptable to thoughtful persons who have had reasonably wide experience, when taken in the light of supporting remarks that can be made, and when compared with the implications of other clearly statable normative theories. It is not required that the implications of a satisfactory theory be consonant with the uncriticized moral intuitions of intelligent and experienced people, but only with those intuitions which stand in the light of supporting remarks, etc. Furthermore, it is not required of an acceptable theory that the best consequences would be produced by people adopting that theory, in contrast to other theories by which they might be convinced. (The theory might be so complex that it would be a good thing if most people did not try their hand at applying it to concrete situations!) It may be a moving *ad hominem* argument, if one can persuade an act-utilitarian that it would have bad consequences for people to try to determine the right act according to that theory, and to live by their conclusions, but such a showing would not be a reasonable ground for rejecting that normative theory.

3. Before turning to the details of various types of utilitarian theory, it may be helpful to offer some supporting remarks that will explain some reasons why some philosophers are favorably disposed toward a utilitarian type of normative theory.

(a) The utilitarian principle provides a clear and definite procedure for determining which acts are right or wrong (praiseworthy or blameworthy), by observation and the methods of science alone and without the use of any supplementary intuitions (assuming that empirical procedures can determine when something maximizes utility), for all cases, including the complex ones about which intuitions are apt to be mute, such as whether kleptomanic behavior is blameworthy or whether it is right to break a confidence in certain circumstances. The utilitarian presumably frames his thesis so as to conform with enlightened intuitions which are clear, but his thesis, being general, has implications for all cases, including those about which his intuitions are not clear. The utilitarian principle is like a general scientific theory, which checks with observations at many points, but can also be used as a guide to beliefs on matters inaccessible to observation (like the behavior of matter at absolute zero temperature).

Utilitarianism is not the only normative theory with this desirable property; egoism is another, and, with some qualifications, so is Kant's theory.

(b) Any reasonably plausible normative theory will give a large place to consequences for welfare in the moral assessment of actions, for this consideration enters continuously and substantially into ordinary moral thinking. Theories which ostensibly make no appeal of this sort either admit utilitarian considerations by the back door, or have counterintuitive consequences. Therefore the ideal of simplicity leads us to hope for the possibility of a pure utilitarian theory. Moreover, utilitarianism avoids the necessity of weighing disparate things such as justice and utility.

(c) If a proposed course of action does not raise moral questions, it is generally regarded as rational, and its agent well advised to perform it, if and only if it will maximize expectable utility for the agent. In a similar vein, it can be argued that society's "choice" of an institution of morality is rational and well advised, if and only if having it will maximize expectable social utility – raise the expectable level of the average "utility curve" of the population. If morality is a system of traditional and arbitrary constraints on behavior, it cannot be viewed as a rational institution. But it can be, if the system of morality is utilitarian. In that case the institution of morality can be recommended to a person of broad human sympathies, as an institution that maximizes the expectation of general welfare; and to a selfish person, as an institution that, in the absence of particular evidence about his own case, may be expected to maximize his own expectation of welfare (his own welfare being viewed as a random sample from the population). To put it in other words, a utilitarian morality can be "vindicated" by appeal either to the humanity or to the selfishness of human beings.

To say this is not to deny that nonutilitarian moral principles may be capable of vindication in a rather similar way. For instance, to depict morality as an institution that fosters human equality is to recommend it by appeal to something perhaps as deep in man as his sympathy or humanity.[1]

4. The type of utilitarianism on which I wish to focus is a form of rule-utilitarianism, as contrasted with act-utilitarianism. According to the latter type of theory (espoused by Sidgwick and Moore), an act is objectively right if no other act the agent could perform would produce better consequences. (On this view, an act is blameworthy if and only if it is right to perform the act of blaming or condemning it; the principles of blameworthiness are a special case of the principle of objectively right actions.) Act-utilitarianism is hence a rather atomistic theory: The rightness of a single act is fixed by its effects on the world. Rule-utilitarianism, in contrast, is the view that the rightness of an act is fixed, not by its relative utility, but by the utility of having a relevant moral rule, or of most or all members of a certain class of acts being performed.

The implications of act-utilitarianism are seriously counterintuitive, and

1 It would not be impossible to combine a restricted principle of utility with a morality of justice or equality. For instance, it might be said that an act is right only if it meets a certain condition of justice, and also if it is one which, among all the just actions open to the agent, meets a requirement of utility as well as any other.

114

I shall ignore it except to consider whether some ostensibly different theories really are different.

5. Rule-utilitarianisms may be divided into two main groups, according as the rightness of a particular act is made a function of ideal rules in some sense, or of the actual and recognized rules of a society. The variety of theory I shall explain more fully is of the former type.

According to the latter type of theory, a person's moral duties or obligations in a particular situation are determined, with some exceptions, solely by the moral rules, or institutions, or practices prevalent in the society, and not by what rules (etc.) it would ideally be best to have in the society. (It is sometimes held that actual moral rules, practices, etc., are only a necessary condition of an act's being morally obligatory or wrong.) Views roughly of this sort have been held in recent years by A. MacBeath, Stephen Toulmin, John Rawls, P. F. Strawson, J. O. Urmson, and B. J. Diggs. Indeed, Strawson says in effect that for there to be a moral obligation on one is just for there to be a socially sanctioned demand on him, in a situation where he has an interest in the system of demands his society is wont to impose on its members, and where such demands are generally acknowledged and respected by members of his society.[2] And Toulmin asserts that when a person asks, "Is this the right thing to do?" what he is normally asking is whether a proposed action "conforms to the moral code" of his group, "whether the action in question belongs to a class of actions generally approved of in the agent's community." In deliberating about the question what is right to do, he says, "there is no more general 'reason' to be given beyond one which related the action ... to an accepted social practice."[3]

So far the proposal does not appear to be a form of utilitarianism at all. The theory is utilitarian, however, in the following way: It is thought that what is relevant for a decision whether to try to change moral codes, institutions, etc., or for a justification of them, is the relative utility of the code, practice, etc. The recognized code or practice determines the individual's moral obligations in a particular case; utility of the code or practice determines whether it is justified or ought to be changed. Furthermore, it is sometimes held that utilitarian considerations have some relevance to the rightness of a particular action. For instance, Toulmin thinks that in case the requirements of the recognized code or practice conflict in a particular case, the individual ought (although strictly, he is not morally obligated) to do what will maximize utility in the situation,

2 P. F. Strawson, "Social Morality and Individual Ideal," *Philosophy* 36 (1961): 1–17.
3 Stephen Toulmin, *An Examination of the Place of Reason in Ethics*, Cambridge University Press, 1950, pp. 144–5. See various acute criticisms, with which I mostly agree, in Rawls's review, *Philos. Rev.* 60 (1951): 572–80.

and that in case an individual can relieve the distress of another, he ought (strictly, is not morally obligated) to do so, even if the recognized code does not require him to.[4]

This theory, at least in some of its forms or parts, has such conspicuously counterintuitive implications that it fails to meet the standard for a satisfactory normative theory. In general, we do not believe that an act's being prohibited by the moral code of one's society is sufficient to make it morally wrong. Moral codes have prohibited such things as work on the Sabbath, marriage to a divorced person, medically necessary abortion, and suicide; but we do not believe it was really wrong for persons living in a society with such prohibitions, to engage in these actions.[5]

Neither do we think it a necessary condition of an act's being wrong that it be prohibited by the code of the agent's society, or of it being obligatory that an act be required by the code of his society. A society may permit a man to have his wife put to death for infidelity, or to have a child put to death for almost any reason; but we still think such actions wrong. Moreover, a society may permit a man absolute freedom in divorcing his wife, and recognize no obligations on his part toward her; but we think, I believe, that a man has some obligations for the welfare of a wife of thirty years' standing (with some qualifications), whatever his society may think.[6]

Some parts of the theory in some of its forms, however, appear to be correct. In particular, the theory in some forms implies that, if a person has a certain recognized obligation in an institution or practice (for example, a child to support his aged parent, a citizen to pay his taxes), then he morally does have this obligation, with some exceptions, irrespective

4 Toulmin and Rawls sometimes go further, and suggest that a person is morally free to do something the actual code or practice of his society prohibits, if he is convinced that the society would be better off if the code or practice were rewritten so as to permit that sort of thing, and he is prepared to live according to the ideally revised code. If their theory were developed in this direction, it need not be different from some "ideal" forms of rule-utilitarianism, although, as stated, the theory makes the recognized code the standard for moral obligations, with exceptions granted to individuals who hold certain moral opinions. See Toulmin, op. cit., pp. 151–2, and Rawls, "Two Concepts of Rules," *Philos. Rev.* 64 (1955), pp. 28–9, especially 25. It should be noticed that Rawls's proposal is different from Toulmin's in an important way. He is concerned with only a segment of the moral code, the part that can be viewed as the rules of practices. As he observes, this may be only a small part of the moral code.

5 Does a stranger living in a society have a moral obligation to conform to its moral code? I suggest we think that he does not, unless it is the right moral code or perhaps at least he thinks it is, although we think that offense he might give to the feelings of others should be taken into account, as well as the result his nonconformity might have in weakening regard for moral rules in general.

6 It is a different question whether we should hold offenders in such societies seriously morally blameworthy. People cannot be expected to rise much above the level of recognized morality, and we condemn them little when they do not.

of whether in an ideal institution he would or would not have. This we do roughly believe, although we need not at the same time accept the reasoning that has been offered to explain how the fact of a practice or institution leads to the moral obligation. The fact that the theory seems right in this would be a strong point in its favor if charges were correct that "ideal" forms of rule-utilitarianism necessarily differ at this point. B. J. Diggs, for instance, has charged that the "ideal" theories imply that:

one may freely disregard a rule if ever he discovers that action on the rule is not maximally felicific, and in this respect makes moral rules like "practical maxims" ... It deprives social and moral rules of their authority and naturally is in sharp conflict with practice. On this alternative rule utilitarianism collapses into act utilitarianism. Surely it is a mistake to maintain that a set of rules, thought to be ideally utilitarian or felicific, is the criterion of right action. ... If we are presented with a list [of rules], but these are not rules in practice, the most one could reasonably do is to try to get them adopted.[7]

I believe, however, and shall explain in detail later that this charge is without foundation.

6. Let us turn now to "ideal" forms of rule-utilitarianism, which affirm that whether it is morally obligatory or morally right to do a certain thing in a particular situation is fixed, not by the actual code or practice of the society (these may be indirectly relevant, as forming part of the situation), but by some "ideal" rule – that is, by the utility of having a certain general moral rule, or by the utility of all or most actions being performed which are members of a relevant class of actions.

If the rightness of an act is fixed by the utility of a relevant rule (class), are we to say that the rule (class) that qualifies must be the optimific rule (class), the one which maximizes utility, or must the rule (class) meet only some less stringent requirement (for example, be better than the absence of any rule regulating the type of conduct in question)? And, if it is to be of the optimific type, are all utilities to be counted, or perhaps only "negative" utilities, as is done when it is suggested that the rule (class) must be the one which minimizes suffering?[8]

The simplest proposal – that the rule (class) which qualifies is the one that maximizes utility, with all utilities, whether "positive" or "negative,"

---

7 "Rules and Utilitarianism," *Amer. Philos. Quarterly*, I (1964), 32–44.
8 In a footnote to chapter 9 of *The Open Society*, Professor Popper suggested that utilitarianism would be more acceptable if its test were minimizing suffering rather than maximizing welfare, to which J. J. C. Smart replied (*Mind*, 1958, pp. 542–3) that the proposal implies that we ought to destroy all living beings, as the surest way to eliminate suffering. It appears, however, that Professor Popper does not seriously advocate what seemed to be the position of the earlier footnote (addendum to fourth edition, p. 386).

being counted – also seems to me to be the best, and it is the one I shall shortly explain more fully. Among the several possible theories different from this one I shall discuss briefly only one, which seems the most plausible of its kind, and is at least closely similar to the view defended by Professor Marcus Singer.

According to this theory, an action (or inaction) at time t in circumstances C is wrong if and only if, were everyone in circumstances C to perform a relevantly similar action, harm would be done – meaning by "doing harm" that affected persons would be made worse off by the action (or inaction) than they already were at time t. (I think it is not meant that the persons must be put in a state of "negative welfare" in some sense, but simply made worse off than they otherwise would have been.) Let us suppose a person is deciding whether to do A in circumstances C at t. The theory, then, implies the following: (1) If everyone doing A in circumstances C would make people worse off than they already were at t (A can be inaction, such as failing to pull a drowning man from the water) whereas some other act would not make them so, then it is wrong for anyone to do A. (2) If everyone doing A would not make people worse off, then even if everyone doing something else would make them better off, it is not wrong to do A. (3) If everyone doing A would make people worse off, but if there is no alternative act, the performance of which by everyone would avoid making people worse off, then it is right to do A, even though doing A would make people relatively much worse off than they would have been made by the performance of some other action instead. The "optimific rule" theory, roughly, would accept (1), but reject (2) and (3).

Implication (3) of the theory strikes me as clearly objectionable; I am unable to imagine circumstances in which we should think it not morally incumbent on one to avoid very bad avoidable consequences for others, even though a situation somewhat worse than the status quo could not be avoided. Implication (2) is less obviously dubious. But I should think we do have obligations to do things for others, when we are not merely avoiding being in the position of making them worse off. For instance, if one sees another person at a cocktail party, standing by himself and looking unhappy, I should suppose one has some obligation to make an effort to put him at his ease, even though doing nothing would hardly make him worse off than he already is.

Why do proponents of this view, like Professor Singer, prefer his view to the simpler, "maximize utility" form of rule-utilitarianism? This is not clear. One objection sometimes raised is that an optimific theory implies that every act is morally weighty and none morally indifferent. And one may concede that this is a consequence of some forms of utilitarianism,

118

even rule-utilitarianism of the optimific variety; but we shall see that it is by no means a consequence of the type of proposal described below. For the theory below will urge that an action is not morally indifferent only if it falls under some prescription of an optimific moral code, and, since there are disadvantages in a moral code regulating actions, optimific moral codes will prohibit or require actions of a certain type only when there are significant utilitarian reasons for it. As a consequence, a great many types of actions are morally indifferent, according to the theory. Professor Singer also suggests that optimific theories have objectionable consequences for state-of-nature situations;[9] we may postpone judgment on this until we have examined these consequences of the theory here proposed, at a later stage. Other objections to the optimizing type of rule-utilitarianism with which I am familiar either confuse rule-utilitarianism with act-utilitarianism, or do not distinguish among the several possible forms of optimizing rule-utilitarianisms.

7. I propose, then, that we tentatively opt for an "ideal" rule-utilitarianism, of the "maximizing utility" variety. This decision, however, leaves various choices still to be made, between theories better or worse fitted to meet various problems. Rather than attempt to list alternatives, and explain why one choice rather than another between them would work out better, I propose to describe in some detail the type of theory that seems most plausible. I shall later show how this theory meets the one problem to which the "actual rule" theories seemed to have a nice solution; and I shall discuss its merits, as compared with another quite similar type of theory suggested by Jonathan Harrison and others.

The theory I wish to describe is rather similar to one proposed by J. D. Mabbott in his 1953 British Academy lecture, "Moral Rules." It is also very similar to the view defended by J. S. Mill in *Utilitarianism*, although Mill's formulation is ambiguous at some points, and he apparently did not draw some distinctions he should have drawn (I shall revert to this historical point).

For convenience I shall refer to the theory as the "ideal moral code" theory. The essence of it is as follows. Let us first say that a moral code is "ideal" if its currency in a particular society would produce at least as much good per person (the total divided by the number of persons) as the currency of any other moral code. (Two different codes might meet this condition, but, in order to avoid complicated formulations, the following discussion will ignore this possibility.) Given this stipulation for the meaning of "ideal," the Ideal Moral Code theory consists in the assertion of the following thesis: *An act is right if and only if it would*

9 M. G. Singer, *Generalization in Ethics* (New York, A. A. Knopf, Inc., 1961), p. 192.

not be prohibited by the moral code ideal for the society; and an agent is morally blameworthy (praiseworthy) for an act if, and to the degree that, the moral code ideal in that society would condemn (praise) him for it. It is a virtue of this theory that it is a theory both about objective rightness and about moral blameworthiness (praiseworthiness) of actions, but the assertion about blameworthiness will be virtually ignored in what follows.

8. In order to have a clear proposal before us, however, the foregoing summary statement must be filled out in three ways: (1) by explaining what it is for a moral code to have currency; (2) by making clear what is the difference between the rules of a society's moral code and the rules of its institutions; and (3) by describing how the relative utility of a moral code is to be estimated.

First, then, the notion of a moral code having currency in a society.

For a moral code to have currency in a society, two things must be true. First, a high proportion of the adults in the society must subscribe to the moral principles, or have the moral opinions, constitutive of the code. Exactly how high the proportion should be, we can hardly decide on the basis of the ordinary meaning of "the moral code"; but probably it would not be wrong to require at least 90 percent agreement. Thus, if at least 90 percent of the adults subscribe to principle A, and 90 percent to principle B, etc., we may say that a code consisting of A and B (etc.) has currency in the society, provided the second condition is met. Second, we want to say that certain principles A, B, etc. belong to the moral code of a society only if they are recognized as such. That is, it must be that a large proportion of the adults of the society would respond correctly if asked, with respect to A and B, whether most members of the society subscribed to them. (It need not be required that adults base their judgments on such good evidence as recollection of moral discussions; it is enough if for some reason the correct opinion about what is accepted is widespread.) It is of course possible for certain principles to constitute a moral code with currency in a society even if some persons in the society have no moral opinions at all, or if there is disagreement, for example, if everyone in the society disagrees with every other person with respect to at least one principle.

The more difficult question is what it is for an individual to subscribe to a moral principle or to have a moral opinion. What is it, then, for someone to think sincerely that any action of the kind F is wrong? (1) He is to some extent motivated to avoid actions he thinks are F, and often, if asked why he does not perform such an action when it appears to be to his advantage, offers, as one of his reasons, that it is F. In addition, the person's motivation to avoid F-actions does not derive entirely from his belief that F-actions on his part are likely to be harmful to him or to persons to whom he is somehow attached. (2) If he thinks he has just performed an F-action, he feels guilty or remorseful or uncomfortable about it, unless he thinks he has some excuse – unless, for instance, he knows that at the time of action he did not think his action would be an F-action. "Guilt" (etc.) is not to be understood as implying some special origin such as interiorization of parental prohibitions, or as being a vestige of anxiety about punishment. It is left open that it might be an unlearned emotional response to the thought of being the cause of the suffering of another person. Any feeling that must be viewed simply as anxiety about anticipated consequences, for one's self or a person to whom one is attached, is not, however, to count as a "guilt" feeling. (3) If he believes that someone has performed an F-action, he will tend to admire him less as a person, unless he thinks that the individual has a good excuse. He thinks that action of this sort, without excuse, reflects on character – this being spelled out, in part, by reference to traits like honesty, respect for the rights of others, and so on. (4) He thinks that these attitudes of his are correct or well justified, in some sense, but with one restriction: it is not enough if he thinks that what justifies them is simply the fact that they are shared by all or most members of his society. This restriction corresponds with our distinction between a moral conviction and something else. For instance, we are inclined to think no moral attitude is involved if an Englishman disapproves of something but says that his disapproval is justified by the fact that it is shared by "well-bred Englishmen." In such cases we are inclined to say that the individual subscribes only to a custom, or to a rule of etiquette or manners. On the other hand, if the individual thinks that what justifies his attitude unfavorable to F-actions is that F-actions are contrary to the will of God (and the individual's attitude is not merely a prudential one), or inconsistent with the welfare of mankind, or contrary to human nature, we are disposed to say the attitude is a moral attitude and the opinions expressed are moral ones. And the same if he thinks his attitude justified, but can give no reason. There are perhaps other restrictions we should make on acceptable justifications (perhaps to distinguish a moral code from a code of honor), and other types of justifications we should wish to list as clearly acceptable (perhaps an appeal to human equality).

9. It is important to distinguish between the moral code of a society and its institutions, or the rules of its institutions. It is especially important for the Ideal Moral Code theory, for this theory involves the conception of a moral code ideal for a society in the context of its institutions, so that it is necessary to distinguish the moral code a society does or might have from its institutions and their rules. The distinction is also one we actually do make in our thinking, although it is blurred in some cases.

(For instance, is "Honor thy father and thy mother" a moral rule, or a rule of the family institution, in our society?)[10]

An institution is a set of positions or statuses, with which certain privileges and jobs are associated. (We can speak of these as "rights" and "duties" if we are careful to explain that we do not mean moral rights and duties.) That is, there are certain, usually nameable, positions that consist in the fact that anyone who is assigned to the position is expected to do certain things, and at the same time is expected to have certain things done for him. The individuals occupying these positions are a group of cooperating agents in a system that as a whole is thought to have the aim of serving certain ends. (For example, a university is thought to serve the ends of education, research, etc.) The rules of the system concern jobs that must be done in order that the goals of the institution be achieved; they allocate the necessary jobs to different positions. Take, for instance, a university. There are various positions in it: the presidency, the professorial ranks, the registrars, librarians, etc. It is understood that one who occupies a certain post has certain duties, say teaching a specified number of classes or spending time working on research in the case of the instructing staff. Obviously the university cannot achieve its ends unless certain persons do the teaching, some tend to the administration, some do certain jobs in the library, and so on. Another such system is the family. We need not speculate on the "purpose" of the family, whether it is primarily a device for producing a new generation, etc. But it is clear that when a man enters marriage, he takes a position to which certain jobs are attached, such as providing support for the family to the best of his ability, and to which also certain rights are attached, such as exclusive sexual rights with his wife, and the right to be cared for should he become incapacitated.

If an "institution" is defined in this way, it is clear that the moral code of a society cannot itself be construed as an institution, nor its rules as rules of an institution. The moral code is society-wide, so if we were to identify its rules as institutional rules, we should presumably have to say that everyone belongs to this institution. But what is the "purpose" of society as a whole? Are there any distinctions of status, with rights and duties attached, that we could identify as the "positions" in the moral

---

10 The confusion is compounded by the fact that terms like "obligation" and "duty" are used sometimes to speak about moral obligations and duties, and sometimes not. The fact that persons have a certain legal duty in certain situations is a rule of the legal institutions of the society; a person may not have a moral duty to do what is his legal duty. The fact that a person has an obligation to invite a certain individual to dinner is a matter of manners or etiquette, and at least may not be a matter of moral obligation. See R. B. Brandt, "The Concepts of Duty and Obligation," *Mind* 73 (1964), especially pp. 380–4.

system? Can we say that moral rules consist in the assignment of jobs in such a way that the aims of the institution may be achieved? It is true that there is a certain analogy: society as a whole might be said to be aiming at the good life for all, and the moral rules of the society might be viewed as the rules with which all must conform in order to achieve this end. But the analogy is feeble. Society as a whole is obviously not an organization like a university, an educational system, the church, General Motors, etc.; there is no specific goal in the achievement of which each position has a designated role to play. Our answer to the above questions must be in the negative: Morality is not an institution in the explained sense, nor are moral rules institutional expectations or rules.

The moral code of a society may, of course, have implications that bear on institutional rules. For one thing, the moral code may imply that an institutional system is morally wrong and ought to be changed. Moreover, the moral code may imply that a person has also a moral duty to do something that is his institutional job. For instance, it may be a moral rule that a person ought to do whatever he has undertaken to do, or that he ought not to accept the benefits of a position without performing its duties. Take for instance the rules, "A professor should meet his classes" or "Wives ought to make the beds." Since the professor has undertaken to do what pertains to his office, and the same for a wife, and since these tasks are known to pertain to the respective offices, the moral rule that a person is morally bound (with certain qualifications) to do what he has undertaken to do implies, in context, that the professor is morally bound to meet his classes and the wife to make the beds, other things being equal (that is, there being no contrary moral obligations in the situation). But these implications are not themselves part of the moral code. No one would say that a parent had neglected to teach his child the moral code of the society if he had neglected to teach him that professors must meet classes, and that wives must make the beds. A person becomes obligated to do these things only by participating in an institution, by taking on the status of professor or wife. Parents do not teach children to have guilt feelings about missing classes, or making beds. The moral code consists only of more general rules, defining what is to be done in certain types of situations in which practically everyone will find himself. ("Do what you have promised!")

Admittedly some rules can be both moral and institutional: "Take care of your father in his old age" might be both an institutional rule of the family organization and also a part of the moral code of a society. (In this situation, one can still raise the question whether this moral rule is optimific in a society with that institutional rule; the answer could be negative.)

123

It is an interesting question whether "Keep your promises" is a moral rule, an institutional rule (a rule of an "institution" of promises), or both. Obviously it is a part of the moral code of western societies. But is it also a rule of an institution? There are difficulties in the way of affirming that it is. There is no structure of cooperating individuals with special functions, serving to promote certain aims. Nor, when one steps into the "role" of a promiser, does one commit one's self to any specific duties; one fixes one's own duties by what one promises. Nor, in order to understand what one is committing one's self to by promising, need one have any knowledge of any system of expectations prevalent in the society. A three-year-old, who has never heard of any duties incumbent on promisers, can tell her friends, who wish to play baseball that afternoon, that she will bring the ball and bat, and that they need give no thought to the availability of these items. Her invitation to rely on her for something needed for their common enjoyment, and her assurance that she will do something and encouraging them thereby to set their minds at rest, is to make a promise. No one need suppose that the promiser is stepping into a socially recognized position, with all the rights and duties attendant on the same, although it is true she has placed herself in a position where she will properly be held responsible for the disappointment if she fails, and where inferences about her reliability as a person will properly be drawn if she forgets, or worse, if it turns out she was never in a position to perform. The bindingness of a promise is no more dependent on a set of expectations connected with an institution than is the wrongness of striking another person without justifying reason.

Nevertheless, if one thinks it helpful to speak of a promise as an institution or a practice, in view of certain analogies (promiser and promisee may be said to have rights and duties like the occupants of roles in an institution, and there is the ritual word "promise" the utterance of which commits the speaker to certain performances), there is no harm in this. The similarities and dissimilarities are what they are, and as long as these are understood it seems to make little difference what we say. Nevertheless, even if making a promise is participating in a practice or institution, there is still the *moral* question whether one is morally bound to perform, and in what conditions, and for what reasons. This question is left open, given the institution is whatever it is – as is the case with all rules of institutions.

10. It has been proposed above that an action is right if and only if it would not be prohibited by the moral code ideal for the society in which it occurs, where a moral code is taken to be "ideal" if and only if its currency would produce at least as much good per person as the currency

of any other moral code.[11] We must now give more attention to the conception of an ideal moral code, and how it may be decided when a given moral code will produce as much good per person as any other. We may, however, reasonably bypass the familiar problems of judgments of comparative utilities, especially when different persons are involved, since these problems are faced by all moral theories that have any plausibility. We shall simply assume that rough judgments of this sort are made and can be justified.

(a) We should first notice that, as "currency" has been explained above, a moral code could not be current in a society if it were too complex to be learned or applied. We may therefore confine our consideration to codes simple enough to be absorbed by human beings, roughly in the way in which people learn actual moral codes.

(b) We have already distinguished the concept of an institution and its rules from the concept of a moral rule, or a rule of the moral code. (We have, however, pointed out that in some cases a moral rule may prescribe the same thing that is also an institutional expectation. But this is not a necessary situation, and a moral code could condemn an institutional expectation.) Therefore, in deciding how much good the currency of a specific moral system would do, we consider the institutional setting as it is, as part of the situation. We are asking which moral code would produce the most good in the long run in this setting. One good to be reckoned, of course, might be that the currency of a given moral code would tend to change the institutional system.

(c) In deciding which moral code will produce the most per person good, we must take into account the probability that certain types of situations will arise in the society. For instance, we must take for granted that people will make promises and subsequently want to break them, that people will sometimes assault other persons in order to achieve their own ends, that people will be in distress and need the assistance of others, and so on. We may not suppose that, because an ideal moral code might have certain features, it need not have other features because they will not be required; for instance, we may not suppose, on the ground that an ideal moral system would forbid everyone to purchase a gun, that such a moral system needs no provisions about the possession and use of guns – just as our present moral and legal codes have provisions about self-defense, which would be unnecessary if everyone obeyed the provision never to assault anyone.

---

11 Some utilitarians have suggested that the right act is determined by the total net intrinsic good produced. This view can have embarrassing consequences for problems of population control. The view here advocated is that the right act is determined by the per person, average, net intrinsic good produced.

It is true that the currency of a moral code with certain provisions might bring about a reduction in certain types of situations, for example, the number of assaults or cases of dishonesty. And the reduction might be substantial, if the moral code were current which prohibited these offenses very strongly. (We must remember that an ideal moral code might differ from the actual one not only in what it prohibits or enjoins, but also in how strongly it prohibits or enjoins.) But it is consistent to suppose that a moral code prohibits a certain form of behavior very severely, and yet that the behavior will occur, since the "currency" of a moral code requires only 90 percent subscription to it, and a "strong" subscription, on the average, permits a great range from person to person. In any case there must be doubt whether the best moral code will prohibit many things very severely, since there are serious human costs in severe prohibitions: the burden of guilt feelings, the traumas caused by the severe criticism by others which is a part of having a strong injunction in a code, the risks of any training process that would succeed in interiorizing a severe prohibition, and so on.

(d) It would be a great oversimplification if, in assessing the comparative utility of various codes, we confined ourselves merely to counting the benefits of people doing (refraining from doing) certain things, as a result of subscribing to a certain code. To consider only this would be as absurd as estimating the utility of some feature of a legal system by attending only to the utility of people behaving in the way the law aims to make them behave – and overlooking the fact that the law only reduces and does not eliminate misbehavior, as well as the disutility of punishment to the convicted, and the cost of the administration of criminal law. In the case of morals, we must weigh the benefit of the improvement in behavior as a result of the restriction built into conscience, against the cost of the restriction – the burden of guilt feelings, the effects of the training process, etc. There is a further necessary refinement. In both law and morals we must adjust our estimates of utility by taking into account the envisaged system of excuses. That *mens rea* is required as a condition of guilt in the case of most legal offenses is most important; and it is highly important for the utility of a moral system whether accident, intent, and motives are taken into account in deciding a person's liability to moral criticism. A description of a moral code is incomplete until we have specified the severity of condemnation (by conscience or the criticism of others) to be attached to various actions, along with the excuses to be allowed as exculpating or mitigating.

11. Philosophers have taken considerable interest in the question what implications forms of rule-utilitarianism have for the moral relevance of

the behavior of persons other than the agent. Such implications, it is thought, bring into focus the effective difference between any form of rule-utilitarianism, and act-utilitarianism. In particular, it has been thought that the implications of rule-utilitarianisms for two types of situation are especially significant: (a) for situations in which persons are generally violating the recognized moral code, or some feature of it; and (b) for situations in which, because the moral code is generally respected, maximum utility would be produced by violation of the code by the agent. An example of the former situation (sometimes called a "state of nature" situation) would be widespread perjury in making out income-tax declarations. An example of the latter situation would be widespread conformity to the rule forbidding walking on the grass in a park.

What are the implications of the suggested form of rule-utilitarianism for these types of situations? Will it prescribe conduct which is not utility-maximizing in these situations? If it does, it will clearly have implications discrepant with those of act-utilitarianism – but perhaps unpalatable to some people.

It is easy to see how to go about determining what is right or wrong in such situations, on the above-described form of rule-utilitarianism – it is a question of what an "ideal" moral code would prescribe. But it is by no means easy to see where a reasonable person would come out, after going through such an investigation. Our form of rule-utilitarianism does not rule out, as morally irrelevant, reference to the behavior of other persons; it implies that the behavior of others is morally relevant precisely to the extent to which an optimific moral code (the one the currency of which is optimific) would take it into account. How far, then, we might ask, would an optimific moral code take into account the behavior of other persons, and what would its specific prescriptions be for the two types of situations outlined?

It might be thought, and it has been suggested, that an ideal moral code could take no cognizance of the behavior of other persons, and in particular of the possibility that many persons are ignoring some prohibitions of the code, sometimes for the reason, apparently, that it is supposed that a code of behavior would be self-defeating if it prescribed for situations of its own breach, on a wide scale. It is a sufficient answer to this suggestion, to point out that our actual moral code appears to contain some such prescriptions. For instance, our present code seems to permit, for the case in which almost everyone is understating his income, that others do the same, on the ground that otherwise they will be paying more than their fair share. It is, of course, true that a code simple enough to be learned and applied cannot include prescriptions for all possible types of situations involving the behavior of other persons; but it can contain some prescriptions pertinent to some general features of the behavior of others.

Granted, then, that an ideal moral code may contain some special prescriptions which pay attention to the behavior of other persons, how in particular will it legislate for special situations such as the examples cited above? The proper answer to this question is that there would apparently be no blanket provision for all cases of these general types, and that a moral agent faced with such a concrete situation would have to think out what an ideal moral code would imply for his type of concrete situation. Some things do seem clear. An ideal moral code would not provide that a person is permitted to be cruel in a society where most other persons are cruel; there could only be loss of utility in any special provision permitting that. On the other hand, if there is some form of cooperative activity that enhances utility only if most persons cooperate, and nonparticipation in which does not reduce utility when most persons are not cooperating, utility would seem to be maximized if the moral code somehow permitted all to abstain – perhaps by an abstract formula stating this very condition. (This is on the assumption that the participation by some would not, by example, eventually bring about the participation of most or all.) Will there be any types of situations for which an ideal moral code would prescribe infringement of a generally respected moral code, by a few, when a few infringements (provided there are not many) would maximize utility? The possibility of this is not ruled out. Obviously there will be some regulations for emergencies; one may cut across park grass in order to rush a heart-attack victim to a hospital. And there will be rules making special exceptions when considerable utility is involved; the boy with no other place to play may use the grass in the park. But, when an agent has no special claim others could not make, it is certainly not clear that ideal moral rules will make him an exception on the ground that some benefit will come to him, and that restraint by him is unnecessary in view of the cooperation of others.

The implications of the above form of rule-utilitarianism, for these situations, are evidently different from those of act-utilitarianism.[12]

12. The Ideal Moral Code theory is very similar to the view put forward by J. S. Mill in Utilitarianism.

12 The above proposal is different in various respects from that set forth in the writer's "Toward a Credible Form of Utilitarianism," in Castaneda and Nakhnikian, *Morality and the Language of Conduct*, 1963. The former paper did not make a distinction between institutional rules and moral rules. (The present paper, of course, allows that both may contain a common prescription.) A result of these differences is that the present theory is very much simpler, and avoids some counterintuitive consequences which some writers have pointed out in criticism of the earlier proposal.

Mill wrote that his creed held that "actions are right in proportion as they tend to promote happiness; wrong as they tend to produce the reverse of happiness." Mill apparently did not intend by this any form of act-utilitarianism. He was – doubtless with much less than full awareness – writing of act-*types*, and what he meant was that an act of a certain type is morally obligatory (wrong) if and only if acts of that type tend to promote happiness (the reverse). Mill supposed that it is known that certain kinds of acts, for instance, murder and theft, promote unhappiness, and that therefore we can say, with exceptions only for very special circumstances, that murder and theft are wrong. Mill recognized that there can be a discrepancy between the tendency of an act-type, and the probable effects, in context, of an individual act. He wrote: "In the case of abstinences, indeed – of things which people forbear to do from moral considerations, though the consequences in the particular case might be beneficial –, it would be unworthy of an intelligent agent not to be consciously aware that the action is of a class which, if practiced generally, would be generally injurious, and that this is the ground of the obligation to abstain from it."[13] Moreover, he specifically denied that one is morally obligated to perform (avoid) an act just on the ground that it can be expected to produce good consequences; he says that "there is no case of moral obligation in which some secondary principle is not involved" (op. cit., p. 33).

It appears, however, that Mill did not quite think that it is morally obligatory to perform (avoid) an act according as its general performance would promote (reduce) happiness in the world. For he said (p. 60) that "We do not call anything wrong unless we mean to imply that a person ought to be punished in some way or other for doing it – if not by law, by the opinion of his fellow creatures; if not by opinion, by the reproaches of his own conscience. This seems the real turning point of the distinction between morality and simple expediency." The suggestion here is that it is morally obligatory to perform (avoid) an act according as it is beneficial to have a system of sanctions (with what this promises in way of performance), whether formal, informal (criticism by others), or internal (one's own conscience), for enforcing the performance (avoidance) of the type of act in question. This is very substantially the Ideal Moral Code theory.

Not that there are no differences. Mill is not explicit about details, and the theory outlined above fills out what he actually said. Moreover, Mill noticed that an act can fall under more than one secondary principle and that the relevant principles may give conflicting rulings about what is

---

13 *Utilitarianism*, Library of Liberal Arts, New York, 1957, p. 25.

morally obligatory. In such a case, Mill thought, what one ought to do (but it is doubtful whether he believed there is a strict moral obligation in this situation) is what will maximize utility in the concrete situation. This proposal for conflicts of "ideal moral rules" is not a necessary part of the Ideal Moral Code theory as outlined above.

13. It is sometimes thought that a rule-utilitarianism rather like Mill's cannot differ in its implication about what is right or wrong from the act-utilitarian theory. This is a mistake.

The contention would be correct if two dubious assumptions happened to be true. The first is that one of the rules of an optimific moral code will be that a person ought always to do whatever will maximize utility. The second is that, when there is a conflict between the rules of an optimific code, what a person ought to do is to maximize utility. For then, either the utilitarian rule is the only one that applies (and it always will be relevant), in which case the person ought to do what the act-utilitarian directs; or if there is a conflict among the relevant rules, the conflict-resolving principle takes over, and this, of course, prescribes exactly what act-utilitarianism prescribes. Either way, we come out where the act-utilitarian comes out.

But there is no reason at all to suppose that there will be a utilitarian rule in an optimific moral code. In fact, obviously there will not be. It is true that there should be a directive to relieve the distress of others, when this can be done, say, at relatively low personal cost; and there should be a directive not to injure other persons, except in special situations. And so on. But none of this amounts to a straight directive to do the most good possible. Life would be chaotic if people tried to observe any such moral requirement.

The second assumption was apparently acceptable to Mill. But a utilitarian principle is by no means the only possible conflict-resolving principle. For if we say, with the Ideal Moral Code theory, that what is right is fixed by the content of the moral system with maximum utility, the possibility is open that the utility-maximizing moral system will contain some rather different device for resolving conflicts between lowest-level moral rules. The ideal system might contain several higher-level conflict-resolving principles, all different from Mill's. Or, if there is a single one, it could be a directive to maximize utility; it could be a directive to do what an intelligent person who had fully interiorized the rest of the ideal moral system would feel best satisfied with doing; and so on. But the final court of appeal need not be an appeal to direct utilities. Hence the argument that Mill-like rule-utilitarianism must collapse into direct utilitarianism is doubly at fault.[14]

14 Could some moral problems be so unique that they would not be provided for by the

In fact, far from "collapsing" into act-utilitarianism, the Ideal Moral Code theory appears to avoid the serious objections which have been leveled at direct utilitarianism. One objection to the latter view is that it implies that various immoral actions (murdering one's elderly father, breaking solemn promises) are right or even obligatory if only they can be kept secret. The Ideal Moral Code theory has no such implication. For it obviously would not maximize utility to have a moral code which condoned secret murders or breaches of promise. W. D. Ross criticized act-utilitarianism on the ground that it ignored the personal relations important in ordinary morality, and he listed a half-dozen types of moral rule which he thought captured the main themes of thoughtful morality: obligations of fidelity, obligations of gratitude, obligations to make restitution for injuries, obligations to help other persons, to avoid injuring them, to improve one's self, and to bring about a just distribution of good things in life. An ideal moral code, however, would presumably contain substantially such rules in any society, doubtless not precisely as Ross stated them. So the rule-utilitarian need not fail to recognize the personal character of morality.

14. In contrast to the type of theory put forward by Toulmin and others, the Ideal Moral Code theory has the advantage of implying that the moral rules recognized in a given society are not necessarily morally binding. They are binding only in so far as they maximize welfare, as contrasted with other possible moral rules. Thus if, in a given society, it is thought wrong to work on the Sabbath, to perform socially desirable abortions, or to commit suicide, it does not follow, on the Ideal Moral Code theory, that these things are necessarily wrong. The question is whether a code containing such prohibitions would maximize welfare. Similarly, according to this theory, a person may act wrongly in doing certain things which are condoned by his society.

A serious appeal of theories like Toulmin's is, however, their implications for institutional obligations. For instance, if in society *A* it is a recognized obligation to care for one's aged father, Toulmin's theory implies that it really is a moral obligation for a child in that society to care for his aged parent (with some qualifications); whereas if in society *B* it is one's recognized obligation not to care for one's aged father, but instead for one's aged maternal uncle, his theory implies that it really is the moral obligation of a person in that society to care for his aged

set of rules it is best for the society to have? If so, how should they be appraised morally? Must there be some appeal to rules covering cases most closely analogous, as seems to be the procedure in law? If so, should we say that an act is right if it is not prohibited, either explicitly or by close analogy, by an ideal moral code? I shall not attempt to answer these questions.

131

maternal uncle – even if a better institutional system would put the responsibilities in different places. This seems approximately what we do believe.

The Ideal Moral Code theory, however, has much the same implications. According to it, an institutional system forms the setting within which the best (utility-maximizing) moral code is to be applied, and one's obligation is to follow the best moral rules in that institutional setting – not to do what the best moral rules would require for some other, more ideal, setting.

Let us examine the implications of the Ideal Moral Code theory by considering a typical example. Among the Hopi Indians, a child is not expected to care for his father (he is always in a different clan), whereas he is expected to care for his mother, maternal aunt, and maternal uncle, and so on up the female line (all in the same clan). It would be agreed by observers that this system does not work very well. The trouble with it is that the lines of institutional obligation and the lines of natural affection do not coincide, and, as a result, an elderly male is apt not to be cared for by anyone.

Can we show that an "ideal moral code" would call on a young person to take care of his maternal uncle, in a system of this sort? (It might also imply he should try to change the system, but that is another point.) One important feature of the situation of the young man considering whether he should care for his maternal uncle is that, the situation including the expectations of others being what it is, if he does nothing to relieve the distress of his maternal uncle, it is probable that it will not be relieved. His situation is very like that of the sole observer of an automobile accident; he is a mere innocent bystander, but the fact is that if he does nothing, the injured persons will die. So the question for us is whether an ideal moral code will contain a rule that, if someone is in a position where he can relieve serious distress, and where it is known that in all probability it will not be relieved if he does not do so, he should relieve the distress. The answer seems to be that it will contain such a rule: we might call it an "obligation of humanity." But there is a second, and more important point. Failure of the young person to provide for his maternal uncle would be a case of unfairness or free-riding. For the family system operates like a system of insurance; it provides one with various sorts of privileges or protections, in return for which one is expected to make certain payments, or accept the risk of making certain payments. Our young man has already benefited by the system, and stands to benefit further; he has received care and education as a child, and later on his own problems of illness and old age will be provided for. On the other hand, the old man, who has (we assume) paid such

SOME MERITS OF ONE FORM OF RULE – UTILITARIANISM

premiums as the system calls on him to pay in life, is now properly expecting, in accordance with the system, certain services from a particular person whom the system designates as the one to take care of him. Will the ideal moral code require such a person to pay the premium in such a system? I suggest that it will, and we can call the rule in question an "obligation of fairness."[15] So, we may infer that our young man will have a moral obligation to care for his maternal uncle, on grounds both of humanity and fairness.

We need not go so far as to say that such considerations mean that an ideal moral code will underwrite morally every institutional obligation. An institution may be grossly inequitable; or some part of it may serve no purpose at all but rather be injurious (as some legal prohibitions may be). But I believe we can be fairly sure that Professor Diggs went too far in saying that a system of this sort "deprives social and moral rules of their authority and naturally is in sharp conflict with practice" and that it "collapses into act-utilitarianism."

15. It may be helpful to contrast the Ideal Moral Code theory with a rather similar type of rule-utilitarianism, which in some ways is simpler

---

15 See John Rawls, in "Justice as Fairness," *Philosophical Review* 67 (1958), 164–94, especially pp. 179–84.

It seems to be held by some philosophers that an ideal moral code would contain no rule of fairness. The line of argument seems to be as follows: Assume we have an institution involving cooperative behavior for an end which will necessarily be of benefit to all in the institution. Assume further that the cooperative behavior required is burdensome. Assume finally that the good results will be produced even if fewer than all cooperate – perhaps 90 percent is sufficient. It will then be to an individual's advantage to shirk making his contribution, since he will continue to enjoy the benefits. Shirking on the part of some actually maximizes utility, since the work is burdensome, and the burdensome effort of those who shirk (provided there are not too many) is useless.

I imagine that it would be agreed that, in this sort of system, there should be an agreed and known rule for exempting individuals from useless work. (For example, someone who is ill would be excused.) In the absence of this, a person should feel free to excuse himself for good and special reason. Otherwise, I think we suppose everyone should do his share, and that it is not a sufficient reason for shirking, to know that enough are cooperating to produce the desired benefits. Let us call this requirement, of working except for special reason (etc.), a "rule of fairness."

Would an ideal moral code contain a rule of fairness? At least, there could hardly be a public rule permitting people to shirk while a sufficient number of others work. For what would the rule be? It would be all too easy for most people to believe that a sufficient number of others were working (like the well-known difficulty in farm planning, that if one plants what sold at a good price the preceding year, one is apt to find that prices for that product will drop, since most other farmers have the same idea). Would it even be a good idea to have a rule to the effect that if one absolutely knows that enough others are working, one may shirk? This seems highly doubtful.

Critics of rule-utilitarianism seem to have passed from the fact that the best system would combine the largest product with the least effort, to the conclusion that the best moral code would contain a rule advising not to work when there are enough workers already. This is a non sequitur.

133

than the Ideal Moral Code theory, and which seems to be the only form of rule-utilitarianism recognized by some philosophers. This other type of theory is suggested in the writings of R. F. Harrod, Jonathan Harrison, and perhaps John Hospers and Marcus Singer, although, as I shall describe it, it differs from the exact theory proposed by any of these individuals, in more or less important ways.

The theory is a combination of act-utilitarianism with a Kantian universalizability requirement for moral action. It denies that an act is necessarily right if it will produce consequences no worse than would any other action the agent might perform; rather, it affirms that an act is right if and only if universal action on the "maxim" of the act would not produce worse consequences than universal action on some other maxim on which the agent could act. Or, instead of talking of universal action on the "maxim" of the act in question, we can speak of all members of the class of relevantly similar actions being performed; then the proposal is that an action is right if and only if universal performance of the class of relevantly similar acts would not have worse consequences than universal performance of the class of acts relevantly similar to some alternative action the agent might perform. Evidently it is important how we identify the "maxim" of an act or the class of "relevantly similar" acts.

One proceeds as follows. One may begin with the class specified by the properties one thinks are the morally significant ones of the act in question. (One could as well start with the class defined by all properties of the act, if one practically could do this!) One then enlarges the class by omitting from its definition those properties that would not affect the average utility that would result from all the acts in the class being performed. (The total utility might be affected simply by enlarging the size of the class; merely enlarging the class does not affect the average utility.) Conversely, one must also narrow any proposed class of "relevantly similar" acts if it is found that properties have been omitted from the specification of it, the presence of which would affect the average utility that would result if all the acts in the class were performed. The relevant class must not be too large, because of omission of features that define subclasses with different utilities; or too small, because of the presence of features that make no difference to the utilities.

An obvious example of an irrelevant property is that of the agent having a certain name (in most situations), or being a certain person. On the other hand, the fact that the agent wants (does not want) to perform a certain act normally is relevant to the utility of the performance of that act.

So much by way of exposition of the theory.

For many cases this theory and the Ideal Moral Code theory have

134

identical implications. For, when it is better for actions of type A to be performed in a certain situation than for actions of any other type to be performed, it will often be a good thing to have type A actions prescribed by the moral code, directly or indirectly.

The theory also appears more simple than the Ideal Moral Code theory. In order to decide whether a given act is right or wrong we are not asked to do anything as grand as decide what some part of an ideal moral code would be like, but merely whether it would be better, or worse, for all in a relevant class of acts to be performed, as compared with some other relevant class. Thus it offers simple answers to questions such as whether one should vote ("What if nobody did?"), pick wildflowers along the road ("What if everyone did?"), join the army in wartime, or walk on the grass in a park.[16] Furthermore, the theory has a simple way of dealing with conflicts of rules: one determines whether it would be better, or worse, for all members of the more complex class (about which the rules conflict) of actions to be performed (for example, promises broken in the situation where the breach would save a life).

In one crucial respect, however, the two theories are totally different. For, in contrast with the Ideal Moral Code theory, this theory implies that exactly those acts are objectively right which are objectively right on the act-utilitarian theory. Hence the implications of this theory for action include the very counterintuitive ones which led its proponents to seek an improvement over act-utilitarianism.

It must be conceded that this assessment of the implications of the theory is not yet a matter of general agreement,[17] and depends on a rather complex argument. In an earlier paper I argued that the theory does have these consequences, although my statement of the theory was rather misleading. More recently Professor David Lyons has come to the same conclusion, after an extensive discussion in which he urges that the illusion

---

16 One should not, however, overemphasize the simplicity. Whether one should vote in these circumstances is not decided by determining that it would have bad consequences if no one voted at all. It is a question whether it would be the best thing for all those people to vote (or not vote) in the class of situations relevantly similar to this one. It should be added, however, that if I am correct in my (below) assessment of the identity of this theory with act-utilitarianism, in the end it is simple, on the theory, to answer these questions.

It hardly seems that an ideal moral code would contain prescriptions as specific as rules about these matters. But the implications for such matters would be fairly direct if, as suggested above, an ideal moral code would contain a principle enjoining fairness, that is, commanding persons to do their share in common enterprises (or restraints), when everyone benefits if most persons do their share, when persons find doing their share a burden, and when it is not essential that everyone do his share although it is essential that most do so, for the common benefit to be realized.

17 See, for instance, the interesting paper by Michael A. G. Stocker, *Consistency in Ethics, Analysis* supplement, vol. 25, January 1965, pp. 116–122

of a difference between the consequences of this theory and those of act-utilitarianism arises because of failure to notice certain important features of the context of actions, primarily the relative frequency of similar actions at about the same time, and "threshold effects" an action may have because of these features.[18]

It may be worthwhile to draw attention to the features of the Ideal Moral Code theory that avoid this particular result. In the first place, the Ideal Moral Code theory sets a limit to the number and complexity of the properties that define a class of morally similar actions. For, on this theory, properties of an act make a difference to its rightness, only if a moral principle referring to them (directly or indirectly) can be learned as part of the optimific moral code. Actual persons, with their emotional and intellectual limitations, are unable to learn a moral code that incorporates all the distinctions the other theory can recognize as morally relevant; and even if they could learn it, it would not be utility-maximizing for them to try to apply it. In the second place, we noted that to be part of a moral code a proscription must be public, believed to be part of what is morally disapproved of by most adults. Thus whereas some actions (for instance, some performed in secret) would be utility-maximizing, the Ideal Moral Code theory may imply that they are wrong, because it would be a bad thing for it to be generally recognized that a person is free to do that sort of thing.

16. I do not know of any reason to think that the Ideal Moral Code theory is a less plausible normative moral theory than any other form of utilitarianism. Other types of rule-utilitarianism are sufficiently like it, however, that it might be that relatively minor changes in formulation would make their implications for conduct indistinguishable from those of the Ideal Moral Code theory.

Two questions have not been here discussed. One is whether the Ideal Moral Code theory is open to the charge that it implies that some actions are right which are unjust in such an important way that they cannot be right. The second question is one a person would naturally wish to explore if he concluded that the right answer to the first question is affirmative: It is whether a rule-utilitarian view could be combined with some other principles like a principle of justice in a plausible way, without loss of all the features that make utilitarianism attractive. The foregoing discussion has not been intended to provide an answer to these questions.

18 David Lyons, *Forms and Limits of Utilitarianism*, Clarendon Press, Oxford, 1965.

8

Fairness to indirect optimific theories in ethics

Various philosophers critical of utilitarianism have indicated that they would find some kind of "rule" or "motive" – a kind of "two-level" – theory less objectionable than a simple act theory.[1] This concession is not ideally helpful, since many different theories can be identified as "rule" or "motive."[2] Some writers are more concerned to criticize the theory of value of utilitarians than the "rule" conception. What I want to do here is consider the "act"/"rule" contrast in abstraction from the theory of value. To mark this, I am calling the theory I am defending an "indirect optimific" theory.

It could be thought inconsistent to talk of an "optimific" theory if one believes there are many quite different intrinsic goods, such as happiness, desire-satisfaction, knowledge, virtue, freedom, equality, autonomy, accomplishment, and personal relationships. Consider specifically the list of values of G. E. Moore, Hastings Rashdall, or James Griffin.[3] Despite the diversity of these alleged goods, if they are commensurable, then some combination of them is preferable to all others. Suppose we have a list of all possible or feasible combinations of this sort. Then we can identify a best state of affairs (say one with a certain level of equality and a given level of average utility). And we can then say that a normative

I wish to thank members of a conference at Loyola University for their comments on an earlier version of this paper, and also members of the philosophy department, and graduate students, at the University of Nebraska. My colleagues have been helpful, and in particular William Frenkena, who has criticized the paper in more than one version; my thanks to them all.

1 S. Scheffler, *The Rejection of Consequentialism* (Oxford: Clarendon Press, 1982), pp. 16n., 52n., 90n.; 1; T. M. Scanlon, "Contractualism and Utilitarianism," in *Utilitarianism and Beyond*, ed. A. Sen and B. Williams (Cambridge: Cambridge University Press, 1982), p. 120.

2 Philosophers who might be (loosely) classified as such would include Bishop Berkeley, Soame Jenyns, William Paley, J. S. Mill, probably John Austin, Roy Harrod, Stephen Toulmin, J. O. Urmson, J. D. Mabbott, John Rawls (in his 1955 article "Two Concepts of Rules"), Kurt Baier, Kai Nielsen, A. MacBeath, C. A. Campbell, L. W. Sumner, Lawrence Davis, R. M. Adams, Richard Wasserstrom, and most notably, John Harsanyi. W. K. Frankena is very close, except for his insistence on distinguishing equality from a "benefit"; as is also David Lyons (sometimes). I have doubtless omitted many, and some of the above have probably changed their minds; and the writers listed disagree with each other to a considerable extent.

3 James Griffin, *Well-Being* (Oxford: Clarendon Press, 1987), passim.

theory is "maximizing" or "optimific" if it holds that what a person should do, or what morality should do, is to bring about this maximally good state of affairs, just as Mill held (roughly) that what is desirable for either a person or a morality is for him (it) to maximize happiness.[4] (An ethical egoist holds a maximizing theory, but with the difference that he restricts what is to be maximized to preferable states of himself.)

In what follows I shall, for the sake of simplicity, discuss only theories which affirm that individuals and/or morality should maximize the *utility* (in the sense of happiness or desire-satisfaction) of sentient beings. I am supposing readers of different persuasions will readily transpose the problems I shall be discussing to the case of the end-states they think intrinsically desirable. Thus I shall limit the discussion to debating the comparative merits of act-utilitarian and two-level utilitarian theories. I shall ignore all objections to utilitarianism that are aimed at both: for example, the claim that utilitarianism "merges" persons, or permits shifting goods from one person to another when this will maximize benefit; or that it ignores the value of equality; or that it violates the "integrity" of agents; or that measurement of utilities and interpersonal comparisons, in the required sense, are impossible. (I shall also leave open the question whether "utility" is to be defined in terms of happiness, or in terms of desire-satisfaction, since this is a problem for both theories – although for the sake of simplicity I shall have the happiness view in mind. And I shall not discuss the controversy whether it is average or total benefit that defines what we ought morally to maximize.)

OPTIMIFIC INDIRECT THEORIES AND THEIR PRAGMATIC JUSTIFICATION

An optimific indirect theory is a *normative* theory that *roughly* holds that any *other-person-involving* act is morally permissible if it would be *best* for the moral motivations of (roughly) all agents to *permit* acts of that type in its circumstances, and that an other-person-involving act is an agent's moral duty if it would be best for the moral motivations of (roughly) all agents to *require* acts of that type in those circumstances. Why say "(roughly) all"? The answer is that, as we shall see, there are moral-problem situations the description of which precludes the possibility of "all." So what I mean by "(roughly) all" is "all except those precluded by the description of some moral-problem situations."

I mean by a person's *moral motivations* a complex consisting of a desire/aversion for some kind of action for itself, in certain circumstances, a

4 J. S. Mill, *Utilitarianism*, chap. 3 (and toward end of chap. 2).

disposition to feel guilty if one does (does not) perform an act of this sort, and a disposition to disapprove or be indignant if someone else does (does not) perform an act of that type, in those circumstances. Thus, a person is manifesting his moral motivations if he decides to add one thousand dollars to his report of income for tax purposes rather than sign a false report, and if he feels guilty if he does perjure himself, and if he does not find it cute or funny but feels indignant or disapproving if someone else saves money by a false report. A person with such motivations will, I assume, be able to come up with some such verbalized principle as "That kind of action is *prima facie* wrong." The moral motivations of a *group* "require" a certain action in certain circumstances if they are for it, would register guilt if an act of their own were not of this sort, and disapprove/be indignant at anyone else whose act was not such.

I take this conception of the "morally wrong" to be essentially that of J. S. Mill when he wrote: "We do not call anything wrong unless we mean to imply that a person ought to [it is desirable that he] be punished in some way or other for doing it – if not by law, by the opinion of his fellow creatures; if not by opinion, by the reproaches of his own conscience. This seems the real turning point of the distinction between morality and simple expediency." On his view, then, it appears that an act is wrong if and only if it is desirable (optimal) that all agents be motivated by conscience to avoid it (a motivation Mill thinks is a result of conditioning by "punishments" but ultimately based on sympathy or "fellow-feeling" in some sense, so that he is not holding a *pure* "punishment" theory of "wrong")[5] and be punished (if they have no excuse) because of it by disapproval of others and guilt feelings of their own (and perhaps by law).[6]

It is manifest that such a normative theory is consistent with most theories about the meaning of moral predicates: with nonnaturalism, with most forms of prescriptivism, and with major traditional forms of naturalism, for example, the Ideal Observer theory. It is not obvious, how-

5 The reader should consult Mill, *Utilitarianism*, chap. 3, for the details of his psychology of morality.
6 Mill, chaps. 2 and 5. Mill should have said that an act is wrong if and only if a moral system ought to punish it, provided it is not *excused*. Mill's account really explains "wrong" only in the sense of "morally blameworthy." (This slip was called to my attention by Allan Gibbard.) We can then define "subjectively wrong" as "would be blameworthy if there were no excuse," and we might explain "excused" as "done in circumstances which preclude a normal inference from acts to traits of character." (The notion of "character" raises problems of its own, but I think they may be ignored here.) If none of the "excuses" consists of a mistake about facts, either about the nature of the particular case or about which moral system would maximize benefit, we can say that the subjectively wrong is also the objectively wrong. I shall not be careful to distinguish between blameworthiness and both kinds of wrongness.

ever, that it is compatible with views that have been put forward about the relations of the principal moral predicates to one another. For instance, it is incompatible with Moore's view that "duty" can be defined just as "maximizes the good."

One could, and should, make an important addition to this account. One could say that an action is morally praiseworthy if it would be optimal for (roughly) all members of the society of the agent to admire actions of that sort although they are not required – actions over and beyond the call of duty, acts that would have been his duty except for the cost to (or preferences of) the agent. (But I shall ignore this supererogation part in what follows.)

Why does Mill use this conception to explain the concepts of the morally wrong and moral duty at all? He seems to be relying on linguistic intuition; he says we *mean* or at least *imply* liability to "punishment" (by guilt feelings and/or reprobation by others) when we say some act is morally wrong.

But there are other considerations one can adduce in support of such a definition. For this conception permits a sharp distinction between "dutiful action" and *best* (maximizing) or even *rational* (maximizing expectable utility) action (whatever the intrinsic values are taken to be). And it is helpful to have a term to mark actions *required* by an (optimal) moral code, just as we need the term "illegal" to mark the kind of action avoidance of which society requires by the system of criminal justice, as distinguished from socially undesirable actions. It is important to mark this distinction: we do not want the social moral code to *require* all ideally desirable behavior, since requiring has its own costs, of teaching, of guilt feelings that may have undesirable effects, and so on.

But why define "moral duty" in terms of optimal moral motivations in a society? Why define in terms of an *optimal* something at all? Since I am discussing only maximizing theories – the merits of an optimal social moral motivation theory versus a utility-maximizing act theory – perhaps I need not say anything more about how one justifies *either* sort of theory. But it seems better to indicate how some theories, at a deeper level, might lend credence to the view that the morally right involves the notion of optimal benefit in some way. Let us see how such a metaethical theory might proceed; it will hardly rely on linguistic intuitions.

First, we might, like Rawls, affirm that a certain moral principle is *justified* if it would be accepted by persons who are rational, and impartial in the sense of choosing behind a "veil of ignorance." This is essentially a *proposal* (not a report of linguistic intuitions), intended to appeal to thoughtful people, partly because its implications fit their moral intuitions. Now Rawls has not argued that such moral principles would or should be benefit-maximizing, and he has relatively little to say about which moral principles for individuals would satisfy his criterion. One he mentions is that a person is "to bring about a great good . . . if [he] can do so relatively easily."[7] John Harsanyi, however, employing basically the same concept of justifiability,[8] has criticized Rawls's derivation of his principles of justice[9] and has argued that individuals will give preference, behind a "veil of ignorance," to a total moral system in which the average utility – defined in terms of corrected desires – is maximal.[10] Alternatively, one might argue that a social moral code is justified if it would be supported by persons who are rational and benevolent to the degree to which this is rational (this could include some wholly selfish people) and fully informed about what life would be like in a society in which such a system were accepted, and that such persons would prefer (perhaps for selfish reasons) a benefit-maximizing system of morality to any other type and to none at all.[11] Somewhat similar to the Rawls-Harsanyi view, T. M. Scanlon's principle of justification urges, "An act is wrong if its performance under the circumstances would be disallowed by any system of rules for the general regulation of behavior which no one could reasonably reject as a basis for informed, unforced general agreement." Scanlon says it is possible that this view is compatible with some form of "rule" or "motive" utilitarianism.[12] Of course, the similarity of Scanlon's view to the other proposals depends very much on the construal of "reasonably." How do these proposals differ in their appeal to a conceptual frame for the definition of moral concepts? One is an appeal to what we would accept if rational and *deprived of all information that might enable us to favor ourselves*, the second to what we would support if fully *informed and rational*, the third to rules which no one could "reasonably reject."

7 John Rawls, *A Theory of Justice* (Cambridge, Mass.: Harvard University Press, 1971), p. 117. The Good Samaritan principle cited might indicate a strain of utilitarianism in Rawls's thinking.

8 John Harsanyi anticipated essentially Rawls's conception of the "original position" in papers in 1953 (*Journal of Political Economy* 61) and 1955 (*Journal of Political Economy* 63). These papers are reprinted in his *Essays on Ethics, Social Behavior, and Scientific Explanation* (Dordrecht: D. Reidel Publishing Co., 1980); see esp. pp. 4 and 14.

9 John Harsanyi, "Can the Maximin Principle Serve as a Basis for Morality? A Critique of John Rawls's Theory," *American Political Science Review* 69 (1975): 37–63.

10 John Harsanyi, "Morality and the Theory of Rational Behavior," *Social Research* 44 (1977): 631–6, "Rule Utilitarianism and Decision Theory," *Erkenntnis* 11 (1977): 27–9, and "Basic Moral Decisions and Alternative Concepts of Rationality," *Social Theory and Practice* 9 (1983): 231–44.

11 See R. B. Brandt, *A Theory of the Good and the Right* (Oxford: Clarendon Press, 1979), chaps. 10, 11, 14, 15.

12 T. M. Scanlon, "Contractarianism and Utilitarianism," in A. Sen and B. Williams, eds., *Utilitarianism and Beyond* (Cambridge: Cambridge University Press, 1982), pp. 110–20.

I do not assert that any of these proposals constitutes a knock-down argument that an action is morally wrong if and only if it would not be permitted by a benefit-maximizing moral system. But, in order to get on with the problems in formulating such systems, I shall assume that they show enough in this direction to make the concept of a benefit-maximizing moral system worth exploring.

WHICH MORAL SYSTEM WOULD BE BENEFIT MAXIMIZING?

We should note that Mill's conception of "moral duty" does not rule out *act*-utilitarianism; what it does rule out is the identity of the *concept* of "duty" with that of "utility-maximizing" or "expectable utility maximizing"; it relates "duty" to the *requirements* (what must be done to avoid guilt, etc.) of an *optimal* moral system. But a benefit-maximizing moral system *could require* a person simply to do what will directly maximize benefit, or at least do what, on her evidence, will maximize expectable benefit – following the act-utilitarian formula. But many philosophers do not feel happy with such a suggestion. Doubtless most of them are moved by the fact that the implications of the theory – that one's moral duty is always to do what, on one's evidence, will maximize expectable utility – are incompatible with deeply held intuitions. However, the objections of many recent philosophers (but also writers at least as early as Bishop Berkeley)[13] have been more pragmatic. Calculating the utilities of various options for action is a somewhat difficult task; moreover it takes time, whereas time is often at a premium when decisions are pressing. Also, many people are just not bright enough, or well enough educated, to make reliable judgments about the utilities of their options; and the calculations are so subtle as to constitute a standing invitation to rationalize in one's own favor. Hence, were individuals to reach moral decisions in this way, it would be difficult to predict where they would come out: We would not know whether a person would keep a promise unless we could see how the different benefits looked to him. As a result, there would not be the security in predicting how others would behave necessary for making personal plans or effectuating schemes of cooperation. Hence a moral system of this sort would hardly be benefit-maximizing, and the proposal an unattractive one, for pragmatic reasons.[14]

13 See George Berkeley, *Passive Obedience* (1712), reprinted in M. W. Calkins, ed., *Berkeley* (New York: Charles Scribner's Sons, 1929), esp. pp. 432–40.
14 R. E. Bales, in a very interesting paper, has argued that such "pragmatic" considerations are irrelevant to the identification of correct principles about the objectively right. They

FAIRNESS TO INDIRECT OPTIMIFIC THEORIES IN ETHICS

This act-utilitarian formulation of an "optimal" moral system does have
a certain advantage of simplicity. All one need investigate, to apply it, is
what the situation is, including what other people are doing, and then
estimate the expectable utilities of the various options for action. It would,
of course, be too much to expect that agents will know enough to maximize actual benefit.

But what would a really optimal moral system look like, one devised
to remedy the shortcomings of an act-utilitarian system?

It would appear that the pragmatic difficulties of act-utilitarianism can
be met, without losing touch with the basic idea that the end of morality
is benefit maximization, if we think that what we ought to do is follow
the requirements of an *optimal moral code* – a benefit-maximizing set of
moral motivations, or conscience. Hence the normative principle I stated
as a definition of an "optimific indirect" theory. What would such a
system be like?

A feature of all such motivation sets is that they will be directed at
types of action: requiring a token of some act-type *A* whenever the circumstances are *C*.[15] There is at least one further restriction that must be
imposed on such a system: that it be relatively simple. Such a restriction
would be violated if we said just that a moral code is benefit-maximizing
only in case *everyone in the society were always to perform a token of
type "A" in circumstances "C,"* social utility would be maximized by the
behavior. This stipulation admits indefinite complication. If there is no
restriction on the complexity of *C*, then the moral code might well take
into account the number of persons who are doing, or will do, either *A*
or not-*A;* it has been argued that if this is the case, there is then no
difference between the implications for behavior of this set of rules and
act-utilitarianism.[16] However this may be, with no restriction, the "rules"

are relevant to another problem: how to decide what is the right thing to do. He thinks
an answer to the first question has no particular connection with decision making. His
view looks much less convincing, however, if we think that what is one's duty is what
one would be required to do by a moral code that would be supported and preferred
by informed rational people, or persons choosing from behind a veil of ignorance. For
why should a person, opting among moral systems, be uninfluenced by pragmatic
considerations, say the impossibility of teaching a certain moral code except at prohibitive
cost? Bales must be supposing that there is some other way of knowing "true" moral
generalizations – very likely by intuition (R. E. Bales, "Act-Utilitarianism: Account of
Right-making Characteristics or Decision-making Procedure?" *American Philosophical
Quarterly* 8 [1971]:257–65). For another criticism of act-utilitarianism, see D. H. Hodgson, *Consequences of Utilitarianism* (Oxford: Clarendon Press, 1967). R. M. Hare,
Moral Thinking (Oxford: Clarendon Press, 1981), pp. 35–52, gives reasons why it is
desirable to have a "two-level" system of moral thinking.
15 The description of the "circumstances" will be restricted to those relevant to the utility
of everyone being motivated to perform the correlated act-type.
16 See David Lyons, *Forms and Limits of Utilitarianism* (Oxford: Clarendon Press, 1965),
esp. chap. 3.

143

everyone is supposed to follow could be so specific and numerous that the moral motivations that would produce a token of an act-type *A* for each different *C* could not be interiorized by human beings. Even if they could be, it is improbable that other persons planning their actions could know which rule the agent would be following. Hence the establishment of such an "optimal morality" would seem to suffer from the pragmatic problems of act-utilitarianism, that nonagents would not know how the agent sees the situation and what rules he would be following – a result that would remove a major benefit of a set of "rules" obtaining in a society. Moreover, in estimating the benefits of a given moral system, we have to take into account the costs (time-consuming trouble) of teaching it; and these costs go up drastically as the complexity increases.

This pragmatic difficulty can be removed by a simple restriction. We can say that "A moral code is benefit-maximizing if and only if it consists of a *learnable* set of moral motivations the prevalence of which (including teaching costs) would maximize value." It is to be included in the notion of a motivation that, when there is moral motivation to do something *A*, the individual will, at least with some prompting, be able to come up with a verbal principle, "One morally ought, *prima facie*, to do things of kind *A*." In consequence, the moral principles held by most people will be rather public; indeed, we should specify some degree of publicity as one of the requisites for an optimal moral system, partly for pragmatic reasons. One advantage of this type of theory is that it at least secures that the code of rules (motivations) is simple enough to be learned at least by most people – see below – (the definition requires this); the *C* with which acts are supposed to vary will normally be limited to circumstances described in terms of abstract properties, hence normally will not include facts about the number of persons already behaving in certain ways. The code will presumably deal with recurrent situations or problems, with which our actual moral code seems to deal.

Possible moral systems must be appraised as wholes, on account of the connections between the individual motivations; ones must be picked which do not conflict with, but support, the others.

The pragmatic advantages of such a moral system, as contrasted with act-utilitarianism, will of course increase with the number of persons subscribing to it. If the number is small, we shall not have the advantage of being able to predict how others will behave; as the number goes up, approaching 100 percent of at least moral and rational people,[17] so will the advantages increase.

17 Harsanyi defines a "correct moral rule" as one, observance of which "by all people concerned with the good of society would maximize social utility." This formulation does not consider costs of teaching or address the problem of "partial compliance" (see

Such a kind of benefit-maximizing moral system requires further explanation. First of all, we should notice that such moral codes can vary in respect of (a) the act-types that are required (prohibited); (b) the relative intensity or strength of the motivations connected with each act-type and varieties thereof, with the effect that the differing strengths may direct what to do in case of conflicts of motivations, and also be more or less successful in directing behavior; and (c) the scope of each motivation (for absolutely everyone, everyone in a particular society, all adults or adults of at least IQ 80, all children, or only persons in a certain profession, etc.). Then we can say that a total moral *system* maximizes benefit when, given all these specifications for a given group, the consequences of its being in force to the extent it is, taken with the costs of teaching and having it, will maximize benefit.

How strong will be the "optimal" level of various motivations in persons of different types? A first approximation: as near the level needed to secure optimal behavior as can be expected in reasonably intelligent well-brought-up adults, without being too costly to teach. (But if a given moral motivation is so strong as to cause prolonged and disabling guilt feelings, the system is not optimal.) How complex may the rules be? Answer: not too complex for reasonably intelligent people to apply, again with the restriction on the costs of teaching. (Presumably some parts of the code affect only professionals: only lawyers need be familiar with some of the details about when promises are binding.) The rules must also be sharp enough so that a person need seldom (except when there is conflict between rules) be in doubt whether one applies – otherwise even conscientious people will give way to the human tendency to rationalize. What all this means, realistically, is that even optimal moral motivations will not always be strong enough to control behavior. So, even in a society with a benefit-maximizing moral system, there will be some *actions* which could be better – partly because some members of the society may not have internalized the rules.

One essential feature of such a conception is that we have to suppose persons enlightened enough to teach it and maintain it in being. One property it seems we must assume in such teachers is an awareness that the purpose of morality is to secure well-being, and a disposition to modify any attitudes, and teaching of attitudes, toward a certain form of behavior if they are seen to serve no purpose – and to develop a requirement when it is seen that conditions demand it. We might put this by saying that what teachers of a moral code must have, and teach to others,

below); John Harsanyi, "Some Epistemological Advantages of a Rule Utilitarian Position in Ethics," *Midwest Studies in Philosophy* 7 (1982): 390.

is a certain amount of *moral philosophy*. It is in virtue of this fact that we may call this theory "two level." At one level, individuals are to have and apply their optimal moral motivations, but, at a different level, teachers are to appraise the system of moral motivations for optimality and "teach" the optimal system to others and themselves. (Undoubtedly, in practice the two levels will get somewhat mixed.)

The above conception of an "optimal moral system" seems to me the one the optimific indirect theorist should adopt, although empirical information would be required to identify what is the benefit-maximizing code for a given group in a given society, all costs and benefits taken into account.

This conception is very similar to R. M. Hare's view of "second-level intuitive" moral thinking.[18] There are some differences. First, Hare (sometimes) identifies an "optimal" system of intuitive thinking as the one that would lead most frequently to utility-maximizing actions, but elsewhere he identifies it as the one that would be utility-maximizing to teach. There is some vagueness here. Second, Hare says that when "intuitive" principles (namely, moral motivations) conflict for a given case, the *agent* should resort to act-utilitarian calculation of benefits. Third, he says that when for some reason an intuitive principle seems grossly unsuitable for a given case, too inflexible, the *agent* should again resort to direct calculation of benefits. The present conception differs. First, the present view holds that the "optimal" moral system is the motivations it would be best for (roughly) all members of the society to share, including all costs, for example, of teaching. Second, while it is consistent with holding that when confronted with a conflict, one should resort to act-utilitarian calculations, one *might* just rely on the relative psychological force of the two motivations. My proposal makes no stipulation about this. Again, in the case of a principle seeming unsuitable or inflexible, what it would seem (I think) most consistent with the general theory (and utility-maximizing) to do, is to require the agent to think out what specification of the "optimal" rule, in terms of abstract properties, it would be best to add to the moral code as a whole, even if such an addition would (in some cases) make the code too complex to be learned. He would act rather like an appellate court deciding a certain case, with the thought the decision would be a precedent, although the principle would be too complex to put into the statutes. (This sort of solution might also be proposed for the case of conflicts of obligations.) In any case, I suggest this would be the long-range, benefit-maximizing way to proceed.

18 Hare, *Moral Thinking*.

We may assume that teachers would start with the moral code of their society as is and prune, add, or modify as seems benefit-maximizing. In this way they could be sure that the moral code they teach would be at least up to dealing with most problems that arise. Teachers will hardly be able to make precise estimates of the benefit of having exactly one code rather than another, and in any case it would be next to impossible to fine-tune the strength of a given moral motivation to just the intensity one would like, particularly in view of the fact that this must be done mostly by building by conditioning, on the sympathetic or other attitudes naturally present in the learners. And, in the case of ethics for the professions (etc.) the teaching would have to be done mostly by specialists in the field.

SOME OBJECTIONS

If we are to be "fair" to this sort of theory, we must note the objections that have been raised and consider how far they can be met. There have been many objections to optimific indirect theories in the literature, of which some half-dozen seem to merit attention. I take some of these roughly in order of ascending importance.[19]

1. The first has to do with the apparent social relativity of the theory. Of course the theory itself is in no way relative: "An act is morally right if it would be permitted by the moral code optimal for the society of the agent." But different societies will be in different situations, with different institutions and conventions. Does this mean there can be no substantive principles of worldwide application? If there are, they may, some of them, need to be very abstract. Unlike a simple imperative such as "no smoking here" there might have to be one like, "Don't do anything disturbing to your neighbor when he isn't free to distance himself from you!" I would guess that any moral system composed wholly of rules so abstract they could be of worldwide application would be costly, or even impossible, to teach. We might then properly say that the substantive moral code optimal for one society would not be so for another.

But this view leaves us with another problem: How do we determine the relevant "society"? Is it to be one's university or professional affiliations, one's city, one's nation, or what? Possibly the issue is not important, since the central moral principles like not injuring others or keeping promises will be roughly invariant. I suggest that the most plausible view is for concrete moral principles suitable for the particular so-

19 I have considered various others in "Problems of Contemporary Utilitarianism: Real and Alleged," in N. E. Bowie, ed., *Ethical Theory in the Last Quarter of the Twentieth Century* (Indianapolis: Hackett Publishing Co., 1983).

cieties to be taught there and that one leave the drawing of lines about which society is which to judgments about which decision would be most beneficial! I propose not to worry about this question.

2. The second problem is not unrelated to the first. Suppose we say that the moral code optimal for a given society is a function not only of its physical (etc.) situation, but of its institutions and customs (including conventions, like driving on the right). For example, it is or was true of the Hopi that they regard themselves as having a duty to support, in their old age, only their mothers and other persons related to them by a female line. Hence the children of a man had no obligation to support him – a regulation less salutary than one in which obligations follow natural affections and one which could leave widowed men very much in need. Now, if we said that the "optimal" morality for the society is the *best* morality, the one that would make children responsible for *both* their parents, the relevant moral principle could lead to unfortunate results in practice, perhaps to children supporting no one. So we want moral rules in some sense to follow institutions; if we have an institution of private property, then it is wrong to steal. If we did not do this, morality would start with a clean slate indeed; to identify the optimal morality we should have to dream up optimal institutions from scratch! For many institutions are constituted, in large part, of certain recognized moral bonds – property, for instance, is composed of the "rights" of the owner, which themselves must be explained in terms of the obligations of others not to take, and so forth. Now are these rights (etc.) to be included in the scope of the optimific indirect theory? If they are, is not a person whose calculations show that private property is not benefit-maximizing not bound to ignore the recognized property rights of others? It looks as if morality has to work on two levels, on one level being free to criticize and attack the institution of private property (marriage, etc.) – this is the level proper for reformers – and on another level being required to accept this institution as a going concern and to support principles regulating behavior on the assumption the institution is there – the morality for everyday life. This duality introduces a complication, which, however, seems to represent what we mostly think. The level on which moral reflection should move will depend on what is at issue. The former is for reform of institutions, the latter for particular actions – although the latter may sometimes involve the former.[20]

How then might we define an "institution"? We might say that it is a social or cultural system, in which individuals occupy offices or stations

20 See Jonathan Harrison, "Rule-Utilitarianism and Cumulative-Effect Utilitarianism," *Canadian Journal of Philosophy* 5, suppl. (1979): 26–7.

with various "duties" and "rights." These rights and duties are *recognized;* behavior in accordance with them is *expected* and *customary.* An optimal morality will take this structure for granted in its provisions for everyday behavior. But a person can challenge an institution, and if he does we have to appeal to the application of the general benefit-maximizing principle, taking into account, among other things, the *other unchallenged* institutions. This is complicated indeed, but no more than actual situations. From the point of view of long-range social utility, this is the best way for moral reflection to go.

3. It is sometimes said that a difficulty act-utilitarianism has, about identifying which course of action will maximize benefit, is exacerbated for an indirect optimific theory.[21] If we cannot, at least as Moore thought, know whether a given lie will be more or less beneficial than a corresponding truth, how can we know that truth telling in general should have *prima facie* moral force in an optimific moral code due to greater benefit? And the more so for more specific principles about which promises to keep. Berkeley's answer was that some such practical rules do "to right reason evidently appear to have a necessary connexion with the Universal well-being."[22] Berkeley's view seems to be seconded by J. D. Mabbott, who raised the question whether life would be tolerable, or a particular kind of society possible, if certain moral rules were not recognized and generally observed.[23] It does seem easy to show that a moral system will best incorporate a general *prima facie* obligation to speak the truth, in view of the importance of being able to rely generally on information from others. Imagine the perils of travel, if the locals, when invited to give directions, felt no obligation to tell the truth but only to maximize benefit as they saw it. Questions about more specific rules are harder: Are promises binding if made on the basis of a deliberate misrepresentation by the promisee? Decisions about the optimal *relative* strength of different moral motivations doubtless will also be hard to support, but it does seem that Ross is right in thinking that the obligation not to injure is generally stronger than the obligation to keep a promise. Giving which rule priority would benefit society more? Actually, we need to break this question down somewhat, in terms of amount of damage, and the kind of promise. There are some problems, but it would

---

21 See R. G. Frey, "Act-Utilitarianism, Consequentialism, and Human Rights," in R. G. Frey, ed., *Utility and Rights* (Minneapolis: University of Minnesota Press, 1984), pp. 73–83; H. J. McCloskey, "An Examination of Restricted Utilitarianism," *Philosophical Review* 66 (1957): 466–85, reprinted in Samuel Gorovitz, ed., *Utilitarianism: John Stuart Mill,* (Indianapolis: Bobbs-Merrill Co., 1971), pp. 209–10.
22 Berkeley, p. 436.
23 J. D. Mabbott, "Moral Rules," *Proceedings of the British Academy* 39 (1953): 97–117, esp. pp. 107–17.

NORMATIVE ETHICS: UTILITARIANISM

be interesting to see what alternative moral theories have to offer. Advice to follow the moral rules one would accept in the "original position" seems no help, if we cannot make some judgment of the relative expectable benefits. Act-utilitarians will doubtless advocate relying, in this context, on "rules of thumb," inductively supported by past correlations between truth telling and public benefit, but if such rules of thumb can be so supported, then the estimates on which the indirect optimific theory relies can hardly be seriously defective.

Matters are more complicated, of course, if we go along with some utilitarians and say that knowledge, autonomy, deep personal relations, and accomplishment are important intrinsic goods. We then do not have the evidence for a definite conclusion that we theoretically would have if hedonistic utilitarianism were true – provided measurement and inter-personal comparison of pleasures were possible. We must simply make some large judgments, but it does seem that a society in which people felt free to tell lies, break promises, and injure other people would be an appalling society in which to live.

4. The above-described form of indirect optimific theory needs to find some reply to the charge of "rule worship," leveled both by utilitarians like J. J. C. Smart and by a nonutilitarian, Philippa Foot (although they doubtless do not have precisely this form in mind).[24] Foot says: "Surely it will be irrational, we feel, to obey even the most useful rule if in a particular instance we clearly see that such obedience will not have the best results."[25] D. H. Monro has wondered why an act that maximizes benefit need not be obligatory on the indirect optimific theory; the theory seems to demand something more, that the act be an instance of a benefit-maximizing rule. He wonders how this can be.[26]

The force of this criticism depends partly on what an optimific moral code will be like and partly on the reasons for following it even if one knows that some action different from the one it prescribes would produce more good. On the first point, it is obvious that an optimific moral code will contain prohibitions of injury to others and an injunction to give aid, just as does Ross's list of *prima facie* duties. So presumably injunctions to do something that fails to maximize benefit will ordinarily occur only when any harm done is relatively small or when aid is not needed – or else when the obligation to do something else is rather strong, for example, to honor a recent promise of loyalty to one's wife or not to commit perjury in a false declaration of income for tax purposes.

24 J. J. C. Smart, "Extreme and Restricted Utilitarianism," *Philosophical Quarterly* 6 (1956): 344–54; Harrison, pp. 24–5; see also D. H. Monro, "Utilitarianism and the Individual," *Canadian Journal of Philosophy* 5, suppl. (1979): 54–5.
25 Philippa Foot, "Utilitarianism and the Virtues," *Mind* 94 (1985): 196.
26 Monro, p. 54.

There is a second fact that may narrow the gap between rule-utilitarians and their critics. This is that a total moral system may imitate the law, which holds that some acts prohibited by the legal code (for example, damage to the property of another) are "justified" when a serious public good is at stake (say prevention of the spread of a conflagration by destroying another's home). So one might say that if following an optimific set of moral rules would cause severe damage, then a person need not follow the relevant rules. Just as the law does not regard such "justifications" as contrary to the rule of law (a criminal code's list of offenses cannot take care of all conceivable contingencies, the rules about "justifications" appearing in the prolegomena), so we might say that a morality that is simple enough to be learned may require being stretched when there is an emergency situation, without departing from the spirit of an indirect optimific theory. Such a reply to critics seems to have been accepted by Mill.[27] Actually, in the case of morality, it would seem that a blanket general "justification" could itself be a special moral principle, one among the several "moral" motivations, something like: "If following an otherwise optimific set of rules would cause a very large utility loss or forgo a very large utility gain on this occasion, the agent is permitted to perform an act that is (close to) utility-maximizing on the occasion." Jonathan Harrison has asked just "how bad the consequences of adhering to a rule must be, before one ought to break it."[28] To this I would reply that philosophers need supply numbers no more than the courts, which seem to have no difficulty with the distinction.[29]

So it would appear that the complaint about irrationality must refer to cases in which a *marginal* amount of good would be done by breaking some principle of the optimific system. Hare, for instance, thinks a rule should be broken in this case, provided we are fairly sure our calculation is correct.[30]

The answer must lie in long-term considerations of benefit: to have agents familiar with moral principles and motivated to follow them, with the effect that their behavior in important contexts can be predicted, with the familiar consequences of possible coordination and incentive.

But might one not say that what it is best to teach and support, from

---

27 About a page from the end of chap. 5 of *Utilitarianism* he says: "Particular cases may occur in which some other social duty is so important as to overrule any one of the general maxims of justice. Thus, to save a life, it may not only be allowable, but a duty, to steal or take by force the necessary food or medicine, or to kidnap and compel to officiate the only qualified medical practitioner."

28 Harrison, p. 22.

29 See Charles Black, "Mr. Justice Black, the Supreme Court, and the Bill of Rights," *Harper's Magazine* (February 1961), pp. 63–8, esp. pp. 67–8.

30 R. M. Hare, *Moral Thinking* (Oxford: Clarendon Press, 1981), p. 133.

the point of view of the indirect optimific theory, is both strong commitment to a certain moral code, as the best long-range strategy for maximizing benefit, and also, for the same reason, advocacy of discrimination? So one might advocate teaching general moral motivations but also, if the learner is intelligent, teaching her to depart from the rules herself (and advocate that she recommend the same to her intelligent friends) when this will clearly maximize utility in the instant case. Yet it is doubtful whether this would be good strategy, despite Sidgwick's recommendation, as Gibbard has pointed out.[31] For it would prevent the benefits of sincere discussion of moral and political matters and undermine one's own firm commitment to the basic principles. It should be conceded that the question whether it would or not is an empirical one, which needs further discussion.

It is possible, moreover, that the critics have given insufficient thought to the incompatibility between strong commitment to follow (with corresponding motivation) a moral code and being always primed to see if there is some public benefit to be gained by ignoring it. Is there not a disutility of the impact, of paying attention to the comparative direct utilities of options open, on the agent's commitment to a specific moral code? So, if there is utilitarian reason to teach a certain moral code, the same reasoning would seem to lead to the view that it will normally not maximize utility for agents to be counting the utilities.

Let us assume for the moment that the critics are right, if they think that even if the benefits of moral commitment to attainment of long-range utility are included in a utility reckoning, there will sometimes be a gap between the requirements of an optimific moral code and what would be recommended by an act-utilitarian. Should they not then formulate at least some kind of principle, however imprecise, about when reflection on such matters should take place? One suggestion that has been made is that we might adopt some rule like, "Do not make a direct appeal to utility unless the loss (lack of gain) is so great that it captures your attention even if you are not looking for it, not trying to make a comparison of utilities."[32] Doubtless this is too vague, and "noticeability" is not enough. But note that the cited rule would not permit appeal to direct utility in *all* cases. The view of the critics seems to make it impossible to sustain an acceptable view of moral rights, if this requires that a person's rights be respected even when it is known that so doing will prevent a marginal gain in utility.

To be fair, we should not overemphasize the relative benefits of an

31 A. Gibbard, "Utilitarianism and Human Rights," *Social Philosophy and Policy* 1 (1984): 101–2.
32 By Sanford Levy, in personal communication, October 2, 1984.

indirect optimific theory in the long run. Act-utilitarians will point to inductively supported "rules of thumb" about which types of actions tend to produce the most good. The agent, according to them, should bear these rules in mind (maybe as built-in aversions, dispositions to disapprove, etc., that are not merely rules of thumb psychologically, even though a justification of them must take the same line as that for a rule of thumb). Heavy reliance on these rules of thumb (or on built-in aversions corresponding to them) may bring the act-utilitarian very close to the plural-obligation code the indirect optimific theory regards as the standard of moral rightness.

There is, however, an important logical point that deserves scrutiny. I have been suggesting, in line with what is often thought, that following optimal rules would be beneficial because it would permit prediction of the behavior of others, hence encourage coordinated activity and provide an incentive to make plans in reliance on what others will do. But there is a complication here. For it is not part of the indirect optimific theory, as such, to tell us which are the optimal rules. The act-utilitarian theory does give us a basic moral principle as the essence of the theory: "Do what will maximize utility" (or, perhaps, "what will maximize expectable utility"). The "pragmatic" objections to this theory, cited above, are clear enough. But is the indirect optimific theory better off? It, too, is a kind of one-principle thesis: "Do only what would be permitted by an optimal moral system!" Does this thesis not also have problems of application? For its application is a two-stage affair – this is why I have called the view a two-level one. First an agent has to decide (in case he has not been taught it so firmly that the question does not arise, except for him in his capacity as teacher) what is the utility-maximizing motivational system and then what this system requires for the case at hand. This is necessarily left to the judgment of agents, just as act-utilitarianism has to leave to the judgment of agents which act will do most good. So it is one thing for there to be benefits in a society having a (roughly) single optimal moral code; it is quite another thing for persons to be committed to the indirect optimific *theory* only. There will be a benefit for people to be committed to the indirect optimific *theory* only if intelligent people will come out at the same place in their judgments about optimal rules, whereas it is not so easy to predict where persons will come out in their judgments of the utilities of various options in an instant case. It seems, then, that if the indirect optimific theorist is to escape the very pragmatic problems of application, which are a main reason for rejecting act-utilitarianism, he will have to say that there is less difficulty in identifying the optimal moral system than there is in identifying which action in a particular situation will maximize utility (or expectable utility). Can he plausibly do this? His answer must be, as I have argued earlier, that it will be obvious, at least to intelligent people, that we shall maximize long-range utility if we all, or virtually all, are strongly motivated (etc.) to keep our promises, refrain from swearing falsely, and so forth. Moreover, one can argue that the *existing* moral codes are time-tested: there are socio-psychological forces which tend to prune away pointless prohibitions, and to some extent to bring about requirements suited to new problems (for instance, about conservation of resources). So one can say that what the intelligent rule-utilitarian wants, in seeking to identify the optimal code, is primarily to expedite this process. He will be an incrementalist in his identification of the optimal moral code. It would have to be admitted, however, that people may not come out at the same place in their estimates of the benefit, say, of some exceptions to be specified in the principle of the bindingness of promises. Moreover, a person committed to optimal rules will want to keep up to date his views about what a benefit-maximizing moral system will be like. It will hardly be easy to predict what he will think the benefit-maximizing moral system will say about the uses of information from amniocentesis, or what to do about seriously defective newborns (say, ones born in the fifth month, who would not survive at all but for modern medicine). So the indirect optimific theorist should not overstate his case for the advantages of teaching exceptionless moral rules (with *prima facie* force). Moreover, I have conceded that in practice act-utilitarians, with their rules of thumb, will often come out at the same place, especially if they think that what they ought to do is maximize expectable utility. Still, there is a substantial difference, and one can think it would be unfortunate if we were left to the mercies of individual judgments about which acts would be most beneficial in particular cases, as contrasted with taking a long-range view about public morality as the basis for such judgments.

5. A further problem, mentioned by Scanlon[33] and others, is raised by the suggestion that there may be, in a society, very partial compliance with the optimal moral code – a problem essentially posed by Lyons under the title of "minimizing conditions," a condition in which it is either counterproductive or useless to follow an optimal rule because so few others are doing so.[34] (This is also a problem for Rawls.)[35] Suppose a certain principle would be part of an optimal moral system, if there were virtually perfect compliance, and intelligent people know roughly

33 T. M. Scanlon, "Rights, Goals, and Fairness," in S. Hampshire, ed., *Public and Private Morality* (Cambridge: Cambridge University Press, 1978), p. 94.
34 Lyons, pp. 138–42; D. H. Hodgson has a discussion of this and related points in the appendix to his book.
35 Rawls, pp. 303 ff.

what it is. But suppose now that a great many people in the society have discrepant moral commitments, for example, embrace racial discrimination. Or perhaps at least a great many people do not conform in behavior to the optimal principles. Might it not cause great harm to follow what would be the optimal moral code if there were perfect compliance? As Feinberg and others have pointed out,[36] fierce intolerance of some features of an optimal moral code could lead to serious strife. Must not a utilitarian, then, urge a person to forsake her rule-utilitarian commitment in this situation?

Is admitting that such a situation is possible even consistent with the definition of an indirect optimific theory, that an act is morally permissible only if an optimal moral system (in the sense of all persons having certain moral motivations) would permit it? It would seem not to make sense to ask what the optimal indirect code adopted by everyone would imply for issues posed by the existence of a dissident constituent group.

It is for this reason that I defined the theory in anticipation of this problem, saying that an optimal moral code consists in the fact that "roughly all" persons – but excluding those whose agreement is precluded by a description of the problem-situation – will share optimal moral motivations. So the problem of inconsistency does not arise.

But, although there is no inconsistency in inquiring what an optimal moral code would prescribe for a situation in which many people either disagree in attitude or at least in behavior, there remains the question how to state what an optimal code would be, for such situations. What we want to know is what is the objective duty here and now of a person who may be moved to do what she thinks is required by the optimal moral system, in the face of such a situation.

I suggest that the solution to the problem is to show that the difficulty arises only if we assume an unduly simple concept of optimal moral rules. (This was the first reply I made to critics like Foot and Smart in the discussion of the rationality of conforming to the theory.) What is needed for a solution is to show that rules can be formulated such that they are both (1) optimific if prevalent in the society as a whole and (2) also optimific if prevalent only among a minority, perhaps a minority of one.[37]

Let us consider an example. Suppose you are living in South Africa. It is clear that the long-range optimal moral system forbids race discrimination, and you accept this moral principle in your conscience. But now? One thing you can do is stand up and be counted as condemning race

36 J. Feinberg, review of *The Forms and Limits of Utilitarianism*, by D. Lyons, *Philosophical Review* 76 (1967): 383–8.
37 In what follows I think I am making use of some of the ideas of Roy Harrod and Donald Regan.

discrimination and refuse to practice it in your own affairs. Another thing that you can do is identify, as far as possible, others with your commitments and join forces with them in a program of education, demonstrations, and so forth. Perhaps the optimal strategy will be something of a compromise: say, avoiding the most offensive things such as interracial sexual contacts but writing and speaking in favor of a completely non-discriminatory system. Then why not say that one's duty is to follow this strategy? (Maybe, because the personal cost would be so great, some such acts must be viewed as supererogatory.)

Is there any way in which we might say that such a strategy can be part of the optimal morality for the society? The answer seems to be that the optimal morality for a society may include disjunctive rules (as part of the basic motivations of the optimal conscience), with the first part of the disjunct having prior force, such as: "Treat everyone equally, without regard to race, religion, or sex; but in case such conduct would produce serious social harm because of massive disagreement, then perform that act which it is benefit-maximizing, for all of society, for you (your group) to do, as a *means to social change in the direction of equal treatment.*" The latter kind of clause could be appended to any otherwise optimal rule following which by the minority, in face of massive disagreement, would be socially very costly. Such an addendum to relevant otherwise optimal rules would be very like the kind proposed in the preceding section for dealing with emergency situations. This kind of rule would be somewhat similar to ones we already, in effect, recognize as necessary in an optimal code, such as "Keep your promises unless your option is . . . , in which case do . . . "; but in this case we normally fill in by reference to another (and for this situation, stronger) *prima facie* obligation of the code, such as "unless it would be very harmful." It would be agreed that we need to have some rule in the optimal code, directive of what to do when the primary principles conflict. I pointed out earlier that this effect might be achieved simply by building in moral motivations of differing strengths; if we look at the matter in this way, the requirement to treat people equally now may be weaker than the prohibition of causing great harm, but the requirement to do what one can to improve matters will be stronger than simple capitulation to the rules subscribed to by the majority. Thus it may be that the problem of partial compliance is resolved simply by taking note of what will be the principles (built-in motivations) of an optimal moral code. Of course, if no harm will be caused, there is no reason why those with the optimal code should not practice and preach it.

Is this proposal about how to deal with the problem of partial compliance really a capitulation to act-utilitarianism, since it is now said that some individuals are to do what it would be benefit-maximizing for them to do, although it would not be but for the disagreement? Not at all. For what the proposal does is simply recognize a powerful moral consideration, that of avoiding serious harm. This is not at all to agree that each case ought to be settled on the basis of the expectable benefits. One is to follow the rule optimal when there is perfect (or near perfect) compliance, except when departing from it will avoid serious harm, and promote general acceptance of the moral code optimal when there is perfect compliance.

But can such a complex set of rules (including priorities between the obligation to keep a promise and the avoidance of a certain degree and kind of harm) be taught, except at a prohibitive cost? If not, one of the criteria for identifying a benefit-maximizing moral code – that it can be taught without prohibitive cost – seems to be infringed. And it may be that we cannot teach such a code to everyone including young children or persons with an IQ below 80. Notice that there is a trade-off here. If the optimific indirect theorist insists that an act is right only if permitted by a moral code the prevalence of which, in a sense requiring that it can be learned by absolutely everyone without prohibitive cost, would maximize the best end-state, he will find himself with a primitive or socially costly moral system. Alternatively, he can say a moral code is prevalent (accepted) even if not all of it can be interiorized by everyone without prohibitive cost, if at all. Then we may have a "prevalent" moral code which is reasonably sensible. Is there any rational basis for making one choice rather than the other? I think the indirect optimific theorist must go for the second option, in order that his general theory, along with his conception of "optimal morality," will permit his theory, and a corresponding morality, to achieve the goal of the institution of morality.

But perhaps we go too far if we disparage the possibility of learning such a morality. Teaching children a complex rule about when promises may be broken seems to offer comparable problems, although the rules are pretty much mastered when children reach maturity. Moreover, it seems that, as things are, reflective educated people have consciences – moral motivations – along the lines I have suggested for the case of race discrimination. Civil rights leaders and civil disobedience groups appear to think exactly in this way. But one must admit that the optimific indirect theory does run into complications when we try to work out the details in a realistic way.

9

Two concepts of utility

1

Utilitarians have agreed that acts, laws, and institutions should be appraised by their actual or expectable consequences, in one way or another, more particularly by whether they maximize the utility or welfare of sentient creatures. The various kinds of act-utilitarians, utilitarian generalizers, and rule-utilitarians agree on this, however much they disagree about whether it is total or average utility, actual or expectable utility, the individual act or the acceptance of a moral rule that counts, and so on.

Utilitarians of all these kinds have a decision to make: how to define "utility" or "welfare," that is, what it is that is to be maximized. In what follows I consider the comparative virtues of two views: the hedonist view, which I shall call the "happiness" theory, and the currently popular "desire" theory. My main conclusion will be that when we spell out the latter theory in its several possible specific forms, we find none to be very attractive.

Of these two, historically the happiness theory came first among utilitarians. Among philosophers generally, the desire theory may have priority, since it was often assumed among the early Greeks that what persons seek or strive for is good. But, if we confine attention to early utilitarianism, which seems to have begun in the writings of Richard Cumberland in 1672 (if not in Epicurus), it was happiness that was thought to be what is to be maximized and to be the sole intrinsic good; indeed Cumberland seems to equate "good" with "happiness." The theological utilitarians generally thought that God aims to maximize the happiness of his creatures.

A desire theory of good or of utility is widely held today among philosophers, and not only among utilitarians but among nonutilitarians. It was urged by R. B. Perry. Recently a form of it has had the support of Rawls. It is defended by R. M. Hare, Jan Narveson, and, essentially, Rolf Sartorius; and it is defended by James Griffin, in an unpublished paper, "Utility

I wish to thank James Griffin for allowing me to use the manuscript of an unpublished lecture "Utility as Satisfaction of Desire," given in 1974, for discussions with him, and for his criticism of a remote ancestor of this paper. Griffin, in his lecture, favored a qualified form of desire theory.

TWO CONCEPTS OF UTILITY

as Satisfaction of Desire." I once defended it myself.[1] It appears to be supported by many economists. One contemporary writer on price-theory (Jack Hirshleifer) says: "What modern economists call 'utility' reflects nothing more than rank ordering of preference. The statement 'Basket A is preferred to basket B' and the statement 'Basket A has higher utility than B' are equivalent."[2] He goes on to write that "the economic utilitarians generally . . . [say] that it is the satisfaction of factually observable wants, whether sensate or 'higher,' that should govern policy" (p. 442). Or, as two other economists[3] put it, "Utility means want-satisfying power. It is some property common to all commodities wanted by a person. . . . A commodity does not have to be useful in the ordinary sense of that word; the commodity might satisfy a frivolous desire or even one that some people would consider immoral" (p. 66). John Harsanyi[4] proposes that we "follow the economists in defining social utility in terms of the preferences (and, therefore, the utility functions) of the individual members of society," with some qualifications, as we shall see.

Utilitarians have sometimes adopted *neither* of these theories: They have thought, sometimes, that the good is not identical either with happiness or with the satisfaction of desire. G. E. Moore and Hastings Rashdall, for instance, held that good is an indefinable supervenient quality that belongs to various things like pleasure, virtuous action, knowledge, aesthetic appreciation, friendship, and a distribution of happiness in accordance with merit. What we are to maximize, then, is just the good, and we are to bring about bearers of goodness like states of pleasure or knowledge, in view of the amount of goodness each bears. An emotivist might hold a variant of this view: He might call various things "good," meaning thereby to express his favoring them, and then say that acts are "obligatory morally," thereby expressing a moral kind of favoring, when they promise to maximize the good in his sense. I propose to ignore all views of this sort.

2

We must begin by getting as clear as we can what might be meant by a "desire theory" and a "happiness theory." We begin with the desire theory.

1 In "The Concept of Welfare," S. R. Krupp, ed., *The Structure of Economic Science* (Englewood Cliffs, NJ: Prentice-Hall, 1966).
2 Jack Hirshleifer, *Price Theory and Applications* (Englewood Cliffs, NJ: Prentice-Hall, 1976), p. 85.
3 D. S. Watson and M. A. Holman, *Price Theory* (Boston: Houghton Mifflin, 1977).
4 "Rule-utilitarianism and decision theory," *Erkenntnis* 11 (1977), 25–53, esp. p. 27.

To begin at the bottom, let us note what it is for a person to have a *desire* at a time. To have a desire is not for some introspectible event, like an itch, to occur, but is roughly to have a dispositional property, as follows:[5] Let us suppose a person at a time t has a desire for a state of affairs S to occur. Then we can suppose there is a disposition at t to *tend more* to perform an action A, if the person judges that doing A will make the occurrence of S more likely; to tend to be pleased, if he learns that S is going to be the case when he has been supposing it would not be the case; to tend to be disappointed, if he hears that S is not going to be the case when he has been supposing it would be the case; and so on, possibly with a *ceteris paribus* clause inserted in each of the hypotheticals. We can then say that a person wants S more than he wants S', or prefers S to S', if and only if, other things being equal, he would tend more to perform A . . . and so on.

It is convenient to consider only the "intrinsically desired" in the sense of what is desired at least partly for itself,[6] that is to say, the disposition at t to tend more to perform an action A, if the person judges that doing A would make the occurrence of S more likely even when the judgment that S is made more likely does not include reference to any prospective consequences of the occurrence of S or to any properties of the obtaining of the state of affairs S beyond what is included in the definition or conception of "S." (The same for the other dispositions constituting desire.)

When "desire" is explained in this way, it is obvious that a person can have many desires at the same time. At the present moment, for instance, I would rather like to have something to eat, to be watching a basketball game on television, to get away for a vacation next week, and so on. Desires need not be future-oriented. I can want it to be the case that my friend in India received a letter from me last week; and I can want it to be the case that I spoke more diplomatically yesterday than in fact I did. If I thought I could do something to effect these changes, I would tend more to do it.

We should note that it does not follow, from the fact that one desires

5 The conceptions of "desire" and "pleasure" are discussed much more fully in chap. 2 of my *A Theory of the Good and the Right* (Oxford: Clarendon Press, 1979).
6 Notice that if we are appraising two courses of action and do not confine utility-assignments to consequences that are desired for themselves, we are apt to get misleading duplications. Suppose we intrinsically want an outcome Z, and we want, because each is an instrument for getting Z, each of Y, X, and W. Suppose also we intrinsically want U, which we can obtain by direct action. Suppose then we are deciding which act will maximize utility A, which will bring about W, X, Y, and Z, or B, which will produce U directly. Now if we want U more than Z, manifestly we should favor course of action B. But if we counted in all the instrumental desires, we might well favor action A. Obviously we should assign utilities only to the extent something is wanted for itself.

at t that S occur – even desires that S be the case at t – that one feels frustrated or disappointed at t even if one knows at t that S is not occurring and probably will not occur. A necessary condition for feelings of disappointment (etc.) is that one thinks consciously, at the time, that S is not occurring and probably will not occur. No unhappiness is caused at t by the failure of a desire to be satisfied unless one thinks about the matter.

Aversions can be explained correspondingly. To say a person has an aversion to a state of affairs S is to say that, if he judges that doing A will make S more likely, he will tend less to perform A than he otherwise would; and so on, *mutatis mutandis*, for the rest of the explanation.

3

If "utility" is defined as "satisfaction of desire," we need to know what is meant not merely by "desire" but by "satisfaction." One, and the simplest, account is this: What it is for a desire for S to be satisfied is for S to occur, or to obtain.[7] According to this account it is not necessary for a person to *know* that S occurred. (Of course, what one might want is for S to occur, *and* to know that it occurred; that is a different desire.) Again, for a desire to be satisfied in this sense is not for the person to be *pleased* that S has occurred, at least in the sense of having been given some pleasure by S or by the thought that S has occurred.

It follows, provided we adopt this conception of "satisfaction," that a person who defines "utility" in terms of desire-satisfaction must say that we put a person on a higher level of welfare at t if we bring it about that there obtains one of the states of affairs that he desires at t. (We shall return to the question whether it is just something he desires at t, or whether desires earlier or later are also relevant.) We put a person on a lower level at t if we bring it about that there obtains one of the states of affairs to which he is aversive at t.

In the case of many desires, satisfaction of them in the foregoing sense brings about a reduction in intensity in the desire, along with various other desires in the same "family."[8] For instance, suppose I want to eat a steak. When I have done so, I normally do not want another steak; my desire for a steak has been reduced to zero. Indeed, I am also likely to

---

7 J. J. C. Smart, in a recent discussion of "satisfaction utilitarianism," in "Hedonistic and Ideal Utilitarianism," *Midwest Studies in Philosophy* 3 (1978):249, writes: "The principle of maximizing satisfaction of desire uses 'satisfy' in a sense related to that in which Tarski says that a predicate is satisfied by a sequence of entities. A person's desire that p (or his desiring-true 'p') is satisfied if 'p' turns out to be true. Presumably Sir Edmund Hillary desired-true the proposition 'Hillary climbs Mt. Everest.' "

8 For the concept of a "family," see my *A Theory of the Good and the Right*, chap. 2.

be less interested in eating peanuts, or fish – although my desire for drinking something may have been increased. One *could* define "desire-satisfaction" so that it occurs only in this syndrome. But it is not necessary, and it is inconvenient to do so. For one thing, aversions hardly occur in families in quite this way. And some normal-looking desires appear not to belong to a family. Suppose I want to help feed hungry people, and I do so on one occasion; it is doubtful whether that reduces my desire to do so again. Or I want to solve philosophical problems; solving one probably does not reduce the desire to solve more. Again, sometimes when I have had a desire satisfied I am glad that it was – I still want it to *have* happened. It looks, then, as though we do not wish to define "desire-satisfaction" generally so as to require reduction in desire-strength, or to occur only when the relevant desire is a member of a "family."

4

The above conception, that what it is for a desire for S to be satisfied is just for S to occur or obtain, is not sacrosanct, and a person who wants to explain "utility" or "welfare" in terms of desire-satisfaction might wish to add some restrictions. (1) We might say that we add to a person's utility at t by bringing about a desired S at t only if the person is alive at t. Some philosophers would not accept this restriction and therefore consider that we are creating utility if we satisfy the past desires of the dead, even those dead long ago. (2) Another possibility is to say that utility is increased for a person with respect to his or her desire for S, only if both S obtains at some t *and* if the person *believes* at t that S has come about or obtains. If a man desires his wife's loyalty, does she add to his welfare-utility if she is loyal, or if she ensures that he *believes* she is, or only if both conditions obtain? (3) Still another possibility would be to add the stipulation that utility is increased with respect to a person's desire for S only if both S occurs or obtains at some t *and* either the occurrence of S at t or the belief that S obtains or occurs at t brings pleasure to the person.[9]

(4) There is another restriction we shall certainly want to introduce, in one form or another, into any desire-satisfaction theory of "welfare" or "utility." For consider altruistic desires, or the aversion to doing anything immoral, or the desire to be a morally ideal person. If I satisfy one of these desires, for example, if I make a contribution to CARE, it is far from obvious that so doing adds to *my* welfare or utility, as distinct

9 The first of the above stipulations was suggested in a lecture by James Griffin in 1974.

from the welfare or utility of the recipients. Perhaps, as Bishop Butler suggested, I may derive some enjoyment from the satisfaction of this desire, just as from that of any other "particular" desire. But, as Professor Mark Overvold points out in a recent paper,[10] if we are to make a distinction between self-interest and self-sacrifice, I must have some desires that it is not in my self-interest to satisfy, and hence desires the satisfaction of which does not, as such, add to *my* welfare or utility. Every action is motivated by desires/aversions and hence, if we do not make this distinction, every successful intentional act, at least unless the motivating desires fail of being "ideal" in some way (see below), must make a contribution to the agent's own welfare – a result certainly at odds with our ordinary concept of a person's welfare. Bringing about my own death for the sake of a moral principle would have to count as adding to my utility or welfare. I shall not attempt to suggest how this stipulation ought to go; Overvold's suggestion is roughly that producing S adds to a person's utility or welfare only if the person "intentionally" or "ideally" wants (wanted) S and the state of affairs S entails that the person is alive.

5

A further class of possible variations is important in desire-satisfaction theories of utility. One might say that utility consists in the satisfaction of just *any* desire, as foolish as you please. Harsanyi, however, holds that only satisfaction of certain qualified desires constitutes an increase of utility. He says:

It is well known that a person's preferences may be distorted by factual errors, ignorance, careless thinking, rash judgments, or strong emotions hindering rational choice, etc. Therefore, we may distinguish between a person's *explicit* preferences, i.e., his preferences as they actually *are*, possibly distorted by factual and logical errors – and his "true" preferences, i.e., his preferences as they *would be* under "ideal conditions" and, in particular, after careful reflection and in possession of all the relevant information. In order to exclude the influence of irrational preferences, all we have to do is to define social utility in terms of the various individuals' "true" preferences, rather than in terms of their explicit preferences.[11]

Harsanyi would also exclude preferences based on sadism, resentment, or malice, but let us pass that. Now there is some doubt whether the conditions he describes distinguish "foolish" desires for *things for them-*

---

10 Marc C. Overvold, "Self-Interest and the Concept of Self-Sacrifice," *Canadian Journal of Philosophy* 10 (1980), 105–18.
11 In his 1977 paper, cited above.

selves, as distinct from "foolish" desires for *means* to things wanted for themselves. But since I believe that some rational criticism can be directed at what we may call "intrinsic" desires, I believe we can follow him in supposing we can distinguish between *actual* and *corrected* or *ideal* intrinsic desires. If we do that, then we might say that one has raised a person's level of utility/welfare only if one has satisfied one of his corrected desires, and not if one has satisfied just any actual desire. For our purposes we can leave the decision between these possibilities open; we shall see later some of the implications of one choice rather than the other.

Thus far I have said nothing at all about what seems a serious problem for the desire-satisfaction theory of "utility," what must be the *date* of the relevant occurrent desire for S, and what are we to say if the person's desire for S varies in intensity from one time to another — and if at some times the person *wants* S and at other times is *averse* to the occurrence of S. I shall come back to this. First let us review the happiness theory.

6

Let us begin with the *concept* of enjoyment or happiness. I am supposing that a person is enjoying (liking) a certain experience if and only if the experience is making him want to continue it (or repeat it) for itself. For instance, I am enjoying a dish of ice cream if the taste is making me want to finish the dish or even order another — for itself, not just to please the person who served it to me. If it is not making me want to eat more, I am not enjoying it. (For very young children, those too young to want continuation of an experience in the sense of "want" explained earlier, it may be more proper to say that what it is to enjoy something is for the experience of it to instigate maintenance activities; for instance, if a child is enjoying an ice cream cone, he will hang onto it hard if someone tries to tug it away.) The definition does not restrict pleasures to so-called sensate ones; a person can perfectly well enjoy reading, or even writing, a paper or book, if the experience makes him want to do that for itself.

This conception differs somewhat from that of Robert McNaughton, who suggested[12] roughly that "x is happier than y" means "x and y are both moments of experience, and x is preferred to y for its own sake," where "prefers" means "one would act to bring about the first experience rather than the second." According to this view, which does not specify the time of the preferring, one could prefer a certain experience at t_1 to a different experience at t_2, with the preference itself obtaining later or

12 "A Metrical Concept of Happiness," *Philosophy and Phenomenological Research* 14 (1953):172–183, especially 172–174.

even before (if one *imagined* a kind of experience at some time), at t_3. McNaughton assumes that a person can make up his mind permanently about which experience he prefers; the one so preferred is the more pleasant. (Mill might have had something similar in mind in his discussion of qualities of pleasure.) In contrast, I have said that the degree of pleasantness of an experience is fixed by the magnitude of the wanting to continue it for itself, which the experience *causes at the time*. So, on this view, an experience E at t_1 is more pleasant than E' at t_2 if and only if at t_1 E is making the person want more intensely to continue E beyond t_1 than E' at t_2 makes him want to continue the quality of E' beyond t_2. (Whether, at other times, he would prefer another experience like E to one like E' is a wholly different matter, although not causally unrelated.) One might ask how we may know about such matters. To which the answer is that sometimes we can make such comparisons fairly directly, since a person can enjoy various experiences at the same time. For instance, a person may be eating a steak, conversing with a friend, and hearing music; if any of these came to a halt he could know that he wants to continue it. If all came to a halt he could, apparently, know which one he wants to continue the most. If, however, the experiences occur at different times, he would need to rely on memory – recall the intensity of frustration, or remember how much he was willing to pay for a continuation. A main problem with McNaughton's view is that in fact there is not a stable preference-ordering of experiences. In some cases there is stability: The experience of reading a certain novel always is rated above a certain bad toothache. But repetitions of an experience make the idea of the earlier experience seems less attractive (also less aversive); acquired associations can change its rating; and the same for the dimming of recollection – a feeling of seasickness is less aversive when we are deciding on the rationality of another ocean voyage. I shall follow my account.

It is worth noticing that, just as we distinguished between actual and ideal desires, we can distinguish between actual and ideal enjoyments. For instance, a person might be enjoying talking with another under the impression that the other person respected and liked him, whereas if he believed the truth, he would not be enjoying himself. If one is moved by this point, one will view the happiness theory of utility sketched below as only a first approximation, although I think, quite a near one.

It is theoretically simple to identify the act that will maximize utility in the happiness interpretation of "utility." To reduce the problem to the bare essentials, let us consider just the case of one person X who can do either A or B at t, and who wishes to maximize the welfare of another person Y, over Y's lifetime. Let us ignore the fact that we can know only with probability what will happen; let us suppose we can talk freely just of what *will* happen to Y if A is done, as compared with what will happen if B is done. (To know this, we might have to know what Y will want, or be averse to, at various moments of his life, since this will affect how happy he will be as a result of what happens to him.) We suppose, then, that for every future moment of time we can know what difference it will make to Y's experience whether A or B is done, and hence can decide how much happier (assuming we can measure the happiness of the different expected experiences) Y is at that moment given one act occurred, than he would have been had the other occurred. Let us represent these results by a broken curve, plotting the moments at which he is happier if A is done above the X-axis, the distance above the axis fixed by how much happier he is than he would have been had B been done; and similarly plotting points below the X-axis representing how much happier he is at some moments if B is done than he would have been had A been done. This operation will give us curve-segments probably both above and below the X-axis. Let us then compute the area under these curves; when we know whether the area above the curve is larger or smaller than that under the curve, we know which act will contribute more to Y's happiness over his lifetime. Whatever the practical difficulties in measurement, this conception is clear.

If we want to maximize welfare in general, on this view, we simply construct curves for the happiness level of everyone concerned, and sum. I anticipate the objection that this summing across persons requires interpersonal comparisons. I happen to think such comparisons are possible, albeit only rough ones; therefore this fact is not an objection to the happiness theory.[13]

7

It could be that an act that maximized utility$_H$ would always be the same act as one that maximized utility$_{DS}$, or that, with a given resource available, what one would do to increase another person's utility$_H$ maximally would be the same as one would do to increase his utility$_{DS}$. We cannot yet be precise on this, pending a discussion of what would count as maximizing utility$_{DS}$. But it will be helpful to consider whether doing what would maximally satisfy a person's desires at t would also produce maximal happiness from t on to the end of his life. Do we know anything about the relation of desires and pleasures that makes at least this coextensiveness plausible or implausible?

Several facts tend to produce a correlation between maximizing satis-

---

13 I discuss such comparisons in *A Theory of the Good and the Right*, chap. 13.

faction as defined by desires at t and maximizing utility$_H$. First, since enjoying an experience is wanting it to be continued, giving a person an experience he enjoys is (roughly) satisfying a desire. Second, people generally just want enjoyment; as Bishop Butler pointed out, you can motivate a person by promising him something nice, without telling him what it is. So, when you produce enjoyments, you satisfy that want. Third, when a person has been wanting something for some time he is to some extent pleased by its occurrence just because it is what he wanted. (One may have been looking forward to an opera at Covent Garden for years and be thrilled by the thought, when one finally gets there, that "Here I am at an opera at Covent Garden!" even though subsequently one is bored by a substandard performance.) Fourth, normally a positive correlation exists between strength of desire and pleasure produced, because of the way we get our desires. Normally, we want things because and to the degree that we have enjoyed them in the past (but there are complicating factors, for example, the frequency of past enjoyments); we want to hear Rampal to the degree to which we have liked his music-making in the past. And, since likings are fairly stable, what we have enjoyed in the past is a good clue to what we shall enjoy in the future (not a perfect clue: tastes do change). Psychologists like P. T. Young, L. T. Troland, and David McClelland have emphasized the role past enjoyments or disasters play in molding present wants and aversions by a process of conditioning.

There are, however, also some notable exceptions to this correlation. It has long been part of the lore of hedonism that some things people want strongly are poor avenues to enjoyment: honor or social status, achievement or success (especially posthumous fame). Desires for these things (or aversions to their absence) often do not come in the normal way, from past enjoyments of them; they arise in the process of "socialization" or "culture transmission." We hear our parents expressing pity for the neighbors whose son has opted to take up motorcycle repair as a life-work; then we associate negative feelings with that occupation. Or a person comes to aspire toward achievement because his middle-class parents rewarded him generously for good marks in school, with embraces and ice cream, and treated him coldly when he came home with poor marks. An aversion to a low-prestige occupation can be very counterproductive as far as hedonic consequences are concerned: One can work hard to avoid this occupation, find little enjoyment in having succeeded in avoiding it, and in fact deprive one's self of what might have been just the happy career for one.

When one reviews these latter facts, it seems doubtful whether maximizing utility$_H$ is necessarily, or perhaps even normally, accomplished by placing a person in the optimal position as fixed by his own preference-ordering at the time of action. The person might even prefer a "successful" life to a happy life, and be quite right that the two are not identical. (Matters might be different if we defined "maximize utility$_{DS}$" in one of the other possible ways, described below.)

We have seen, however, that some advocates of a desire-satisfaction theory would argue that "utility" should be defined not in terms of actual but of "ideal" desires. And it could be that desires/aversions acquired from parental preachments (and similar contingencies) are to be ruled out as not "ideal." In that case, maximizing utility$_H$ and maximizing utility$_{DS}$ might correlate much more closely. To become clear on this point, we require an account of how to identify "ideal" desires. It is not *obvious* that satisfaction of these is going to produce happiness to an extent that maximizing utility$_H$ will *exactly* coincide with maximizing utility$_{DS}$. In any event, if we define "utility$_{DS}$" this way, economists in particular should be put on notice that determining utility-maximizing courses of action is getting complicated and we are moving far away from a simple behavioral test for "ideal" preference-ordering.

The foregoing remarks show that it is at least doubtful whether a program of action that will maximize utility$_{DS}$ will maximize utility$_H$. If the argument is well taken, however, it does not show that either of these programs is *mistaken;* it merely shows that they may be different – that the program of maximizing utility$_{DS}$ will likely comprise different actions from the program of maximizing utility$_H$.

8

I come now to the main argument of this paper: I shall show that the desire-satisfaction conception suffers from a puzzling defect, when we try to work it out in detail.

In Section 6 I explained how in principle to decide, given ideal information, which of two courses of action will maximize utility$_H$ for a person. What we must now do is consider whether we can similarly explain in principle how to decide, given ideal information, which of two courses of action will maximize utility$_{DS}$. I shall argue that there is no plausible way of doing this.

For the sake of simplicity let us set aside the conception of "ideal" desires, and confine ourselves to actual desires.

We can see the problem by looking at a simple example.

Let us suppose I am considering what to do, to maximize utility$_{DS}$ with the funds at my disposal, for my son on his twentieth birthday next week. I am considering two courses of action. He has recently manifested a strong desire to learn Greek, and has avowed a wish to possess a Greek lexicon. So one course of action is to order a Liddell and Scott. I am also considering contributing to his nonintellectual life, specifically by purchasing a ten-speed bicycle. We assume the costs of the options are substantially the same. Which will maximize his utility$_{DS}$?

What sort of information may we assume to be available? To parallel the generous information assumed when we discussed the theoretical question of how to maximize utility$_H$, let us suppose that we have a profile of all his intrinsic desires for each moment of his lifetime, and all the consequences of an act we might perform (as compared with an alternative) that would satisfy some one of these desires (aversions). (There is a complication, because a projected action may *change* his desires, for example, if we start a person on a career of morphine addiction. Should we consider his desires as they would be if we performed an action rather than an alternative, or if we performed the alternative, which of course might be *in*action? Presumably the former. But we must remember to count the change of desires as a consequence, and there may well be "second-order" desires/aversions directed at the having/not-having of these desires.) We assume that each of these desires is for some state of affairs to obtain, at some particular time or stretch of time, or perhaps at some indefinite time. We may assume also that to each desire we can assign a number, unique up to a linear transformation, measuring its strength at the time of measurement, determined by some procedure such as that suggested by von Neumann and Morgenstern or more recent writers. If we have these numbers, for any moment, we can rank-order alternative biographies for a person or the world by means of them, for *any particular moment t_1*, if we think of these biographies as combinations of occurrences or states of affairs in which the desires are gratified or frustrated.

It would seem, then, that my project in deciding what to do for my son is to scan all the desires he may have at some time over his lifetime, and take the course of action that will satisfy the strongest set of these desires. But when we scrutinize this conception in detail, it becomes elusive. Let us see why.

The fundamental difficulty for the desire-satisfaction theory is that desires change over time: Some occurrence I now want to have happen may be something I did not want to have happen in the past, and will wish had not happened, if it does happen, in the future. Desires for something may also vary in intensity.

We should not underestimate the extent of such changes. Notice that one acquires some desires and loses others as one matures: One loses one's desire to be an airline pilot, and gains the desire to have a family or at least to provide for it after it arrives. There are temporary fancies: A person suddenly wants to learn Greek, works at it, and then loses interest before achieving mastery. Most obviously, some desires are cyclical, in the sense that after satiation there is a period of no desire for a whole family of events, after which interest is recovered. Some desires, as in morphine addiction, are a result of an earlier sequence of activities. Again, as a person grows older and realizes he has only a finite amount of time to live, he may lose many of his hedonistic interests, acquire a stronger desire to achieve something and make some contribution to the world, and perhaps a desire to have done things differently in the past. (Of course, an equal variety exists in the sources of a person's happiness; and to know what will give him happiness, we need to know, among other things, what his desires are at any given time. But, if the earlier account was correct, this raises no difficulty in principle for deciding which of two courses of action will maximize utility$_H$.)

To see the problem of principle in this situation, let us revert to the example of a choice between ordering a Greek lexicon or a ten-speed bicycle for my son. Let us suppose, for simplicity, that we can lump together his intrinsic desires for getting/having the lexicon, and for the consequent ability to look up words conveniently when occasion arises; and, in the case of the bicycle, the desires to own it and for the consequent ability to go places rapidly. We suppose that we have a picture of the intensity of these desires at every moment over his lifetime. Certain segments of this time span are of special interest: (1) the period before the time t_1 when I make my decision and order the present; (2) the desires he has at the time t_1; (3) the desires he has at the time t_2, his birthday, when he receives the present; and (4) the desires posterior to t_2. Now suppose some change occurs in these desires. For instance, let us say that from age six to eighteen his desire for a bicycle is to be assigned the number 10, compared with 0 for the Greek lexicon, on his von-Neumann-Morgenstern scale. Then, from nineteen until some time after twenty, his desire for a Greek lexicon is 15 and the interest in a bicycle down to 5; and thereafter the interest in a Greek lexicon declines to 1, with the desire for the bicycle remaining stationary. How do we decide whether we maximize utility $_{DS}$ by giving the lexicon or bicycle?

(a) One possible procedure is to identify the utility number for having the lexicon for each day (or hour?) of the person's whole life – past, present, and future – sum the numbers, and then compare with the like sum for the bicycle. This procedure is complicated. It is also artificial. For the relative utility of something will depend on how long one wanted something (even though no frustrating experiences occurred, since the matter did not cross the person's mind) before getting it, and on how long one was glad retrospectively to have had it, afterward, even though again one never gave thought to the matter and was not pleased by the thought. (It is true, of course, that we think the gift of the lexicon better justified if the gladness to have had it stands up for five years rather than one day, and this procedure gives place to that conviction.)[14]

There are two somewhat more simple procedures. The first (b) is to proceed as in (a) except that all desires before the time t_1 are to be ignored. The second (c) is the same except that now all desires before t_2 are to be ignored. In favor of these alternative procedures is their relative simplicity as compared with (a) – although one is still committed to thinking of desire-levels for the rest of the person's life after either t_1 or t_2. Also, we think that what a person didn't want at age eight is no clue to what it is rational to give him at age twenty. If a person is deciding what to do for himself, we should think it strange for him to decide on the basis partly of what he wanted or did not want ten years ago (unless he thinks this is evidence for what he does want now or will want later).[15] Nevertheless, it is not obvious why there should be this asymmetry in the treatment of past versus future desires, on the desire theory. If satisfaction of a desire is for the desired event to occur, whether the person knows about it or not, why has a desire not been satisfied even if it occurred some time ago? (The justification of the asymmetry is clear enough on the happiness theory. For past happiness is irrelevant to action at t_1, since it is beyond change at t_1. But past desires *can* be satisfied by action at t_1.) Moreover, for some cases it does not seem plausible, or at least definitively convincing, to ignore past desires altogether. Consider the following example (for which I am indebted to Derek Parfit and James Griffin): A convinced skeptic who has rebelled against a religious background wants,

14 This procedure sets no limit on the date on which the desired state of affairs is brought about; thus it is consistent with saying that an event a deceased person wanted during his lifetime adds to his utility – a view held by some. Since I personally do not feel inclined to maximize "utility" in this sense, I hasten to point out two facts. First, it is consistent to deny that one adds to welfare/utility of a deceased person by what one does after his death, and at the same time to concede that the law possibly ought to take account of the known wishes of the decedent at certain points, say in construing his will. But the reason for this is to give living individuals ability to control the disposition of their estates. Second, much the same is true about morality. It may be that people ought to pay some attention to the wishes of a deceased person, again for the reason that it is a good thing for living people to control the execution of their desires after their death. But this point about morality does not show that we are adding to a person's welfare or utility, after his death, by paying attention to his living wishes. My attention was drawn to these two points by W. K. Frankena.

15 I think we happen to know that a person's actions are a function of his desires and beliefs at the time of action (t_1), so the question whether his act should be determined to some extent by past (or future) desires does not arise – except for second-order desires to be "rational" in some sense, or to satisfy past or future desires.

most of his life, that no priest be called in when he is about to die. But, when he is on his deathbed he weakens as he feared he would, and asks for a priest. Do we maximize his welfare$_{DS}$ by summoning a priest, or not? If we ignore his desires before t_1, we shall send for the priest. (This may be what a person would do who was aiming at utility$_H$.) Some persons will not feel comfortable about this, although one can avoid this consequence (also on the happiness theory) by claiming that the present desire is not "ideal" and hence should be ignored.

The reasons that favor procedure (b) as compared with (a) are also reasons for preferring (c) over (b). Of course, in practice, a person's information about another's desires at the time t_2, available to him at the time of action t_1, will normally be the person's avowals of desire at t_1. So in practice the procedures usually amount to the same, although there can be differences if the interval between the two times is great, as there usually is when one is writing a will.

(d) Both the two preceding programs are somewhat simpler than procedure (a), since there is a large segment of times, with associated utility-numbers, that they propose to ignore. But they are still complicated, and face much the same problem of artificiality as procedure (a). These problems are largely resolved if we decide to ignore *future* desires along with past desires. One can do this by making decisions *solely* on the basis of desires at some particular time, either t_1 (call this program dt_1) or t_2 (call this program dt_2). We have discussed whether it is plausible to ignore *past* desires; the question now is whether it is plausible to ignore *future* desires. If it is, then we might opt for one of these (d) programs.

The first point to notice is that a complication arises about the date t_2. Consider the proposed gift of a Greek lexicon. What is desired is not only the *getting* of the lexicon, but the having of it, and the ability, over a period of time, to look up words conveniently. If we take this fact into account, then "t_2" should refer not to a point of time, but to a stretch of time, and what we should perhaps be considering is not the utility number of the lexicon at the moment of receiving it, but the average utility number over the whole period of its possession (as compared with the average utility number of the bicycle over the same period). This process gets complicated, but of course much of it can be avoided for a relatively durationless event like an expensive wedding. Suppose that a person at t_2 (and at t_1) wants an expensive wedding badly, but thereafter wishes very much that the money had been spent on some durable goods. Our question is whether it is convincing to adopt a procedure that ignores these latter desires, which were relatively weaker (than the desire for the wedding) earlier, and relatively stronger later.

Some philosophers would certainly hold that the later desires (the regrets, the being glad in retrospect) are not to be ignored. We may recall that some philosophers have thought it irrational to expend effort for pleasure, since the pleasure lasts only a moment and then is gone; they presumably also would be moved to agree that a wedding that lasts one hour and is intensely wanted during that hour (and at the time the decision to have it was being made) is worthless, at least if the parties are not glad it occurred for some period of later time. Indeed, it is possible to think that preference among alternative biographies, at the very end of life, is important for assessing choices, if not decisive. This last proposal, if taken as affirming that utility is fixed *solely* by preferences among possible biographies, just before one's death, is unconvincing. Suppose we provide a person with something that he likes very much and is glad to have over a long period of time; but toward the end of his life he wishes intensely that he had not had it, but had lived a spartan life of sheer intellectual achievement. I do not believe we want to say that we made a mistake in giving him this thing. Utility, viewed as what a rational person would want to maximize, apparently should be defined so as not to leave desires after the event (t_2) matters of indifference, or so as to make all other desires matters of indifference except the preference-ordering just before death.

If we had to make a choice between dt_1 and dt_2, it appears that the reasons for which program (c) is preferable to program (b) could be adduced in support of dt_2. An implication of dt_2 is that a person's utility is not enhanced by what happens after his death; the same holds for program (c).

From a practical point of view, the desire-theory program that would, I think, arouse most sympathy is dt_1. The idea, of course, is that, at the time of decision between two courses A and B, I adopt the recipient's set of priorities at the time (or, alternatively, his set of corrected or ideal priorities). To the extent to which he ignores his own past desires, I ignore them. To the extent to which he ignores his own future desires (or would do so, if his present desires were corrected), I do so. Of course, if we are to consider "corrected" desires, we need to decide how much information we are to require the ideal other person to have and other corrections that should be made; and if we find that he has a second-order desire to maximize his own utility$_{DS}$, *he* will have to be considered as facing the very problem we have been discussing.

It might be argued that this program is practically the most likely or efficient way of maximizing utility$_{DS}$ as defined by one of the other methods, (a), (b), or (c). But it has to be made plausible that this is so, and these other methods themselves we have seen to have serious shortcomings.

Given all these options, how are we to define – and justify defining – "utility$_{DS}$" for any contemplated event S? When choosing between two courses of action, what is it we want to maximize? Perhaps the despised happiness theory is not so bad after all.

9

There is an interesting puzzle that the desire theorist might pose, as a rejoinder against the happiness theory, at least as framed above. He might say: "You take a motivational, or reduction-to-desire, view of the nature of pleasure, so that in the end the happiness theory of utility reduces to a variety of desire-theory. The difference is that the happiness theory assigns utility only to *moments of experience*, with a degree of utility depending on how intensely the experience is wanted (or its continuation wanted) for itself at the time (of course, with summing over relevant periods of time). So does not this proposal have to be justified by showing that it is somehow preferable to the other desire-analyses that have been proposed? Why should we want to maximize happiness as compared with utility defined in some of these other ways?" Of course, since in fact everyone wants moments of happiness, happiness does have utility according to the other theories.

Is the happiness theory a form of desire theory? Strictly not: for utility is assigned to an experience E at t not on the ground that it is wanted at t (or some other time), but on the ground that its *continuation* is wanted. The point is a fine one, however, and it would seem mistaken to place weight on it. How may the theory be compared with some of the other desire theories already considered? (1) It is like plan (c) in considering no desires for the occurrence S at any time before t_2, the moment at which S occurs. (There might be added any pleasures of anticipation.) (2) Later desires for the event S are taken into account only to the extent to which they play a role in moments of pleasant retrospection about S; and what is taken into account is not the intensity of the desire for S, but only the intensity of the pleasantness of the reflection about S. Thus no latent regrets, but only actual pangs of regret (and the same for being-glad-that) are taken into account, so that if a person is the type who never looks back, the event that one would regret if one did look back is not made worse by the mere "aversion after the event." In this respect the happiness theory is rather like desire-theory dt_2. (3) The theory is unlike the desire theories in confining utility to moments of experience.

Why might the happiness theory be thought superior to the desire theories?

(1) It is consistent with the intuitions of the many philosophers who

174

have thought that only experience can be intrinsically worthwhile. (2) Pleasure is motivationally basic, in the sense that all our intrinsic desires for a state of affairs S owe their existence to an experience of S having been pleasant, or to something similar to S having been pleasant, or to the association of an experience of S with something else that was pleasant. In that sense Bentham was right that pleasure and pain are on the throne.[16] If the preceding discussions have been correct, the happiness theory is clear and relatively simple; and it does not suffer from the artificial and implausible features of the various desire theories. We might, then, be moved to go along with Sidgwick's statement (made, however, for a slightly different context): "If we are not to systematise human activities by taking Universal Happiness as their common end, on what other principles are we to systematise them? . . . I have failed to find – and am unable to construct – any systematic answer to this question that appears to be deserving of serious consideration."[17]

10

There is, however, another option for desire-theorists. They might take a pragmatic line and simply abandon the ideal of applying the theory to *all* types of cases. They might concede that the theory can be applied plausibly only in case the relevant desire is approximately stable (so that the artificial multiplying of moments by utility numbers is unnecessary). They might argue that these special situations are the most frequent and most important, and that the application of the notion of maximizing utility$_{DS}$ to them is all, or almost all, we need for practice. Or at any rate, if that is not all we need, it is all that it is possible to get, and we have to learn to live with no more. A person who is thus willing to cut his suit to fit the cloth might then go on to say that program dt_1 is a reasonably good guide to the action that will maximize utility$_{DS}$, for the cases to which that concept is applicable. Incidentally, it might be argued with some force that this program is not a bad rule of thumb for maximizing utility$_H$, especially if the desires are "corrected."

Some philosophers and economists appear to think that some form of desire definition of "utility" is much simpler than any form of the more traditional hedonist theory. An implication of the above reflections surely is that this confidence is misplaced.

16 I have surveyed the evidence for this thesis in *A Theory of the Good and the Right*, chap. 5.
17 Henry Sidgwick, *The Methods of Ethics*, 1922, p. 406.

C

Utilitarianism and rights

10

The concept of a moral right and its function

The noun "right," as in "a right to," appears in many contexts: in talk of legal rights, but also in talk about the rights of club members and at commencement ceremonies in talk of "the rights and privileges pertaining to that degree." But we also speak of "a moral right" (sometimes we say, "morally he has a right to"), and it is with the concept of a moral right that I shall be concerned. One might think that to have a moral right is just for it to be true that morally one ought to have a legal right.[1] This is not the case. We speak of a moral right when it is not thought that there should be a legal right, for instance, when we speak of the moral right of a child to equal treatment in a family. I shall assume that the concepts are distinct and focus on the concept of a moral right, ignoring the concept of a legal right.

It is important for the normative theory of moral rights that there be an adequate understanding of the concept. When it is thought that the concept is clear enough without explication, perhaps so simple as to be indefinable – as H. J. McCloskey appears to think when he explains "rights" simply as "entitlements"[2] – the way is left open to think, as some philosophers do, that a person's having a right can be a *reason* why someone else is morally obligated to do something. This is a mistake, which encourages thinking that a creditor X's having a *right* to his money from his debtor Y is a reason why Y morally ought to pay, on a par with X's needing the money being a reason why Y morally ought to pay. If one person's having a right *logically entails* some other person's(s') having an obligation, then it is just confusion to cite the right as a *reason* for the obligations; the fact of the right just is, or includes, the fact of the obligation.

But if we are to seek an explication of "moral right," we have to ask what kind of explication we are looking for, what we accept as criteria of a good explication. It seems unlikely that philosophers any longer hope

This paper is a revised version of a paper read at a conference on rights, held at Virginia Polytechnic Institute and State University, May 22–25, 1980.
1 See the papers of John Kleinig and Christopher Arnold in E. Kamenka and Alice Tay, eds., *Human Rights* (New York: St. Martin's Press, 1978).
2 "Rights: Some Conceptual Issues," *Australasian Journal of Philosophy*, 54, 2 (August 1976): 99–115.

to find an explication of any moral term in the sense of an obviously synonymous expression that analyzes the meaning of the term being explained, in the way "a brother of my father or my mother" explicates the term "my uncle." It is true that there are some helpful things to be said in the case of "moral right," of this sort; we can point out that "her moral rights" means the same as "those things to which she has a moral right," but this fact only reminds us that the basic term to be explained is "has a moral right to." And the same for some other expressions that can be helpfully explained in terms of other moral expressions, for example, "moral obligation *to*" in terms of "moral obligation regarding" and the notion of a beneficiary, although in this case the explanation is subject to debate. But in other cases, and "a moral right to" is one, we must be satisfied with something else, a showing that the explaining expression is an *adequate replacement* that contains only words with which we are relatively comfortable, words that we understand better. But in what sense "adequate replacement"? A full answer to this question would be a long story; I shall abstract from this just two remarks. First, a necessary condition for adequacy is that speakers of the language – at least those who have reflected on the nature of morality and its function in society, the place of moral discourse in morality, and the psychology of moral commitments in the individual – will not find any question they might raise with the old unexplained terminology which use of the definition or explanation would prevent them from raising. Second, a replacement is more convincing if it enables us to understand the role the term has in moral discourse, why there needs to be such a term in our moral vocabulary. In this we may largely agree with a passage in Rawls, where he says, "explication is elimination: we start with a concept the expression for which is somehow troublesome; but it serves certain ends that cannot be given up. An explication achieves these ends in other ways that are relatively free of difficulty."[3]

We want, then, an adequate replacement for the term "a moral right to," which uses terms more clear, less troublesome, more satisfactory than our definiendum. Which kinds of terms qualify as "less troublesome"? One thing we might do is view terms like "morally wrong," "moral obligation to," "moral duty," as terms that are better off than "a moral right to," just as, if we were attempting to analyze the concept "a legal right" we might take the term "legal duty" as being less troublesome. But we need to make a distinction between what we may call a "surface" definition of "a moral right," that is, one which makes use of ordinary moral terminology ("right"/"wrong" etc.) in an *unexplained*

3 *The Theory of Justice* (Cambridge, MA: Harvard, 1971), p. 111.

sense, plus nonmoral concepts, just as "legal right" might be explained in terms of "legal duty" in an unexplained sense. That is, a surface definition is one that does not require us to analyze the concepts of the morally right or obligatory, but can just take them for granted. (In the legal case, a surface definition of "legal right" might use "legal duty," but not go into the question whether "legal duty" has to be defined in terms of power or sanctions, or in some more complex way.) In contrast, a "deep" definition of "a moral right" requires us to go back a level, so as to give an analysis of "morally wrong" and "morally obligatory." The analysis need not be complete, in the sense of giving an account in terms of an "empiricist" vocabulary, say the language of science or of fact statement, or perhaps performative terms like prescriptive ones. (I shall in fact suggest alternative paths: one that employs the term "justified" in a further unexplained sense, and one that replaces this term by an expression that clearly belongs to an "empiricist" language. It might be suggested that "justified" is itself a "moral" term, so that explanation that employs "justified" qualifies as a "surface" explanation. It does not seem worth while to pursue this point.) Why might one insist on a "deep" analysis? One answer is that in the end philosophy must go all the way in any case, and there is no harm in making a start. But another answer, more important for the present context, is that there are certain things it is important to do that it is impossible to do short of going beyond a surface definition. In particular, there are at least three such things. First, the concept of a moral right requires a more elaborate system of explanatory notions, as compared with "moral duty" – notions that help to explain how "a moral right" plays a special role and is useful in an optimal moral vocabulary. Second, such analysis will make clear why the term "a moral right" is closely related to "moral obligation" and has implicative relations to it; it will also show why we have to introduce the notion of a *prima facie* right. Third, the deeper analysis will help clarify and answer some perplexing questions about moral rights, for instance the relation between "has a moral right to" and "it is causally possible that."

I A FRAMEWORK FOR ANALYSIS OF MORAL TERMS

As a first step toward a "deep" analysis of "*X* has a moral right to *Y* against *Z*," let us consider a conceptual framework I suggested, in a recent book,[4] as adequate for the analysis of moral language generally. The general idea of this framework can be made clear by considering the expression "It is *morally obligatory* for *X*, in his circumstances, to do

4 *A Theory of the Good and the Right* (New York: Oxford, 1979), chap. 10.

A." I proposed, as a first approximation to an explication of this phrase, that it be construed as "A *justified moral code* for *X*'s society would require a person to do *A* in his circumstances." To understand this, we need to have the concepts of a social moral code and of a code being justified. Let us begin with the former.

It seems relatively uncontroversial that for there to be a social moral code of a certain kind is for something to be true of the *personal* moral codes of the society's members – all of them, or most of them, or on the average. We need not worry about the details of this; the more important question is what it is for an individual to subscribe to a certain personal moral code or to a certain "plank" of the social code. I urged, in the book, that a primarily *motivational* account be given of this. The type of account can be explained by an example: what it is for a person to subscribe to the wrongness of hurting another person unnecessarily. I suggest that what it is for a person to subscribe to the wrongness of this is for him (a) to be motivated to avoid hurting any other person, for no further reason and especially for no reason of personal advantage; (b) to tend to have uncomfortable emotions, guilt feelings, if he comes to believe he has hurt another person without justification or excuse (these last notions also requiring to be spelled out motivationally, a task here omitted for lack of space); and (c) to tend to disapprove of persons when he believes they have hurt others without justification or excuse. (There may be other aspects typical of moral codes, for example, for a person to tend to *admire* persons who benefit others at cost to themselves over and beyond the call of duty.)

These motivational dispositions are the basic part of a person's subscription to a moral principle. There is also a cognitive part: that a person believes that his motivational dispositions are *justified*, in some way or other that is appropriate. We can generalize this account of what it is to subscribe to the principle that injuring another is wrong, to all the moral principles to which an agent subscribes.

The second concept employed in the above account of "moral obligation" was that of a social moral code being *justified* (or of a personal moral code, in particular the motivations constitutive of it, being justified). It is not essential, for the present purpose of explicating "has a moral right to," that there be agreement that there is one proper analysis of this concept. Some people may well have meant by "justified" something like "is commanded by God." We can leave this open. But it will be helpful to have one reasonably plausible suggestion in mind. What I suggested in the book was roughly that we may construe "A certain social moral code is justified for a society" as "A fully rational and informed person who expected to live in that society would support bringing about

182

and keeping in place that certain moral code, more than any other moral code, including none at all." Or, to spell this out in terms of motivations, "A fully rational and informed person who expected to live in that society would support bringing it about and keeping it true that the typical motivations of persons in that society would require/permit/prohibit certain actions" (as specified in the "certain moral code"). This explanation needs complication if one thinks that not all fully rational and informed persons would support the *same* moral code.

A point worth notice is that this conception of "justified" is not necessarily utilitarian – obviously, if the sense of that term is left open, but also if the suggested construction is adopted. For the suggested construction leaves one free to go with Mill and insist that long-range utility is the test for all institutions including morality, since a fully rational and informed person would support utility-maximizing institutions; but it also leaves us free, at least until after more consideration of what rational persons would do, to go in some quite different direction, for example, that of John Rawls or W. D. Ross.

If a framework like this (with or without the suggested special proposal for "justified") is correct for moral language in general, it is obvious that all moral terms have close affinities. For the claim just is that *every* moral statement can be construed, at least roughly and as a first approximation, to affirm that the moral code (motivational and emotional dispositions) justified for the society of the agent requires/permits/prohibits something. (The motivational/emotional dispositions have been depicted so far as dispositions directed at acts or agents in view of their acts – sometimes, say, in the case of guilt feelings, the agent being the person who has the attitude – but we shall see shortly that there are other possible directions.) It follows from this view of moral language in general that "has a moral right to" must be construed as functioning to claim that some emotional/ motivational dispositions, partly constitutive of the moral code of a society, are justified.

Reasoning from some metaethical thesis about moral language in general to a conclusion about rights language may seem dubious. But the reasoning appears not so shocking, or at least not very novel, when we consider some recent metaethical theories. Charles Stevenson did not develop a theory of rights language, but since he held that moral language expresses moral approval or disapproval and that moral approval and disapproval are the only moral attitudes, presumably he would construe rights talk as expressive of the same thing, in one way or another. Much the same may be said of the prescriptivist theory of R. M. Hare. Hare regards moral statements as primarily prescriptions, expressing desires and other motivational/emotional attitudes, directed at agents. Rights language, as he makes explicit in his recent book, can be construed only in a similar fashion, and accordingly he regards "a moral right to" as definable in terms of "moral obligation."[5] Much the same may be said of the ideal-observer theory. Moral terms are construed by it as assertions that an "ideal observer" would have an attitude of approval or disapproval toward something, or experience a "requiredness-characteristic" in connection with it. If we reflect on how the ideal-observer theory might construe moral-rights language, it appears that there are no plausible options other than to construe it, roughly, in terms of the approval/disapproval (etc.) of the "ideal observer" toward someone or some act. Even a nonnaturalist, who thinks that "duty" or "is right" or "fitting" designates a simple property, will presumably at least want to define "has a right to" in terms of this property, in order to avoid a proliferation of simple properties.

If we think that all moral terms have close affinities, in the sense of being adequately construed in terms of roughly a common conceptual framework, it will not be surprising that many philosophers have thought that "X has a moral right to Y against Z" can be explained roughly as "Z has a moral obligation to X with respect to Y." I shall be suggesting, however, that this type of proposal is not wholly adequate.

II AN IMPLICATION, AND A FIRST DEFINITION OF "RIGHTS"

The general conception set forth so far has an interesting implication; at least it does if we suppose that the several motivational/emotional dispositions of individuals who subscribe to a moral code may vary in strength, as a result of their psychological genesis say through conditioning, and also are not indefinitely strong. Of course, it is logically possible that some moral motivations be so strong that in no circumstances could any contrary motivation control behavior. But we do say, perhaps untruly, that everyone has his price, and if this is true it implies that some set of selfish motivations will in conceivable circumstances be strong enough to outweigh any moral motivation. And this is probably as it should be, for it would not be cost-productive for society to go to the length necessary to build into children moral motivations that would win out in absolutely every contest with selfish motives. So moral motivations must be of finite strength, and presumably differ somewhat in strength, among themselves. Thus the moral motivation

5 *Moral Thinking: Its Level, Method and Point* (Oxford: University Press, 1981), chap. 9.

to render aid to a person in danger of death may normally be much stronger than the moral motivation to keep one's promise to attend a tea party. This conception raises two questions. The first is: Should we not expect that the motivation expressed by saying "X has a right to Y" will vary in strength from one right to another, so that we must find a way to say that in a corresponding sense the right to speak freely on political matters may be stronger than the right to own capital goods, and both weaker than the right not to be tortured? We must, I think, answer this question in the affirmative. And we certainly do want to say things of this sort; for rights often conflict with one another (for example, the right to free speech and the right not to have hatred preached against one), and when they do we wish to say that one right is somehow weightier than the other. The second question is: Must the motivation expressed by rights language always be stronger than moral motivation of any other sort? For instance, if there should be a conflict between my right to speak and the national security, is the right always going to be stronger? To this the answer should very likely be negative, although the motivation concerned with free speech will be stronger, in a justified moral system, than marginal considerations of public welfare. (I shall propose to incorporate this fact in the explication of "moral right.") From all of this it follows that we shall have to say that all rights (at least, all but at most one, or at least one small set of rights that cannot conflict with one another) are only *prima facie*, not only in the sense that they may be overridden by other rights in certain circumstances, but also that they may be overridden by other moral considerations that are not matters of rights at all. Thus I find Joel Feinberg's terminology at least awkward, when it leads him to say that "the notion of a '*prima facie* right' makes little sense" and that "Rights . . . do not differ in degree; no one right is more of a right than another."[6] It would be difficult for a moral philosopher to jettison the concept of *prima facie* obligation/duty, and, if rights language is as closely related to this as I suggest, it is better to employ corresponding terminology in the case of moral rights. In any case, we may say a person has a right to X, and someone also a right to Y, but the justified motivation in the two cases might well be of different strengths. There is no point in obscuring this fact by a choice of terminology. The motivation theory of moral codes implies all this. That is one reason for moving to a "deep" analysis of "rights."

There is a point, in the literature of moral philosophy at least since the

6 Joel Feinberg, "The Nature and Value of Rights," in David Lyons, ed., *Rights* (Belmont, Calif.: Wadsworth, 1979), p. 88.

work of W. D. Ross, about *prima facie* moral obligations and their force, which we may well bear in mind for the case of rights. Ross pointed out that if we have a *prima facie* obligation, say, to keep a promise, and this obligation is overridden by another *prima facie* obligation of greater stringency, the situation is not, or at least often is not, as if the first *prima facie* obligation had not ever existed. For one thing, the agent properly will feel compunction about the situation. For another, he may have a new obligation arising out of the total situation, perhaps to apologize or explain or do something to make it up to the person the promise to whom has been broken. The same seems properly said of moral rights. Some philosophers have said that, if a right has been *violated*, that is, infringed *without* justification, then *compensation* of some sort is due the right-holder. We need not consider here whether this is so, and if so, how much compensation is due. But suppose a right is infringed, but *with* justification, because of some conflicting right or some weighty consideration of public interest. *Then* is something due him? It does seem that matters are not the same as if the person had never had a right at all. At least what Ross said about the infringement of a *prime facie* obligation holds also for this context; and perhaps more so.

If we accept all this, how might we, as a first approximation, construe the expression, "*X* has a moral right to do, have, or enjoy *Y*"? Let us begin with a brief formulation of essentially Mill's account in *Utilitarianism,* and then rephrase this into the conceptual scheme I have been suggesting. Mill thinks that, when *X* has a right to do, have, or enjoy *Y*, several things are true. (1) Some person or persons *Z* have a moral obligation to do something for, or avoid doing something to, *X* (and, of course, others in the same situation, for example, all adult women). (2) This moral obligation must be relatively *strong*, a high-priority obligation. (3) The obligation is to provide some benefit or avoid some harm or deprivation for *X* (or possibly others, too, on the nomination of *X*). We must widen the notion of "harm" to include states of affairs likely to produce later harm. Thus there might be an obligation to provide a trial by jury for everyone accused of having committed a crime. It is no direct harm not to have a trial by jury, but that device is a protection that decreases the probability of harm. (4) Mill thinks the benefit or harm must be important to *X*. So he concludes that rights (he *says* "justice") concern "certain classes of moral rules, which concern the essentials of human well-being more nearly, and are therefore of more absolute obligation, than any other rule for the guidance of life. . . . To have a right, then, is I conceive, to have something which society ought to defend me in possession of" (chap. v). We may take the last sentence to be saying that a *moral* right is something the *moral* code of society, if not the legal code, should defend one in possession of.

How, then, shall we transpose this into our motivation conception of the meaning of moral language? I suggest the following: "*X* has a right to *Y*" is to be construed as "It is justified for people in *X*'s society to be strongly motivated, overridingly so normally and always when in conflict with concern merely for marginal benefits in a given case, and to disapprove others who are not so motivated, to enable *X* – always by refraining from interference, but when necessary also by cooperating substantially to bring about the opportunity – to do, have, or enjoy *Y*, primarily because of the importance to people in *X*'s situation of being able to do, have, or enjoy things like *Y*." Usually the "substantial cooperation" will be to set up institutions that guarantee that persons in the position of *X* will be enabled to have *Y*.

We should notice that this terminology does not require that rightholders be morally compelled to take advantage of any opportunity to enjoy *Y* (neither does it exclude there being justifiable compulsion to do so, on other grounds); a person's right to education is in part for society to be obligated to provide the means for an education, but whether the person is compelled to take advantage of it is another matter unconnected with his having a right. Some writers have emphasized that it is characteristic of a right that the right-holder is free to waive, or not to exercise, the right if he chooses; our definition is intended to reach this result by saying that others are to *enable* a person to do or enjoy something, not to require him to.

III   A SECOND APPROXIMATION: AN AUGMENTED ACCOUNT

At an early point in the argument I said that "a moral right" needs a "deep definition." One reason I offered was that the concept of a "moral right" simply requires a somewhat *augmented* system of explanatory notions as compared with what is satisfactory for "moral duty." Let us consider this point.

I have asserted above that an individual's subscribing to a moral code consists primarily of his being motivated to avoid certain act-types for no further reason, to feel guilt if he himself acts contrariwise, to disapprove of others who do not show a standard level of motivation of this sort, and so on. But is this all? I now wish to suggest something else, harking back to a statement made by Ross[7] (which I echoed in *Ethical*

---

7 *The Right and the Good* (Oxford: Oxford University Press), 1930.

Theory[8]). Ross said, "There hangs about the notion of a 'right' the notion of its being not only something which one person should in decency respect but also something which the other person can in decency claim, and we feel that there is something indecent in the making of a *claim* to beneficence" (p. 53). David Lyons[9] developed the point more forcefully: He wrote that right-holders may "demand respect for them [their rights], to challenge those who threaten to infringe them, to be indignant and perhaps noisy or uncooperative when their rights are violated or threatened, and so on" (p. 184). Joel Feinberg, Richard Flathman, and Richard Wasserstrom have said, or implied, much the same thing.

How can we absorb this idea into the conceptual scheme developed so far? Morality, as I have described it, is a feature of agents – their motives, dispositions to feel guilt – and of the attitudes of the generality of other persons toward agents – approval or disapproval of them. In my account nothing has been said about the patients, the targets of the behavior of agents. I now suggest that we should extend our description of moral codes, to include something about patients. First, patients may have a disposition to *resent* infringements of the rules we have been talking about when these impinge on them, when they are the parties injured, or deprived, or threatened. Of course, people tend to resent *any* deliberate injury, so this reaction is not specific to rules of rights.[10] Second, persons who resent it when they are injured or deprived in one of these ways or even when they are threatened because of the nonexistence of institutions able to protect them, may also be inclined *not* to feel *ashamed or embarrassed* to protest on their own behalf. This feature need not occur, and in societies in which individuals have felt it is their place to be downtrodden, ill-treated, and so on, it was not the case. Of course there are several levels of this. The first is expression of resentment to the injuring party. A second level is public protest, or joining in a public protest, calling attention to the situation and inviting sympathy and support, particularly for the institution of legal devices for prevention of what has occurred or redress or punishment when it already has occurred.[11] A third level is that of passive disobedience, lack of cooperation, perhaps nonviolent economic pressure that causes inconvenience or discomfort on behalf of a cause. Finally there is violent action, willingness

---

8 Englewood Cliffs, NJ: Prentice-Hall, 1959, p. 441.
9 "Human Righs and the General Welfare," *Philosophy and Public Affairs*, 6, 2 (Winter 1977): 113–29; reprinted in Lyons, op. cit.
10 P. F. Strawson has interesting things to say about natural resentment in *Freedom and Resentment* (London: Methuen, 1974).
11 I have introduced emphasis on the role of legal devices here and in the definitions, where in earlier drafts it did not occur, in response to persuasive reasoning by Henry Shue and Paul Vernier.

to cause personal or property damage, in order to bring about a change in those who are infringing moral obligations or to bring about legal institutions to prevent or punish such infringements. Presumably the level of protest will normally correlate with the strength of the obligation being infringed and the seriousness of the damage or threat. The practice of company stores might elicit one level of protest, the practice of lynch law on members of a racial minority quite another.

A full description of this part of a moral system might be complex. For one thing, it would include a description not only of this resenting and being unashamed to protest on the part of targets of unjust action; it would also say something about the sympathetic attitudes of others toward this resentment and its expressions in protest. That is, third parties may not only disapprove of *agents* for what they do or fail to do; they may also have attitudes toward patients: sympathy, willingness to encourage or help in protest – and possibly disapproval of patients of an unjust act if they fail to resent the act and protest (or if they do not disapprove of such patients, they may fail to do so only if certain excusing grounds are present, such as that protest is too dangerous, or that the individuals have been brainwashed and cannot be expected to resent the maltreatment).

What I am suggesting is that, when these attitudes of resenting and protesting without embarrassment (and so on) are present, when a person is treated or not treated in a certain way – and when the attitudes of third parties toward these attitudes are roughly sympathetic – then it is natural to use the language of *rights*. So we might say that a person has a right when we think it justified, not only for some agent or agents themselves to feel averse to behaving toward him in a certain way and for third parties to feel disapproval of them if they do, etc., but when we think it is also justified for the right-holder to resent what has happened, protest without embarrassment, demand institutional protection where appropriate, and so on.

If one agrees with this, one will want to enlarge our first definition of "a moral right," so as to double its length. The definition would then read as follows: "*X* has a right to *Y*" is to mean: "It is *justified* for people in *X*'s society to be strongly motivated, overridingly so normally and always when in conflict with concern for merely marginal benefits in a given case, and to disapprove others who are not so motivated, to enable *X* – always by refraining from interference, but when necessary also by cooperating substantially to bring about the opportunity, when appropriate by legal means – to do, have, or enjoy *Y* primarily because of the importance to people in *X*'s situation of being able to do, have, or enjoy things like *Y; and* it is *justified* for *X* to feel resentment if he is hurt or

189

deprived because of the failure of others to have this motivation, and for him to feel unashamed to protest, and for him to take reasonable steps of protest, calculated to encourage others to have the motivation to enable anyone in a similar situation to do, have, or enjoy things like Y."

I suggest we have missed some of the content of rights affirmation unless we add this second half to our explication.

One might ask what the implication of the definition is for whether infants, fetuses, or animals have rights, in view of the fact that they do not feel resentment and cannot make a protest. The definition of course does not affirm that they must be *able* to do so; it says only that it is *justified* if they do. It seems, however, not to make much difference how this issue is resolved, since in any case people may be morally obligated to treat infants, fetuses, and animals in certain ways, irrespective of whether we say they have rights. One might think the issue matters in the case of a fetus, on the ground that, if it has no rights, then it has no rights that can override a pregnant woman's right to control her own body; but this conclusion is unwarranted, since her right to control her body can be overridden by other moral considerations, not necessarily only by the moral *rights* of others.

IV   A PROBLEM: "RIGHTS," "CAN," AND RELATIVISM

I promised earlier that the definition I put forward would be of help in clarifying and solving some puzzles, and held out this promise as a reason for going to a "deep" definition. I shall now try to make good on that promise. The puzzles I have in mind concern whether "a right" implies "can," and the sense in which a moral right is relative to a society. The two issues are interrelated.

One implication of the definition as stated is that there can be no moral right, not even a *prima facie* right, to Y in a society where there is *no* possibility of any person or group of persons in the society enabling X (and others with equal rights) to have Y, say an income above the poverty line. The reason is that there is *no point* in people having moral motivations of whatever strength, when *no* degree of motivation, however high, would bring about the goods or avoid the evils that are the whole point of the motivation being present. Where such motivation would be useless, presumably it is *not justified*, certainly not in the sense that a fully rational person who expected to live in that society would support a moral system with such motivation. In *that* sense "ought" implies "can," and "a right" implies "can" (not that there is a *logical* entailment; the implication, according to my special account of "justified," arises from the empirical fact that a fully rational being would not support something). For instance, suppose the society happens to be India, and we think that no amount of moral motivation on the part of even everyone in India would make it possible either now or in the near future to provide everyone with a decent livelihood. Then our definition implies that there is now no moral right to this in India. This conclusion is embraced by various philosophers.

It could be, however, that if the moral motivation in India were strong enough, means could be found to provide a decent livelihood for everyone, but possibly at a cost to other things, say police or fire protection, which we might also think to be a right. Or it might be thought there are rights to reproduce, or to be protected by an army or by atomic weapons, and that these rights conflict with a prospective right to a decent livelihood. In that case we might be able to say that there is a *prima facie* right to a decent livelihood in India, but, depending on the rights to other things which a fully rational person would want to support if he expected to live there, there might be no right, *everything considered*, to a decent livelihood.

It follows, of course, that what is a moral right, *prima facie* or everything considered, in the United States of America may not be so in India. This kind of relativism seems required by the conceptual framework I have outlined. This result is consistent with the thought, which seems plausible, that what is a right in a society must depend on the institutional and economic structure of the society.

Nevertheless, we may be left a bit uncomfortable with the conclusion that there may not even be a *prima facie* right, in India, to a decent standard of living. For we are well aware that there is something that *could* be done, even if not by the effort of residents of India alone. There could be a unified effort on the part of other people in the world, perhaps via some kind of world organization, the result of which could be, at least if there were cooperation by the Indians (say by restricting the birth rate), tomorrow or sometime in the near future, a decent level of welfare for everyone in India. Is there any way in which this fact, if it is a fact, could imply that there is now a right to a decent standard of living in India? Not, I think, within precisely the conceptual framework I have outlined. But there are other frameworks within which it would, one of them only slightly different from the one I sketched. Let me develop this latter possibility. I have been talking of the social moral code of "the agent's society" and of the question of which moral code would be justified in the sense that it would be supported for *that society* by fully rational persons who expected to live in *it*. Now it is well known that there are problems with identifying "the agent's society." If we restrict

191

our attention to primitive societies, maybe not. But if we ask what is the society of a professor at the University of Michigan, the atmosphere gets murkier. Moreover, a person might say that some moral problems are essentially *worldwide* problems, and that we don't get at them intelligently by talk of what would be a good moral code for a particular society. Indeed, it can be said that there are some moral problems that even young children must be taught to think about in worldwide terms. Now, if we can identify some moral problems of this sort, we might wish to change our conceptual framework so that "the agent's society" becomes relative to the scope of the problem in question. In that case we might say that a moral right, relative to a problem of worldwide scope, in India is *the same* as the same moral right everywhere else. Thus a person might say that there is a right in India to at least the diet and housing that a given individual could purchase for say eight rupees a day, because a fully rational person, who knew how world resources might be allocated (with all the problems of stimulus for production, etc.), would support a world-wide moral code requiring at least that level of real income for everybody everywhere, perhaps because that institutional structure for allocating resources would maximize the general expectable welfare or utility. So, with this small change in the conceptual scheme, we can arrive at some worldwide rights, and the relativity of rights to a particular social system, for matters that are essentially world problems, would be rejected. According to the suggested change, "a right" still implies "can," but the locus of the power (can) has been broadened to include society as a whole.

The possibility of such a change raises a rather deep issue of strategy. Should our conceptual scheme be changed to accommodate our moral intuitions "in reflective equilibrium"? In the present case that proposal might not be very useful, because different philosophers appear to have different intuitions about what is a moral right in India, and about which group is the group that must have the "ability" in order for there to be a right within that group. In any case, however, there are reasons for modifying a general conceptual scheme in metaethics other than sensitivity to moral intuitions. One possibility is that such changes are called for by an adequate view of what moral codes are, how they work, how far at present a given code may transcend the borders of one "society" owing to the level of communication, the extent to which moral problems are international in scope, when a moral rule covering a given problem can be of benefit only in the context of a rather specific set of institutions, and how a rational person would appraise all this, and what strategy he would adopt for supporting one or more moral codes in order to achieve his ultimate objectives. All of this is doubtless a long story, at which I can only hint.

One advantage of insisting on a "deep" analysis of "rights" terminology is that it brings all these problems out into the open and shows that whether we are to say there is a moral right to a decent standard of living in India is not a simple matter.

V THE FUNCTION OF THE LANGUAGE OF MORAL RIGHTS

At the outset of this paper, I suggested that one feature of an explication that makes it more plausible as an "adequate replacement" is that it makes possible an understanding of the function the explicandum plays in moral discourse, why it is useful for there to be such a term in the language.

It appears that "rights" talk does have a role different from that of talk of duties, obligations, right and wrong, and that our explication brings out nuances of the meaning which make clear why.

First, the account of "a right" sets at the center what it is that a person is to be enabled to do, have, or enjoy, and that it is important for the welfare of the person. We might call this the "focusing" function of rights talk, as contrasted with talk of duty or obligation. Consider the right of women to equal treatment. Corresponding to this right are a great many duties, the legal ones of which are gradually being spelled out in court and administrative decisions. "It is one's duty to employ the best qualified person for a certain job, irrespective of sex." "It is a husband's duty not to press menial chores on his wife, but to seek for her equal opportunities for development." We could go on and on. A manifesto of the women's movement might list innumerable duties of men, corporations, or government, in respect of women. But such a list would lack focus. After all there is a target here: that women have an equal opportunity for a good life. That is what all these duties are aimed at; the duties are what other people must do if women are to have an equally good life. In talking of a right to equal opportunity, we focus attention on the intended good. The above explication makes this clear. (So would an explication that identified rights with interests, but this explication would be overly simple. For not every interest is a right; I have an interest in my own happiness, but I have a right only to freedom to pursue it. Only those interests are rights that other people can do something to secure, and which it is desirable for the moral code of society to be invoked in securing.) Listing the various things persons must do, or avoid doing, in order not to harm or threaten or deprive others is by implication to list rights; but listing these does not provide much of a manifesto. But if we focus, as rights talk does (according to our explication), on important interests, or their necessary conditions, we can draw on human under-

193

standing and sympathy in a way we cannot do by just talking of duties and obligations. Talk of rights can start a revolution – but hardly talk of duties.

Second, the phrase "has a right to" implies quite strong moral force, as compared with "obligation." Notice that we can say, "I have an obligation to go to tea, since I promised I would," but we should only in very special circumstances say that the prospective host "has a right" to my appearance. Similarly we can say that one has an obligation to do something for a certain friend, but hardly that he has a right to it. (It is true that this difference may arise from something other than the normally overriding force of rights.) It would widely be agreed, now, perhaps partly because of the influence of Ronald Dworkin's writings, that rights have greater moral force than even substantial increments to the general welfare. This is consistent with supposing, of course, that the reason for the force of moral rights is the benefits of a moral system providing such guarantees. The above proposed explication makes this special moral force explicit.

It is true that it is only convenient, not necessary, that there be a special term with these connotations, as distinct from "moral obligation"; we could simply speak of certain obligations as being very strong.

There is a third benefit of the language of rights, in that, if the explication is correct, it encourages the patients of right-infringing actions to feel resentment, to protest, to take a firm stand. To say "You have a right to this" seems to imply that these attitudes/behaviors are justified.

It hardly needs pointing out that encouragement of the oppressed and maltreated to stand up in their own behalf is beneficial for society, in the long run. The sympathy of impartial spectators may be a fairly strong motivation in the direction of beneficent change, but it may not be enough, or the reflections that excite it may not occur, where there is not the support of protest by those who are injured or deprived or threatened. The history of rights movements shows that sympathy, even of enlightened people, moves the public conscience or at least custom and legal institutions only slowly when there is not supporting motivation from protests, nonviolent noncooperation, and sometimes violent action. Historically talk of "rights" has occurred in the context of complaint or revolution or lawsuits. Some civil rights leaders have asserted that no gain for their cause has come from morality or altruism of the well off; gains come only from the action of the oppressed. Doubtless this goes too far: witness aid to underdeveloped nations and future generations, and laws about cruelty to animals. Nevertheless the moral system is not healthy and effective unless both sympathy for the oppressed *and* a readiness of the threatened to protest on their own behalf cooperate in social change.

One may say that what is important is not the *concept* of rights, but that the oppressed are resentful and willing to protest, and do so without any feeling of shame – or even disapprove of those among the oppressed who do not speak out. One may say that the *concept* of something's being one's right is not important. This sounds plausible. But the concept and the attitudes are not so easily pried apart. For, if the explication is right, to say that someone has a right is to say, in part, that these attitudes on the part of the oppressed are *justified*. And to say that an attitude is justified is to support it, just as to think an attitude is unjustified is to undermine it. We may wonder how many civil rights leaders would have taken a strong stand in protest if they had believed that their resentment etc. was *un*justified. The very concept of moral rights, then, seems to play a role in the development of a more humane morality and society.

It seems, then, that an optimal conceptual scheme for morality needs the notion of a moral right in the sense our explication makes explicit.

11

Utilitarianism and moral rights

I

Virtually all philosophers now agree that human beings – and possibly the higher animals – have moral rights in some sense, both special rights against individuals to whom they stand in a special relation (such as a creditor's right to collect from a debtor), and general rights, against everybody or against the government, just in virtue of their human nature. Some philosophers also think, however, that anyone who is a utilitarian ought not to share this view: There is a fundamental incompatibility between utilitarianism and human rights. Most utilitarians, of course, have not thought there is such an incompatibility. John Stuart Mill, for instance, espoused utilitarianism at the same time that he defended rights to free speech and freedom of action except where it injures others. In what follows I wish to explore some reasons recently put forward to show that the utilitarian who wishes to affirm that there are moral rights faces a serious logical problem; and I shall argue that further analysis shows the alleged difficulty is unreal.

The first thing to notice is that utilitarianism is a general normative theory *either* about what is *desirable*, or about what conduct is *morally right*, but in the first instance not a theory of rights at all, except by implication. A philosopher can be a utilitarian without offering any definition of "a right" and indeed without having thought about the matter. It is true that *some* definitions of "a right" are so manifestly incompatible with the normative theses of utilitarianism that it is clear that a utilitarian could not admit that there are rights in that sense. For instance, if someone says that to have a right (life, liberty) is for some sort of thing to be secured to one absolutely, though the heavens fall, and that this is a self-evident truth, then it is pretty clear that a utilitarian will have no place for rights in his sense. Again, if one follows Hobbes and says, "Neither by the word *right* is anything else signified, than that liberty which every man hath to make use of his natural faculties according to right reason," one is not going to be able to accept a utilitarian normative theory, for a utilitarian is not going to underwrite a man's absolute liberty to pursue his own good according to his own judgment, in the way Hobbes had

196

in mind. Hobbes can use the word "a right" as he pleases, but the utilitarian will say that a man exercising his rights in that sense may be immoral. So, while some definitions of "a right" are such that a utilitarian will deny that there are rights in that sense, the major definitional views being advocated today, say among H.L.A. Hart, David Lyons, and Joel Feinberg, do not imply that there being rights in their sense is incompatible with utilitarianism. So I think it is fair to say, although I think not *quite* true to say, that utilitarianism is neutral about the major proposals today for the definitions of "a right," not committed to any.

What concept of "a right," then, shall we bear in mind for our discussion of utilitarianism and rights? What normative affirmation, not making use of the term "a right," corresponds to the claim we, now, are normally making when we say "X has a moral right against Z to do, have, or enjoy Y," at least when this expression is taken in its most important sense? I suggest the following: "Some Z – either individual or individuals or sovereign body – has a strong moral obligation *not overridable by marginal or even substantial but only by extreme demands of welfare, both* to refrain from interfering with X's having or doing or enjoying Y, *and* to *enable* X to do, have, or enjoy Y; *and* it is not wrong for X to feel resentment if he is hurt or deprived because of the failure of Z to discharge that obligation, and for him to be unashamed to protest, and there is some obligation for X to take reasonable steps of protest, calculated to encourage persons to discharge that obligation in this and similar situations."

Our main question is whether utilitarianism has room for moral rights as explained, that is, for affirmations of moral obligations of the kind stated. Of course, the answer to this question will depend on what one means by "utilitarianism." The theory is usually defined as a general normative theory about what actions are morally right or wrong. I am not going to define it this way, however, to avoid begging some important questions. So I am going to follow J.S. Mill (who in this is seconded by David Lyons), who wrote: "The utilitarian doctrine is that happiness is *desirable*, and the only thing, desirable, as an end; all other things being desirable as means to that end." Mill then goes on to offer a proof of this doctrine, and having done his best on this, he says: "If so, happiness is the sole end of human action, and the promotion of it the *test* by which to judge of all human conduct; from whence it necessarily follows that it must be the *criterion of morality*, since a part is included in the whole" [italics all mine]. It is also the test of legal institutions, so that a legal system will be adjudged desirable if it will produce (or probably produce) maximal happiness.

Utilitarianism, then, is a general theory about when actions and institutions are (instrumentally) *desirable;* and the idea is that they are so in view of their promotion of actual or expectable happiness, or better, actual or expectable *utility.*

There are, of course, various brands of utilitarianism. For one thing, utilitarians differ among themselves about what is to count as happiness or utility. Some say the only thing having utility is a state of mind, one a person likes for itself at the time he has it, the idea being that a state of mind is happier or more utile the more strongly the person likes it. Other utilitarians say that *any* state of affairs *wanted* for itself by a person – or sometimes a rational and fully informed person – has utility, and that one state of affairs has *more* utility than another just if the person *prefers* it. Still other persons (sometimes called "ideal utilitarians") think that we know that various states of affairs are good in themselves, independently of anyone wanting or liking them. I would wish myself not to count this last view as utilitarian since it can turn out to be only semantically different from a deontology such as that of W. D. Ross. But I believe the quarrel between the first two views can also be ignored now, as unimportant for present purposes.

A second disagreement among utilitarians, however, is more important. So far I have said that the basic idea of utilitarians is that acts and institutions are to be appraised as desirable if they are productive of utility or happiness (or expectable utility or happiness). So far I have said nothing at all about *morally right* and *wrong* acts. But utilitarians always do bring in a concept of the morally right and wrong somewhere, and then wind up with different proposals about which acts are morally right or wrong. Some of them say that an *act* is morally right, or wrong, depending directly on the utility (or expectable utility) of *its* consequences. This view, at present usually called "act-utilitarianism," has been held by J. J. C. Smart and many others. A second species of utilitarianism holds that the moral rightness of an act is much less directly related to utilities. This second theory, often called "rule-utilitarianism," has itself several varieties, and I shall now describe just one that I find most convincing. First, this view affirms that a morality, or moral code, for a society is *most desirable* (here it follows the basic idea that desirability of an institution is fixed by utility) if and only if there is no other moral code, the acceptance of which – in the sense of substantial prevalence of which among adults of a society – would have greater expectable utility, when we count the cost of getting the code accepted and kept so, as well as its total effects. Now this second theory goes on to hold that the moral rightness of an individual act is fixed by – or even *defined* as – whether it is permitted or required by the *most desirable* (not necessarily the *actual*) moral code for that society. This theory, incidentally, seems to have been held by Mill. Notice that it holds that an act is not made morally right by the utility of *its* consequences; Mill would say that the act whose own consequences are most desirable is just the "expedient" act, not necessarily the morally right one. What I mean by talk of the "moral code permitting or requiring" something is this: A person's moral code *requires* him to do something, say *A,* if and only if (1) he has strong, normally overriding, motivation to perform acts of the type *A* for no further reason and especially reason of self-interest, (2) he tends to feel guilt if he fails to do *A* without justification or excuse, (3) he tends to think less of others not motivated to perform acts of the type *A* up to a standard level, and (4) he thinks all the foregoing dispositions on his part are justified in some appropriate way.

Now, if we adopt a *rule*-utilitarian theory of the morally right and wrong, or the morally obligatory, of this type, then it seems to me clear that there is no *inconsistency* in claiming that people have rights, that is, in subscribing to the thesis about obligations which I suggested is what rights-claims amount to. Where could the inconsistency be, if one is a utilitarian in *this* sense, in holding that some persons Z have strong moral obligations, *not overridable by marginal or even substantial but only by extreme demands of welfare* (in the case at hand), both to refrain from interfering with *X*'s doing *Y* and to enable him to do *Y,* and so on as stated earlier? To say this is only to say that the most desirable moral code for the society would require that one refrain from interfering with others' doing certain things, and positively to *enable* them to do them, sometimes when so doing will not maximize expectable utility in a particular situation. Quite obviously there is no *inconsistency* in a rule-utilitarian affirming that people – and animals – have moral rights. So, if utilitarians have some problem about rights it must lie deeper.

Before turning to possible "deeper" difficulties, let me make just one point favorable to the utilitarian view, that it tells us, in principle, *how to find out* what are a person's rights, and how stringent they are, relative to each other, which is much more than can be said of most other theories, unless reliance on intuitions is supposed to be a definite way of telling what a person's rights are. How does one do this, on the utilitarian theory? The idea, of course, is that we have to determine whether it would maximize long-range expectable utility to include recognition of certain rights in the moral code of a society, or to include a certain right with a certain degree of stringency as compared with other rights. (For instance, it might be optimific to include a right to life with more stringency than a right to liberty and this with more stringency than the right to pursue happiness.) Suppose, for instance, one wants to know what should be the *scope* of the "right to life." Then it would be proper to inquire whether the utility-maximizing moral system would require people to refrain from taking the life of other adults, more positively to support life by providing adequate medical care, to abstain from life-termination for seriously defective infants or to refrain from abortion, to require abstaining from assisting a person with terminal illness in ending his own life if he requests it, to refrain from assisting in the discharge of a sentence of capital punishment, or to refrain from killing combatants in war time and so on. If one wants to know whether the right to life is stronger than the right of free speech on political subjects, it is proper to inquire whether the utility-maximizing moral code would prefer free speech to the cost of lives (and in what circumstances). It may, of course, be raised as an objection to the theory that it is difficult, or impossible, actually to carry through the assessments of comparative utilities which this program involves.[1] That is a large issue, but I do not propose to worry about it in the present context. I shall also not worry about a somewhat opposite objection, to the effect that we know what utilitarianism permits or requires well enough, and some of the actions it permits or requires are manifestly immoral. For instance, it is said that there are conceivable circumstances in which the utilitarian would condone slavery. These objections seem to me just unsympathetic, although they do need to be taken up one by one. I think Professor Hare's recent paper, "What is wrong with slavery?,"[2] says most of what should be said in defense of the utilitarian on that score. I would concede that the problem of just distributions is worrisome, but it has been much discussed, and there is no point in saying more about it here, in the short time at my disposal. I do not claim to be in the majority, in my optimism for the utilitarian program; I take note, with respect, of Professor Lyons' recent remark that "the idea that Utilitarianism might account for *moral* rights would generally be rejected, even by those who assume that utilitarianism can give some account of legal rights."[3]

II

Let me now turn to one of what I regard as the "deeper" problems, one that agitated Sidgwick in the penultimate chapter of *The Methods of Ethics*, and comprises the central objection to utilitarianism in two subtle

1 Richard A. Posner, "Utilitarianism, Economics, and Legal Theory," *Journal of Legal Studies*, 8 (1979) 103–40.
2 R. M. Hare, "What Is Wrong with Slavery?" *Philosophy and Public Affairs*, 8 (1978–9) 103–21. See also David Lyons' remarks in "Nature and Soundness of the Contract and Coherence Arguments," in Norman Daniels, ed., *Reading Rawls* (New York: Basic Books, Inc. 1975), pp. 141–67.
3 David Lyons, "Utility as a Possible Ground of Rights," *Nous*, 14 (1980) 19.

recent papers by David Lyons.[4] As there presented it is a criticism of the utilitarian account of the *moral force* of *legal* rights, such as one's right not to have access to one's driveway blocked by a car whose owner does not have one's permission to obstruct.

I shall explain why, if successful, the argument also works against a utilitarian account of *moral* rights in general. Incidentally, as Lyons points out,[5] if successful the argument undermines not only a rule-*utilitarian* account of the moral force of rights, but also any other *rule*-theory of rights, say a theory according to which a person has a right if and only if a legal moral system that maximized *equality* would require it.

What is the Lyons argument? The gist is as follows. He agrees that the utilitarian will view the existence of certain *legal* rights as justified in the sense of being desirable – such as the right of Mary, the owner, having unobstructed use of her driveway. Such rights are desirable when the legal system involving them maximizes expectable utility. But then Lyons asks whether such *desirable legal* rights necessarily carry over into *moral* rights. More particularly, he asks whether, if Mary has a desirable legal right to unobstructed use of her driveway, she necessarily has a moral right, in the sense that others are morally bound not to obstruct her access, and that police officers are morally bound to give tickets to one who fails to respect her legal right. Lyons doubts this. He argues, rightly, that an act-utilitarian like Smart will take the legal rights as part of the background that fixes the utilities of various possible acts, but will hold that a person's *moral* obligation is just to maximize utility for that context – and that may involve infringing Mary's legal right to unobstructed access. He also argues, again rightly, that rule-utilitarianism of the kind I am defending need not imply that utility-maximizing legal rights or obligations carry over directly to moral rights or obligations. More is required; one sometimes has a moral obligation to ignore a legal obligation. What more is required? The answer is, *I* think, that it must be shown that a *moral system* requiring the relevant behavior would maximize expectable benefit. If a moral system requiring that one respect Mary's right to access to her driveway is shown to maximize expectable utility, then respect for her legal right has been shown also to be a moral right, with all the implications thereof for the moral duties or obligations of persons like policemen and would-be parkers of cars.

But here Lyons does not go along. Why? Lyons defines "utilitarianism" as the thesis that an *act or institution* is *desirable* if it serves the end of happiness. And I have adopted this definition in order not to beg questions

---

4 Ibid., and "Utility and Rights," in J. R. Pennock and J. W. Chapman, eds., *Ethics, Economics, and the Law. Nomos* 24 (New York: New York University Press 1982).
5 Lyons, "Utility and Rights," p. 131.

against Lyons. So the utilitarian will regard a happiness-serving legal system, or moral system, as *desirable*. Now Lyons is prepared to agree that *desirable* legal or moral systems may call for unimpeded access to a driveway. But he does *not* agree that when a desirable moral system calls for this, it is therefore morally obligatory on a person or police officer to conform his behavior to the requirements of the system. Why, he asks, does the fact that a certain moral *system* is *desirable* because happiness-maximizing prove that a person has a *moral obligation* to conform to it, especially if there is some other act he can perform that will produce *more* benefit? That a person does have such an obligation will follow only if there is some true proposition connecting being required by a *desirable moral system* and being morally obligatory. And Lyons questions whether a utilitarian needs, in consistency, to recognize any such proposition. A consistent utilitarian can regard both *acts and* moral systems as desirable if they maximize expectable utility, and therefore he can perfectly well hold that a utility-maximizing *act* has a claim to be recommended by the utilitarian, even though a moral system, which he also recommends, prohibits it. So, he thinks a utilitarian will be *consistent* if he says that it is all right, or even a duty, to park one's car obstructing Mary's driveway, if it will do more good, the fact of preferable contrary legal and moral systems notwithstanding. And that, he thinks, shows that legal and moral rights, as I have explained them, have no moral force for the utilitarian. Why not recommend good-producing *acts,* and also an institution maximally good-producing as a whole, even if the latter implies a prohibition of some good-producing acts?

It is easy to see that this reasoning carries over to important human rights. For suppose I have a right not to be tortured. Lyons can say that my prospective torturer can argue, in case he is clear it will maximize expectable utility for me to be tortured, that a utilitarian must regard this act as desirable, irrespective of the desirability of any legal or moral system. And why may he not claim to be morally in the clear?

What are we to say to this, if we are utilitarians? The form our thinking must take will naturally follow from how we have defined "utilitarianism." If we had *defined* it as some thesis linking utility-maximization with moral obligation, we would have one problem. But the definition I adopted earlier, in order to go along with Lyons (and Mill), was that utilitarianism is the thesis that an *act* or *institution* (including morality) is *desirable* if and only if it maximizes utility or expectable utility. Then, however, since "desirable" is one predicate and "morally right" is a different one, utilitarianism as a theory about what is desirable is not yet a theory about the morally right at all. So how do we get from the utilitarian's thesis about when something is desirable to *any* thesis about what is morally right? Historically utilitarians have taken different routes to close this gap. G. E. Moore, in *Principia Ethica*, held that a proposition linking the two is an analytic truth; in his *Ethics* he affirmed there is a true a priori synthetic proposition linking the two. Mill *may* have regarded the connection as a kind of conceptual point. He said

We do not call anything *wrong* unless we mean to imply that a person ought to be [it is desirable that he be] punished in some way or other for doing it – if not by law, by the opinion of his fellow creatures; if not by opinion, by the reproaches of his own conscience. This seems the real turning point between morality and simple expedience.[6]

So Mill connects the *morally wrong* with the *desirability* of being punished in some way, on the ground that we call something wrong only if "we mean to imply" something about desirability. None of these modes of making a connection seems very convincing.

There is, however, another line of thinking that connects desirability with moral obligation for the utilitarian, and in fact shows why a utilitarian requires a concept of moral obligation and what the concept will be. This line of reasoning goes as follows. We begin with the assumption that the utilitarian wants to maximize happiness in society. Now, he knows that one important means to his goal, indeed the only one within our control, is human actions with that effect. So he will want acts that produce welfare, ideally ones that will maximize it as compared with other options. Let us say, then, that he will want expedient acts as a means to happiness. But the thoughtful utilitarian will further ask himself how he can bring it about that people perform acts which, taken together, will maximize happiness. One way, and surely a good way up to a point, is to employ moral education to make people more sympathetic or altruistic; if they become so, they will tend to act more frequently to produce happiness in others. It looks, however, as if such educational encouragement of sympathy is not enough, mainly because people are ill-informed about the probable consequences of what they do, and in any case because the intent to do as much good as one can may lead to action at cross-purposes rather than to more beneficial cooperative behavior. So the utilitarian, who wants maximal happiness, will do something more than just try to motivate people to aim directly at it. It will occur to him that a legal system, with its sanctions and implicit directives, will both guide people what to do, and at the same time provide motivation to conform to the legal standards. He will want, with Bentham, a legal system which as a whole will maximize happiness by producing pro-social conduct at the least cost. Moreover, the imaginative utilitarian

6 J. S. Mill, *Utilitarianism*, chap. 5.

will also think of a *moral* system. It will occur to him that he can educate children to find certain *act-types* aversive, by conditioning; and that he can educate them to feel guilty if they act in some forbidden way except in special (excusing) circumstances; and that he can educate them to disapprove of others who act so, again except in special (excusing) circumstances. And, just as in the legal case, he will want a moral system which as a whole will maximize happiness by producing as much pro-social behavior as possible at least cost. All of this he will view as desirable, not for itself, but as a means to happiness.

Now where, in all this, will a utilitarian need a concept of the morally right or obligatory? One answer is that in the law it is convenient to have a term like "illegal" or "criminal" to mark the kinds of actions society is prepared to punish, barring absence of responsibility. And it is equally convenient, as the utilitarian will see, to have a term to mark the kinds of behavior it would maximize expectable happiness to have required or forbidden, by the moral system, on pain of some sort of penalty (except when justified or excused), perhaps only by the pangs of the agent's own conscience. Given that the utilitarian finds it desirable to have a moral system to guide and motivate pro-social behavior, he will need some term or other to classify those act-types that the utilitarian ideal will require through the medium of the moral code.

It is certain the utilitarian will need some term *other* than "expedient" or "desirable" for speaking about act-types and their status. For one thing, he does not want the moral system to *require* all ideally expedient behavior; for requiring has costs of its own: the cost of teaching, the occurrence of undesirable guilt feelings that may have psychological ill-effects, and so on. Moreover, an act which itself is expedient may not be of an act-type it is expedient to require; a given breach of promise may maximize utility, but it may not maximize utility to try to incorporate a recommendation of that specific act-type into a moral system. So the utilitarian will want a clear conception of the difference between desirable behavior and behavior required by the moral system.

The utilitarian, then, needs a term for required-by-optimal-moral-system, in the sense explained. If we co-opt the term "morally obligatory" for this purpose, we shall be following in Mill's footsteps, I think with better reasons than he gave.

Let us now return to Lyons' problem about a possible moral obligation not to obstruct Mary's driveway. Let us assume that the optimal moral system will at this point roughly support the optimal legal system. But now suppose a utilitarian driver knows that utility will be maximized if he obstructs the driveway; and suppose a police officer knows that most good will be done if he does not ticket the offender. What should these persons do, as consistent utilitarians? One thing should be clear: If the moral system has been carefully devised, there will not be *gross* disparity between what it requires and conduct that promises to maximize benefit. To avoid such disparity, an optimal rule-utilitarian moral code will contain "escape clauses." For instance, it will permit a driver to obstruct a driveway illegally when there is an emergency situation. But suppose there is a minor disparity between the requirements of the moral code and what will do most good: suppose Mary will have to walk to work tomorrow, but the gain in convenience to the person who obstructs her driveway will be greater than the loss to her. Will the consistent utilitarian then advise the driver to park illegally? Let us suppose the utilitarian has decided that a utility-maximizing moral code will *not* direct a person to do what he thinks will maximize expectable utility in a particular situation, but to follow certain rules – roughly, to follow his conscientious principles, as amended where long-range utility requires. If he has decided this, then it is inconsistent of him to turn around and advise individuals just to follow their discretion about what will maximize utility in a particular case. Of course, the utilitarian will want everyone to be sensitive to the utility of giving aid to others and avoiding injury; requirements or encouragement to do so are part of our actual moral code, and it is optimal for the code to be so. But once it is decided that the optimal code is not that of act-utilitarianism, the utilitarian will say it is desirable for a person to follow the optimal moral code, that is, follow conscience except where utility demands amendment of the principles of the code. So it seems the consistent utilitarian *will* conclude that there is a moral obligation not to obstruct Mary's driveway illegally, in accordance with the optimal code.

Now where does Lyons think the defect is in this reasoning? I think he means to insist that the utilitarian's ultimate aim is to maximize well-being, by *acts and* by *institutions.* He favors the whole moral system as a means to happiness. But now, suppose a utilitarian knows that his best means to maximize happiness *now* is to obstruct Mary's driveway, thereby ignoring the moral system. Would it not, Lyons seems to ask, be irrational and inflexible in him, as one who supports the moral system only because it will maximize happiness, to be unwilling to deviate from it, when he knows that so doing will maximize happiness? Should he not recommend this as preferable? I think this is Lyons' basic puzzle.

What is there to say in response to this? In the first place, the argument does not show there is no *moral obligation* not to obstruct the driveway. For the terms "moral obligation" and "morally wrong" have been introduced precisely to mark those occasions on which the optimal moral code requires or prohibits something. This was Mill's view. So, if Lyons thinks there is *not* a moral obligation not to obstruct the driveway, one would like to know what sense he is going to give to the term "moral obligation." It looks to me as if he may be confusing "moral obligation" with "desirable" or "expedient."

There is a second point. Lyons seems to be assuming that a consistent utilitarian can combine two strategies: first, *preaching* generally, publicly, even sometimes to himself, a morality that calls on him to avoid certain act-types like breach of promise, so that people are encouraged to feel guilty if they fail, etc.; and at the same time *doing*, and recommending to selected others to do, whatever reflection indicates will maximize expectable utility in any particular situation, irrespective of the requirements of the moral code he is preaching. (Incidentally Lyons might argue that a consistent egoist could adopt a parallel strategy. Any sort of *rule*-theory might be combined with a case-by-case strategy.) Now the question I want to raise is: Will the combined strategy probably maximize expectable utility as contrasted with the pure rule-strategy? Notice that one can't preach publicly the combined strategy; that would be to subvert the pure strategy one has already decided is the best moral system. The most one can do is practice it, and let a few of one's friends in on the secret. I believe the feasibility of this combined strategy deserves more attention. But, as Professor Gibbard has pointed out recently,[7] there will be some inevitable unhappy consequences of such a strategy. The strategy works only if one deceives others, keeps one's views a secret, operates in a way incompatible with mutual trust once it gets known. One essentially must be insincere in one's ethical discussions with others. And once one cannot have sincere discussions with other persons on ethical topics, one cuts one's self off from one of the most important sources of ethical knowledge: sincere dialogue with others. So it looks as if the combined strategy Lyons thinks a utilitarian might take would not be an effective one, as compared with the pure strategy of the rule-utilitarian.

I conclude that Lyons' argument ought to leave the utilitarian unmoved.

III

Lyons' objection, nevertheless, is very instructive. I believe that some forms of rule-utilitarianism, such as the kind I defend, are not open to his objection. But the theories of some rule-utilitarians are, I think, open to it. It is worthwhile to see which types of theory are open to it, and which are not. I propose to discuss this by commenting briefly on the

7 Allan Gibbard, "Utilitarianism and Human Rights," *Social Philosophy and Policy* I (1984), 100–2.

present theory of R. M. Hare, as most fully represented in his book, *Moral Thinking*.[8] His view is especially interesting because of an article in *Nomos*,[9] criticizing Lyons' attack on utilitarianism. The view also merits discussion because some philosophers find his combination of act- and rule-utilitarianism quite attractive.

Professor Hare is an act-utilitarian, although, as we shall see, he is also a rule-utilitarian of a sort. He is an act-utilitarian in the sense that he claims the *right* act is the act that will in fact maximize utility in the sense of happiness or desire-satisfaction. (He says that the *rational* act is one that, on the agent's evidence, is *probably* the right act.) Hare thinks that this kind of act-utilitarianism can be established by appeal to the *logical* features of normative language, of such words as "ought" and "must" and "right," to the effect that use of such terms is to issue a universal nonoverridable prescription, for all possible worlds. I think myself that one may entertain doubts about his theory here, but I do not wish to discuss that point, and shall simply take for granted that he is an act-utilitarian about "right."

But now Hare also thinks that a person who wants utility-maximizing acts performed, the strictly *right* acts, will want, as a means to this, to have a system of moral education that will instill in people, including the educator himself, certain moral principles different from the act-utilitarian principle, "Do what will maximize expectable utility!" The reason is that the thinking required to identify the really right act is complex; more information is required than agents are likely to have; the very complexity of the reasoning opens the agent to a temptation to favor his own interests, and so on. What the moral educator should do, then, is teach some rather general principles, prescribing certain *act-types,* roughly like Ross's list of *prima facie* obligations but doubtless somewhat more complex. These principles will be associated with strong feelings of repugnance toward prohibited acts, a disposition to feel guilt if one infringes one of the principles without excuse, a disposition to be indignant with others who do so, and so on. It is these principles, Hare thinks, that talk of "moral obligation" and "moral rights" expresses – "moral rights," by the way, being defined by him in terms of "moral obligation" almost exactly as I have done. Thus when we say, "You have a moral obligation to do *A*," what we are doing is issuing a universal prescription to do *A* in situations like yours, and at the same time expressing repugnance to failure to do it, and the other dispositions I have mentioned. Hare proposes that a utilitarian moral educator will select these principles so that people living

8 *Moral Thinking* (Oxford: Clarendon Press, 1982).
9 R. M. Hare, "Utility and Rights," in J. R. Pennock and J. W. Chapman, eds., *Ethics, Economics and the Law, Nomos* 24 (New York: New York University Press, 1982).

by them will *usually* bring about the *really right* act, or at least the *rational* act. An action that follows the agent's *own* moral principle Hare calls a "morally good" action.

Hare does not, however, say that following one's *actual* moral principles will necessarily lead to the right act. Our actual moral principles are often misguided. He cites as an example of a misguided principle the conviction that a woman's place is in the home.[10] For the most part our actual principles are ones that a utilitarian educator would recommend, but not all of them. So the fact that we have intuitive moral principles need not always relieve us of thinking about our moral principles, given the situation we are actually in, with knowledge that our principles are the product of a history not controlled by utilitarian educators. There is a further complication. Hare thinks that even the principles a utilitarian educator would try to instill in us are bound to be defective in certain ways, just because they have to be general and relatively simple so that the average person can learn them. As a result, intuitive moral principles will not tell us what to do when our principles give conflicting advice for a particular situation. Not never; for undoubtedly we can and do also have some intuitive moral principles about how to deal with *some* conflicts of principle. We are quite clear that we should break a promise to attend a tea party if it so happens we are in a position to save someone's life only if we miss the party. But other conflicts are not so easily resolved by the principles we have. Take, for instance, one Hare mentions, a conflict between the right to free speech, the right of racial minorities not to have hatred preached against them, and the right of the public to be protected against outbreaks of violence.[11] Or even in the case of the poor but well advertised sheriff, who has to decide whether to frame and hang an innocent man, or to allow five hostages to be killed by an angry mob.

What does Hare think we ought to do when faced with such conflicts of principle? His answer is that we should revert to *act-utilitarian* thinking, decide the conflict on the basis of which action will do the most good in the long run. Now I think this is the wrong recommendation. For one thing, it risks collapsing his two-tier theory of moral thinking into just a one-step theory, act-utilitarianism. In any case, surely there are other and more convincing options. First, since certain types of conflict of intuitive principle often recur, we can ask ourselves to which principle we, as utilitarians, would want the agent to give priority, in general. Our decision on this will define a second-order rule. Second, we

10 Ibid.
11 R. M. Hare, *Moral Thinking*, p. 155.

might try to resolve the conflict by considering whether our intuitive principle needs refinement. Suppose our intuitive principle is that there is a right to free speech, but on reflection we may see that morality should surely not, in general, protect inciting a riot, or a stampede in a movie theater, under the principle of protection of free speech. It is true that if we are to think along these lines, some time is needed, and decisions sometimes need to be made quickly; but if there is a conflict of intuitive principles, the agent will have to stop and think anyway, if he wants to know the objectively right thing to do. (We shall not blame him, of course, if he just does the best he can, as he is.) It is also true that the principle the thoughtful utilitarian will want to see prevail may not be one it is easy to teach everyone, but we should not underestimate the capacities of the beings who are able to master English grammar and vocabulary. And it is also true that, if the above two lines of thinking fail to resolve the problem, it may be the best rule to follow, *then,* is just to do the most good. But I believe long-range utility will be maximized if agents are taught that, in case of conflict of intuitive principles, they must try their best to find a *principle* they themselves, as utilitarians, would want to see prevail for the type of case at hand. We should recall that Hare does not think such reflection is beyond most people, since he thinks parents must indulge in it when trying to decide which moral principles to try to instill in the minds of their own children.

Hare's view is that we must have recourse to the basic principle of act-utilitarianism in three contexts: first, when deciding what moral principles to teach ourselves and our children; second, when our intuitive principles conflict with each other; and third, when an intuitive principle, even one an omniscient utilitarian educator would advise teaching, does not do its job very well in an individual case and will not lead to maximizing utility, primarily just because intuitive principles must be simple and unspecific in order to be learned and applied easily to a large range of cases. In this last situation, provided we are sure of our facts, Hare thinks we should desert our intuitive principles and decide on the basis of act-utilitarian considerations, by inquiring which act will do most good.

Now what is the implication of this for our basic question concerning Mary's driveway: whether there is a moral obligation for her legal right to be respected by the would-be parker and the policeman? What Hare says in his paper responding to Lyons is that both motorist and policeman should follow their intuitive principles in this case, and respect her rights. I do not believe, however, that this view is coherent with Hare's general theory. The reason is that Hare thinks that the *really* right thing to do is to maximize utility, so that if utility is *manifestly,* or very probably, increased by obstructing her driveway in this case, one is free, or even duty-bound, to ignore her legal rights. Just as one must resolve conflicts of intuitive principles by reverting to act-utilitarian thinking, so one may revert to act-utilitarian calculation where intuitive obligations conflict with manifest utilities.

In case anyone thinks Hare does not generally take this line, let me point out that he says[12] that people may "supplement" intuitive thinking, "when they have to and when they dare, with such archangelic [act-utilitarian] thinking as they are capable of." He says that good men,

the nearer they approach archangelic status [i.e., full knowledge of the facts], the more, on unusual occasions, they will be able to chance their arm and do what they think will be the right act in defiance of their principles; but most of us ordinary mortals will be wise to be fairly cautious. . . . For some . . . the greater danger may be too much rigidity in the applications of level–1 [intuitive] principles; but perhaps for more . . . it is a too great readiness to let them slip. It is a matter of temperament; we have to know ourselves (empirically); the philosopher cannot tell each of us which is the greater danger for him.[13]

A person who *follows his moral principles* may well sometimes perform "a wrong and indeed irrational act."[14] In a recent book he says the same, although having reservations about how often an agent can be adequately sure of his facts. He says that we may have moral principles "while allowing that in particular cases one may break them."[15] Indeed, he says that

what is fanatical is the determination in principle to think with one's blood: that is to say, to put one's ingrained convictions beyond the reach of critical thought even when we are in a position (have the facts and the leisure) to examine and appraise them.[16]

But sometimes he is hesitant about whether agents are ever in a position to identify the really right utility-maximizing, or even the expectable-utility-maximizing act. When discussing whether doctors should murder an apparent bum who has been brought into a hospital drunk, in order to use his heart and kidneys to save the lives of two other patients, his answer is that the doctors should commit the murder if they really are *sure* of the facts. (It could be that the apparent bum is an important public official having a relaxed weekend!) He says the requisite level of assurance "will not be forthcoming in many actual situations, if at all." Hare thinks

12 R. M. Hare, "Ethical Theory and Utilitarianism," in H. D. Lewis, ed., *Contemporary British Philosophy* (London: Allen & Unwin, 1976), pp. 113–32.
13 Ibid., 129; cf. also *Moral Thinking*, p. 45.
14 Hare, "Ethical Theory and Utilitarianism," p. 127.
15 Hare, *Moral Thinking*, p. 59; but cf. also pp. 51–2.
16 Hare, *Moral Thinking*, p. 176.

that perhaps the notorious sheriff *should* hang the innocent man if he really knows it will maximize expectable utility, but, he says, "in practice he never will know this."[17]

Where does this view of Hare's leave him with Mary's right to an unobstructed driveway? In his response to Lyons, one reason Hare gives for respecting her legal right is "that in the case described the probability is that to follow such intuitive principles would yield the optimific act."[18] Now it seems to me that we can well imagine a situation in which a would-be parker *would* know quite well that utility would be served by *ignoring* her legal rights. Suppose Mary lives in Washington, say near Dupont Circle, where night-time parking spaces are virtually impossible to find. Suppose I work late, and find, just before leaving my work, that I must take a plane fairly early in the morning – say, at an airport not served by the subway system, nor, at that hour, by a limousine; and suppose past experience has taught me that taxi service at an early hour is highly unreliable. So, unless I am to park my car half a mile away and carry my luggage that distance to it early in the morning, I must park illegally. Mary's driveway is a tempting possibility. I know that she uses her car only to drive to work; so, if her driveway is blocked, she has to walk only eight blocks – no big thing. It may be quite clear, as I reflect on these matters while driving to my apartment, that I shall maximize utility by parking in her driveway. It would be nice, of course, to get her permission, but her lights are out and she obviously has gone to bed; in any case, she is a stickler about such matters and probably would not give permission anyway. I shall take into account the fact that she will be quite angry, but since I rarely see her, the disutility of that side-effect seems rather small. So, if I were an act-utilitarian, I would park in her driveway. Now I think that I ought *not* park in her driveway, and that I must inconvenience myself to the degree necessary to avoid obstructing her – perhaps by parking in her driveway but arising and going to the airport at 4 A.M. And the *principle* I should want to recommend on my kind of rule-utilitarian grounds would require just that. So Mary's legal right will be respected.

As I understand Hare's view, however, he does not take this line. According to him, Mary's right in this case will be respected if the agent is unsure of what the facts are, or has little confidence in his ability to sum up the situation in terms of utilities. But when the agent is quite clear that expectable utility will be maximized by obstructing her driveway, as an act-utilitarian he will not find her legal right to have any force.

17 Hare, *Moral Thinking*, pp. 132–64.
18 Hare, "Utility and Rights."

And, I think, for a theory to allow this is for it not to provide for rights, as not overridable by marginal gains of utility.

I am not saying there may not be good moral reason for obstructing Mary's driveway. As Lyons agrees, a medical emergency would be a justification. What I do *not* wish to grant is that Mary's right can be overridden by knowledge that so doing would make a marginal contribution to the general welfare. It seems to me that Hare's theory permits this to be the case.

My conclusion is that if we are to be utilitarians in the sense that we think morality should maximize long-range utility, and at the same time think that a utilitarian morality should have room for recognition of rights that cannot be overridden by marginal gains in utility, there are two positions we must espouse. First, we must hold that a person does the *right* act, or the obligatory act, not by just following his *actual* moral principles wherever they may lead, but by following the moral principles the acceptance of which in society would maximize expectable utility. Of course, this means that people who want to do what is right may have to do some thinking about their moral principles in particular situations. Second, we must emphasize that the right act is the one permitted by or required *by the moral code* the acceptance of which promises to maximize utility, and not compromise, except in extreme circumstances, in order to do what in a particular situation will maximize utility, where so doing conflicts with the utility-maximizing code. Only if we do this will we have room for a concept of "a right" which cannot be overridden by a marginal addition to the general welfare. It is clear that acting morally in this sense will never be very costly in utility; and where it is costly at all, that is the price that has to be paid for a *policy*, a morality of principle. If my exegesis of J. S. Mill is correct, these recommendations are ones in which he would join.

Addendum (1991): This criticism of Hare's views about the case of Mary may overlook the fact that some rights are relatively weak.

D

Determinism, excuses, and character

12

A utilitarian theory of excuses

If we aim to formulate and defend a utilitarian theory of excuses, we should begin with a rough indication of what the "theory" is to be about – what, in broad terms, an excuse is – and with a statement making clear what kind of theory is to be offered – whether a definition or explication, or a normative statement, or what. The following introductory remarks are intended to do these things.

We speak of something as excused or inexcused only when something has gone wrong. If a boy goes to school on time, is there all day, and works hard, the question whether something is excused does not arise. It arises only if he is absent, comes late, dawdles, and so on. Suppose he is tardy and presents an "excuse." What does he do? If the excuse is a good or valid one, he presents some explanation of his lateness that shows the tardiness was not a result of lack of diligence in conforming to the school's rules (and so forth). As a consequence he does not have to stay after school, do extra homework, or be otherwise disciplined. The excuse, while not a denial that something untoward occurred, prevents both the imputation of some kind of fault to the agent and the application of punishment or sanction. We may generalize this, and say that excuses are offered only when some form of behavior – "behavior" taken very broadly, we shall see – is in some way out of line; and a good excuse is some story or explanation that prevents an imputation of some fault to the agent, and just application of a penalty.

Excuses in this sense comprise that part of criminal justice usually discussed in legal textbooks under the heading of "responsibility." Suppose, for example, a woman has shot her husband. In the normal course of events she would be charged with homicide and be punished if found guilty. She can, however, admit that she shot her husband, but offer an explanation of the event that prevents the imputation of a guilty mind (*mens rea*) and the application of the penalty; she can say that the shooting was accidental, or that she mistook her husband for a burglar, that she was temporarily of unsound mind, and so on. These replies to the charge of homicide constitute the offering of an excuse, in this case a legal excuse.

The particular variety of excuses I wish to consider are what we may call "moral" excuses, although one must admit that the term "morally

215

excused" has little currency in common discourse. The kinds of excuses I have in mind, however, will be familiar; indeed, the legal excuses just mentioned would also count as moral excuses. The same is true of most of the important excuses recognized in the criminal law: mistake of fact, accident, coercion, provocation, insanity (but not necessarily duress or infancy). Of course it is no accident that the lists largely coincide.

What do we mean when we say that some consideration "excuses morally" or shows that a person is not "morally responsible"? Very often when we use "morally" as a modifier, we are drawing a contrast with something else, usually with "legally." For instance, we may say that while Mr. X was legally responsible for the accident, morally he was not. Thus, if a driver damages a car in front of him that made an abrupt and unsignaled stop, we may concede that legally he is liable for the damages, but we may say that *morally* he is not. For we may think that the liability for damages *should* lie with the party at fault; and in this case, despite any rule of law that a following driver is always liable for damage to a car in front of him, we think it was the driver in front whose substandard performance resulted in the accident, and hence that he ought to pay. In this case the talk of "moral responsibility" draws a contrast with the rather clumsy but simple rule employed by the courts. Much the same distinction is sometimes made in the area of the criminal law. A boy of seventeen and a boy of eighteen may join in a vicious crime, in which the younger and more intelligent boy is the guiding spirit. The law, however, may prescribe a criminal penalty for the older boy, while turning the younger boy over to a juvenile court for treatment according to the recommendation of psychological consultants. In this case, we may say that *morally* the younger boy was more responsible, whatever the law may say. Again, we are using the term "morally responsible" to draw a contrast between the rules of our legal institutions and a system of finer discriminations which embodies an ideal which the legal system, we think, should aim at even though it is impracticable for the courts.

But "morally" does not *just* contrast with "legally"; to say that behavior morally is "excusable" is not just to imply that legally it should not be punished. Indeed, sometimes we think that behavior that is morally without taint ought legally to be punished; we may think it is desirable for minor traffic violations to be punished whatever the excuse. The concepts of moral excuse and moral responsibility stand on their own feet; at least some important uses of them can be explained without reference to a set of concepts other than moral ones. What then is a *moral* excuse? A moral excuse is *needed* only if something has gone wrong morally, if someone has done what is morally wrong, either objectively or subjectively – some behavior which in the normal case would be a

216

reflection on the person. A sound moral excuse is an explanation that, while not contesting that behavior in some respect has not been morally up to par or morally correct, averts an imputation of *moral fault*, as well as the propriety of *moral blame, condemnation, disapproval,* and so on. (An excuse may be offered which is a bad one – one which purports to do this but does not succeed.) All this needs to be spelled out, of course, especially if we are not to be charged with circularity.

It is helpful to contrast moral excuses with moral justifications, just as excuses are contrasted with justifications in the criminal law. In the law, there are special circumstances in which an act that normally is wrong is not considered wrong at all. It is illegal to kill another person, but if an officer of the law kills someone in the course of executing his duty, the homicide is said to be *justifiable*. If a homicide – or other offense – is justifiable, the legal defenses listed in the chapters on "responsibility" are unnecessary: The policeman need not plead insanity in order to avoid punishment for killing a burglar attempting to escape apprehension. Something parallel is true in morals. We think it is normally wrong to lie, or to break a promise. But it is only *prima facie* so. There are times, in special circumstances, when it is right or even obligatory to tell a lie or break a promise. If one is charged with having told a lie, one *justifies* one's act by showing that in the total circumstances it was the right thing to do. And while justifying oneself in this way "lets one off the hook," all right, to do so is not to offer an excuse. For there is no charge left, no defective feature of one's behavior, that even looks like a reflection on one. And an excuse, of course, is an explanation such that, given that something was in some way out of order that would normally be a reflection on one, it is shown that one is in fact not open to moral criticism, condemnation, or disapproval. It must be admitted that the line is not perfectly obvious; later it will be argued that it is theoretically very convenient to draw it in this way.

What kind of *theory* of moral excuses are we looking for? What is here being sought is a set of correct or acceptable universal statements, describing circumstances in which the agent of an action that is morally questionable in some way is properly free from moral criticism or condemnation or disapproval – either entirely free, or at least free from the normal severity of criticism or disapproval. Such a set of statements would comprise only part of a theory of moral responsibility. A complete theory would include, in addition, universal statements about when an agent is blameworthy *at all*, and when he deserves *more* than the usual severity of disapproval – in other words, a theory of aggravating rather than excusing circumstances. Indeed, ideally a complete theory would consist of statements from which could be inferred the degree of blameworthiness for all possible types of actions. And the same also for praiseworthiness: a complete theory would comprise statements from which the relative degree of praiseworthiness of agents could be inferred, for all types of actions – from which one could infer the circumstances in which the normal degree of moral admiration or praise is properly either reduced or augmented. It is clear, then, that the theory of moral excuses is only part of a much larger whole. But we shall confine ourselves to it, very largely.

A "theory" of this sort is an expedition into normative ethics, and not just an exercise in the analysis of meanings or of definitions, since it consists of universal statements in which moral terms like "morally blameworthy," "morally praiseworthy," and so forth are *used*. Thus the utilitarian theory of excuses has the same epistemological status as the utilitarian theory of right and wrong conduct. It is true that some philosophers might wish to regard this "theory" as a case of analysis of meanings, thinking that the universal statements of which the theory consists are analytic, because of the meanings of the moral terms involved, or of the term "moral excuse." Such a view seems implausible, but a discussion of the matter is out of order here. I shall, however, conclude the whole discussion with some remarks in support of the utilitarian theory of excuses.

It may be useful to conclude these introductory paragraphs by commenting on the importance to moral philosophy of *any* theory of moral excuses, utilitarian or otherwise. One is apt to say to oneself that the important questions for the guidance of conduct are about what things or activities are worthwhile or desirable, and what kinds of behavior are right or wrong. If we know what kinds of activities are worthy of choice, and what kinds of actions are wrong, what more of importance do we need to know? Is not the question of what counts as a moral excuse, and even the more general question of what is a fitting object of moral admiration, blame, praise, or disapproval merely a minor matter for curiosity? If we already know what are desirable activities, and what is right or wrong to do, it would seem that we have all the information we need for practical decisions. In earlier days, we incline to say, the questions had a point. For if we regard a person who is subject to moral criticism as having committed a *sin*, and as therefore subject to divine wrath and vengeance, then the question of what moral excuses are valid is important; it is highly relevant to predictions about how, or where, one will spend eternity. One can see how St. Thomas and the Church Fathers were exercised about it. But why disinter the subject now?

In fact, the subject is more important than it looks at first, for two reasons. First, the concept of the morally obligatory, or the morally right, probably cannot be explained without reference to the concepts of moral disapproval, condemnation, and so on. (For instance, one possible although too simple suggestion is that "it is morally obligatory for x to do A" means "it would be proper to disapprove of x morally if he fails to do A without an excuse.") One can, of course, say that the concept of moral disapproval is needed without saying that the concepts of the morally blameworthy and of excuse are needed; and one can say that some of these concepts are needed without saying that they are the *only* concepts required – matters may be rather complex. But, just as the term "legal duty" may not be definable solely by reference to the power or sanctions of a sovereign authority, but can hardly be explained *without* use of these concepts, the same with "moral obligation." On this point J. S. Mill was nearly, but not quite, right when he said: "We do not call anything wrong, unless we mean to imply that a person ought to be punished in some way or other for doing it; if not by law, by the opinion of his fellow creatures; if not by opinion, by the reproaches of his own conscience. This seems the real turning point of the distinction between morality and simple expediency." If we are to recognize a sharp distinction between the morally obligatory act and the merely desirable act, we have to bring in the concepts of moral disapproval and perhaps blameworthiness and even punishment. One might argue, however, that despite this close conceptual tie, the set of acceptable universal statements about what is morally obligatory will be, or may be, quite different and disconnected from the set of statements about what is morally blameworthy. This leads to the second point: that at least a plausible rule-utilitarian theory of what is right or wrong will hold that a determination of what conduct is wrong cannot be made independently of determination of what kind of misbehavior may be morally excused. The reason for this is essentially the same as the reason why a utilitarian will not wish to approve of the scale of punishments in a system of criminal law until he has learned what excuses, or defenses against criminal charges – such as insanity – are going to be allowed. I shall develop this point in a moment. But obviously, if a utilitarian must say that we cannot decide what is right or wrong without deciding what are sound moral excuses, the subject of moral excuses cannot be without importance.

I A TRADITIONAL UTILITARIAN THEORY OF EXCUSES

We now turn to the topic of utilitarian theories of moral excuses. I shall begin with what I call a "traditional" theory, although I should not claim that any theory of excuses is *necessarily* part of the traditional utilitarian theory, and indeed do not wish to say that the general type of utilitarian theory I shall describe first is properly called "the traditional" utilitarian theory at all. What I wish to discuss first, however, is a type of utilitarian theory of excuses that has been *a* way of viewing the matter, that is worth examining, and has been typical of important utilitarians.

I shall define the "traditional" utilitarian view as essentially that held by Sidgwick, and also by Moore, Rashdall, Laird, and Smart. A "traditional" utilitarian, then, is a person who says that an action is morally right if and only if it will – or probably will – do as much good in the total circumstances as any other act the agent could perform instead. The utilitarian, then, holds that the right act is the optimific act, or at least the probably optimific act; or, in other words, the utility, actual or probable, of an act determines its rightness or wrongness.

So far the theory is not yet a theory of excuses, a theory about which considerations should or should not excuse a person from imputations of moral fault and from moral disapproval. But most of the writers listed assimilate the theory of excuses to the general theory of right and wrong actions, by the following maneuver. They take for granted that what it is for a person to be open to imputation of a fault, or to moral condemnation or disapproval, is for it to be *morally right* for persons to perform a certain *action:* that of condemning, reproaching, upbraiding, or reproving a person for his deed. (The condemning, of course, may be done before an audience of other persons, not the accused himself.) Sometimes it is said that what it *means* to say that an action is morally blameworthy is that it is right for people to condemn the agent for his deed; and that what it means for an action to be morally praiseworthy is that it is right for people to praise the person for what he did. The utilitarian will then be at pains to point out that an act that is wrong is not necessarily one it is right to condemn, on utilitarian grounds. For it may well be true that an action is wrong in view of the harm it does, everything considered; but at the same time there may be reasons why it would do no good to condemn it. A moral *excuse,* for such utilitarians, will be explained as follows. Suppose an act is wrong on utilitarian grounds. In the normal case, we may suppose, it will be right, on utilitarian grounds, to express condemnation of the act. Nevertheless, there may be considerations such that in view of them it clearly will do no good, and may do harm, to express condemnation of the deed. Such considerations may be called "excuses." On the "traditional" utilitarian theory, then, an excuse is a consideration that shows it useless or bad to blame an agent for a deed, even though his act was wrong.

There is some room for variation of opinion within the general framework of this theory. For instance, I have suggested that the *act* which is central to the theory of excuses is that of condemning, or expressing condemnation. But what exactly is this? So long as it is some *act*, one can vary its description and still remain within the general type of theory. One might say it is some *verbal* performance; J. L. Austin classified some such verbal performances as "behabitives." J. J. C. Smart suggested that blaming a person is grading him, with the implication that the behavior for which we grade him unfavorably is a result of some trait of his that can be influenced by threats, promises, and punishment. Blaming a person for something, according to Smart, is partly informative; it gives information about what the person is like. But it has a secondary function of discouraging the person from repeating the kind of conduct in question, since people do not like to have themselves advertised as persons with low moral marks. We can, if we like, understand all this as comprising, or partly comprising, the act of blaming, or condemning, or expressing condemnation. It is still an *act*, albeit a piece of verbal behavior, which can be assessed as right or wrong by utilitarian standards.

The foregoing utilitarian theory has objectionable consequences. For instance, it has the consequence that a person is properly held morally responsible for an action if he did not even perform it, provided that for some reason it is useful to perform this blaming act. The theory also implies that a person has a sound moral excuse, if it would be a bad thing for someone – say, me – to condemn him for it. This can hardly be true. Suppose a vindictive and tyrannical king does something we think deserving of most severe disapproval, but would be provoked to even more objectionable behavior if he were personally reproached in public, or even if the news came to him that he had been criticized in private. According to the theory, he is morally excused. We must agree that an *act* of overt condemnation is something the rightness of which has to be assessed with its consequences in view; but a piece of behavior is not morally excused just because such condemnation would have bad consequences.

A second objection to the theory is that it focuses on *acts*, saying that a person is excused if certain acts should not take place. As such, it pays little or no attention to the *state of mind* which these acts express and which gives them their force. There is such a thing as the *belief* that an act would not have been performed if the agent had not been a certain kind of person (say, a selfish person); and there is such a thing as an unfavorable *attitude* – we may call it moral disapproval – toward an agent taken up because of one's explanation of his behavior by an unfavorable hypothesis about his character or motivation. If there were no such thoughts and attitudes, verbal criticisms, normally taken to be expressions of such thoughts and attitudes, would have no force. It would seem that

221

any adequate theory of excuses must explain when and why certain considerations make it unjustified to think such thoughts or take up an attitude of disapproval toward an agent – and, what is equally important, why certain considerations make it unjustified for an agent to feel guilty or remorseful about his own behavior. Now I suppose that, if we are going to concentrate attention on thoughts and attitudes, the utilitarian might still regard these as *acts*, and assert that they are justified according to the utilities of their occurrence. But it is surely questionable whether the coming to an opinion (or having it) about someone, or the taking up (or having) an attitude of disapproval toward him, is an act at all. And if it *is* an act, one can wonder if its justification is a matter of its individual utility. Perhaps we would be better off if I stopped disapproving of people generally; but we might be better off if you disapproved of them more.

II A RULE-UTILITARIAN THEORY OF EXCUSES

Rather than pursue further this type of utilitarian theory of excuses I propose to explore the possibilities of a different type of utilitarian theory, which looks more promising for the topic of our interest. If I am right in thinking that moral disapproval is not an act, however, and hence if I am right in thinking that to be morally excused is not to have a reason why some act should not be performed, we shall be looking for a utilitarian theory which is not just a theory about which acts are right or wrong. It may therefore seem, at least at the outset, that we are looking for a queer type of utilitarian theory.

Some contemporary (and also traditional) utilitarians hold that an act is wrong, not if the performance of *it* would produce less good than some other act the agent could perform, but because it would have bad consequences for actions of the same kind to be *generally* performed. Some writers of this general persuasion do not call themselves utilitarians because they deny that an act's general performance having *good* consequences can generate any obligation to perform it; they think an act is shown to be wrong only if the general performance of it would have bad, or disastrous, consequences. Other writers are closer to the tradition of utilitarianism, and count both good and ill consequences of actions as morally relevant; they hold roughly that an act is obligatory, or wrong, if and only if the general performance of an act of that kind would make the world better, or worse, respectively. All these writers have in common the view that what makes an act right or wrong is not *its* consequences, good or bad, but the utility or disutility of performance of a whole *class* of actions of the same type as the one in question. This type of view is generally called "rule-utilitarianism."

One variety of this type of theory has certain advantages, among them the fact that it leads naturally into a plausible theory of moral excuses. The essence of it is the thesis that the rightness or wrongness of an action is fixed by the utility of the currency of a *moral code* which prescribes or proscribes the action. We might say its thesis is this: "An action is right if and only if it is not proscribed by a moral code, the currency of which in the society of the agent would produce at least as much good per person as the currency of any other moral code, in view of the situations that may be expected to arise in the society." Later, I shall propose adding to this a thesis about praiseworthiness and blameworthiness, which entails a theory of excuses, when we have seen that the thesis about right and wrong leads to it.

The reason this particular theory leads to a theory of moral excuses becomes clear when we have seen what it is for a moral code to have currency. What it is for a moral code to have currency in a society is for it to be accepted or interiorized, by most of the adults of the society, to about the extent to which moral codes generally are interiorized.[1] For an individual to accept or interiorize a given code is for him to accept and interiorize, or subscribe to, the rules constitutive of the code. What it is for an individual to subscribe to a rule of a moral code is for something to be true of the thinking, experience, and attitudes of the individual. What exactly is true of a person when we wish to say that he subscribes to a rule of a moral code cannot be described here, but we can sketch informally what is true, in terms of an example. What facts about a person would make us want to say of him that he accepts the rule "One ought, *prima facie*, to keep one's promises"? The following, doubtless among other things: First, if he thinks that his doing A would result in his breaking a promise, he is motivated to some extent *not* to do A, and would, if asked, cite the fact as a reason for not doing A. Second, if someone breaks a promise to him or his friends he will be inclined to be annoyed, and to complain on that account, other things being equal. Third, if he breaks a promise for whatever reasons, he will feel uncomfortable about it, unless he has made up for it, explained the difficulties to the promisee's satisfaction, and so on. Fourth, if a person sees behavior he construes as evidence that some agent has only a weak and substandard attitude about promises, he will think this attitude in the other person a defect, and he will tend to admire the person less as a person. Finally, he will regard all these attitudes or dispositions on his part as well justified

---

1 I have explained this whole concept in somewhat more detail in "Some Merits of One Form of Rule-Utilitarianism," in *University of Colorado Publications in Philosophy* (1967), pp. 48–9. This paper is obtainable in anthologies, and as a separate reprint in the Bobbs-Merrill series in philosophy.

in some sense. For a moral rule to have currency in a society, then, is for most adults in the society to accept it in this sense, to an ordinary degree, on the average. But something else is involved. We would not say that a moral rule had currency unless adults in the society were *aware* of the fact that the rule was generally accepted – at least aware of it to the extent that, if the question were put to them, they would answer it correctly.

Now once we have the concept of a person subscribing to a rule in the foregoing sense, we can see that he *can* be trained to make certain discriminations, and not to develop feelings of discomfort (guilt or remorse, and so forth) in certain circumstances, and so on for the other phenomena. For instance, suppose a person breaks a promise to me, but honestly does not realize that what he has done constitutes a breach of promise; I might be so trained that in this situation I would feel no annoyance and not be inclined to complain. Again, suppose someone fails to do something that my moral code requires him to do, but fails because his own moral code requires him to do something incompatible with it – or at least he honestly thinks it does. Again, I may be so trained that in this case I am disinclined to be annoyed or to complain or to count his failure as evidence of a defect in him, and so on. Now, in case I am so trained, we can say that while I subscribe to a moral rule prohibiting breach of promise, I also subscribe to the rules that a person is excused from moral criticism if he does something in ignorance, or from a sense of obligation. An anthropologist wishing to give a complete account of the moral code of a society would list not only the *prima facie* rules of obligation accepted by most adults in the society, but also the accepted rules about excuses from moral criticism despite breach, in some way or other, of the rules of obligation – just as a description of a system of criminal law would list not only what kinds of behavior are penalized and how much, but also such facts as that insanity is an accepted defense against any criminal charge.

It should be noticed that, as I have described what it is for a person to subscribe to a rule of obligation, a person's disposition to feel remorse or guilt and to have condemning or anti attitudes toward others because of their behavior are central features. Such features distinguish subscription to a rule of obligation from thinking that something is desirable or expedient, or wanting it as a means or as an end, roughly in the way J. S. Mill suggested in the passage already quoted. These features play the role in the moral code that punishment plays in a system of criminal law.

It may not be clear why an anthropologist describing a moral system must keep the rules of obligation and prohibitions separate from the system of excuses. The reason is roughly the same as that which requires a legal historian to keep penalties and excuses separate in the criminal law. The reason is that there are certain forms of behavior that are *prima facie* grounds for application of the penalties in both law and morals: breach of promise, deliberate injury to the persons of others, and so on. But there are two types of cases in which the penalties are not, or need not be, applied despite the presence of a *prima facie* ground. The first case is that of the agent incurring *prima facie* liability to penalty because he could not fulfill some more stringent obligation of law or morals unless he did: for instance, he broke a promise in order to avoid injuring another person, or in order to render assistance in an emergency. In this situation, the breach of a rule is said to be *justified* and the penalty is not applied. The second case in which the penalty is not applied is one of some general feature being present, such as ignorance, mistake of fact, and so on, the presence of which prevents the penalty irrespective of which *prima facie* ground for penalty happens to exist. So, in moral systems as in law, there are rules of *prima facie* obligation; there is justification when such rules conflict; and there are general conditions in which there is release from condemnation irrespective of the kind of breach involved. Naturally, the descriptive anthropologist will keep these three things separate.

We can see now why we can say, of a moral system or a legal system, that what it is for an action to be wrong, all things considered (that is, all justification taken into account), is for it to be subject to condemnation except where there is a valid excuse. This statement may look empty, but since we can identify obligations and justifications and excuses independently, it is not empty but an important statement of the relations of the three features of moral, and legal, codes.

Thus far I have explained only how it is *possible* that people should be so trained that their moral system would contain both subscription to rules of obligation, and also to excuses. Obviously, people in our society actually *are* so trained. But I have not yet made good my earlier claim that the rule-utilitarian theory of right and wrong leads naturally to a theory of excuses. We can now see why this claim is correct. For the rule-utilitarian holds that the right action is the one that would not be prohibited by the moral code the currency of which in the agent's society would (roughly) maximize utility. But which moral code will maximize utility is partly a function of the system of excuses it contains – just as the utility of a legal system is partly a function of its system of legal excuses. For when we are seeking to determine the utility of a certain moral system, we are not merely inquiring what would be the advantage in a certain kind of *prohibited behavior not occurring;* we are trying to answer a much more complex question about the gains and losses, partly from the decrease of prohibited behavior, but also from the very existence of the moral system – the costs

225

of teaching it, the psychological burden and risks of living with it, and so on. Therefore, different sets of excuses will be features defining different moral systems, some of which will have more utility than others just on this account. So if a rule-utilitarian affirms that an act is objectively right if it would be permitted by the moral code that will have the best consequences, then, since the best moral system will also contain a system of excuses, the utilitarian will presumably say that behavior in some way out of line *should be excused* if its excuse would be provided for in the total moral system that would have the best consequences. There are two types of excuses the rule-utilitarian presumably can and should recognize. First, total excuses, exculpations: an action is totally excused if the moral system with best consequences would not condemn it at all. Second, mitigating excuses: an action has a mitigating excuse if, in view of some feature, the moral system with best consequences would condemn it *less severely* than where this feature is not present.

To see the reasoning more clearly, let us pursue a bit further the analogy with the law. Let us suppose a utilitarian is considering what should be the penalties affixed to the act of homicide. He will follow Bentham in deciding such matters by applying the principle of marginal utility to punishment, or what might be called the principle of "least necessary punishment." For, since punishment is an evil, the utilitarian will want to inflict it only in order to avoid a greater cost. In the case of homicide, the utilitarian will insist on having *some* penalty for the offense; otherwise, everyone is invited to indulge in homicide when it suits his ends. The utilitarian will consider successively more severe penalties, and each time he will count the loss of the punishment against the predicted gain, primarily in crime prevention because of the threat of punishment. When he arrives at a degree of severity such that the utility of the crime prevention just equals the disutility to society of the punishment itself, he will decide that the punishment is just severe enough. In making the calculations, the utilitarian will take into account how the utility of the system is affected if certain defenses (such as insanity) are allowed and if certain circumstances are regarded as mitigating (different degrees of homicide recognized). Whether such defenses or mitigations are allowed will make a great deal of difference to the utility of the system as a whole. Obviously, if every homicide were a capital offense, and no defenses of mistake or accident or insanity were admitted, the total effect would be intolerable; anyone who drove a motor car would be continuously under the shadow of a threat to life no voluntary act of his could remove. Of course, there are also disadvantages in having such defenses, since their existence is something of an invitation to crime, in that a person may hope that skillful maneuvering and a clever lawyer may prevent a deliberate crime from being punished. Nevertheless, it seems clear that the utilitarian will conclude that the best system of criminal law will combine a fairly heavy penalty for homicide with a system of exculpations and mitigations for certain circumstances. This system will yield a high degree of deterrence combined with lower social costs, as compared with any system that had no provision for excuses.

Moral systems must be evaluated in a similar way. A moral system produces both social gains and social costs. It provides gains to society in many ways: for instance, by preventing personal injury of sorts that the law cannot prevent; consequently by enhancing feelings of personal security; by making possible benefits of cooperative behavior by motivating people to play the roles to which they are committed by their position in an institution or to which they have obligated themselves in some other way. But there are also costs. For instance, one cost is that many people are burdened with excessive feelings of guilt. Another is that some are so concerned about their obligations, and about possible moral criticism by others, that they fail to make firm decisions important for their own well-being. Moral excuses provide a certain easing of these costs. Take, for instance, the excuse of accident or mistake. If persons were made to feel guilty about accidental injury to others, and if they were targets of condemning attitudes toward them for accidental injury, there would be much needless anxiety and discomfort in the world.

Let us consider more in detail the kind of reasoning by which a rule-utilitarian would decide whether a given consideration should be accepted as an excuse from moral blame.

It will be agreed that there is always some gain in any consideration being recognized as excusing, since persons are saved the distress of guilt and of being targets of criticism by others. The serious question about the acceptance of a consideration as excusing is whether acceptance will produce a compensating, or more than compensating, loss in the effectiveness of the moral system. In analyzing a moral system to answer this question, one finds that matters are somewhat different from what they are in the criminal law; for the gains and losses are to be found in different places, since the moral system does not work primarily by deterrence through threat of punishment. It is true that the moral system does operate in part by threats: the threat of disapproval by other persons. It is part of socialized human beings that they cherish the good opinion of other persons, or at least of other persons whom they admire or respect. They also dislike being held in contempt by others, or being rated low by others as to traits of character, or being the target of others' indignation. Just as they do not like others to regard them as stupid or dirty, with corresponding attitudes, they do not like others to regard them as immoral, unreliable, or cruel. Moreover, there is a palpable aspect to the disapproval of other persons. Persons who are indignant at us, or hold us in contempt, do not treat us well. An indignant employer may not raise one's salary, or give a recommendation. But the moral system does not work primarily in this way. It works through the fact that a person with a well developed conscience has a built-in aversion to doing things of a certain sort. The mere thought of doing these things stirs up faint rumblings of anxiety or guilt. And the actual doing of them leaves one most uncomfortable. Moreover, people with well developed consciences dislike having to think of themselves as persons of a certain sort. They have ego ideals: They do not like to have to view themselves as ones who fall short of an ego ideal by being persons who take their pledged word lightly, or are callous about the welfare of other persons.

The moral system works, then, by aversions, mostly aversions just to doing something of a certain kind or acting like a certain sort of person. Now this machinery cannot prevent certain types of actions. And there is hence no point in marshaling condemning attitudes of others or guilt and anxiety feelings in the agent, for the purpose of preventing them. Take, for instance, injuring another person accidentally. Evidently it is useless to blame a person for, or for him to have been trained to feel guilty about, injuring others accidentally. (Or, more exactly, since training presumably could produce a higher level of heed, what we must say is that the training necessary to produce a level of heed that would succeed in preventing certain accidents would, if possible at all, be more costly by far than the damage the heed would avoid.) There is no point, in general, in a moral system condemning failure to do the impossible, or the accidental, or what is done when a person is hypnotized or paralyzed by fright. If the utilitarian theory of excuses is correct, such considerations must entirely exculpate from blame. The preventive capacities of the moral machinery are in no way reduced by excepting such kinds of behavior from moral blame.

The rule-utilitarian, then, may be led to a thesis like the following, from which principles about excuses can be derived: *An agent is morally blameworthy (praiseworthy) for an act if, and to the degree that, the moral code the currency of which in that society would maximize utility would condemn (praise) him for it,* where "condemn" and "praise" are construed as indicated above.

III   EXCUSES AND CHARACTER

Is it possible to infer, from the general rule-utilitarian principle about blameworthiness just stated, any more definite statement about which kinds of behavior are morally excusable? I think it is; and the more definite statement is that an objectively wrong action (or an action in some way out of order) is excused if it *does not manifest some defect of character.* This implication strikes the writer as intuitively plausible; at any rate, it does not seem possible to find counterexamples to it. If philosophers generally on reflection find this result intuitively acceptable, this is a point in favor of the general rule-utilitarian theory.

It must be admitted that there are various obscurities in the notion of "manifesting a defect of character."[2] It needs to be explained in what sense any action "manifests" a trait of character. It needs to be explained how to identify a "defect" of character – whether, for instance, to have a defect is simply to be below average in some respect (a suggestion on this is offered below). Perhaps more important, the notion of "character" is somewhat fuzzy, as becomes obvious when we try explain how a trait of character differs from just a trait of personality. On this point, it may be helpful to suggest that, for example, whether kleptomania is a trait of character or just a trait of personality is a question that the ordinary concept of "character" is not sharp enough to enable us to decide. And in this instance, the most helpful way to decide is to classify so as to make true the very thesis we are discussing: so that a defect turns out to be a defect of *character* precisely if it is one an action manifesting which a utility-maximizing moral system would not excuse. This suggestion may seem queer, but it is parallel to an important case in law: If a judge, required to interpret the Durham Rule, asks himself what is to count as a "mental defect" or "mental illness," it seems the only satisfactory answer is that it is the sort of mental condition that may be treated as an excusing condition without harm to the deterrent capacity of the legal system.

Conceding that there are some conceptual questions needing clarification, the thesis here defended is that it follows from the rule-utilitarian proposition that an agent is blameworthy for an act only if the utility-maximizing moral code would condemn him for it, that an action is morally excused if it manifests no defect of character, or, in other words, that an agent of an action is morally blameworthy because of it only if it manifests a defect of character. Otherwise put, it is contended that in a utility-maximizing moral system, people would feel guilty (be trained to feel guilty) about an action, and others would feel disapproval of them for it, condemn them for it, think less of them as persons for it, only if the action manifested a defect of character.

But how could it be shown that a utility-maximizing code would "condemn" (in the above sense) a person for an action only if it manifested a defect of character? Would making this point not at least involve an

---

2 Some of these I attempt to remove in a paper, "Traits of Character: a Conceptual Analysis," below, Chapter 14.

elaborate discussion of the possible gains and losses from various arrangements, perhaps involving vast empirical research about gains and losses? It is true that the question how severely a particular type of dereliction should be reprehended is a question the answer to which requires empirical evidence and calculations. But the particular problem with which we are here concerned is fortunately a purely conceptual problem the philosophical analyst is competent to solve. All that is needed is to get the problem precisely in mind. Let us proceed with this.

The fundamental issue is whether it is or is not true that in a utility-maximizing system people would be trained to be motivated, and to feel, in certain ways about certain things – namely, to have an aversion to breaking a promise, to feel guilty about doing so, to think less of others who take their pledged word lightly, and *at the same time* be trained not to feel guilty say about breaking a promise, or to think less of others who break their promises *when the action in question does not manifest a defect of character.* Would a utility-maximizing moral system have precisely this second feature along with the first – just as a utility-maximizing legal system might admit just certain excuses and no others?

The central move in the solution of the problem is the recognition that a defect of character is, or includes, *a defect of motivation.* That this is indeed so many not be evident, and some philosophers would deny it.[3] A few examples may make the thesis clear and perhaps plausible. One might hold, then, that honesty is essentially an aversion to deception and to appropriation of the property of others; that sympathy is an aversion to others being unhappy or in distress; that considerateness is an aversion to causing or permitting even minor distress or discomfort in others; that courage is absence of an overwhelming aversion to personal injury or loss of status, when certain other things are at stake; and so on. A *defect* of a given trait of character, then, would be a defect in motivation – an insufficient degree of the corresponding wants, aversions, needs, motivations (which term we choose makes little difference), in the dispositional sense of these terms.

Exactly how much motivation of a certain kind constitutes an "adequate" amount and how little constitutes a "defect" is a question we cannot here even discuss. *This* question requires detailed balancing of advantages and disadvantages, like the question of the proper sentence to be meted out in punishment of a certain crime. Obviously, it would not serve utility to have people so strongly motivated to avoid any discomfort in others that they were perpetually ignoring their own concerns, allowing themselves to be disadvantaged, and so on. In principle it seems

---

3 The matter is discussed below, in Chapters 14 and 15.

there is an "ideal" amount of motivation, although the problem of what precisely it would be cannot profitably be discussed without an account of the measurement, or ordering, of different degrees of motivation.

If we construe "defect of character" as suggested, our present thesis is that a utility-maximizing moral system would not condemn a certain action – the agent would be trained not to feel guilty about it, and others would be trained not to feel disapproval of it – unless it manifested insufficient motivation (want, desire, aversion, in the dispositional sense) of a kind of importance for the moral system. In other words, the suggestion is that, unless the agent has shown an unsatisfactory level of motivation, his action is not open to moral criticism.

Why not? Roughly, the answer is that if a person's level of motivation to do certain sorts of things is adequate, the "moral system" has done its job. The "adequate" level of motivation is what we want, in general, neither more nor less; this level, we have seen, is the one that maximizes utility. On the other hand, if a person fails to do what he ought on account of an inadequate degree of motivation in the appropriate directions, the "moral system" has not done its job in his case. For such instances, it is a good thing if the agent has guilt feelings and if others disapprove, in a number of different ways. The details of the reason for this involve controversial issues in the theory of the learning of motives, and what I can say on this may be only roughly correct; the central idea, however, is that guilt feelings and disapproval of others *increase* motivation in the desired direction – that is, improve the corresponding trait of character. For one thing the guilt feelings, which are unpleasant, become associated with the idea of the action (which the agent wrongly did or wrongly failed to do), and the unpleasant associations provide a "boost" in the right direction for similar situations in the future. And roughly the same if the agent acquires the unpleasant information that others disapprove of what he did. Knowledge that the agent feels guilt, or that he is disapproved of, will produce a smaller but similar effect in the minds of third parties. In addition, all these experiences may have a purely cognitive function: of impressing on all the parties, more firmly, the conception of what the standard behavior is.

Where motivation is approximately at the optimal level, then, and hence where there is no defect of a related trait of character, nothing is needed to improve the agent's motivation; so there is no call for guilt feelings, or knowledge of criticism by others, and so forth. But where the motivation is below the optimal level, the operation of these mechanisms is beneficial – or, at least, it looks as if it is in many or most types of cases, and even if it were not, the negative point about when it is useless is what is important for the theory of excuses.

All the considerations traditionally recognized as exculpating excuses are ones evidencing adequate motivation – or at least showing absence of evidence of inadequate motivation. If a person damages through inadvertence (not negligence), or through mistake of fact (not culpable mistake of fact), through defect of memory (when the failure to remember does not show inadequate interest in remembering), through the effect of drugs or fatigue (since these leave open the possibility of adequate motivation in the dispositional sense), there was no failure of motivation. Provocation may or may not show an adequate aversion to performing a forbidden action; it depends on the degree of provocation – whether it was such that it goes beyond what could be withstood by a person with as much motivation as it is useful for people to have.

In the case of the mitigating excuses, presumably the considerations provide evidence, not that an adequate degree of motivation was present, but that the shortcoming was possibly not serious, and hence that the action need not be "condemned" by an ideal moral system to a very severe degree.

A rule-utilitarian, then, will say that an agent is blameworthy for an act only if it would be "condemned" by a utility-maximizing moral system, and hence that an act will be excused unless it shows a defect of motivation (defect of character). I do not mean to suggest, however, that *only* a rule-utilitarian can defend a conclusion somewhat of this sort. One might simply assert that acts should be excused unless they exhibit a defect of character, with no attempt to explain or derive one's assertion. In any case, part of our conclusion can be defended without reference to any utilitarian considerations. For part of what it is to *blame* a person[4] is to impute a *defect* to him – and a defect is a dispositional feature of him, an incapacity or deleterious tendency. In so far, then, as an action shows no incapacity or deleterious tendency, its agent cannot be condemned for it. Therefore some behavior – for example, accidental injury of another person – must be excused because it shows no incapacity or objectionable tendency in the agent. So, if I am right about the concept of blaming, there are some kinds of actions that cannot be blamed except through misunderstanding.

IV   WHY THE UTILITARIAN THEORY OF EXCUSES?

I conclude with some scattered remarks on the subject whether one should accept the rule-utilitarian theory of excuses.

---

4 See my "Blameworthiness and Obligation," in A. I. Melden, ed., *Essays in Moral Philosophy* (Seattle, 1958).

(1) The utilitarian theory has the virtue of being a general theory, which tells us in principle how to determine, for odd and unusual cases, how to go about deciding whether the action is morally excused. For instance, there is the question whether kleptomanic behavior is morally excused. The debate on this is interminable as long as it proceeds on the level of a decision whether kleptomania is a trait of character or a disease. But if we ask ourselves whether, given all we know about kleptomania, it would maximize utility for a moral system to excuse it, we know in principle how to get an answer to our question. Whether the answer is one with which we shall all feel satisfied we need not decide. At least the theory is general, and its implications for the answer of particular questions may be illuminating and general. It thus differs from a collection of unrelated intuitions that give no guidance for novel problems.

Utilitarianism is not, as a genus, much less as the specific variety described, the only possible general theory of the matter.

(2) The utilitarian theory described is not only a general one, but one the implications of which coincide with our intuitions, in so far as these are clear and definite. It implies that those circumstances are exculpating, or mitigating, or neither, just as we think they are, in the clear cases. One of these implications of special importance is that not all conduct that is an instance of a causal law is excused – and no conduct is excused for that reason. On the rule-utilitarian theory, determinism and blameworthiness are compatible.

This is not to say that there is an exact parallel between ordinary moral thinking about excuses and the logic of the utilitarian theory. For instance, we may excuse a wrong action because it was a result of an invincible error about fact; in doing so, we may think that the consideration adduced is sufficient to settle the point, and that no complicated reflections about utilities need be adduced in support. This fact, however, is no objection to the theory. The fact that people do not ordinarily feel the need for going behind an established principle for more support does not show that support cannot be provided or that it is not desirable for some purposes.

(3) The rule-utilitarian theory also *explains* our intuitions by presenting them in a certain light, showing how the fact that excuses are embodied in a moral code ministers to human welfare. By presenting them in this light, the theory recommends our intuitions to human sympathy. Moreover, just as it is generally regarded as rational for an individual to act, in a personal matter, to maximize his expectable utility, it can be argued that society's "choice" of an institution of morality is rational if and only if it will maximize expectable social utility. As such, a utilitarian morality can be recommended to an unselfish person because it maximizes the

expectation of the general welfare, and to a selfish person because, in the absence of special evidence about his own case, it maximizes his own expectation of personal welfare. Either way, a moral institution of a utilitarian kind can be vindicated as a rational choice. In so far as an actual moral system embodies the utilitarian ideal – as ours seems to, at least in the matter of excuses – it can be recommended as a rational institution.

(4) The rule-utilitarian theory of moral excuses, because it is so parallel with the utilitarian theory of legal excuses, avoids some criticisms that have been leveled at the theory of moral blame and excuses. It has been claimed that the theory of moral blame and excuses tries to consist of self-evident propositions, clear, totally free of arbitrariness, and unentangled with earthy questions about policy desirable for society. The thought has been that this is too high an aspiration. Now this accusation cannot be entirely true if one thinks, with the writer, that in some respects morality *is* superior to the law. But, however that may be, on the utilitarian theory it is not true that which behavior is subject to blame and which is excused is a matter of clear, self-evident propositions. The theory rather requires an analysis of the conditions and effects of blaming other persons, and of having anxiety or guilt feelings about one's deeds, as a prerequisite to a decision whether a given level of motivation is adequate from the point of view of society, and hence whether an action is excusable for having manifested adequate motivation. Indeed, it *could* be that society would be better off if *no one* were educated so as to suffer from feelings of guilt, and if no one ever disapproved of others for their behavior. And to decide whether a certain sort of wrong behavior should be excused is, on the utilitarian theory, a difficult matter. Thus, whatever be true of other theories, the utilitarian cannot be justly accused of even trying to produce a clear, simple theory, unentangled with earthy questions about policies good for society. Whether there is force in this criticism, in any case, I leave to others to decide.

13

A motivational theory of excuses in the criminal law

The central contention of the following paper is that criminal liability requires a *motivational fault* in the agent. More fully, persons who have unjustifiably broken valid law should be exempt from punishment unless their behavior is a result of some defect of standing motivation (one might say "character" instead) – "should be" in the sense that the exemption is required by any reasonably adequate general theory of criminal justice.

I shall suppose that we need four concepts in the criminal law. First, the law prohibits certain types of actions (call an instance of one, *actus reus*) such as arson, larceny, rape, assault. The traditional view is that these forms of behavior are forbidden because they are thought to be normally harmful, or threatening, or bad in themselves. Some kinds of behavior the law forbids or has forbidden are not harmful, or threatening, or bad, in fact; but let us pass this. Call this forbidden behavior, this violation of "primary" (Hart) legal norms, "unlawful."

Second, in particular circumstances an instance of one of these forbidden types of actions may not be, or at least is reasonably believed by the agent not to be, harmful, or bad, on the whole, from the point of view of society; on the contrary, it may be or at least is reasonably believed to be preferable to other options open to the agent. In this case the law permits an exception. Thus whereas arson is forbidden by the law, an agent will not be punished if he sets fire to a house in order to prevent a general conflagration. Call behavior that is unlawful but falls into this special class, "justified unlawful action."

Third, an act may be unlawful but *not* justified in this sense, but nevertheless may not manifest any defective motivation of the agent. Thus, if a person commits a rape, we can normally infer that he has no strong aversion to using violence for obtaining sexual gratification, or to producing fear and shock in his victim, or to forcing a woman to have

I have learned a great deal from the comments of various individuals who kindly read and responded to an earlier draft of the present paper: William K. Frankena, Bruce Frier, J. Roland Pennock, Adrian M. S. Piper, Louis Michael Seidman, Heathcote Wales, and Peter Westen. Needless to say, they are not responsible for the errors that may remain. I am also indebted to Peter Tague, whose course on substantive criminal law I audited while a visiting professor at the Georgetown University Law Center, and to conversations about the topic of the present paper with Patricia D. White and Silas Wasserstrom.

intimate relations she does not want, and to infringing the prohibitions of the law. (We might add that the person does not have a strong aversion to the risk of incurring severe legal penalties, but I think we should not include lack of such self-interested aversion among the "defects" of motivation; it would make no difference to the argument if we did.) But sometimes such an inference is blocked. A person who has raped may have honestly believed that he had the woman's consent. In this case a circumstance may or does block the normal inference to substandard motivation; the action in this situation is compatible with the agent having an adequate standard level of motivation in all respects. Now, say of such a case that the behavior is "excused," and the relevant circumstance that blocks the inference we can call "an excuse." So accidents and mistakes of fact are excuses.

Fourth, there is behavior that is unlawful, unjustified, and not excused in this sense, but nevertheless thought not properly punished. For instance, behavior of infants or persons suffering from some forms of insanity. (But unlawful, unjustified behavior arising from a delusion may be excused, as involving mistake of fact.) Say that such behavior is "not responsible." Thus we need four terms: "unlawful," "unjustified" (behavior that is unlawful and unjustified may be called "legally wrongful"), "unexcused," and "responsible." An unlawful unjustified act is done with *mens rea* only if responsible and not excused; at least I propose we talk this way, giving a clear meaning to *mens rea*.

It should be noticed that the foregoing conceptual framework deliberately diverges from familiar legal categories in some ways. First, the *actus reus*, or unlawful conduct, is defined so as *not* to require such mental elements as purposefulness, recklessness, and the like, although in order to be conduct at all, it must be different, for instance, from sleepwalking; that is, it must be guided by *some* beliefs and desires. Thus absence of the mental elements is included among excuses. In this and also in the matter of how to explain "justification" I am happy to have the support of Glanville Williams;[1] he notes that the inclusion of mental elements in the definition of an offense raises problems about the liability of accessories. I also note that Herbert Packer pointed out[2] that the Model Penal Code's procedure is clearer and simpler in some ways, but that it is more perspicuous to identify the kinds of overt behavior the law aims to prevent, and then to list the various mental elements that serve to exempt

---

1 Glanville Williams, "The Theory of Excuses," *Criminal Law Review* (1982): 734 ff. As will be clear in what follows, however, I do not accept his definition of "excuse," p. 735.
2 Herbert Packer, *The Limits of the Criminal Sanction* (Palo Alto: Stanford University Press, 1986), chap. 6. Packer points out rightly that *mens rea* is also relevant to mitigation. See the discussion of provocation below.

violators from punishment. In this respect my term "excuse" is more inclusive than it is for such writers as George Fletcher. But on the other hand, my use of excuse is in other respects narrower than is usual. Whereas infancy and insanity are often viewed as excuses, I propose not to call them so because they differ from other excuses in important ways, which the following discussion will make clear. I am not suggesting that infancy or insanity should not exempt from punishment; but the reasons are different. I am calling sanity and noninfancy conditions of "responsibility" – and the list could be expanded. Whether we define *mens rea* so as to imply both absence of excuse in my sense, and responsibility, or only the former, is a semantic issue to which little importance should be attached. In earlier times, excuse was not even distinguished from justification; this failure to distinguish was a manifest confusion.

The main contention of this chapter departs both from tradition and the Model Penal Code. The motivation theory does have something in common with an earlier period of the law when, for example, Bracton said that "desire and purpose" distinguish "evil-doing,"[3] and "desire to injure" was a part of the definition of arson, and a child of eight was hanged for arson because of "malice and revenge" in him.[4] The law at that time seems to have overlooked that a person's motivation in acting involves not only desires for certain outcomes but also *aversions* to being motivated not to do certain things, and overlooked the central importance of the latter. But the law has moved from identifying the mental element of a crime from something about motivation, to *intent*. There are different intentions comprising the mental element for the various offenses, so that F. B. Sayre, at the conclusion of his historical study, opined that it is futile at present to seek "any single precise meaning" for *mens rea*.[5] (Of course, that is exactly what I am proposing to do.) The Model Penal Code groups together several unrelated "general principles of liability," namely, that the agent has acted "purposely, knowingly, recklessly, or negligently, as the law may require," but then, in the same Article, lists various specific defenses, including ignorance or mistake of fact or law, involuntary intoxication, duress, entrapment, etc., and separates all this from a section on justification and a further section on responsibility (insanity and infancy). If any general principle underlies the various excuses listed in the Code, it is not made clear; perhaps the motivation theory is wrong, but at least it puts forward a general principle to be assessed. Incidentally, the movement of the law from motive to intent may be more verbal than real, since a person's intent reflects his moti-

3 *De Legibus*, 136b.
4 Francis Sayre, "Mens Rea," *Harvard Law Review* 45 (1932): 974–1026, at p. 1010.
5 Ibid., p. 1023.

vation; this "movement," unless I am mistaken, reflects an overly simplified psychology. But I agree that the motivation theory is a departure from mainstream thinking and therefore has to be defended.

In the course of my argument I explain why certain circumstances (for example, duress, accident, mistake of fact) excuse an action according to the motivation theory, and point out that these circumstances in fact exempt from punishment according to current law. But I am not suggesting that *because* my definition implies that certain circumstances that are standardly regarded as excusing by the courts, do excuse is a *confirmation* of my proposal. Sociology of the law, or explanatory history of the law, aims to explain actual laws and court decisions ideally in the same way as astronomy explains eclipses; such theoretical frameworks *are* refuted by disconformity with the actual laws and decisions. Not so the theory I shall provide. In any case the conformity is inexact: The theory to be proposed does not follow the law's view that, roughly, nonculpable ignorance of the law is no excuse, or that *mens rea* considerations may be ignored in connection with the offenses of bigamy or statutory rape, or that a strict felony-murder rule is justified. (Since many lawyers are uncomfortable with the law at these points, perhaps an element of fiction is present in talk of "the law.") I wish to say, however, that the rough conformity of actual law to the proposed general principle is enough to give plausibility to the view that the principle is in some sense implicit in the law; I also point out that where principle and law in principle are discrepant, there is reason to doubt that the law is justified.

WHAT KIND OF THEORY DO WE WANT?

I am urging the general position that legally wrongful acts ought to be subject to legal punishment only if they are at least partially caused by a defective state of the agent's (long-term) motivation. But how is one to support such a contention?

A full explanation and defense of an answer to this question would be too large a project to be undertaken here; what will be possible is only to outline a view, a parallel to which for the closely related field of ethics the writer has defended in detail elsewhere.[6] What we may say briefly is that we are looking for *justified* legal principles about excuses. But what is it for a legal principle to be "justified," and how do we identify one that is? I make use here of a proposal defended elsewhere for ethical principles: A legal system is justified if and only if all factually informed

6 *A Theory of the Good and the Right* (Oxford: Clarendon Press, 1979); and "The Explanation of Moral Language," above, Chapter 4.

and rational[7] adults would choose or prefer it to be obeyed and enforced in the society, with its institutions, if they expected to live in it. Or, what may be very nearly the same thing, legal principles are justified if that *moral system*, which factually informed and rational persons would prefer to any other if they expected to live under it, would call on individuals to obey and require officials to enforce them. I hope and anticipate that most readers will be favorably disposed toward this conception of justified principle; I think most if not all persons will be more favorably disposed toward a legal principle or system if they think it is justified in this sense – or better justified than alternatives.[8]

Among the "institutions" of a society like ours is the political system, with legislative and executive branches roughly democratically chosen, with a Constitution, a Supreme Court, and a division of powers among the three branches of government (not to mention all the pressure groups such as unions, the Moral Majority, etc.). It might be that all rational persons would want any legal system, adopted and supported by this political organization, to enjoy a defeasible presumption of authority – a presumption that might be defeated by a clear showing that some feature of the system must be expected to work contrary to the long-range welfare of people in general.

Can we say anything about what kind of legal/moral system informed rational persons would prefer for a society in which they expected to live? I believe the answer is that they would prefer a legal/moral system the currency of which in the society would maximize general benefit – general happiness, if you like. In other words, a rule-utilitarian system. This chapter is not the place for any extensive argument for this answer. It is admittedly controversial today, and unpopular in some quarters. Among those with whom it is unpopular are neo-retributivists about the criminal law. These writers, however, seldom or never work out a theory of their alleged moral knowledge; nor does the retributive theory ever get a precise statement. Those who lean toward the more traditional

---

7 See the writer's "The Concept of Rational Action," and ten other essays by various authors, on the general topic of rational decision, in the September 1983 issue of *Social Theory and Practice*.

8 It is logically possible that not all rational persons would prefer one and the same set of legal principles for a society in which they expected to live, and in that case we should have to adopt a more person-relative conception of "justified" such as, "If I were fully rational, *I* would choose or prefer this set of legal principles to be obeyed and enforced in that society, with its institutions, if I expected to live in it." For our purposes we can ignore this complication, which will hardly arise for the problem with which we are concerned. Another possible complication is that the moral system that all rational adults would prefer for a society in which they expected to live might condemn the very laws that they would want obeyed and enforced in that society. I ignore this logically possible complication.

utilitarian view need not worry for fear they are out of date.[9] For the present purposes I feel free to suppose that utilitarianism is sufficiently plausible today[10] to make it worthwhile to develop the implications of a utilitarian theory of the criminal law, as I shall do in the final section of this chapter.

What we are specifically concerned with here is those legal principles that rational persons would want as principles governing exemption from punishment when a legally wrongful act has been committed. The motivation theory of excuses is such a possibility: that a legally wrongful act ought to be subject to punishment only if the act manifested a defect of motivation. (A person who has acted wrongfully should also be exempt from punishment if he is insane, an infant, etc.)

The motivational theory, as stated, is a restricted principle; it states only what is a necessary condition for being punished at all. It could be expanded, in combination with a principle of proportionality, into the thesis that the severity of punishment for a given crime should be proportional to the gravity of the defect displayed by the criminal act. Retributivists might approve this, unless they think that the punishment inflicted must somehow equal the evil done. Thus, if a worse defect of motivation is shown by intentional homicide than by reckless homicide, one might infer that the punishment for murder should be more severe than for manslaughter. The "gravity" of a defect is not obvious, except for some cases: willingness to kill is manifestly worse than willingness to *risk* a killing. Mostly our thoughts about relative defects of motivation seem to go with our thoughts about how objectionable is the type of act that typically manifests it. We do have opinions on such matters, shown by how relatively severe a punishment we think acceptable, and also by our thoughts about which kinds of benefit will justify; thus we think and the law holds that use of a lethal weapon is justified to defend one's own life (or that of wife or children), but not to prevent a theft, much less to prevent trespass on one's land. The Supreme Court evidently thinks that murder is more heinous than rape.

However this may be, it is certain that suppositions about the character (= system of motivations)[11] of a defendant play a considerable role both

9 For a criticism of some recent retributive theories, see R. W. Burgh, "Do the Guilty Deserve Punishment?" *Journal of Philosophy* 79 (1982): 193–210; and D. F. Thompson, "Retribution and the Distribution of Punishment," *Philosophical Quarterly* 16 (1966): 59–63. For Kant, see D. E. Scheid, "Kant's Retributivism," *Ethics* 93 (1983): 262–82.
10 For support of this view see John Harsanyi, "Morality and the Theory of Rational Behavior," *Social Research* (1977): 623–56, and his *Essays on Ethics, Social Behavior, and Scientific Explanation* (Dordrecht: Reidel, 1976). See also Brandt, *Theory of the Good and the Right*, chaps. 11, 14, and 15.
11 See R. B. Brandt, "Traits of Character: a Conceptual Analysis," *American Philosophical*

in actual sentences to imprisonment and in normative statements in the Model Penal Code about the principles that should govern sentences.

We should note that some writers think that the dangerousness of a person, as revealed by his criminal act, does and should play a large role in the criminal law. How dangerous a person is, of course, is closely related to the particular defect of motivation shown by his criminal behavior; information about a person's standing motivation is an important guide to prediction of future behavior.

WHY THE MOTIVATIONAL THEORY?

Why should we think that an agent ought to be exempt from punishment for a wrongful act if a defect of motivation is not among the causal conditions of the act? We shall go into this more deeply in the final section, when we survey the rationale of legal punishment as a whole, but certain considerations merit attention at this point. We can at least call on the authority of ancient tradition if we think that an act is liable to punishment only if it springs from an "evil heart" or "vicious will." According to Sayre, about 1600 the "malice" required for a charge of murder involved "general malevolence or cold-blooded desire to injure."[12] As Sayre puts it,[13] the moral blameworthiness of a criminal deed

Quarterly 7 (1970), esp. p. 34, below, Chapter 14. Contrast Feinberg, *Doing and Deserving* (Princeton, NJ: Princeton University Press, 1970), pp. 126–7, 190–1.

12 Sayre, "Mens Rea," p. 997. The present writer has argued that to say an act is morally blameworthy is to affirm that the act would not have occurred but for a defect of character (motivation). See "Blameworthiness and Obligation" in A. I. Melden, ed., *Essays in Moral Philosophy* (Seattle, WA.: University of Washington Press, 1958); and *Ethical Theory* (Englewood Cliffs, NJ: Prentice-Hall, 1959), chap. 18. For the connection between character and motivation, see note 11 above.

Professor Fletcher appears to be mistaken when he says "The only way to work out a theory of excuses is to insist that the excuse represents a limited, temporal distortion of the actor's character." See George Fletcher, *Rethinking Criminal Law* (Boston: Little, Brown, 1978), p. 802. Assuming we identify character with standing motivation, there is no such thing as a "limited, temporal distortion" of it. Anger might seem an example, but if a person acts from extreme reasonable anger (provocation), we think his character is all right – that is, his standing aversions – it is only that the temporary angry desire to hurt was stronger. In the case of mistake of fact, or duress, there is no defect of character (motivation) at all. (See Brandt, "Traits of Character.") Fletcher remarks, however, that "an inference from the wrongful act to the agent's character is essential to a retributive theory of punishment" (p. 800). Further, "[I]f someone violates a legal prohibition under an unavoidable mistake about the legality of his conduct, we cannot infer anything about his respect for law and the rights of others. The same breakdown in the reasoning from conduct to character occurs in cases of insanity."

It should be noted that moral blameworthiness, as a commonsense term, is no better off than *mens rea*. I have argued (see "Blameworthiness and Obligation") that it is useful to define it in a certain way, but in fact the term is hardly in active use at all by ordinary speakers (nonlawyers, or more likely, nonlaw professors), and the most obvious candidate, "deserves to be blamed," raises more questions than it answers. What is it to

241

(and *mens rea* required this) was "necessarily based upon a free mind voluntarily choosing evil rather than good." This view, if we include the talk about a "free" mind choosing evil, appears to be burdened with a heavy load of questionable metaphysics. We get the picture of a mind, free in the sense of causally undetermined, opting for what is evil rather than what is good. This picture must be modified to some extent if the conception is to deserve a serious hearing today. The first thing we have to do is construe free choice in the ordinary sense, such as when a person says, "You married me of your own free will," meaning in the absence of coercion (it was not a shotgun wedding) and perhaps after an opportunity to deliberate on the options and their probable consequences, and to take the option one most wanted to take, everything considered. This is far from free choice in the sense of causal indeterminism, and is compatible with a science of motivational psychology (a science about lawfulness in action, or causation in action). Suppose, then, we take free choice to mean uncoerced action determined by the desires and aversions of the agent and his conception of the options open to him and their probable consequences. Then we can construe an evil will in terms of the (objectionable) desires or aversions of the agent, from which his actions spring, in part. So we might mean by an evil will the presence of desires to do harm to someone, and the like, or, more important, indifference to the prospect of harming others or running the risk of so doing. If we do this, we can regard human agents as causal systems, of which desires/aversions are an important part. If we make this change, and go along with tradition in identifying *mens rea* with an evil will, then we can claim the support of tradition in holding that *mens rea*, the mental element necessary for liability to punishment, at least in large part concerns the motivation of the agent, as a consequence of which he chose to do what he did, in the situation as he saw it. Indifference to the welfare of others, then, may be a major part of what it is to have an evil will.

Recent writings, however, emphasize that the mental element of a crime has to do with intention, whether something was done knowingly or purposefully. In the case of *Regina* v. *Cunningham* (Court of Criminal Appeal, 41 Crm. App. 155, 1957), the court proposed that to show that a defendant acted "maliciously," it suffices to show that he "foresaw" that what he did might injure. This seems a departure from a motivational conception of *mens rea*. But it is not; the psychology of motivation

blame someone for something? To reproach him face to face? To criticize him behind his back? To affirm that some defect in him is a cause of his act? ("The engine's performance must be blamed on the plugs.") Evidently the meaning of this term does not lie on the surface.
13 Sayre, "Mens Rea," p. 1004.

appears to have been widely misunderstood. If we turn to psychological theory, we find that what a person does at a given moment is a function of at least five variables: (1) his beliefs (possibly partly unconscious) about the options open to him; (2) his beliefs about the situation he is in; (3) his beliefs about consequences that might occur if he takes any one of these options and how likely they are (how likely he thinks the consequences would be); (4) the vividness of his representation of these matters at the time; and (5) his desires and aversions for these consequences (taking each action as being a consequence of itself, so that an aversion just to doing something of a certain sort is included). The theory asserts that a person will have a *tendency* to perform an action he thinks open to him, according as it promises to have consequences he wants with how great a probability; the person will actually perform that act he has the strongest tendency to perform, as fixed by the desires/aversions associated with the anticipated consequences, their influence diminished by the anticipated improbability of a consequence occurring if he performs the act. Some writers put this by saying that people act roughly so as to maximize their expected utility – "utility" being defined in terms of their desires/aversions at the time.

A surprising fact then emerges: The motivation and belief are entangled in the production of an action in a way seemingly overlooked by some writers on the law. Suppose we say Jane is guilty of a crime because she tampered with the brakes of her husband's car, expecting it would bring about his death. Our legal scholar says Jane has *mens rea* because she knowingly acted so as to bring about a death. (Presumably Jane brought about her husband's death not because she wanted this for itself, but because his death would enable her to collect his insurance and elope with someone else.) Now, when we take psychological theory into account it is clear that what is responsible for Jane's tampering with the brakes and thereby producing her husband's death is not merely her wanting the insurance money along with knowing that tampering with the brakes in order to get it would bring about his death; what is responsible is her relative indifference to bringing about her husband's death. Our legal scholar could as well have said that Jane is guilty of a crime because she tampered with the brakes, relatively indifferent to the prospect that so doing would bring about the death. But for that indifference, her action would not have occurred. So it is clear that while the Model Penal Code makes the normal mental condition of criminality that the agent purposefully or knowingly or recklessly do a forbidden thing, it could as well be said that the normal condition of criminal action is *failure to be motivated to avoid* a foreseen forbidden consequence or to be indifferent to a substantial risk that it occur. Thus talk about intention or foresight is misleading; the intentions we have are a function of our desires/aversions, and what a person foresaw is evidence about what he was indifferent to. What is novel in the motivation theory, as compared with the ordinary view, is simply the looking at another side of the picture.

If we speak of "defects of motivation," the question arises which kind of defect we have in mind. Would some moral defect, like lack of generosity or sympathy, or sadism, be enough? (If we answer affirmatively, a judge might have to draw on the positive morality of his day to identify a defect, or, if he happens to be a scholar in the history of philosophy, he might speculate as to "true" defects.) A more plausible view would be to identify as defects those stated or implied by the prohibitions (in statutes or precedents) of a given legal system; so, if the law forbids intercourse with a girl less than ten years of age, absence of an adequate aversion to intercourse with a child, or at least absence of an adequate aversion to obedience to the relevant prohibition of the law, would count as a defect. Sometimes the law specifies that a crime of a certain sort is committed only if the agent intended something, for example, if he enters a building for the purpose of committing some crime; the defect then is not only that of being unaverse to entering a building not one's own, but also that of being unaverse to the prospect of committing some other wrongful act. So our list of defects is essentially taken from the law. Of course, the law may be bad law, in which case the "defects" will not really be defects from any point of view other than that of bad law. The law is always subject to improvement from the standpoint of reflective morality.

When we speak of a "defect" of motivation, we need to specify some degree of strength. A person might have some degree of aversion to killing another, or breaking the law generally, but go ahead anyway because the prospective victim stood in his way. How much motivation is adequate? It need not be of infinite strength, enough to overcome every possible contrary motivation; to use terminology some favor, it must only be enough to resist contrary motivations that a person of ordinary firmness would resist. So the aversion to cooperating in an armed robbery should be greater than any desire to do what might win the affections of a lady, but it need not be enough to overcome an aversion to having a bullet in one's head, instantly, if one refuses to go along (excuse of duress). One finds some of these comparisons spelled out in cases in which it is debated whether an offense is "justified." One will also get a rough ordering of the expected strength of aversions for various offenses, by looking at the severity with which the corresponding offense is punished. (This correspondence is, however, certainly rough: In *Rummel* v. *Estelle* the Supreme Court upheld Texas statutes that inflicted life imprisonment on a person whose three nonviolent felonies, for example, a forged check, involved a total of $240.)

If the motivational theory of *mens rea* is correct, in holding that an unlawful and unjustified act is subject to punishment only if it manifests a defect of motivation, then an excuse must be some showing, in the face of knowledge that the accused acted illegally and without justification, that the action was compatible with there being no defect of motivation – the normal inference from act to motivation is blocked. If we hold that this theory of excuses is essentially embodied in the law, we expect to find that the recognized excuses (and, *mutatis mutandis*, at least some mitigations) are of this kind.

It may be thought that obviously a legal excuse is no such thing, for, if it were, judges would be required to dabble in speculations about motivation in order to apply the law. (But according to the motivational theory, a judge is not required to sum up the virtues and vices of a person and decide whether on the whole he is a virtuous man, or at least up to average. Also, he is not required to decide whether a given action would be morally blameworthy – manifest a moral defect – if it were not contrary to law.) But judges in fact necessarily do make some judgments about motivation. (And judgments about the intent or beliefs of the accused need be no less speculative.) If we follow the Model Penal Code, a judge, in order to decide that a voluntary act was performed at all, must conclude that the bodily movement was not a result of a convulsion, made during sleep or unconsciousness, or as a result of hypnotic suggestion, but rather that it was "a product of the effort or determination of the actor, either conscious or habitual" (Art. 2.01).[14] The conclusion clearly requires inference beyond observable bodily behavior. Moreover, according to the Code, in order to decide that an act meets the general conditions of criminal culpability, it must be shown that either (1) the "conscious object" of the agent was to behave in a certain way or produce a certain effect, or (2) that the agent was "aware of" or "practically certain" of all material elements of the offense, or (3) that the agent consciously disregarded a substantial and unjustifiable risk "such that its disregard involves a gross deviation from the standard of conduct that a law-abiding person would observe in the actor's situation," or (4) he acts as if he were disregarding a risk, but is unaware of the risk although his failure to be aware of it is itself a "gross deviation from the standard of care that a reasonable person would observe in the actor's situation" (Art. 2.02

---

14 Actually, a judgment is required about a causal relation to beliefs and desires. See A. I. Goldman, *A Theory of Human Action* (Englewood Cliffs, NJ: Prentice-Hall, 1970), p. 72. Scholars of the criminal law should be familiar with this book.

245

(2)). With the possible exception of (2), if this is not speculation about motivation, what would be?

The motivational theory of excuses requires only that someone decide whether a certain feature of the case rules out an inference to a defect of motivation, given the other facts surrounding what the defendant did.

It may be objected that the theory implies that, when illegal behavior is unexcused, there can be inference from behavior to defect of motivation, whereas no such inference is ever possible. But this is absurd. Once we assume, as we must, that action is a function roughly of the beliefs and desires/aversions of the agent, we are in a good position to reconstruct the motivation, and we do so all the time. If a person does not interrupt a friendly game of tennis to make inquiries when a child falls off a bicycle in the next court and is screaming and covered with blood, and no one else is around to render succor, we infer that he is defective in sympathy or empathy. Of course a further story might provide a justification or excuse. And the inference does require commonsense familiarity with how people ordinarily behave in certain circumstances, and why they do the things they do. But we do know these things.[15]

THE MOTIVATION THEORY
AND RECOGNIZED EXCUSES

The motivation theory will appear more plausible if it is clear that the standard excuses recognized are excuses in my sense. I have suggested earlier that this fact does not strictly confirm the theory, but it does show the theory is in touch with the realities of the law. Let us therefore survey the major excuses, and see how well they fit the motivation theory.

Accidents. An accident occurs when some untoward event occurs because a causal process has unforeseeably gone awry: A bullet ricochets and kills a bystander; a child darts out from between parked cars in front of a motorist; a cable breaks. (The event is not accidental if negligence is involved, for example, if the driver could have stopped had he not been

15 For a view similar in many ways to the motivation theory of excuses, see Michael D. Bayles, "Character, Purpose, and Criminal Responsibility," *Law and Philosophy* (1982): 5–20, especially pp. 9 ff. Bayles attributes a form of the theory to Hume. One might object that a man may be guilty of manslaughter if he kills his brother who has a terminal cancer, is in pain, wishes to die, but cannot find a physician with the courage to give a lethal dose. How is this possible, if criminality requires some defect of motivation? In fact, most people do not think the man a criminal, and are not surprised or shocked if he receives probation or a nominal sentence, perhaps just a fine. The judge is in a dilemma: He cannot himself regard the man as a criminal whom the law ought to punish, but he does not wish to encourage other people to make decisions about the lives of others, possibly in a less discriminating way. Much the same may be said about conscientious objectors to many laws.

talking with a passenger or waving to a friend.) In such cases, when an event occurs that the law prohibits, the agent is legally excused. The motivation theory implies this conclusion, for in such cases (negligence aside) no inference to a defect of motivation is possible. In some special circumstances, however, the agent is not legally excused. For instance, if a person is committing a felony and accidentally discharges a weapon, killing someone, he is not excused, since the context of the attempted felony provides "presumption" that the death was caused "recklessly under circumstances manifesting extreme indifference to the value of human life" (Model Penal Code 210.2 (1)(b)). The "presumption" need not correspond with the facts, but the explanation offered by the Code fits the motivation theory, in that the total event is said to "manifest extreme indifference to the value of human life" – certainly a defect of motivation of high degree.[16]

Mistake of fact. The motivational theory affirms that an agent is not liable to punishment for a wrongful act (unjustified breach of the law) if the breach was not at least partly caused by a standing defect of his motivation. So, is a woman guilty of a crime if she kills her husband, shooting through a closed door, in the honest belief that she is firing at someone attempting to break into her bedroom to rape her? What would be the defect of motivation? The law does not condemn willingness to use a lethal weapon to protect one's self from being raped. So, in the circumstances, there is no reason to suppose her action was caused by defective motivation, and, according to the theory, she must be excused. That is also the conclusion of the law. (See the Model Penal Code, 2.04, 233.1(1) and 212.4(1)(a).) It can be, however, again as the law affirms, that, given a person's mistaken belief, his action shows some other defect of motivation different from that which would have been shown had he not entertained a mistaken belief, and then he can be guilty of a lesser crime.[17]

It may be objected that the motivational theory does not reflect the law since, according to the motivational theory, an honest mistake of fact could block inference to a defect of motivation, whereas at least the

---

16 For a useful discussion of the history and logic of the status of accidents, see George Fletcher, *Rethinking Criminal Law*, pp. 276 ff. and 487 ff.

17 This remark supposes that the defect of motivation is to function not merely as a condition for nonexemption from punishment altogether, but as a clue to the permissible degree of punishment, as it does in those theories that hold that the severity of punishment should be proportional to the blameworthiness of the agent. If this view is rejected, as it would be by the writer, for a largely treatment view of criminal justice, once guilt (some offense + *mens rea*) is established, then degrees of defect would be of little functional importance. The role of considerations of deterrence will be discussed in the following section.

common law tradition requires that the mistake be reasonable, and in some cases (bigamy, statutory rape, abduction, attacking an officer of the law), a mistake of fact is no defense, reasonable or not. (The motivational theory will concede that the reasonableness of a belief is important evidence for whether the belief was actually held.) A view closer to the motivational theory (Texas statute, see *Green* v. *State*)[18] requires that the belief arise from want of proper care, which of course implies a defect of motivation, but possibly a minor defect. Contemporary legal opinion, however, appears to have moved into substantial agreement with the motivational theory, requiring only actual belief rather than reasonable belief, for serious crimes.

Mistake of law. The motivation theory appears to be in conflict with the practice of courts on the question whether mistake of law is an excuse. On the whole, at least in theory, courts have held that mistakes as to criminal law (as distinct, for instance, from property law) are no excuse. For example, a native of Baghdad committed an unlawful "unnatural offence" on board an East Indian ship anchored in an English harbor. The act was no crime in his native country; he did not know that it was in England; and he presumably did not think the action immoral. But his conviction was upheld. How could this be, if liability to punishment requires a defect of motivation? It would be unreasonable to suppose that he should have inquired as to the legality of the act in England; thus there was no evidence of defect of diligence in inquiring into the law, so no lack of respect for the law of England. It may be that in the England of the time (1836), it was thought manifest that "unnatural offences" were immoral and that the man should have been put on notice thereby that the law might well prohibit them;[19] or it may have been thought that absence of an aversion to sodomy was itself a defect of motivation. Public opinion today, however, is probably better summarized in an opinion of the Iowa Supreme Court, in part as follows: "Respect for law, which is the most cogent force in prompting orderly conduct in a civilized community, is weakened, if men are punished for acts which according to the general consensus of opinion they were justified in believing to be morally right and in accordance with law."[20] Nevertheless, a line of distinguished jurists has offered arguments to the effect that allowing ignorance of the law as an excuse would be impracticable and undermine the efficacy of the law. Even an opinion of the U.S. Supreme Court,[21]

18 153 Tex. Crim. 442, 221 S. W. 2nd 612, 1949. See citation in P. W. Low, J. C. Jeffries, Jr., and R. J. Bonnie, *Criminal Law* (New York: Foundation Press, 1982), p. 264.
19 The case was *Rex* v. *Esop*, 173 Eng. Rep. 203 (Cent. Crim. Ct. 1836).
20 *State* v. *O'Neil*, 147 Iowa 513, 126 N.W. 454 (1910).
21 *Lambert* v. *California*, 1957, 335 U.S. 225.

delivered by Justice Douglas, while overturning a conviction of infringing a California law that the defendant could not have known about, stated that "We do not go with Blackstone in saying that 'a vicious will' is necessary to constitute a crime, for conduct without regard to the intent of the doer is often sufficient. There is wide latitude in the lawmakers to declare an offense and to exclude elements of knowledge and diligence from its definition." The Court managed to distinguish the case at hand on the ground that it was "conduct that is wholly passive – mere failure to register. It is unlike the commission of acts, or the failure to act under circumstances that should alert the doer to the consequences of his deed." The Court found that in this type of situation a conviction violated the constitutional requirement of due process. Oliver Wendell Holmes argued at length that the tests of criminality are external behavior, except for cases of infancy and insanity.[22]

I believe we must concede that some decisions of the courts in denying ignorance of the criminal law as an excuse tend to show that the motivation theory is not entirely in accord with judicial practice. On the other hand, the justification of this practice is open to serious question. The dictum even of the Supreme Court does not justify it. The arguments offered by legal writers, in defense of the practice (for example, that allowing the excuse would be unacceptably burdensome for the courts, that it would encourage ignorance of the law, and stand in the way of efficacy of the law in preventing objectionable forms of conduct, or in effect that it would make the law identical with whatever the defendant thinks it is) seem without merit. If what the courts had to decide, in the terms of the Iowa decision, were whether the defendant was "justified in believing his conduct to be morally right and in accordance with the law," the burden on the court would not be too heavy. Nobody would convince a jury that he thinks unjustified murder is morally right and also in accordance with the law. And a person will hardly be justified in thinking his conduct in accordance with the law, unless he has diligently made inquiries, when he is aware at least that there are or may well be differences of moral opinion about an action, so that he is put on notice that the law may contain a relevant provision. It is true that if the Iowa principle were followed, a defendant must be excused when he infringes some unadvertised regulation about which moral considerations give no warning. But such a practice would not undermine the law, especially if it were understood to apply only in the case of serious charges involving possible imprisonment. Here we should go at least part way with Professor Hart when he writes that "[W]e should restrict even punishment designed as

---

22 See *The Common Law*, chap. 2.

'preventive' to those who at the time of their offence had the capacity and a fair opportunity or chance to obey the law: and we should do this out of considerations of fairness or justice to those whom we punish."[23] We need go only part way with Hart in that we should, I think, replace his phrase about "capacity and a fair opportunity to obey" with an expression about defect of motivation, and replace his reference to reasons of "fairness or justice" by one to long-range utilitarian considerations, as we shall see below.

It should be noticed that the motivation theory does not imply that all ignorance of law should constitute an excuse, but only that kind of ignorance, or ignorance in such circumstances, as to make clear that the defendant's conduct did not spring from a defect of motivation.

Voluntary Intoxication. The law understands "intoxication" to refer to a state brought on by drugs as well as alcohol; it will do no harm to confine ourselves to the case of alcohol. Let us suppose, then, that a person has become drunk and commits an offense, and that the offense and circumstances are such that, had he been sober, his conduct would undoubtedly have manifested a defect of motivation. Now the law says, in effect, that even if, in his state of intoxication, one cannot assume a defect of motivation, he is nevertheless liable to punishment (barring crimes the definition of which includes "specific intent"), unless he took the alcohol for medical reasons, or does not know (and need not know, morally or legally) that the amount ingested would cause intoxication (see Model Penal Code, 2.08). Is this what the motivation theory implies?

Evidently we must distinguish two acts, what the agent did after he was already drunk, and his acts (one or more) of drinking a quantity of alcohol. Drinking is not a crime, and unless one thinks it morally wrong the taking of a drink does not permit inference, by itself, of a defect of motivation. However, on the basis of past experience of his own reaction to alcohol, or by inductive generalization from the reactions of others, the agent might well have reason to believe that in drinking what he did, he was running a risk – that an ordinary law-abiding person would not run – of becoming drunk and committing an offense in that condition (for example, driving his car). In that case, his initial act showed some defect of motivation: indifference to taking this risk. He might even know he is running a substantial risk of acting violently. In that case we can say that his subsequent offense arose out of this initial defect of motivation, but only indirectly. The offense for which he is culpable is running the risk. If a person runs the risk of acting violently and kills someone,

23 Review in *Yale Law Journal* 74 (1965): 1325 ff.

he might well be charged with manslaughter – his behavior could be classified as reckless. However this may be, a person who has demonstrably run a serious risk will have done something that, if one adopts the modified Wootton-like view of punishment defended by H. L. A. Hart and Joel Feinberg, justifies his being placed at the disposal of the system for dealing with criminal offenders. New York State has a statute forbidding reckless endangerment.

The motivation theory, then, is out of line with the law when the law refuses to count voluntary drunkenness as any kind of excuse (except for the case of specific intentions). But then, in this the law is inconsistent: On the one hand it declares that an act must be voluntary (controlled by beliefs and desires), in order to be criminal, and then in effect affirms that acts not so controlled (a drunken act) may be fully liable. The motivation theory has implications identical with those the law ought to have. There is another way of viewing the total situation that might reconcile the law and the motivation theory. Suppose it is agreed that what the law should punish is reckless endangerment (by taking a drink in circumstances such that the agent should know he is taking a risk). The law might wish to deter such recklessness by suitable punishment, but the problems of detection make this impracticable. However, the law might say that, in this situation, the sensible thing to do is to punish quite severely those who cause real damage; this is a kind of selective punishment (like punishing every tenth person), and it would serve the purpose of deterring from reckless endangerment, if the law is known. If lawmakers do view matters in this light, it would be helpful if the fact were well publicized.

I am not familiar with any full phenomenology of drunkenness; it could well be that behavior when drunk (depending somewhat on how drunk the person is) could reveal, or be caused by, standing defective motivations.[24] The motivation theory need not object to punishment in some such circumstances.

Duress. My theory gives a clear account, superior in simplicity and plausibility, of why and when duress is an excuse. The theory, we recall, holds that wrongful behavior is liable to punishment only if it manifests a defective level of motivation. But how strong must be the motivation to avoid a certain offense, or to act in a law-abiding fashion? It depends on the offense. For instance, aversion to killing one's wife is expected to be strong enough to outweigh a desire to be free to elope with one's secretary. But aversion to breaking some laws is not expected to be able

24 See the learned and helpful discussion in Herbert Fingarette and Ann F. Haas, *Mental Disabilities and Criminal Responsibility* (Berkeley, CA: University of California Press, 1979), chaps. 6, 9, 11, and 12.

to compete with certain other motives, such as a present, immediate threat of death or serious bodily injury either to one's self or others close to one. So the Model Penal Code (2.09) states that if a person is threatened with unlawful force "which a person of reasonable firmness in his situation" would be unable to resist, there is a valid defense. The standard of motivation expected by the law falls short of the requirement of proving one's self a hero, more dedicated to avoiding illegal acts than persons of reasonable firmness. What a person may do, then, depends both on the unlawful act he is coerced to perform, and also on the nature of the threat.

Matters are more complex if the defendant was responsible for being in his dilemma: if, for instance, he voluntarily joined a group that he knew might later threaten him if he refused to perform violent acts. In that case the situation must be viewed from a longer time-span, as in the case of unlawful behavior when drunk, and the whole situation may lead to an inference of defective motivation at the time of joining, so that inferences comparable to those in the case of drunkenness are authorized.

Provocation. Provocation is not an exculpating excuse in the law, but only a mitigating one, reducing a charge of murder to one of manslaughter. But its legal status is sufficiently similar to that of intoxicated behavior to merit dicussion.

A rather plausible (perhaps unrepresentatively progressive) principle, stated in *Maher* v. *People* (10 Mich. 1962), is that there is legal provocation if "reason should, at the time of the act, be disturbed or obscured by passion to an extent which might render ordinary men, of fair average disposition, liable to act rashly, without due deliberation or reflection, and from passion, rather than judgement." This is somewhat similar to the Model Penal Code rule (210.3 (1)(b)) that a homicide is only manslaughter when "a homicide which would otherwise be murder is committed under the influence of extreme mental or emotional disturbance for which there is reasonable explanation or excuse. The reasonableness of such explanation or excuse shall be determined from the viewpoint of a person in the actor's situation under the circumstances as he believes them to be."

Strong emotional disturbance is known to primitivize thinking (much as does alcohol). A state of anger notoriously enhances one's aggressive tendencies, and reduces one's empathetic or sympathetic concern about injuring its target. So the law has traditionally looked sympathetically at homicide brought on by discovering one's spouse in the act of adultery, or by a violent blow. Why? Herbert Wechsler and Jerome Michael opined[25] that the reason is that the fact of anger blocks inference to a

---

25 Herbert Wechsler and Jerome Michael, "A Rationale of the Law of Homicide II," *Columbia Law Review* 37 (1937).

deficiency in the agent's character (standing level of motivation, in my terms); the more an ordinary man, of "fair average disposition," would incline to do the same, the less reason there is to think that the agent falls short, in his normal standing motivation, of a satisfactory level of moral/legal motivation. Not just any strong emotion will do this job: as the Model Penal Code puts it, there must be a "reasonable explanation or excuse," traditionally the objectionable conduct of the victim, presumably because anger not understandable to the average person would be a manifestation of irascibility, which is itself a defect of motivation of a sort.

The law on this topic has puzzling features. Why does provocation not exculpate, and merely mitigate, if the provocation shows that the motivation of the accused is not demonstrably less acceptable than that of the reasonable man? Perhaps the law is best read as suggesting that the standing motivation of the provoked man is not so very far from that of the ordinary man (but surely he is a difficult person with a hot temper!), and hence, combined with a theory of proportionality, that his punishment should be less.

In general, the legally mitigating effect of provocation fits in reasonably well with a motivational theory of excuses (mitigations).[26]

We should notice that the law governing the punishment of attempts fits nicely with what the motivational theory implies. If a man announces to a woman that he is going to rape her, and is in a position to do so, and then abandons his venture, the law takes a very different view of his behavior if his abandoning it is brought about by the unexpected appearance of a policeman, as compared with his saying to her, "No, I simply cannot do a thing of this sort. Please forgive me." Manifestly the latter behavior shows a level of motivation much nearer to what the law expects than does the former.

Somewhat the same might be said of the law in jurisdictions where a

---

26 I omit discussion of entrapment. It seems impossible to give a coherent account of it as an excuse, since the very seductions to crime that are a defense when they are provided by the police, do not serve as a defense when provided by private parties. (The law does suggest the motivation theory, however, when it speaks of entrapment as providing inducements to crime "by persons other than those who are ready to commit it." Does "ready to" refer to a substandard level of aversion to the offense or to lawbreaking in general?) Maybe what is behind it is the idea that we are all likely to commit a crime if we are tempted often enough, or severely enough, and it may be the victim's bad luck, not his less-than-adequate character, if he is seduced by the police. Or perhaps it is that we do not think the law-enforcement agencies ought to be in the business of tempting people to break the law. J. Feinberg, in *Doing and Deserving*, pp. 191 and 213 ff., gives helpful suggestions. I am indebted to L. M. Seidman's paper, "The Supreme Court, Entrapment, and Our Criminal Justice Dilemma," *Supreme Court Review* (1981): 111–55.

crime is punished less severely if the defendant has a low level of intelligence. The intellectual defect leaves open the possibility that the character – motivation – of the agent is not below, or not far below, what the law expects.

Insanity. I shall consider two questions about the insanity defense: first, whether it adds anything to the excuses already considered, for example, mistake of fact or law; and second, if it does, whether this defense may be viewed as an excuse in the sense explained above, as a consideration blocking inference from a person's unlawful behavior to a defect of motivation. We may follow the Model Penal Code (4.01(1)) definition of the defense: that a person is exempt from punishment for legally wrongful (unlawful, unjustified) conduct "if at the time of such conduct as a result of mental disease or defect he lacks substantial capacity either to appreciate the criminality [wrongfulness] of his conduct or to conform his conduct to the requirements of law." It is added that "mental disease or defect" does not include abnormality manifested only by repeated antisocial conduct.

We may assume that we are considering only "voluntary" acts within the meaning of the Model Penal Code (2.01), limited to bodily movement that is "a product of the effort or determination of the actor, either conscious or habitual," and thus excluding convulsions, automatisms, movements during sleep or unconsciousness, or resulting from hypnosis. Our questions are not easy to answer because "mental disease or defect" can take many forms, or be manifest in many ways.

One widespread form of insanity is the occurrence of delusions or distortions of judgment, so as (to use terms of the older M'Naghten rule) "not to know the nature and quality" of one's act. Suppose, to take an example that appears to be a favorite of law professors, a man strangles his wife in the honest belief that he is squeezing a lemon. In this case the agent is acting on the basis of a mistake of fact; if the facts were as he believes them to be, his conduct is perfectly lawful. So this kind of "insane" behavior is already covered under "mistake of fact," and no additional insanity defense is needed. The same goes for all behavior that would be lawful or justified if the agent's delusional beliefs were true.[27]

The older M'Naghten rule distinguishes something else from such factual mistake, namely, "if he did not know he was doing what was wrong," echoed by the Model Penal Code as "if he lacked substantial capacity . . . to appreciate the criminality [wrongfulness (moral?)] of his conduct." In both cases it is stipulated that the ignorance must be the product of mental

---

27 See Heathcote W. Wales, "An Analysis of the Proposal to 'Abolish' the Insanity Defense in S.1: Squeezing a Lemon," *Univ. of Pennsylvania Law Rev.* (1976): 687–712.

disease or defect. This conception is puzzling. Perhaps the agent is deficient in capacity to visualize the impact on others of what he does. Presumably, if this were intended, the defense would seem to recognize a showing that the inability is a result of some other defect, like brain damage, since some studies have shown prison populations to be relatively deficient in a capacity for visualization. Some interpreters of the law construe the moral knowledge or appreciation to include emotional appreciation. But then such interpretation might classify most criminal conduct as insane, if we construe, as apparently we must, thinking that an act is wrong or appreciating its wrongness, as essentially not cognitive but a matter of attitudes – essentially aversion to an act, disposition to feel guilty about performing it, and disapproving of others who do. But if that is what is true, then that kind of insanity consists precisely in failure to have adequate moral/legal motivation. And it is puzzling how that could serve as an excuse; adequate moral/legal motivation (or, in other words, character) is exactly what the law expects of people; behavior that must be explained by absence of adequate motivation is precisely unexcused. Another possible interpretation of these passages is that it is suggested that a person's conceptual scheme is so primitive that his concepts of the criminal/morally wrong are too undeveloped to serve as the basis for motivation to avoid criminal forms of behavior. But this is speculation; the meaning of the legal conceptions does not seem clear enough for an answer to our two questions.

The Model Penal Code also, as noted, exempts from punishment if, as a result of mental disease, an agent "lacks substantial capacity ... to conform his conduct to the requirements of law." This could be a cognitive defect but not a mistake of fact or law, if we follow Sir James Stephen in his account: "The man who does not control himself is guided by the motives which immediately press upon his attention. If this is so, the power of self-control must mean a power to attend to distant motives and general principles of conduct, and to connect them rationally with the particular act under consideration, and a disease of the brain which so weakens the sufferer's powers as to prevent him from attending or referring to such considerations ... deprives him of the power of self-control."[28] If one attempts to apply this interpretation, one faces the difficulty of discriminating between incapacity deriving from a "disease of the brain" and that incapacity common, more or less, to us all, or at least to many criminals.

More frequently, however, the incapacity of an agent to conform his conduct to the law is explained in a different way. Courts have recognized

28 *A History of the Criminal Law of England* II (1883), p. 170.

an "irresistible impulse" to do something, for example, steal, as relieving from responsibility. What seems to be meant is that the desire to steal was so strong that it would overcome even a satisfactory level of moral/legal motivation. If so, there could be no inference from the criminal act to defective motivation, and this insanity defense could be incorporated as an instance of the motivational theory of excuses, rather like duress. But perhaps this is not what is meant by an irresistible impulse, for in cases of kleptomania it is known that the desire is not a normal desire; it is for things that apparently do the agent no good, and can hardly be a source of satisfaction.[29] But the psychological literature on kleptomania is minute, and it may be that any sensible theory of it would require a different account.

Other types of cases apparently fall within this "inability to conform" conception of legal insanity, for instance, a man who suffered brain damage and who mutilated himself and killed others in sudden fits of rage.[30] Or a woman, in what was diagnosed as a psychosis brought on partly by repeated ingestion of drugs, who repeatedly stabbed her mother with no apparent motive.[31] One might say that the psychiatrist's account does block an inference to defective moral/legal motivation. But one is left puzzled about the possible state of the defendants' moral/legal motivation. One can hardly say that the evidence raises no doubt that the motivation system is normal/adequate, in the way no doubt is raised when we learn that criminal behavior arose from a nonculpable mistake of fact. I suggest that this kind of insanity defense not be viewed as an excuse.

THE BASIS OF THE MOTIVATION THEORY: THE GENERAL THEORY OF PUNISHMENT

What sort of justification can be given for the motivational theory, that persons who have unjustifiably broken valid law should be exempt from punishment unless their behavior is a result of some defect of standing motivation (one might say "character" instead)?

One way to answer this question would be to affirm a certain form of the retributive theory of punishment, and point out that the motivation theory follows from it. That is, one might subscribe to that form of retributivism which holds that a person should suffer punishment for lawbreaking to a degree corresponding to his moral blameworthiness, or

---

29 *State* v. *McCullough*, 114 Iowa Supreme Court, 532 (1901). See the interesting discussion in Joel Feinberg, *Doing and Deserving*, pp. 281–88.
30 *People* v. *Robles*, 1970, 2 Cal. 3d 205.
31 *People* v. *Kelly*, Supreme Court of Calif., 1973, 10 Cal. 3d. 575, 111 Cal. Rptr. 171, 516 P. 2d 875.

at least that he forfeit his right not to be used for purposes of deterrence, and to the extent of his blameworthiness. This theory entails the motivation theory if, as I think, "*X* is morally blameworthy for doing *A*" should be explained roughly as "*X* did *A*, and he would not have done *A* but for a defect of standing motivation (character), and as a result it is fitting for persons to disapprove of *X* because of his doing A." Thus, this retributive theory implies that a person should be punished for an act only if it showed a defect of motivation. The retributive theory of course goes beyond the motivation theory in implying a principle of proportionality: of quantity of punishment and degree of blameworthiness.

It seems likely that few philosophers (but perhaps relatively more legal theorists) take the retributive theory very seriously at the present time, despite the popularity of some kind of intuitionism in some circles. Some writers, who would draw back from asserting the retributive principle as just a basic moral principle known intuitively, have tried to derive some forms of it from different principles of justice that they find congenial, but their views are open to serious criticism.[32] In any case, the retributive theory at best gives only an ordinal theory: it tells us that *X* should be punished more for *A* than *Y* should be for doing *B*, but gives no clue exactly how much either one should be punished. The utilitarian theory has the virtue of yielding, in principle, some quantitative guide.

It seems worthwhile, then, for this and more general reasons suggested earlier, to examine what a utilitarian theory would imply with respect to the motivational theory of exemption from punishment.

We may recall that utilitarianism is a theory roughly that the whole system of social institutions should be appraised for its impact on well-being or happiness. The system of criminal justice is one of these institutions. One important cause of unhappiness, of course, is harmful behavior, and hence one of the aims of an optimal system of institutions, according to the utilitarian, will be to minimize harmful behavior, to the extent that so doing does not impair realization of more important goals. Among the other features of a society that affect happiness are such things as freedom to plan one's own life and implement the relevant decisions, the preservation of personal privacy, a considerable degree of social and economic equality, knowledge and its utilization in personal planning, and so on. The system of criminal justice is an institution especially aimed to reduce harmful or antisocial behavior, but, according to the utilitarian, it is open to criticism if it accomplishes this special aim at too great a

---

32 For a critical review see R. W. Burgh, "Do the Guilty Deserve Punishment?" *Journal of Philosophy* 79 (1982) 193–210.

cost, for example, loss of freedom and privacy; some loss in preventing harmful behavior must be accepted if avoiding it would cost more in loss of other benefits. Certain other institutions should aim, among other things, at preventing antisocial behavior: the economic system by removing incentives to crime and the crime-fostering conditions of the ghetto; the educational system; the church; the system of medical care for the mentally defective or ill; and positive morality if we want to call that an "institution." In view of these points, it is clear that the system of criminal justice must operate under some constraints. In order to avoid intolerable intrusion, or undue interference with freedom of planning, the system cannot give everyone psychological tests to determine whether, to maximize the general safety, he or she should be in custody; a person must be left alone unless he or she actually does something contrary to law – rather like allowing a dog one bite before its dangerousness is scrutinized. So a person cannot be held criminally liable unless there is an *actus reus* – a proved unlawful act.

What can the system of criminal justice do, within these constraints, to achieve its primary function of reducing harmful or antisocial behavior? I mention three things.

1. Partly it can be educational; it in effect announces, in a forceful way because the announcement is accompanied by a threat, which forms of behavior the society (or its representatives) considers harmful to the extent of being socially intolerable.

2. It can operate as a deterrent to harmful behavior. We should be clear just what can be expected of the system in this respect. Most people have well interiorized moral standards, and hence, to a large extent, will conform their conduct to the law in any case. But if there were no parking meters, even very decent people would be inclined to take more than their share of that scarce commodity of parking space; and if the Internal Revenue Service never prosecuted, it is doubtful whether so many even generally decent people would pay their share of taxes. So while, for most people, the deterrent threat of the law is unnecessary for most kinds of harmful behavior (most people would not consider murder, quite apart from the law), a threat of punishment is beneficial, for some types of cases, to help the average person behave properly. This is not to say that severe penalties (long prison terms) are needed for the average person; the reader need only ask himself for what conceivable gain he would risk being arrested, tried, having his shortcomings spread in the newspaper, being fined or imprisoned for six months, or even just being put on probation. The writer can think of few gains worth such a risk; and one need not escalate the risk to that of twenty years in prison in order already to have maximized deterrence. On the other hand, many people are not

deterred by the law, even with the relative severity of its threats in the United States.

Why? For one thing, people with little or no income have little incentive to stay out of jail, where they receive three square meals a day; they may think they are better off in than out. Again, some do not read a newspaper and know little about the threats of law, or perhaps they have never learned to evaluate prospective behaviors in terms of consequences and costs. The law also needs help from morality: If an agent's group does not proscribe violence or crimes of passion, or even idealizes power in a system of organized crime, the targeted deterrence is in for problems.

3. The system of criminal justice can operate to prevent repeaters. If a person is imprisoned and kept out of circulation, there is no danger of further criminal behavior (at least, outside the prison). Moreover, no one will doubt that a substantial fine for running a traffic light will, at least for some weeks, render the convicted motorist more cautious about obeying traffic signals. Is lengthy imprisonment effective as far as future behavior of the criminal is concerned? Not unless it gets at the causes of the original misbehavior. It would seem that the prison system should aim to return inmates to normal life as soon as is compatible with public safety – and that means such things as treatment for drug addiction, job training, assistance in finding a job on leaving a prison, and so on.

With these general background considerations in mind, we can now understand the justification of exempting persons from punishment when they have committed an unjustified offense by an action not caused, even in part, by a defective system of legal/moral motivation.

The utilitarian's general answer, and I suggest it is the right answer, is that the motivation theory of exemptions will maximize benefits. Let me summarize the reasoning.

1. If a person has broken the law but with no defect of motivation, no benefit is gained from punishing him, as far as his own future behavior is concerned. To allow him to circulate in society is no more dangerous than in the case of those who have not broken the law. It may be that punishment will attach an additional negative affect to the idea of doing that because of which he was convicted, but if his level of motivation is already satisfactory, so far as is known, to build up more negative affect is pointless. So the person (and presumably his family) is penalized without any benefit, at least as far as his future impact on society is concerned. Of course, a system of excuses different from the motivation theory (like the present one which emphasizes lack of intention, knowledge, recklessness, or negligence as an excuse) may have much the same effect, but the point of identifying excused behavior for these reasons must be that the indirect effect is that people already adequately motivated are excused.

But the motivation theory gets to the central point directly, and points the way to a desirable reform of law, by way of abolishing strict liability conjoined with serious penalties, as well as various irrational anomalies in the law such as, possibly, the felony-murder rule.

2. What is the alternative to the motivation theory, or something essentially identical with it? One possibility is a system of strict liability: A person convicted of unjustifiably breaking the law (or perhaps just breaking the law, justified or not) would be given a specified sentence, depending on the offense (or at least turned over to the detention system for treatment, as Lady Wootton would have it). Such a system could well be a nightmare, intolerable from the point of view of the average law-abiding citizen. What would life be like if one must anticipate a year in prison for accidentally running down a child, with no fault whatsoever on one's own part? The nightmare would be less bad if Lady Wootton's version were adopted, but even so the life of anyone unlucky enough to break the law by accident, or because of nonculpable mistake of fact, would be grossly damaged.

3. That punishment for excused crimes is pointless because not needed, and that the impact of a pure strict-liability system would be disastrous, might not be totally convincing, if it were not that exempting adequately motivated persons from punishment does not diminish the deterrent impact of the system of criminal justice. The issue is important, since the reason for legal punishment, according to most writers, is the deterrent effect of threat of punishment on potential wrongdoers. Many writers think that in fact the incorporation of excuses in a system of criminal law does diminish the deterrent effect of the system, and therefore hold that the consistent utilitarian would be opposed to a legal system with excuses.

If it were true that a strict liability system would be a more effective deterrent, that would be a utilitarian point in its favor – but only one, to be weighed against the preceding ones just mentioned. But why should it be thought that allowing excuses diminishes deterrence? As far as I know, no comparative studies show that excuses increase the crime rate. So we must simply think the matter through in a commonsense way. Let us ask: What class of crime would be deterred by a strict liability system but not by a system with excuses (roughly as the motivation theory advocates)? Not those committed by persons who do not know the law, so we must limit the effects to persons relatively informed on the system of criminal justice. Suppose we think of an informed rational person, who for some reason wants his wife out of the way and is deliberating whether to make an attempt on her life. How will the fact of the system of excuses affect his thinking? Perhaps he can manage to have a bullet ricochet? Perhaps he can convince a jury that he mistook his wife for a burglar, or that he was acting under hypnotic suggestion, or that someone threatened to kill him if he didn't, or that the episode was the result of a delusion, of schizophrenia? I think the rational prospective murderer will do better to spend his time thinking how to commit the crime so that the jury will not be convinced that he actually did it. So how much deterrence will be lost, for rational informed persons, from knowledge of the system of excuses? The rational person will see that it is going to be very difficult for him to escape punishment by the excuse route. I think we may agree that people may be encouraged to commit crimes by knowledge that persons who commit crimes are mostly not punished. Perhaps they know that most murderers are never brought to justice. How many of these escape via the excuse route? Perhaps two percent? Will this two percent have a detectible effect on deterrence, given the general situation? Suppose we think, as may be true, that the deterrent effect of the criminal law comes through vicariously attaching negative affect, by conditioning, to the thought of a given offense. Is there any reason to think this conditioning process will be significantly affected by the knowledge that a very small proportion of persons escape punishment by the excuse route?

Nevertheless, various writers at present, as far as I can see without support from either observation or psychological theory, airily assume that we know that allowing excuses must reduce deterrence. Not that these writers advocate that excuses be abolished in view of the alleged impact on the deterrent force of the system. Quite the contrary. What they want to do is pin on utilitarians a commitment to strict liability in the law, because they do, of course, in principle favor a system that on the whole will maximize utility. In fact, these critics fail to show that a strict liability system would actually increase the deterrent effect of the law. Even if it did, the foregoing two reasons, especially the second, are weighty; in view of them, one could hardly advocate a strict liability system on utilitarian grounds even if such a system were somewhat superior in efficacy of deterrence. Thus a utilitarian system of punishment will necessarily exempt from punishment those who have acted wrongly but in so doing manifest no defect of motivation or character.

My conclusion is that a rational and informed person, if he were to be given a choice among possible systems of criminal justice for the society in which he expected to live, would opt for a system exempting from punishment those persons who have committed an unjustified unlawful act, but did not thereby manifest any defect of standing motivation, or character. But I do not suggest that a person would feel happy about the total situation, even if the system of criminal justice were made as humane as possible, compatibly with a reasonable degree of protection of society from harmful actions. This is because of the great inequalities in our society, not only economically, but in intelligence, health, energy, and the type of family in which a person is reared. Many persons with a high level of intelligence and the good fortune of upbringing in a good family and a good education are never put in a position where they are strongly motivated to disobey the law. With others the opposite is the case. Even a humane system of excuses, one that punishes a person for a crime only when it is "his fault," does not remove the unjustified inequality in the lottery that bestows good things on some and bad things on others. It is true that we should say to ourselves, "There but for the grace of God go I." I suggest we all have an obligation to work toward the amelioration or removal of these inequalities, but that is not the job of the criminal law. What justifies the criminal law is that it is the best compromise among unhappy alternatives, for the world as it now is. On the one hand, life would be intolerable if no criminal law existed and no one was deterred from doing as he pleased by the threat of punishment; on the other hand, with the system, many have to suffer who would not have had to suffer had the lottery of life not put them where they are. So the criminal law has to remain an uneasy compromise, attempting to accommodate both the need to protect society from harm, and the obligation to avoid imposing suffering on those who have broken the law. A system that exempts from punishment offenders who are not "at fault" – defective in moral/ legal motivation – is an advance toward humanity without significant loss in protection of society.

14

Traits of character:
A conceptual analysis

Recent philosophical psychology has paid scant attention to the concept of traits, either of personality in general or more specifically of character, in comparison with that devoted to concepts of choice, desire, will, and intention. This is unfortunate, for several reasons. Trait-names play a large role in the practical discourse of the ordinary person, whether in back-fence commentary or in letters of recommendation, and there is always a danger that things may go wrong if the speaker is totally vague about the analysis of the term. The same danger is run by historians who make free use of trait concepts in explanations of events (the collapse of a nation may be ascribed to things like the queen's vanity). Furthermore, there is currently a large literature on traits by psychologists (the work, for example, of writers like Cattell, Eysenck, McClelland, Allport, Heider, and Norman). Despite the mathematical sophistication of these writers, particularly the factor analysts, it seems that a little philosophical spadework at the foundations can serve at least to suggest interesting questions relevant to the large theoretical edifices that have been raised. Finally, and most important, the moral philosopher has a considerable stake in the understanding of character-trait concepts. Some philosophers, like Ross and Hartmann, have included character traits among the things that have intrinsic value. Other writers, concerned with the issue of determinism, have thought that the determinist thesis about human conduct arises from a confusion about the nature of traits of character. Last, there is the thesis that an act is morally blameworthy only if it would not have occurred but for some defective trait in the moral character of the agent, and that it is morally praiseworthy only if it would not have occurred but for some superior trait in the moral character of the agent – a view that is a development of Aristotle's suggestion (*Nicomachaean Ethics*, Bk. II) that a necessary condition of an act's being virtuous is that it "be based on a fixed and permanent quality" in the agent's character. Obviously this view makes no sense if the concept of a trait of character, or of degrees of such traits, makes no clear sense – or if it cannot be made clear how it can be, and be known, that a certain action would not have occurred but for the presence in the agent of some trait to a defective or superior degree. So, concern about the analysis of character-trait concepts can hardly be written off as aimless devotion to lexicography.

In what follows I shall attempt to delineate the common logical structure of a class of terms I shall call "character-trait names." More exactly, I shall offer a *schema*, as definite as possible, for the definition of all character-trait names such that, by filling in the blanks appropriately, one would get illuminating explications. This statement of a program obviously needs explanation.

First, I assume that there are terms which it would be agreed are character-trait names, including such terms as conscientiousness, considerateness, courage, generosity, honesty, kindness, modesty, prudence, reliability, responsibility, self-control, sympathy (compassion), truthfulness, and unselfishness. In contrast, there are terms designating traits of personality that I should not classify as names of traits of character, at least not as traits of *moral* character, such as adventurousness, calmness, credulity, emotional instability, energy, fussiness, good nature, gregariousness, imagination, inflexibility, intelligence, optimism, pedantry, poise, polish, shyness, talkativeness, tenseness, timidity, and warmth. The *schema* to be offered may fit some of the latter group as well as the former group; what is here attempted, however, is simply a *schema* that fits all, or at least most, of the former group. Obviously it does *not* suit some of the latter group, for example, "energetic."

It is important to notice that the *schema* is not in any sense intended to provide an analysis of the term "trait of character"; what is intended is a *schema* which will enable illuminating analyses of various terms that are in fact names of traits of character.

It may be objected that the suggested dichotomy of personality-trait terms into those designating traits of moral character and others is questionable, and there is no reasonably definite intuitively acceptable class of names of traits of moral character. To this complaint several concessions should be made. First, possibly there is a use of "character" very close to that of "nature," so that almost any feature of a whole person can count as a trait of character in that sense. Moreover, when we say a person is "quite a character" we mean that he has distinctive eccentric features of some sort, and on the other hand when we say a person is a "man of character" we mean that he is a person of *good* character. But there surely is a use of "trait of moral character" which applies to a fairly definite set of traits, roughly identical with the set of what have traditionally been called moral virtues or moral vices, and in which "moral character" is used in a sense different from any of the foregoing. It is this sense of the term "character" (= "moral character") that philosophers have had in mind when they have accused Aristotle and Hume of discussing, in their accounts of virtues, some traits which are not traits of moral character at all, for example, being witty. This sense is a familiar one; printed forms for testimonials often contain a space for comments on "character," in which evidently something else is to be described than intelligence, flexibility, emotional stability, etc., to which topics other spaces are devoted. Traits of character in this sense appear to have two features in common: (1) Each is a trait of personality that is normally, in *any* adult (not just in a person with a certain role such as a mother or a nurse or a lawyer), either an important asset or an important liability for cooperative living, from the point of view of society. (2) An expression of any of them in action is within voluntary control, in the sense that a person always can produce it given appropriate interests (wants, aversions) on his part.[1] Accordingly, some trait that might be counted a virtue in a military commander or a burglar, say daring, is not usually classified as a trait of character, certainly in the sense of "moral character." It cannot be denied that the phrase "trait of character" carries rather specific implications for some people. Some would not count the natural sympathy of a six-year-old, shown on the playground, as a trait of character; they would say that a trait of character must be learned through practice based on moral reflection.

We may have to accept the fact that there are terms (perhaps "patience") about which our linguistic intuitions are mute, about which it is not clear whether they do or do not have the features characteristic of traits of moral character. If so, our success in attaining our present objective is not threatened, for the chief goal of the analysis is illumination of paradigm, well-recognized examples. For the same reason we need not be perturbed if, as I think is the case, evaluative judgments are required for some decisions about what is to count as a trait of character.

But in what sense is it proposed that our *schema* will provide an "illuminating explication" of these terms? It will not be asserted that all the features of our *schema* are required by the "conscious meaning" of these terms in the way in which the definition in terms of "unmarried male" is required by the conscious meaning of "bachelor." It is claimed that the *schema* is consistent with such conscious meanings, and at least roughly consistent with intuitions about the application of the terms by language users in concrete cases. More important, however, the *schema* is intended to be consistent with the conceptual framework employed by both common sense and scientific psychology; it is intended that the terms, as defined, are ones we shall be happy to continue using, given

---

1 See the writer's *Ethical Theory* (Englewood Cliffs, NJ, Prentice-Hall, Inc., 1959), pp. 466–8. The proposal is somewhat similar to that of P. H. Nowell-Smith, *Ethics* (Baltimore, MD., Penguin Books, 1954), pp. 300–6.

our total psychological theory. As such, our proposed definitions may expand, make precise, or possibly even somewhat change our present intuitive use of the terms, it is hoped in a useful way.[2]

I CHARACTER TRAITS AS DISPOSITIONS; REJECTION OF THE "SUMMARY" VIEW

It is natural to regard trait names as naming dispositions of a person. Just as we might explain "x is soluble in water" as meaning "if x were placed in water it would dissolve," so it is natural to propose – roughly following one of Ryle's suggestions – that "x is vain" amounts to a set of subjunctive conditionals, one of which might be, "if it occurred to x that doing A would likely secure the admiration and envy of others, he would be strongly tempted to do A."[3] Such a formulation implies that trait attributions support counterfactuals: even though x were not in fact to find what he thinks is a device for arousing the admiration of others, he *would* be strongly tempted to utilize it, if he did.

A dispositional view of trait names will here be defended, but with the reservation that a more precise account would construe them as theoretical terms. Exactly how this would be will be indicated later. But for the purpose of getting clear the reasons for preferring one type (what I shall call a "motivational dispositional" analysis) of analysis to some other quite different types, extended pursuit of this rather subtle refinement is unnecessary and would only be confusingly complicating.

It should be noticed that a dispositional analysis along the above lines does not exclude the use of probability or frequency notions in the analysis. One might, for instance, propose an analysis such as "if it occurred to $x, \ldots$, then he *probably* (or "very frequently" or "relatively frequently") would..." How the term "probably" (etc.) should be construed naturally would need explanation, by an advocate of such a proposal. In fact, however, one of the things I shall be doing is offering reasons for rejecting probability/frequency ideas from the analysis.

A dispositional analysis of some form would, I believe, be acceptable to most psychologists interested in the theory of traits of personality. Some philosophers, however, are disposed to adopt a form of what I shall call the Summary Theory. The first thing I wish to do is to give reasons for dropping the Summary Theory.

2 Some writers seem to think that the main content of trait names is just the evaluative, or praise–blame element. This has been shown to be mistaken by Dean Peabody, "Trait Inferences: Evaluative and Descriptive Aspects," *Journal of Personality and Social Psychology*, vol. 7 (1967), pp. 1–18.
3 See Gilbert Ryle, *The Concept of Mind* (London, Hutchinson's University Library, 1949), p. 89. Ryle offers somewhat different formulations.

The Summary Theory may take either of two forms: *pure,* or *mixed.* The *pure* form holds that to ascribe a trait to a person is simply to affirm that a certain corresponding form of behavior/experience has occurred, in the person, frequently or relatively frequently in the past – perhaps with the "implication" in some sense that the same frequency may be expected to continue. Thus, to say that a person is witty is to say that he has relatively frequently succeeded in making amusing sallies in the past and perhaps to imply that this frequency may be expected to continue.[4] The *mixed* form construes trait names partly as dispositional, thus adopting some subjunctive conditional expression as *part* of the analysis, but insists that to this we must *add* some expression to the effect that in fact manifestations of the trait have occurred in the individual's past, either frequently or relatively frequently.

Three main types of reasons appear to be offered in support of some version of the Summary Theory. First, it is said that "normally" we make trait ascriptions only when we know about actual manifestations of the trait. And this seems true; but it is hardly an objection to a dispositional theory. For it is obvious that *normally,* say, in the absence of test information like the Rorschach, or the MMPI, etc., we do and must base our trait ascriptions on observations of relevant behavior manifesting the trait. But this would be true even if the dispositional analysis were correct, and it can hardly be an objection to the dispositional analysis. Second, it is argued that we can be *certain* of a trait ascription only when we are able to cite numerous instances of past behavior, and that such information, and only such, has *conclusive* force in appraising a trait ascription. In the case of this argument, we can concede that *other* evidence may not be conclusive or lead to certainty; psychological tests, for instance, are not that reliable. Even if a psychologist had a battery of test results in front of him – Rorschach, Thematic Apperception, MMPI, etc., – and also biographical data about traumatic experiences in the person's childhood, rejection by his parents, etc., and even if all this evidence pointed firmly to the likelihood that the individual was an anxious person, it is still *possible* that he would respond to life-situations with less anxiety than the normal person. Highly unlikely, but possible. But there is no reason why the dispositional theorist need deny this; he can admit that past real-life reactions are a more certain guide to present dispositions than any psychological test, but go right on affirming that what trait ascriptions do is affirm present dispositions and not facts about the past. (Inciden-

4 Something at least like this view has been defended by Stuart Hampshire, "Dispositions," *Analysis,* vol. 14 (1953), pp. 5–11; George Pitcher, "Necessitarianism," *The Philosophical Quarterly,* vol. 11 (1961), esp. pp. 207–8; and Betty Powell, "Uncharacteristic Actions," *Mind,* vol. 68 (1959), pp. 492–509, esp. pp. 500, 502.

tally, past real life reactions are not necessarily conclusive, or certain, evidence about traits. For instance, a really anxious person may meet a situation that would be anxiety-arousing even to a normal person, after some elating experience such as an unusual achievement on his part, and he may *not* react to it with anxiety. It could well be, for such reasons, that a mass of psychological tests would be better evidence for a given person's traits than data about his actual past behavior in real situations. Third, and finally, there is an argument that is simply an appeal to meanings: It would be contradictory to say that a person is *T* (has a certain trait) but has never behaved in a *T*-like manner. As W. P. Alston has put it, "A person who has never obeyed any orders might be correctly called 'potentially obedient,' 'an obedient type,' or 'a person who would be obedient if he had the chance'; but we could not be justified in terming him 'obedient' *tout court*. The occurrence of some instances of the correlated manifestation category is a necessary . . . condition for the application of the trait term."[5]

Is it *contradictory* to affirm that a person is *T*, or, on the evidence probably *T*, and at the same time to say that certainly or probably he has never acted in a *T*-like way in the past? I fail to see that it is, at least for the traits of moral character with which we are concerned. Such questions are, of course, difficult. But take "courageous." Suppose we knew a given person had lived a very sheltered life and had never been required to act in the face of a serious threat. (It is not easy to imagine comparable situations in the case of most traits; for the normal life situations of human individuals are such that, in the case of most traits, if a person has the trait he cannot have failed to manifest it in behavior.) Would we infer of such a person that he *cannot* be courageous? Surely not. Indeed, there are conceivable psychological tests such that, given a certain result on these tests, we would say that the person is *probably* a courageous person. (Suppose there were a known high correlation between this trait and the presence of a certain chemical element in the blood, and tests showed this chemical to be present in the blood in ample quantity.) It is true that, as things now stand, we would hesitate to affirm roundly, without any "probability" reservation, that a person was courageous without any behavioral evidence; but this fact shows something, not about the meaning of "courageous" (or other trait names of interest to us), but about our convictions on what is adequate evidence for trait ascriptions; and if that is the point, then this argument reduces to the second argument. There is no evidence

5 W. P. Alston, *Toward a Logical Geography of Personality: Traits and Deeper Lying Personality Characteristics* in *Contemporary Philosophic Thought, Conferences at Brockport* (Albany: State University of New York Press, 1970), pp. 59–92, esp. p. 62.

to suggest that it is self-contradictory to say that a person is T but has not behaved in a T-like way.

The objections to a dispositional theory, then, seem at best highly dubious. There is also, however, an argument that appears to show that the Summary Theory is simply wrong. This argument adduces as its premise the fact that we often draw inferences about a person's traits of character on the basis of a *single* piece of behavior.[6] For instance, if a young boy is threatened with a beating by larger boys if he fails to do a certain thing, and he steadfastly refuses, we justifiably assert that he is courageous. It is true that we do need a good deal of information to eliminate other hypotheses – such as that he mistakenly thought he had nothing to fear, or that he had just taken a courage drug, etc. But how could we draw such an inference with high confidence, from any amount of information about a single situation if trait affirmations were assertions about the frequency of behavior in the past? (The present behavior is one case; but to say that a person is courageous is surely not to say merely that he has acted courageously once.) It is true that we could draw such inferences on such evidence *if* we were assured of some general proposition to the effect that people do not behave in *this* way unless they have frequently behaved in a comparable way in the past. But we do not have evidence that such generalizations are true when we are drawing such inferences; and it is doubtful whether they are true. (It seems there could be a first time when a person manifested his courage.) Surely we do not appeal to any such generalization in drawing or justifying our inference from the behavior. We make the judgment of courage because that hypothesis is the most plausible explanation in view of our total information about the situation and about how people generally behave; and we justify our judgment as being such. The mode of our inference, and of our justification of our inference, simply does not jibe with the Summary Theory.

II TRAITS OF CHARACTER ARE RELATIVELY PERMANENT DISPOSITIONS

Traits of character are relatively permanent features of a person. So, if we are to give a dispositional account of character trait names, we must begin with some such phrase as "It is a relatively stable and permanent feature of X that, were he . . . , he would. . . . " There is none of the trait names of interest to us that we would apply to a person in virtue of some

6 This point was noticed by Maurice Mandelbaum, *The Phenomenology of Moral Experience* (New York, The Free Press, 1955), p. 147.

relatively unstable and temporary feature. Furthermore, traits of character do not undergo cyclical modifications like the "needs" for food or water or sex; it is not as if, having acted sympathetically (assuming being sympathetic is a trait) at noon, I shall have a desire for more sympathetic action at six o'clock and not before. Traits do change; we often have occasion to say that when a boy Mr. X was so-and-so, but as an adult he has become such-and-such, where the latter is incompatible with the former.

III TRAITS OF CHARACTER ARE INTRINSIC WANTS/AVERSIONS

I now wish to claim that traits are relatively permanent dispositions *of a specific kind* – the kinds of dispositions that wants and aversions are. We shall see that there is more to be said; for instance, a given trait name implies that the relevant desire/aversion reaches a certain level of intensity. These refinements will be discussed later. In the present section I shall discuss the central claim that trait names designate desires or aversions (or some structure of these), and indeed ones that are *intrinsic* in a sense to be explained.

This claim is certainly controversial; it would be contradicted not only by many philosophers but by many (by no means all) psychologists interested in traits. That it is a defensible claim is a central thesis of this paper. I shall call the claim "the motivational theory" of character traits.

The motivation theory of character traits, in claiming that traits are dispositions of the want/aversions kind, is assuming that wants/aversions are themselves dispositions (subject to a refinement already noted, that will be discussed further below). I do not know that this assumption needs any apology.

Let me begin by pointing out that there is some *prima facie* reason for thinking that a motivational theory of character traits must be correct. Traits of character, as contrasted with "stylistic" traits like being affected, analytical, cheerful, clumsy, energetic, enthusiastic, excitable, or expansive, are concerned with *intentional actions*. Now, if we assume that character traits are wants/aversions, we shall be in a position to do what we think we can properly do – *explain* intentional behavior by reference to character traits. Notice that we do sometimes, or often, explain behavior (which is unusual enough to call for an explanation) by appeal to such things as that the person is unusually conscientious, or sympathetic, or considerate. So, *if* we adopt the motivational theory, we can properly explain intentional behavior in the way we do explain it, at least in thoughtful moments. That is some reason for adopting the motivational theory. Of course, it may be that if we construe character traits in some different way, it will still be possible to appeal to them as in some sense explanatory of intentional behavior. This is one thing we shall be looking into.

If we look at the literature on the theory of action and motivation,[7] we find a list of variables, of which intentional action is thought to be a function; the function it is of these variables is the law or laws of behavior. Now if we assume that traits of character figure in the explanation of actions, and if we look among the psychologists' list of factors for items that might represent specific traits of character, the most plausible candidate is surely what is sometimes called "need" or "drive" or "want," of which the "need" for food or affiliation or achievement or security or freedom from pain (aversion to pain) are prime examples. If traits are construed as specific kinds of need (want/aversion), at least an understanding of the role they play in action would be a straight forward matter; we could see how they fit into a widely accepted pattern of psychological explanation of intentional action.

What kind of "pattern of explanation of intentional action"? It must be admitted that motivation theorists talk somewhat different languages, for example, the behavioristic learning theorist emphasizing "anticipatory goal responses." We can ignore these differences, however, if we assume, as seems plausible, that these languages are intertranslatable. The "pattern of explanation," put in one kind of terminology, consists in acceptance, as a general law of behavior, of the thesis that (roughly) a person always acts (moves his body) in such a way as to *maximize expectable utility for himself;* and in assimilating all actions, given the context of beliefs/needs of the agent, to this law as instances of it. To spell out a bit what is meant, we construe "expectable" in the following way: The organism believes itself to be in a certain location and situation, and it believes that there are various states of affairs that could be produced by various basic actions (movements) it could produce, with varying degrees of probability. Or, in other words, the organism associates various outcomes as connected with various of its possible actions, with differing degrees of firmness or confidence. We construe "utility" as follows: Various needs (wants/aversions) of the agent are *in force* (see below) at the time of action, with different degrees of strength. These needs make "contact" with various ones of the conceived possible outcomes, which are states of affairs toward which the organism has wants/aversions; as a result there

7 For instance, J. W. Atkinson, *An Introduction to Motivation* (Princeton, NJ, D. van Nostrand and Co., 1964); or E. C. Tolman, "A Psychological Model" in Talcott Parsons and E. A. Shils, eds., *Toward a General Theory of Action* (Cambridge, MA, Harvard University Press, 1954).

is generated a psychological "valence" of that state of affairs, positive or negative, with a strength corresponding to the degree of strength of the respective need at the time. Different outcomes that make contact with the same need, however, somehow have different incentive values (for example, a choice steak having more incentive value in relation to the hunger need than does goulash), and these differences are also reflected in the size of the "valence." (There are difficulties, definitional and otherwise, in this concept of lumping need–strength and incentive value together in the "valence.") Now we think of assigning numbers to the valence of an outcome and to the subjective probability of that outcome, given a certain action; and the product of these numbers represents the "expectable utility" of the action thought to lead to the outcome. (The same action might lead to several outcomes; the expectable utilities then have to be summed.) The size of the expectable utility may be represented as a force-vector in the direction of a given action. The "law" of behavior says, roughly, that the organism will take that action that conforms to the strongest force-vector. If we employ this kind of law as our pattern for explanation, then we shall, for instance, explain my walking to the refrigerator by such things as how thirsty I am, what kind of drink I think is available in the refrigerator (beer, warm water), how anxious I am not to be interrupted in writing a given paragraph or finishing some job, how likely I think it is that if I walk toward the refrigerator I shall be able to open it, etc. Similarly for traits of character. If, for instance, we construe sympathy as an aversion to other people being in distress, we shall fit it into the pattern of explanation much as we do thirst; what I shall do if I see a child fall off his bicycle will be a function of the strength of this aversion, how serious the distress I take it the child is in, how little I want to be interrupted (maybe I am in the midst of a crucial game of tennis), and how likely I think it is that I shall be able to relieve the distress if I move to the rescue; and so on.

The foregoing is only a simplified sketch of the relation between the intentional basic movements of a person and the values of certain variables characterizing him at the time. Even as such, a few further points should be noted about it. For one thing, "expectable" has to be defined as "subjectively probable" and explained in such a way that what is expectable for a person can be ascertained, at least partially, independently of what he does at the moment, else the "law" is analytic. Furthermore, a certain need (want or aversion) may characterize a person at a time but, because he has forgotten about it, it may fail to influence his behavior. It seems necessary, for this and other reasons, to distinguish between "latent" and "active" needs (ones *in force*) of a person at a time; and the needs in force, again, must be determinable by reference to other phenomena than the person's consequent behavior (or, at least, partially by reference to other phenomena), again in order to avoid rendering the "law" of behavior analytic. Again, it appears that motivation theory somewhere has to allow a place for such variables as "impulsiveness," which are not identifiable either with needs or beliefs. Moreover, it has to be admitted that psychologists are much more at home in behavior theory applicable to nonsymbol-using animals than for men, and do not have much to say about a process of reflection issuing in behavior. In general it seems necessary to distinguish between a simpler model for the explanation of behavior and a more complex one in which symbolic processes play a significant role, as was argued by the writer and Jaegwon Kim in an earlier publication.[8]

Fortunately it is not necessary for us here to be clear about the nature, or even the general form, of an acceptable theory of human action. For our purpose is simply to get clear what is intended by saying that a character-trait name designates some need (want/aversion) or, more exactly, by saying that ascription of a character trait functions to assert something about the needs, or level of intensity of needs, of a person; and to get clear in what general way the ascription of character traits (or, more generally, needs) can function in the explanation of behavior.

It may be that we must acknowledge various differences between the needs designated by character-trait names and those most familiar in behavior theory. Compare, for instance, the need thirst and the trait sympathetic. First, intensity of thirst seems to be correlated with the dehydration of the body cells, etc., hence a function largely of hours since water intake, exercise, etc., whereas sympathy is not a function of such variables. Again, thirst decreases in strength rather rapidly as the consummatory activity goes on; after a couple of glasses of water the thirst of a human being in normal circumstances drops to zero and resistance to further drinking develops. This satiation phenomenon is evidently not so marked, if it exists at all, with the sympathy need; if a second child falls off his bicycle five minutes after the first one, one does not find it overpoweringly repulsive to go to his rescue also. (Needs like affiliation and achievement are less variable than thirst, although satiation is clearly observable in their case, too.) In this respect sympathy rather resembles the aversion to pain, since it appears that a continuous dose of pain does not decrease one's interest in avoiding it. In general it seems more plausible to construe character traits as aversive needs than as positive wants.

8 R. B. Brandt and Jaegwon Kim, "Wants as Explanations of Actions," *The Journal of Philosophy*, vol. 60 (1963), pp. 425–35.

My proposal has been (as a first approximation) that character-trait names designate dispositions; and it follows from this that (at least as a first approximation) they can be explained by appropriate subjunctive-conditional statements. Since I am also suggesting that the disposition in question is a kind of need, it follows that the subjunctive conditionals by means of which trait names can be explained will be of the type by which need concepts can be explained. So, *if* to say that a person *wants* something of a certain sort is to say that under certain conditions he would be disappointed (if he didn't get a thing of the kind, when he thought he would) or feel joy (if he did get a thing of the kind when he thought he wouldn't) or tend to act in a certain way (which he thought would bring him a sample of the situation wanted and would not prevent other things he wanted more), etc., then to say that a person has a certain trait of character will be to make a statement that can be explained along similar lines.

There is, however, a complication; and it is time to state more explicitly what would be claimed if we were not limiting ourselves to a "first approximation." In an earlier paper (see footnote 8), the writer and Jaeg-won Kim defended the view that "want" and "aversion" are not, strictly speaking, disposition terms but theoretical terms, and hence that in principle no producible set of statements relating them to experiences like disappointment will provide an explicit definition of them. It was argued that many important single statements of this sort are neither analytic nor synthetic. Moreover, it seems impossible to spell out exactly the conditions under which a given want/aversion will lead to disappointment, etc., certainly if there is permitted no reference to *other* wants/ aversions, or to *beliefs* – a concept with a status like that of "need." These strictures presumably hold for character trait names. Hence my suggestion is that for them, as for need statements generally, true statements relating them to experience have to be regarded as correspondence rules, or dictionary statements, in the sense in which these terms are used of theoretical language, rather than as explicit definitions. These statements cannot be construed as giving an acceptable explicit definition; on the other hand, they are not simply synthetic, since the meaning of the theoretical terms is determined by their role in such true statements.

Having said this, however, I propose from now on mostly to ignore it, and to write as if character-trait names name dispositions that can be explained by means of counterfactuals. It should not be forgotten, however, that when such things are said, it is intended that the statement be viewed only as a first approximation.

It may be helpful, as an illustration of the present conception of traits, to indicate how an expression like "*X* is sympathetic" might be partially explained by a set of subjunctive conditionals. (One might translate "X is sympathetic" into "X has an aversion to people being in distress"; but this translation does not provide the kind of explanatory account we are looking for.) Subjunctive conditionals that we might regard as partial substitutes for "is sympathetic" would presumably include the following: (1) "would feel disturbed, other things being equal, if he perceived some sentient being to be in acute distress." (2) "would feel relieved, if he perceived a being in distress in process of being helped, provided he had earlier felt discomfort at the person's distress." (3) "would be motivated to relieve the distress, if he believed that he could do so and that no one else would if he did not."[9] (4) "would feel guilty, other things being equal, if he perceived distress he thought he could relieve but did not, provided justifying or excusing considerations were absent." (5) "would notice a case of distress, if he were presented with it perceptually." (6) "would remember a previous case of distress, if he had noticed it before, and were now in a position to give relief." Doubtless the reader will be able to think of various qualifications that must be added, before he would regard any of these statements as true of a person who is sympathetic.

Expressions like the above cannot be used to explain all character-trait names, for some of them, for instance, "*dis*honesty," refer to the lack of a trait that might be explained as above. Dishonesty is a trait name, but it designates the absence of honesty, so that if we are to try to explain it in terms of statements somewhat like the above, they have to take the form, "It is not the case that if X..., then X would...." Moreover, just as this vice has to be viewed as the absence of a virtue, so some virtues have to be viewed as the absence of a vice, for example, courage as the absence of cowardice (as will be explained below). There may have to be more complications still. All that is here claimed is that character-trait names function as ascriptions of *some* state of the person's *system of wants/aversions,* and can be explained accordingly. Only in this sense is our theory "motivational."

One perplexing question that may be raised about the motivational proposal is appropriately mentioned at this juncture. Why is it that the analysis of most character-trait names involves the notion of guilt feelings? Guilt feelings do not appear in the analysis of most personal wants and aversions, for example, wanting a drink or wanting a raise in salary, or aversion to bananas. In the case of personal wants/aversions, the notions of disappointment and anxiety may well occur in the analysis, but not

---

9 This explanation is circular, if, as appears to be the case, "is motivated" has to be taken to mean, in part, "would take action... if he did not *want more strongly* to do something else." In the present context, this circularity is not an objection.

guilt feelings. Why is there this disparity? I raise this question, without knowing the answer to it.

In the title of the present section, it was indicated that the wants/ aversions which are identical with traits of character must be "intrinsic." What was meant by this is that the truth of the "if . . . then" statements that constitute the explanation of the trait name is not *derivative*, or at least *not wholly* derivative, from some other want/aversion. For instance, a person might be motivated to give to charity, and as such we might be inclined to call him generous. But if his willingness to give to charity were dependent on his desire to be in the public eye, or to improve his reputation, or to be elected to public office, we should not call him generous. (The term "derivative" might here be defined in various ways; I propose to ignore problems of its definition.)

So much for the statement of the proposal. It should be noticed that the proposal has an implication for psychology of some interest, which might permit empirical testing of it: for it appears that wants/aversions, when they are learned, are learned in ways different from behavioral responses. So, if traits of character are needs (wants/aversions), the development of them will follow the same laws as the general laws for learning needs.[10]

The foregoing motivational construction of character-trait names is not self-evidently true, and I shall now produce some support for it. But first, what is the alternative, assuming we have dismissed the Summary Theory? Consideration of this will bring out the distinctiveness of the theory here proposed.

Strictly, there is not just *one* alternative. One could even hold – indeed it has been held – that character-trait names are primarily evaluative, and that the cognitive content is minimal, even negligible. Again, it might be said that the proper lines have not been drawn with respect to the definition-theoretical term distinction. I think, however, that these possibilities are unimportant, and I shall ignore them. Where will important differences lie? Presumably there can be differences of opinion about specific proposals I shall make below about specific traits; but if the disagreement is about a pattern of analysis, it must be about some broader feature common to the analysis of the whole set of traits. Obviously *any* theory of traits of character is going to construe them as especially related

10 See, for instance, E. C. Tolman, "There Is More Than One Kind of Learning," *Psychological Review*, vol. 56 (1949), pp. 144–55; R. B. Cattell, *The Scientific Analysis of Personality* (Chicago, Aldine Publishing Co., 1965), chap. 10; D. C. McClelland et al., *The Achievement Motive* (New York, Appleton-Century-Crofts, 1953), pp. 89–96; O. H. Mowrer, *Learning Theory and Personality Dynamics* (New York, Ronald Press, 1950), *passim*.

to, and in some way explanatory of, intentional behavior (among other things); so the contrast must be between the motivational theory and one or more other theories with this feature in common. What is characteristic of the motivation theory is that it construes traits of character as like (as playing a role in common sense and scientific psychological theory alike), say, the need to achieve, or the aversion to the disapprobation (or disapprobative behavior) of other persons. As such, the motivation theory relates traits to intentional behavior rather indirectly; it holds that, under conditions not fully understood, they become active and generate "force vectors" in the psychological field of the person, their direction and degree depending partly on the person's beliefs; what the person actually does is a function of the force vectors in his psychological field at the moment of action. Furthermore, as was pointed out by A.F. Shand many years ago, the existence of needs/aversions brings with it relevant changes in many of the prospective/retrospective emotions of a person, as his psychological field changes – such emotions as joy, anxiety, sorrow, despair, disappointment, and hope. There is, then, a large and fairly definite conceptual framework that traits must fit, if they are what the motivation theory says they are. The point about how motives are learned, mentioned just above, is a part of this. But, if we abjure motivation theory, *what* will be the connection between traits and behavior (or something else), which presumably will be definitive of that conception of traits? One thing is clear; such a theory will not make use of the explanatory framework of motivation theory: the conception of a psychological field in which there are behavior forces that are a function of the whole set of needs active at the moment, and also of the agent's beliefs. In forming a conception of a more positive competing theory, it would be foolish to suggest that there may not be many, and possibly of quite different types. But the obvious alternative – at any rate the one that seems actually to be espoused, as an alternative to the motivation theory – is a theory that proposes that *for various trait names a form of behavior typical of that trait can be identified* (as talking for talkativeness), and that what it is for a person to have a certain trait is primarily for him to be *disposed to behave in the correlated typical way, in certain conditions, relatively frequently.* (Another way of putting it is to say that to have a certain trait is for the probability to be relatively high that the person will behave in the correlated way in certain conditions.) A trait can then be construed as a *set* of dispositions; not only as a disposition to act, but, under certain conditions, to have certain emotions relatively frequently – in this way absorbing whatever truth there is in the motivation theory hypothesis that when a person has a certain trait he will *feel* in certain ways in certain conditions. On this view, a trait is not a motive that may issue in a certain type of goal-seeking behavior depending on what other motives are present; it is a disposition for a relatively specific type of behavior to occur.[11]

It should be noticed that this theory, which I shall call the Direct Disposition Theory, is a loosely defined theory, and it could be stretched so as to be scarcely distinguishable from the motivation theory. For instance, the "behavior" in question might be to do something from a certain motive, or for itself, or with some end in view. Or, more broadly, the phrase "in certain conditions" could be explained in such a way, in specific cases, as to specify all the beliefs and motives that must be present or absent for the behavior to (probably, or frequently) take place; in this case, the theory would be only terminologically different from the motivation theory. A type of Direct Disposition Theory, to be different in substance from the motivation theory, must propose explications of character-trait names that do not in substance incorporate the conceptual framework of motivation theory; it will not, in substance, construe traits as playing the role of needs in motivation theory, or appearing in laws or general statements, or implying these, just as would be done if the traits were construed as needs/aversions.

On this alternative theory, it should be noted, explanation of behavior will take a different form, being more like the kind of explanation solubility in water gives of the soluble thing's actually dissolving in water. It is not suggested that such explanations are unimportant. Indeed, there can be and is a "science" of traits in this sense. For – but I am not suggesting there are not other possibilities – there is factor analysis that can/does discover interdependencies among traits and analyzes human personality in terms of a few statistical creations called "source traits."

I shall devote the remainder of this section to supporting the motivation theory. I shall proceed as follows. First, I shall consider two important objections to the theory, and meet them; I shall then show how one of the objections backfires and provides support for the motivation theory, and I shall then adduce another powerful reason for accepting the latter. Finally, I shall discuss some important character traits that look initially like counterexamples and consider whether they may be construed as compatible with the motivation theory. We should remember, however, that I am not necessarily arguing that the motivational theory is true for *all* traits of character; it could be an illuminating and sound proposal for some but not all. Of course, if it is the account we must adopt for all, its interest is considerably increased.

I begin with two objections to the motivation theory. It is useful to

11 In this contrast between the two types of theories, I have benefited from Professor Alston's paper referred to above, and from numerous discussions with him, about this and related problems.

cite a passage from R. S. Peters which incorporates the two objections in question, and at the same time appears to be a defense of a form of Direct Disposition theory.

We can explain a man's action in terms of traits of character, like considerateness, and punctuality. These may be reasons why people act; but they are not motives. For such terms do not indicate any definite sort of goals toward which a man's actions are directed.[12]

Such terms express simply a correlation between typical situations and behaviour appropriate to them. To say that man acts because of indolence, vanity, or honesty is to relate his behaviour in a certain situation to a host of similar responses in similar situations – predominantly social ones. The man may be motivated in different ways while exhibiting the same trait; he may exhibit the same or different traits in bringing about a variety of aims. . . . The "trait" is a typical low-level concept useful for social intercourse, valuative assessments of character novelist's descriptions of character, and so on.[13]

Here there are two main arguments against the motivational theory: first, that trait ascriptions obviously do not imply any particular goals (in our terminology, "needs") at all; and second, that one may exhibit a given trait (for example; act considerately) from very different motives so that having a given trait could not be identified with any particular want/aversion.

The first of these criticisms takes as being obvious the falsity of the motivation theory, except possibly as a "reforming" analysis of trait names – the "reform" presumably being undertaken in the interest of construing trait names so that traits can play a significant role in the explanation of behavior. But is it *obvious* that character-trait names indicate no definite sort of goal? Surely we need to examine a representative list of such terms and consider whether they can plausibly be construed to refer to goals or wants/aversions. In the case of "considerateness," one would think that concern for discomforts, embarrassments, etc., of other persons precisely is implied by use of the term. Peters' other example in this context, punctuality, is not a trait of character at all. Peters' contention may seem plausible because most character-trait terms name aversions rather than wants/desires, and hence it is true that in a sense they are *aiming* at nothing specific, as distinct from simply *avoiding* something specific, in *some* way or other. Still, aversions do have specifiable goals in an appropriate sense; for instance, while in a sense the aversion to pain has no goal, it is still true that there is a goal – there being *no* pain. Peters may have overlooked these facts, assuming that any

12 *The Concept of Motivation* (London, Routledge and Kegan Paul, 1958), p. 32; see also p. 5.
13 *Proceedings of the Aristotelian Society*, Supplementary Volume 26 (1952), pp. 156–7.

need/want motive must have a structure like the physiological needs, with a definite consummatory occasion after which the "tension" is diminished.

Peters' second criticism, that character traits are dispositions to perform certain sorts of actions and are not wants/aversions, since several actions may manifest one and the same trait but be motivated in diverse ways, is found also in M. H. Mandelbaum's work. Mandelbaum says:

When we hold that a man is courageous we do not attribute any particular motive to him: his courage may be due to ambition, to emulation, or even to a fear of certain forms of opprobrium, and yet his action may be justly called courageous. ... This trait [courage] may be grounded in such disparate conditions as combativeness, a calculated use of daring to attain certain personal ends, a craving for self-aggrandizement through social approbation, or a readiness to sacrifice one's self to an ideal.[14]

Mandelbaum lists fidelity, prudence, temperance, and sloth as further traits of this sort.

In reply to this objection I shall shortly suggest that some of Mandelbaum's examples can after all be construed straightforwardly as aversions. But first let me point out why, in the case of *some* traits, a diversity of motivation is quite compatible with the motivation theory. This fact derives from the polarity (already adverted to) of some trait pairs. For instance, suppose honesty is construed as aversion to certain things such as appropriation of the property of others, deceit, etc. But honesty has a polar opposite: *dis*honesty. But what is dishonesty? Presumably it is just the *absence* of the kind of aversion that constitutes honesty. As such, dishonesty is not identical with any particular want or aversion. Not, for instance, with acquisitiveness, which may be present in an honest man. Therefore behavior manifesting dishonesty *of course* will be variously motivated; the reason why it is called dishonest behavior is simply that it is behavior that would not have occurred had the aversion distinctive of the honest man been present. Any character trait that consists in the *absence* of some kind of aversion typical of its polar opposite will necessarily be manifested by behavior motivated in all sorts of ways – by desires to do all sorts of things, which would not have controlled behavior in the presence of the aversion typical of the opposite trait. Among Mandelbaum's examples, both sloth and courage appear parallel with dishonesty in this respect; sloth being the absence of the aversion that constitutes ambitious industriousness, and courage being the absence of

14 *The Phenomenology of Moral Experience* (Glencoe, IL., The Free Press 1955), pp. 142 ff.

the aversion that is cowardice – the aversion to death, bodily injury, or damage to fundamental features of one's position. (I shall return to courage.) When we take this polar relationship into account, certain traits that look like counterexamples to the motivation theory turn out really not to be so.

I suggested above that the second objection backfires and points to something that is support for the motivation theory. What I mean is this. If the motivation theory is correct, then behavior manifesting the trait will be *any sort of behavior* that requires to be explained by reference to the need identical with the trait. So, if the motivational theory is correct, we may expect it to be impossible to work out a thesis of the alternative theory: that some *definite kind of behavior* may be identified, correlated with a given trait. What one may expect is that no such definite correlated type of behavior can be identified, except by some reference to needs/ aversions. What are the facts?

The Direct Disposition Theory is at its best with traits like talkativeness (not, of course, a trait of character). For one may construe "*X* is talkative" as "whenever *X* has an audience, he is apt to talk a lot." In this case the behavior manifesting the trait seems easy enough to specify. Even here, however, some complications arise, for we do not regard a hotel clerk as talkative just because the conditional is true of him; we need at least some further clause like "in a normal situation."

When we consider some traits of character, however, the situation is more complex. Let us consider whether we can state what specific kind of behavior, identified without reference to motivation, may be expected to be relatively frequent, in specifiable conditions, in the case of a *generous* person. (The same would be true with virtually all the traits listed in the third paragraph of this paper.) One might say that a generous person is one disposed,[15] among other things, to make frequent gifts or perform services for others. But this cannot be right: for a generous person might not have contact with needy persons or causes, or might not have the means to make gifts or perform services. So at least we must introduce a condition: "*If* the person recognized a need, and believed he had requisite means at his disposal, he would, relatively frequently, make a gift or perform a service." But must one really do this *frequently* to be generous? Suppose one saves one's resources over many years to make

15 There are complications if one follows O.E.D. in distinguishing several senses of "generous," such as magnanimous and liberality in giving. I think it more plausible to recognize just one sense: a relative lack of concern for personal possessions, status, advancement, etc., combined with a relatively strong interest in persons or causes not involving one's self directly. If this is correct, then liberal gifts are one manifestation one might expect, given appropriate circumstances.

one large gift; this would seem to show generosity. It is at once clear that any one of a great variety of forms of behavior is enough: *any* form of behavior intended to reach some goal of a certain type. Again, a person with large means or capacities must do more to show himself generous than a person with limited means or capacities. (Example: the Widow's mite.) How much more? Apparently the answer is: Enough to prove the strength of one's motivation! Moreover, the making of gifts does not establish one's generosity unless they are made in a certain spirit, without ulterior motives; a person is not generous if he is disposed frequently to make gifts to establish a favorable public image, avoid income tax to a government he hates, and so on. But what is it to make a gift "without ulterior motives?" Apparently it is to make a gift with such an understanding of the circumstances as not to rule out – or rather so as to imply an important role for – motivation by an *intrinsic* (as it was called above) desire to assist, that is, a desire at least not wholly derivative from a desire to advance one's self in some way. It appears, then, that when we try to describe behavior which is to be expected if a person is generous, we cannot do so without bringing in reference to the person's desires/aversions/motives/goals in some way or other. And *any* kind of behavior that is testimony to the requisite kind of motivation is reason for calling a person generous. This result is precisely the opposite of what one would expect if the Direct Disposition Theory were true, at least for the trait generosity.

There is a further serious difficulty with the Direct Disposition Theory, which again should incline us toward the motivation theory. This is the fact of how we make, or revise, trait estimates in view of single pieces of behavior. Consider an example. Suppose a person, whom we have deemed kindly and sympathetic, does a mean thing. We do *not* then say: "This is one of the cases permitted by the trait of sympathy, since to be sympathetic is only to be disposed to do kindly things on relatively frequent occasions" – as the Direct Disposition Theory implies we should. On the contrary, the mean action constitutes a problem for us, and we revise our assessment of the person's character unless we can find some plausible explanation that permits us to reconcile the behavior with a strong aversion to hurting other people. (Sometimes we are satisfied that there *must be* some explanation, although we have no idea what it is.) We do not concede that a sympathetic person, just occasionally and with no strong countermotivation (or other explanatory circumstance) does a mean thing; we do not think of traits of character as statistical facts. Consider again how we make our original assessment. It is true that information about frequency of behavior is relevant, if we happen to have it; if we know that a person relatively frequently performs services for others, apparently with no ulterior motive, we infer a trait of generosity – and this is consistent with the motivation theory, since relatively frequent behavior of this sort is testimony to a relatively high motivation of a permanent sort, in normal circumstances. But we also infer traits on the basis of behavior in a single situation, when this can be explained only by the presence of a strong motive presumably of a relatively permanent kind. For instance, if in circumstances of very great temptation to do something else, for instance, acquire the desired property of another when there is no possibility of being detected, one does not do so, one is assigned the trait that consists in desire/aversion that would explain one's behavior. In other words, given our knowledge of the situation and of what may be presumed to be various motives operating, we reconstruct the "psychological field" and motivation of the individual so as to explain his behavior, and where called for we assign a character trait. A relative frequency is not what we determine before we assign a trait; evidence for assignment of (relatively permanent) wants/aversions is what we do determine.

One other line of possible objection to the motivation theory may be considered in concluding the present section. It may be objected that the motivation theory has some plausibility for traits like generosity, considerateness, etc., but very little for others that are important and universally recognized as traits of character.

It is clear, however, that various other important character-trait names, not hitherto considered, can be construed as natural along the lines of the motivation theory. Callousness is a lack of sympathy. Honesty is an aversion to deceit and/or the appropriation of the property of other persons. Conscientiousness is an aversion to failure to do one's duty. Unselfishness is a relatively high interest in the welfare of other persons. Kindness is aversion to causing any kind of distress in others. Truthfulness is aversion to deviation from the truth, or to the kind of interpersonal relationship which results when one party indulges in deception.

But possibly other important traits of character cannot easily be so construed. How about courage, temperance, prudence, reliability, and modesty? Let us consider just two of these, courage and temperance, which seem likely to be as difficult cases for the motivation thesis as we shall find.

What then is courage? It is not just a matter of standing (or being disposed to stand) in the face of dangers – for a man might do this because he does not recognize dangers for what they are, or because, in view of his skill or power, they are not really dangers for him. Courage is at least a disposition to stand up against what the person *thinks* are serious threats of some kind. Courage is not a matter, as Aristotle seems to have thought it partly is, of not feeling fear; for a person who trembles from fear need not be short of courage if he stands his ground, however useless he may be in combat. What courage requires is primarily a negative feature of the system of desires/aversions, *not* setting the highest store by personal safety and position in life. Courage is not, of course, a matter of setting *no* store by these things; that would be foolhardiness in the highest degree. There is something in Aristotle's suggestion that courage requires a desire to maintain one's honor, or an aversion to disgrace; the point is that there are *some* values that have priority over personal safety in a courageous man, whereas a cowardly man will back down on any issue when a serious personal threat arises. Suppose a person has a scale of values, of priorities – involving the obligations of his position, the welfare of other persons, his long-range goals in life – in which presumably personal safety does not outweigh everything else. A person is cowardly, then, in the highest degree if any risk to his personal safety and position will impel him to a course of action divergent from that implied by his scale of values. The more courageous a man is, the less he will be swayed, when something he deems important is at stake, by even serious and imminent threats of personal harm or status. Courage, then, is essentially the absence (the general question of what level or degree is discussed below) of an all-absorbing attachment to personal safety and position.

Let us turn now to temperance or self-control, in the sense in which they contrast with self-indulgence. Philosophers have sometimes thought of this as having to do, at least primarily, with the bodily appetites, especially for food, drink, and sex. This is too narrow. A man is self-indulgent if he omits his daily exercises in favor of the morning paper; a student is self-indulgent if he spends time watching football games on television when he should be devoting it to his studies. We can put it generally: A person exhibits temperance or self-control when he forgoes immediately enjoyable experiences that he knows conflict with his long-term welfare, or when he engages in immediately unpleasant activities (like doing push-ups) when his long-term welfare calls for it. Now, what kind of person is apt to behave in this way? The answer seems to be: a person who has a strong aversion to impairing his long-range prospects for a good life. The self-controlled man is one whose aversion to risking these is sufficiently great to overcome very considerable attractions of immediate enjoyment and the irksomeness of unpleasant activities. His aversion is strong enough so as to bring to mind the relevance of present activities to them, and to control behavior when this relevance has been brought to mind.

IV TRAITS ARE DISPOSITIONS OPERATIVE IN A NORMAL FRAME OF MIND

So far our (first approximation) proposal has been that what it is for X to have a trait of character T is for it to be a relatively permanent feature of X that, were X in situation S he would . . . , and were X in situation S' he would . . . , and . . . ; and furthermore, for these dispositions not to be derivative from other needs/aversions. We have sketched what might replace the 'S's, and how the blanks might be filled in, for the case of sympathy.

It is now necessary to complicate this proposal somewhat further. For we do not necessarily withdraw our judgment, for instance, that X is sympathetic, just because he fails to respond in the specified way even when his situation satisfies the antecedent of one of these subjunctive conditionals.

The most obvious type of situation in which failure of behavior specified in the consequent does not lead to withdrawal of trait ascriptions is that of severe emotional disturbance. We do not call a person unsympathetic if he fails to respond sympathetically five minutes after being discharged from his post. We tend to regard this phenomenon as one of the "primitivizing" or "regressive" effects of strong emotion. In this respect character traits are very like intellectual capacity; a person with a high I.Q. may, in a state of emotion, do very poorly on a standard test. And emotional disturbance may affect the influence any need/aversion may have on action.

The effect of recognition of someone's emotional condition on our ascription of traits to him is, however, rather more complex than the preceding paragraph suggests. There are degrees of emotional upset. A given state of upset will permit some trait attributions to stand unrevised despite absence of the behavior specified in the relevant consequent, but not necessarily every attribution; in a given state of shock ungenerous behavior might not lead us to withdraw the attribution of generosity, whereas forging a check in the same state probably would lead us to withdraw the attribution of honesty. Moreover, if we assign a man a trait in a high degree we expect it to manifest itself even in abnormal situations; we expect a highly considerate man not to act in a mean way, virtually irrespective of his emotional situation. And so on.

States of emotion are not the only situations that make us hesitant to revise trait ascriptions in view of a person's response failing to satisfy the consequent of one of the subjunctive conditionals. Information that the person is intoxicated, or under the influence of tranquilizers, or just extremely fatigued, has the same effect.

We cannot incorporate all such complications into our illustrative account, say, of sympathy. Nor, of course, can we incorporate it into our pattern of analysis, except in some crude way that simply points to the fact that certain complications would have to be taken into account in any complete analysis of a particular trait. One way of doing something to recognize the complication officially I propose to adopt: that of introducing the phrase "if in a normal frame of mind" into the antecedent part of any subjunctive conditional functioning as the partial analysis of a trait name. Thus we shall insist that the analysis of "is sympathetic" will be of the form, "would feel disturbed, *if he were in a normal frame of mind* and perceived some sentient being to be in acute distress."

V TRAITS ARE WANTS/AVERSIONS WITH A STANDARD LEVEL OF INTENSITY

For all that has been said so far, a person might be assigned a trait of character if the intensity of the want/aversion that constitutes the trait were as small as you please, anything above indifference. This is surely counterintuitive. We do not call a person "sympathetic" if in the most severe cases of distress he manages only the slightest inclination to relieve it, not enough to motivate substantial expenditure of effort. Obviously some standard level of want/aversion is required for attribution of a trait; we must consider this.

We do not need conclusions about the degree of want/aversion proper for ascription of a trait in its absolute form, for the purpose of comparative statements. It is clear that a person has a given trait in *higher* degree than another, if the data indicate a stronger want/aversion. X is *more* sympathetic than Y if he gets *more* disturbed at the sight of distress in another, feels more relief when the distress is removed, would expend more energy in relieving the distress, would feel guiltier about doing nothing to help someone in distress, and so on (all the appropriate exceptions and reservations being taken into account).

Our present concern, however, is with trait attributions in their *absolute* form: judgments just that a person is honest, conscientious, etc. It should be noticed, however, that we do not really need to be clear about this matter, as distinct from judgments in comparative form, for some of the purposes of moral philosophy mentioned in the introductory remarks; for the purpose of explaining what it is to have a *defect* in some trait of character it is enough if we understand what it is to say that a person has *more* or *less* of a trait than he ought to have. Nevertheless, an understanding of the use of trait names in their absolute form is of interest.

286

It is obvious that trait attributions in their absolute form do not give very precise information. What they do is say that a person *at least barely qualifies* as having a trait, no more. If we want to be a bit more definite, we can say that a person is, say, highly sympathetic, or moderately sympathetic, or perhaps sympathetic enough typically to do a certain kind of thing. What, however, is the minimum to which a person must come up in order to qualify as having a certain trait at all?

One possible proposal is to say that a person qualifies as having a trait, if he has it at least to the degree to which the average person does (or, if we gave tests, came out in the top 60 percent). But this is implausible, since it forbids us to say that there is any trait of character everyone or nearly everyone has.

What seems the correct answer may best be explained by an example. Take sympathy. Each of us has a conception of what a sympathetic person will do in a situation of a certain kind. For instance, we may think a sympathetic person will interrupt a friendly tennis game to tend to a child who has fallen off his bicycle. If he won't do that, we do not call him sympathetic. Each of us could give an answer as to whether a person would or would not be reckoned sympathetic by us, if he did or didn't take pains of a certain degree when needed to relieve distress in a given type of situation. This range of situations, and the range of degrees of trouble a person is willing to take, define the least a person has to do to qualify, for a given speaker, as being sympathetic. What ascription of the term "sympathetic" does is assert that the person's desire/aversion is at a level to produce the required degree of effort in these circumstances, or stronger. We may put this by saying that what a person does, who assigns a certain trait, is affirm that the person has a disposition identical with a relevant desire/aversion up *at least to the standard level.* I suggest this is true of all trait ascriptions.

We must complicate this suggestion slightly. In the first place, we make allowances for how the agent in question perceives the situation. For instance, we do not regard a young lady as unsympathetic if she fails to rush to assist a victim of an accident, if we know that she knows she always faints at the sight of blood. Furthermore, the effort required for one person to do a certain thing may differ greatly from that required for another. A nervous person in a demanding business post may find it much harder to give up cigarettes than does someone else; and the temptation to watch a baseball game on television may be much greater for a young boy than for his little sister. We make such adjustments in deciding whether a trait name may be applied, but what is expected of a normal person in response to a correct perception of a situation remains a kind of baseline.

An interesting question is whether the criteria that define the lower limit of applicability of a trait name are roughly the same for speakers of a given language community, or whether they vary from person to person, or from group to group. There is presumably a limit to a personal variation, since the terms are learned mostly by hearing them applied to persons in concrete situations. The conditions of learning do not guarantee uniformity throughout a speech community, however, since terms are learned by hearing their use by a small group, especially the family group. And use by different groups may differ somewhat, particularly in view of the fact that character-trait names have a flavor of moral praise or blame about them, so that attribution of the term carries a certain moral commitment. Thus businesspersons might not call a man dishonest for failing to report profits on expense accounts for tax purposes, whereas government employees might call him so. So we may expect some variations in the criteria for the lower limit of applicability of some traits.

Thus the criteria for assigning trait names are probably both somewhat variable and fuzzy at the borderline. We might add that the actual degree of the want/aversion in a given person is probably not perfectly precise, either. There may be some things a person would always do, some he would never do; there may be other things he would do on one day, but not on another. Character traits are possibly somewhat like physical abilities; and athletes have their off days and we cannot predict precisely how well a given high jumper will do on a given day.

15

The structure of virtue

We think a man's virtue may (partially) explain his action. "He would not have done this if he had not been courageous" – or compassionate, and so on. A virtue, then, is often, if not always, some feature of a person that, at least partially, can *explain* his intentional behavior (often also his emotions and thoughts). Aristotle says "virtue . . . is a state of character concerned with choice."[1] In what follows I want to defend a part (only) of Aristotle's spelling out of his view on this. A virtue, he says, is a settled state of the person that is *manifested* in emotions (he mentions desire, anger, fear, confidence, joy, friendship, etc.),[2] some of these involving an appetitive element (for example, fear involving a desire for safety),[3] the emotions being "in a mean . . . determined by a rational principle" that a person of practical wisdom would identify.[4] Again, he says that virtuous *acts* must be chosen for their own sakes and "proceed from a firm and unchangeable character."[5] I omit the part about emotions and virtue being in a mean. What I want to defend is his view that a virtue is a (certain kind of) relatively unchanging disposition to desire an action of a certain sort (for example, helping one in distress, not stealing) for its own sake.[6]

Before trying to answer our question what a virtue is, let us look at the picture of the determinants of action with which motivation theory and common sense provide us.

I A SKETCH OF THE DETERMINANTS OF BEHAVIOR

Let me preface my account of this theory by observing that, while this theory is widely accepted by writers on the theory of motivation (and in

I am grateful to Marcia Baron and William Frankena for criticisms of an earlier draft of this paper.
1 *Nicomachean Ethics (NE)* 1106b36, translated by W.D. Ross, in W.D. Ross, ed., *The Works of Aristotle* (Oxford, 1915).
2 *NE* 1105b20–5.
3 See J. O. Urmson, "Aristotle's Doctrine of the Mean," *American Philosophical Quarterly* 10 (1973): 224, 226, 229. Urmson proposes this interpretation as a possible one.
4 *NE* 1107a1–2.
5 *NE* 1105a30–5.
6 *NE* 1105a30 ff.

other social sciences) as an empirical supposition (and not a thesis about what is rational), it may be only an approximation to the truth: further knowledge about the physiology of the brain, and more detailed knowledge of the phenomenology of action may require modifications and additions. Moreover, the theory is only partially quantitative, and hence does not compare with physics for confirmability. However, the theory at present stands as follows:

First, the theory holds that intentional (not reflex or "instinctive" or habitual) behavior is restricted to options the agent thinks, at the time of choice, are open to him. Second, action is influenced by the agent's view, at that time, of the consequences of his behavior (counting the kind of act as itself a consequence – and one consequence could be the deviation of an action from preexisting intention), and how likely these consequences are, given the act. Third, the action is a function of the "valence" (being desired or aversive), at the moment of decision or action, of the complex act-plus-consequences, that is, of the intensity of the desires (or aversions) toward members of this complex, including the force of any already established intentions. Finally, it is influenced by the salience of one or'more features of the situation as apprehended, whether clearly before the mind, or only dimly so. We might break all this down as follows.[7]

Say that an agent's *tendency*, at a given time, to perform a given act is a sum: the sum of the intensity of his desire/aversion toward any consequence of that action (as explained above), reduced by the subjective improbability of its occurring if the action is performed, and reduced again by the lack of salience of that consequence and its relation to action in the awareness of the agent – the sum over all the anticipated consequences of the act. Then we can affirm that what an agent actually does is adopt whichever option is the one he has, at that time, the strongest *tendency* to adopt – for which this sum is greatest.[8]

7 There is criticism of the theory in Albert Bandura, "Self-regulation of motivation and action through internal standards and goal systems," in L.A. Pervin (ed.), *Goals Concepts in Personality and Social Psychology* (Hillsdale, NJ.: Erlbaum, 1989), pp. 19–85.
8 Readers who suspect there are no experimental data bearing on these matters should consult Douglas G. Mook, *Motivation: The Organization of Behavior* (New York, 1987), chaps. 5, 7, 9–11. I have reviewed the evidence for the theory in *A Theory of the Good and the Right* (Oxford, 1979), chaps. 2 and 3. See also A. I. Goldman, *A Theory of Human Action* (Englewood Cliffs, N.J., 1970), chaps. 3, 4, 157–69; D. Davidson, *Essays on Actions and Events* (Oxford, 1980), chaps. 1, 3, 5; and W. P. Alston, "Wants, Actions, and Causal Explanation," in H. N. Castaneda, ed., *Intentionality, Minds, and Perception* (Detroit, 1967).
    Some philosophers would reject this type of causal conception of human action altogether. See R. M. Chisholm, "The Agent as Cause," in M. Brand and D. Walton, eds.,

This is not to say that an action follows automatically, according to this function, from all the agent's *dispositional* beliefs roughly at the time of action. To say this would be to ignore the fact that dispositional beliefs may not all be before the mind at the time of choice, and, among other things, to overlook the role of deliberation. Usually one option open is to postpone decision and reflect further. The deliberation that follows may eliminate some options for one reason or another. When more deliberative procrastination has become aversive, one chooses among the remaining alternatives on the basis of the salient beliefs about them – in consciousness or in short-term memory, and salient – at the moment of decision, and the valences (at the time) of the expected consequences (including the action itself). There is reason, however, to doubt that all choice reflection is that simple.[9] Whether the valences are always consciously represented is doubtful; at least it seems hard to deny the influence of unconscious desires.

Many philosophers who would not question the above as a piece of psychology would want a good many details filled into the above sketch. What the details should be is controversial. But something like the following is probably as near as we can get to an agreed view. First, it will be said that the tendency to adopt a particular course of action strongest for a person (in view of all the factors described above) will *result* in the formation of an *intention* – acquisition of a disposition to follow a relevant plan of action. (Some philosophers have said that an intention *is just* an

Action Theory (Dordrecht, 1975), 199–212; "He Could Have Done Otherwise," in M. Brand, ed., *The Nature of Human Action* (Glenview, IL., 1971), 293–301; "On the Logic of Intentional Action," in R. Brinkley et al., eds., *Agent, Action, and Reason* (Toronto, 1971), 38–69; and "The Structure of Intention," *Journal of Philosophy* 67 (1970): 633–47; also Richard Taylor, *Action and Purpose* (Englewood Cliffs, NJ, 1966). For a critique, see I. Thalberg, "How Does Agent Causality Work?" in *Action Theory*, 213–38.

I do not accept the account of maximizing behavior offered by David Wiggins in "Weakness of Will," *Proceedings,* The Aristotelian Society (1978–79): 271–2.

9 See, for example, Albert Bandura, *Social Foundations of Thought and Action: A Social Cognitive Theory* (Englewood Cliffs, NJ, 1986), 231, 465, 473, 477. Experimental data show that individuals do not very reliably estimate the probabilities of outcomes, given their evidence. Moreover, we are not equipped with any summing device which enables us to know which sum comes out highest, as is obvious to anyone who has bought a car or even a sandwich. There are all sorts of strategies individuals use to solve this problem, and all sorts of proposals what these strategies are. See Mook, *Motivation*, and various review articles in the *Annual Review of Psychology:* J.R. Bettman, "Consumer Psychology," 37 (1986): 257–89; G.F. Pitz and N. J. Sachs. "Judgment and Decision," 35 (1984): 139–63; H. J. Einhorn and R. M. Hogarth, "Behavioral Decision Theory: Processes of Judgment and Choice," 32 (1981): 53–88, especially 69–77; and P. Slovik, B. Fischhoff, and S. Lichtenstein, "Behavior Decision Theory," 28 (1977): 1–39. Also see D. Kahneman and A. Tversky, "Prospect Theory: An Analysis of Decisions under Risk," *Econometrica* 47 (1979): 263–91.

291

everything-considered preference or pro-attitude toward an action plan, as compared with alternatives;[10] but others would insist that formation of an intention is more than this, partly because intentions persist and mold future plans.)[11] This intended plan of action will presumably fix when it should be executed, and when that time is (believed to be) *now* the agent will (possibly partly just because of the intention, but also supported by the underlying desire for the outcome and possibly antecedent intentions) begin to execute the plan by trying, or willing, to bring about an initial *basic* bodily action (one he can bring about without it being caused by some other bodily action) – a "willing" sometimes thought of as being the focusing of attention on the prospective basic action or a prescription of it ("Do so-and-so now!"), and perhaps involving an image of the sensations characteristic of the intended movement, any of which will, with the cooperation of the nervous system, cause the intended action. This basic action will set an appropriate next stage of the action, or even produce the wanted outcome.[12] (If one wants more light in the room, the act of pulling the drapes aside will be enough.) The intention will, unless there is a change of mind, remain through the period necessary for reaching the desired outcome, monitoring the sequence of actions in view of the feedback resulting from earlier members of the sequence, and other information.

All of the foregoing can be construed in a way compatible with the major theories of the relation of body and the mental. It appears, however, to be an analytic reduction of what it is for "the self" to act. All of this is consistent with holding that, directly or indirectly, acts are caused by a complex of beliefs and desires/aversions.

How might virtues possibly fit into such an account? Obviously, it

10 Davidson, *Essays on Action and Events*, 98–100. For more clarification of this view, see the following note on his reply to Bratman, and pp. 220 ff.
11 See Michael Bratman, "Davidson's Theory of Intention," in B. Vermazen and M. Hintikka, eds. *Essays on Davidson: Actions and Events* (Oxford, 1985). Also his forthcoming (Harvard) *Intentions, Plans and Practical Reason;* and his "Taking Plans Seriously," *Social Theory and Practice* 9 (1983): 271–87. Davidson replies lucidly in *Essays on Davidson*, 195–201.
12 See, for example, Bruce Aune, *Reason and Action* (Dordrecht, 1977), chaps. 1, 2, and 137–42; A. I. Goldman, *Theory of Human Action* and "The Volitional Theory Revisited," in Brand and Walton, *Action Theory;* Hugh McCann, "Volition and Basic Action," *Philosophical Review* 83 (1974): 451–73; L. H. Davis, *Theory of Action* (Englewood Cliffs, NJ, 1979), 38 ff., 59–93; John Searle, *Intentionality* (Cambridge, 1983): 83–135; Wayne Davis, "A Causal Theory of Intending," *American Philosophical Quarterly* 21 (1984): 43–54; G. A. Miller, E. Galanter, and K. H. Pribram, *Plans and the Structure of Behavior* (New York, 1960), especially chap. 4; William James, *The Principles of Psychology* (New York, 1913), II 487–92; A. G. Greenwald, "Sensory Feedback Mechanisms in Performance Control: With Special Reference to the Ideo-Motor Mechanism," *Psychological Review* 77 (1970): 73–101.

could be that a virtue is a relatively permanent *desire or aversion* (or complex of these) directed at some action-type and/or some expectable kind of consequence of an action (which can be included in the description of the action, for example, helping the distressed), with a strength up to a certain (acceptable) level, and furthermore being good in some sense.

But what are desires and aversions? These are (unlike longing) not primarily introspectible "felt" items of experience. A person is said to "desire" some situation S if his belief that S will occur if he does a certain thing will increase his tendency to do that.[13] This proposal may seem to render analytic the above statement that a person's tendency to act is a function of his desires/aversions; but in fact it does not, in view of the fact that the above statement says, not that a tendency to act is a function of one's desires/aversions simply, but only of these in conjunction with subjective probability judgments and degree of salience. In any case there are other features of a desire which suffice to make the statement synthetic. For example, when one thinks of something one wants, the thought of it tends to have an attractive aura.[14] Or, if a desire is frustrated (and its intensity above a certain level), one will experience some discomfort, like thirst, what Karl Duncker called "the sorrow of want."[15] Again, if one wants a given situation but has been in doubt whether it will occur, information that it will occur (provided the desire has a certain level of intensity) will cause joy. Conversely, if one has believed that the situation will occur, but then hears that it will not, she will (provided the desire is strong) feel disappointed. Moreover, the occurrence of a desired event of the kind E, or the belief that it has occurred, tends to be pleasant. Again, if one desires E, one will tend to notice possibilities for getting it, maybe daydream pleasantly about its occurrence. Further, at least in the case of physical desires (hunger, thirst, sex, etc.) there is a satiation effect: When an event of the kind E occurs, all the symptoms of the desire vanish, for a time (to recur after a certain time interval), and indeed desires for related states of affairs are diminished – as, for instance, when consumption of some item of food reduces interest in other kinds of food. This last feature is not wholly limited to physical desires: It seems that a desire for the company of others, and a desire for expressions of approval or admiration by others, also vanish after satiation, and recur after an interval (varying with the individual person).[16]

13 See Mook, *Motivation*, 59.
14 See Goldman, *The Theory of Human Action*, 49–50, 94; Karl Duncker, "On Pleasure, Emotion, and Striving," *Philosophy and Phenomenological Research* 1 (1941): 416; J. C. B. Gosling, *Pleasure and Desire* (Oxford, 1969), 97, 105, 121, 124.
15 Duncker, "On Pleasure, Emotion, and Striving," 417–18.
16 For instance, R. Eisenberger, "Is there a Deprivation-Satiation Function for Social Approval?" *Psychological Bulletin* 74 (1969): 255–75.

Aversions are a bit different. An aversion to S is not exactly a desire for *non-S*, although a person is said to have an aversion to S if his belief that S will occur if he does a certain thing will increase his tendency *not* to do that thing. An example is having an aversion to one's child being injured or to being thought stupid. To some degree, the concept of aversion is the mirror image of the concept of desire, except that desires aim at a target, whereas aversions are aimed at just getting away from something, anywhere.[17] If one thinks of an event occurring to which one has an aversion, one may feel repugnance at the idea (not an "attractive aura"); but in the case of aversion it appears there is no parallel to the "sorrow of want" which occurs when there is frustrated desire. If one has been in doubt whether an aversive event will occur, and one learns that it will not, one will feel relief (provided the aversion is strong) – not be pleased, as would be true if there were a desire for *non-S* – but the aversion is not a desire for this feeling of relief. If one has been expecting it wouldn't occur, but learns that it will, one will be (provided the aversion is strong) disturbed. But, different from the case of desire, one normally does not reflect on what might produce any one of various possible aversive events, or daydream (unpleasantly) about them. (One could, if some one of highly aversive events is threatening; but there is normally not motivation to have unpleasant daydreams.) And there is no satiation effect reducing aversions toward events of the same general kind, when an aversive event has occurred (though repetition reduces dislike, and there is some recovery of the dislike after a time-lapse).[18]

With this contrast in mind, it might make sense to say that an agent may have an *aversion* to acting dishonestly, or deceptively, but less obviously a positive desire to act honestly and truthfully. The virtue of benevolence might be a *desire* to give to others, and the virtue of compassion might be a desire to help – or to see others help – those in severe need. (Alternatively, one might say one has an *aversion* to other persons suffering, and hence a tendency to help relieve it – perhaps arising out of the emotion of pity, along a line suggested by Aristotle.) Again, one might have an *aversion* to unfairness: failure to adhere to standards of truthfulness in a trial, or lack of correspondence between merit and reward, or of equal consideration of persons, and so on. A virtue might be a desire for some action or state of affairs just for itself and not for any further reason – in that sense an intrinsic desire – and so like a desire for achievement or for human company; or it could be an aversion to

17 See Mook, *Motivation*, 172, 310.
18 R. B. Zajonc, "Attitudinal Effects of Mass Exposure," *Journal of Personality and Social Psychology* 9 (1968), monograph supplement; and S. P. Grossman, *A Textbook of Physiological Psychology* (New York, 1973).

some state of affairs like stealing, or telling lies, also for no further reason; and it could be both. (We might speculate that when Kant spoke of acting out of "respect" for the moral law, what he should have had in mind was an intrinsic *aversion* to acting in disconformity with moral law.)

The strength of these desires/aversions will presumably vary from one person to another. As we shall see, such desires/aversions will not be called "virtues" unless they are thought good in some sense, and their strength reaches a certain acceptable level.

If we speculate that what are usually regarded as virtues can, at least some of them, be so conceived, we can ask about the corresponding vices. It would seem that, in the case of at least some of the aversions, the corresponding vice is just *lack* of the aversion; for instance, dishonesty or mendacity seems to consist in just lack of an aversion to theft or deception. Dishonest people normally do not desire dishonesty for itself, only behavior expected to lead to wanted outcomes, which they know is dishonest. And in the case of compassion, again lack of aversion to the suffering of others seems enough – a person is said to be "lacking in compassion." However, in the case of benevolence the vice would seem to be a contrary desire: malevolence, a desire for others to be unfortunate. (A person might, however, be thought to have a vice if he merely wholly lacks benevolence.) Things are more complex with the virtues of courage and self-control, as we shall see.

Most of these motivations are concerned in some way with interactions with other persons. But there are other relatively unchanging motivations: for instance, ambition. "Ambitious" might be explained, following the Random House Dictionary, as "eagerly desirous of obtaining power, superiority, or distinction." This concept is obviously motivational.

There are some interesting personality traits, affecting action or at least a style of behavior, which do not obviously fit easily into this pattern: gentleness, grouchiness, sulkiness. The behavior patterns characteristic of these traits are obvious enough, but it is not clear what the motivation is. Possibly these are not dispositions having to do with *intentional* action, but are just traits of personality (not of character), dispositions of some other kind.

Somewhat the same may be said for intelligent behavior, behavior showing at least an average ability to be aware of a full range of options, an ability to identify their probable consequences with a justified belief about the likelihood of the consequences on the agent's evidence, an ability to represent all this vividly. This capacity cannot be analyzed motivationally. Intelligence in behavior instantiates a *capacity*, one which to some extent can be learned. (There may be, of course, motivation to think, to try to balance valenced consequences, etc.) Aristotle was right in distinguishing intellectual from practical virtues. (He would also classify wisdom as an intellectual virtue; I shall discuss wisdom below.) Let us call such qualities "intellectual excellences."

So much, initially, for the concept of a motivational analysis of various nonintellectual kinds of virtue.

II IS SELF-CONTROL A MOTIVATIONAL VIRTUE?

According to G. H. von Wright, virtues are not dispositions at all, hence not dispositions of the kind desires/aversions (roughly) are. The master virtue is "Self-control . . . [which is] a feature of character which helps a man never to lose his head, be it for fear of pain or for lust after pleasure, and always lets his action be guided by a dispassionate judgment as to that which is the right thing for him to do."[19] Von Wright does not explain what he means by "character," not considering, apparently, that a motivational theory of character is possible. What is self-control? Perhaps, as we shall see, it can be given a motivational analysis.

A more restricted proposal is made by R. C. Roberts, to the effect that at least *some* virtues are *capacities* whereby to "resist adverse inclinations."[20] "The most important distinction between kinds of virtues is that between the virtues of will power and those that are substantive and motivational"[21] (the latter, including honesty and compassion, being those of which roughly a desire/aversion account can be given). The virtues of will power are "capacities to manage our inclinations,"[22] are "skills of self-management." Exercise of these is a matter of the agent's own "achievement, his own choice, and thus reflects credit on him as an agent."[23] That they are skills is shown by the fact that they can be learned, by instruction, as a child learns self-control by being advised to put off minor gratifications for a short period of time, gradually enlarging the time-span and the scope.[24] Emotions can be controlled by learning to act contrary to their behavioral impulses, and by "self-talk," for example, "the power of positive thinking."[25] (But, as we shall see, desires/aversions can also be learned, and the details about how to do so can be fitted into a belief-desire framework.)

Similarly, Stephen Hudson says that a virtuous person "must be prin-

19 *The Varieties of Goodness* (London, 1963), 149.
20 R. C. Roberts, "Will Power and the Virtues," *Philosophical Review* 93 (1984): 227–84.
21 Ibid., 228.
22 Ibid., 233.
23 Ibid., 234.
24 Ibid., 243.
25 Ibid., 245 ff.

cipled and must have the capacity, the strength of will, to act as he should despite temptations."[26]

Again, James Wallace says some virtues are tendencies or *capacities*, that are *not* skills, to act in ways that constitute living well as a human being.[27] They involve a "positive capacity for acting rationally when certain motives are apt to incline us to do otherwise."[28] Thus courage is a capacity or tendency to overcome excessive (disabling) fear, as temperance (self-control) is a capacity or tendency to overcome disabling indulgence in easy pleasures. But, *in contrast*, some virtues like honesty, veracity, fidelity, and fairness are intrinsic (in the sense of not being for any further reason, such as self-interest) desires/aversions, different from just a desire to maximize one's own benefit, toward certain forms of behavior – so fitting in with a motivation theory. There are other clearly motivational virtues: of kindness, generosity, humaneness, and compassion, all involving a direct concern for the happiness and well-being of others.

The question I wish to raise about these writers is whether their conception of the relation of self-control (and courage) to motivation is probably correct. Can the former be explained in terms of the latter? Let us consider self-control.

There are various areas in which we think self-control is often called for: to restrain indulgence too often or inappropriately in eating, liquor, sex, and watching television; to avoid losing control of oneself in emotional states like anger, grief, or fear; to avoid self-gratifications like those involved in boasting or putting other persons down; to overcome a tendency to daydream or be distracted when trying to work. Persons are often so aware of deficiency in self-control in these areas that they seek therapeutic advice.

We should notice that there is motivation here, even in those dissatisfied with the degree of their self-control – enough to seek therapy and try to follow a constructive program. The motivation is usually specific: to overcome bad eating habits, alcoholism, losing one's temper.

Since there is motivation here, why is therapeutic advice necessary? The answer seems to be that goals, like that of being self-controlled or even weighing only 115 pounds, being either remote in time or abstract, are not, relatively, strongly motivating. Whether this is a basic fact, or a result of difficulty in visualizing vividly, we need not try to decide. (Psychologists seem not to have an opinion on this.) Much more is this the case with a recollection that one has judged a constrained line of action

26 Stephen Hudson, "Character Traits and Desires," *Ethics* 90 (1980): 539–49.
27 James D. Wallace, *Virtues and Vices* (Ithaca, NY, 1978), 40 ff.
28 Ibid., 61.

to be "the best thing to do," in some sense or other – a situation that is essentially the problem of "akrasia." Even if it is supposed that "is best" serves, as the internalist will have it, to express an overall preference for that course of action, a judgment that some action "is best" may be "remote" in the sense of being a recollection of an *earlier* judgment. If the "is best" judgment, in the suggested internalist sense, is made *now*, then what is judged best may of course be done, but the fact of experience, that we sometimes fail to do something at the very moment we are judging that it would be "best," is some evidence that "is best" at most expresses a strong motivation but not an overall preference.

What does the therapist do to help? The kind of "treatment" recommended varies somewhat depending on the particular problem. To control eating habits, it is agreed that there should be adoption of a program of sub-goals, one for each day, and, if possible, involvement of others (in a "weight-watchers" group) and making a pledge to them to submit periodic progress reports. Moreover, the plan should include daily evaluations of how well one is succeeding, and rewards for oneself, for success, either by some indulgence (going to a movie to celebrate) or at least by congratulating oneself verbally. How does all this work? Well, first, motivation to abstain may not be strong enough to adhere to a long-range program, but possibly be sufficient for success just today; moreover, this motivation will be supported by one's explicit resolution and the pledge to others (not to mention the anticipated shame in having to confess one's failure). Moreover, reinforcement by rewards will enhance motivation to adhere to the program, including the long-range target. Furthermore, the agent will often have sought therapy because he is convinced he cannot manage on his own, and if he is convinced there is something he cannot do, the motivation to do it will be less effective (the goal seeming not probable). The day-to-day success, however, will change this view, being replaced by the thought that he can cope with the problem.[29]

For other problems, like loss of temper, a slightly different regimen may be recommended. First, it is suggested that the agent take two or three deep breaths, when he gets angry, before doing anything. (It is not too much to be motivated to do this.) This gives time to think. Second, the agent is invited to notice the internal talk that tends to arise in such situations, such as "He's trying to push me around again, and I'm not going to stand for it!" that raises the level of anger. The agent is urged, after having noticed this, to substitute different thoughts: about what the problem really is, what actions he can take, how well he will like the

29 See Bandura, *Social Foundations* and "Self-Regulation of Motivation and Action."

probable consequences of each. He is then to adopt a plan of action. (His desire to vent his anger may not be strong enough to prevent these steps from being taken.) In all this, he will be motivated by the thought of self-censure if he fails. And, afterwards, he will evaluate how successful he has been in following the adopted plan. If he has been successful, he will reward himself, as in the previous case, and have his sense of ability to cope enhanced.

After a time, the self-rewards can be "faded," the meetings with weight-watchers dropped. So what is the resulting motivational situation? This seems unclear: perhaps the temptation of suboptimal behavior has lessened, or perhaps the moving power of one's motives not to overeat, or to avoid losing one's temper, has been strengthened.[30] My own experience is that the attractiveness – in prospect, not necessarily enjoyment of the act – of consuming chocolates diminishes after three or four weeks.) Whichever it is, it appears that the "problem" calling for self-control has been abolished. "Temptations" are no longer stronger than the desire to reduce, not to give vent to one's anger, etc.

Will such regimens tend to establish a *general* trait of "self-control" – adequate motivation, in case one recognizes *any* inclination to an immediate and pleasurable good that conflicts with beliefs about what one "ought" to do or is "best" for one to do, to do the latter? Some psychologists doubt whether such a general trait develops, wondering how much *generalization* there will be as a result of the "training"; but there is some suggestion that the idea of self-control may become a part of a person's ego-ideal.[31] It is possible that a person master the temptation to eat, but not master the temptation to watch television when he knows he should be working. So he can act akratically in one area, but not in another. We might say a person is not akratic, but self-controlled, if he is not akratic *in as many types of situations* as the average person is.

The writers cited above seem to be right in distinguishing the role of motivation in "self-control" from motivations such as manifest truthfulness or sympathy. How much difference is there? One difference is in the specificity of the target. In the latter cases one is motivated to avoid telling lies, and to help other people. In the former, there is initially inadequate motivation to do what the agent thinks he "ought" to do, followed by adoption of a plan for specific situations, with rewards, and then development of motivation so that the problem calling for self-

---

30 See Douglas Meichenbaum, "Teaching Children Self-Control," in B. Lahey and A. Kazden, eds., *Advances in Child Clinical Psychology* (New York, 1986); also D. Meichenbaum, *Cognitive-Behavior Modification: An Integrative Approach* (New York: 1977); and Albert Bandura, *Social Foundations*, chap. 8.

31 Bandura, *Social Foundations*, 240 ff.

control does not exist (and possibly generalization to a general motive of self-control). So there is some difference between the type of *plural* motivation (plural in the sense of relatively stronger motivation to this, and that) characteristic of "self-control" and that of these other virtues; but it is not true that self-control is not "motivational" – there has been learned a total motivational situation so that motives effective in controlling specific kinds of situations have been established.[32] Incidentally, the other virtues may be somewhat more like such self-control than at first appears, for example, if sympathy is stronger for some types of situations than for others where it does not lead to helping behavior.

There seems to be phenomenological support for a further observation about self-control (and other virtues). For there are things we want, like sensory pleasures, the company of other people and their respect, and it is easy to think of desire for these things as controlling behavior. We actually seem to feel the pull of such opportunities.[33] The same for many states of affairs to which we are averse. We do not like electric shocks, or drinking castor oil, or visiting a dentist. Here, again, we seem to feel an aversive push. But there are also things we do not do by inclination, where, as James said, we seem to be acting "in the line of greatest resistance."[34] I want to eat a sweet, but control my impulse by reflection on the undesirability of more weight. I want to go to a party, and can hear the good time everyone is having; but I do not because I know I need a good night's sleep in order to be in shape for demanding tasks tomorrow. I want to help myself to another piece of cake, but desist because I know other guests will be arriving later. These cases seem very different from refraining to act because I have an aversion to shocks, castor oil, or public criticism. In the latter cases I may feel a "pushing" inclination to avoid imminent personal discomfort. In the former cases this is not true: At least there is nothing aversive or uncomfortable *now*, or in some cases even a personal loss at all, about later getting too little sleep, putting on more weight, and allowing late-arriving guests to go without goodies. There is no "felt" desire involved.

Nevertheless this phenomenon has been stated too simply. When self-control (courage, etc.) is involved, a choice is being made between two options. If we assume the main idea of the belief-desire theory of mo-

---

32 Contrast much of the foregoing with David Wiggins, "Weakness of Will, Commensurability, and the Object of Deliberation and Desire," *Proceedings*, The Aristotelian Society (1978–79): 251–78, especially 255–8.
33 See Alexander Pfaender, *Phenomenology of Willing and Motivation*, translated by Herbert Spiegelberg (Chicago, 1967): 17.
34 James, *Principles of Psychology* II, 549.

tivation, we shall hold that a person always does (roughly) what he *prefers* to do. How is it possible that a person *prefer* (that is, be *more motivated* to do, or get) something that does not promise enjoyment, or the avoidance of pain, now, to something that does? How is it possible for one's own long-range good, or the well-being of others, to be a motivating consideration? Presumably there is some brain *representation* of a future state of affairs – expressible in either images or concepts – that is motivating. (The representation may be of outcomes of a kind of action, or the kind of action itself.) So one can ask, must a representation be of something that is an immediate or pleasurable good (or an immediate or unpleasant bad), and be *felt* as an inclination, in order to be motivating? If not, if behavior can be otherwise motivated, then we have to say that *felt* inclinations are not all that important as indicators of effective causal processes, and of course we shall want a story about how this is.

How in particular can we be averse to acting dishonestly – perhaps with no felt aversive push at all, of the sort we feel when we consider drinking castor oil? The most plausible view is that the *representation* has become motivating as a result of conditioning by prior pleasant or unpleasant (or other) experiences. Take, for example, the case of giving aid or avoiding lies. The best explanation seems to be that, for evolutionary-survival reasons, young children find the cries of distress of others distressful. When they relieve the distress, the relief of their own distress reinforces the behavior of relieving the distress of others – representation of the goal of relief of distress becomes more strongly motivating. This motivation is supported by the praise of others (or criticism if the individual ignores the distress of others); and there is further support from observation of others with whom the agent identifies. Then, as a result perhaps of parental explanations, the motivating force of relieving distress spreads, by conditioning, to bring about intrinsic motivation not to lie, or act dishonestly, in view of the fact that these behaviors are normally hurtful.[35] So there is a proliferation of aversions – a result of conditioning by association – supported by praise or blame, and by identifications. The development of sympathy (and empathy), then, has a major role to play in the development of moral aversions.[36] (Of course, response to categories like truthfulness – "That would be deceptive" – requires development of corresponding concepts.) Thus we can see how it can be that the idea of certain behavior or its consequences is attractive – the

35 See Martin Hoffman, "Moral Development," in P. Mussen, ed., *Carmichael's Manual of Child Psychology* II (1970), 261–359.
36 Jonathan Bennett, "The Conscience of Huckleberry Finn," *Philosophy* 49 (1974): 123–34. And various early figures.

representation of that behavior, or its consequences, motivating – even though the representation is not of some pleasant or immediate good or ill, and there is possibly no felt pull of inclination at all.[37]

This phenomenon needs to be unpacked a bit further. When some representation of an option for action is aversive enough so that the individual "prefers" to act in a self-controlled way, nevertheless there may be left a feeling of regret for the pleasures, or safety, forgone; *that* is why we feel, in James's terms, that we are "acting in the line of greatest resistance."[38] This feeling makes us think we are *not* doing what we *prefer* to do, but what is shown is simply that such feelings are not necessarily a guide to what is really motivating.

This view, and the foregoing account of how one "learns" self-control, may be contrasted with that of Aristotle (and St. Thomas[39]), to the effect that virtues are learned by habit – perhaps by parents inducing a child to act in a certain way, with the effect that he finds acting in that way pleasant (perhaps we should say, more accurately, not irksome[40]), and then in some sense sees the point of it all – that such a life is best.[41]

It can be that two persons may have differing degrees of self-control or sympathy although both are called "self-controlled" or "sympathetic." But the success of one person may be less frequent than that of another, owing to the different degrees of strength and the specific directions of the motivation.

III   ARE ALL THE VIRTUES MOTIVATIONAL?

We have noticed that various writers agree that some traits naturally invite a motivational analysis, that is, invite the view that to have the trait is for the person to be motivated positively or negatively toward a represented situation. Thus for sympathy/compassion, generosity, honesty, veracity, promise-keeping, apparently justice and conscientiousness. These are what R. C. Roberts called "substantive" virtues.[42] But I concede that other virtues, at least at first glance, appear to be different: virtues like self-control, and perhaps courage, patience, reliability, perseverance, industry, tolerance. I have now made a general proposal to the effect that the virtue of "self-control" can be viewed as motivational – a (plural)

37 See notes 35 and 51.
38 James, *Principles of Psychology* II, 534, 549.
39 *Summa Theologica* q. 51, a. 2; q. 52, a. 3.
40 Gabriele Taylor and Sybil Wolfram, "Virtues and Passions," *Analysis* 31 (1971): 82.
41 See M. F. Burnyeat, "Aristotle on Learning to Be Good," and Richard Sorabji, "Aristotle on the Role of Intellect in Virtue," both in A. O. Rorty, ed., *Essays on Aristotle's Ethics* (Berkeley, 1980).
42 Roberts, "Will Power and the Virtues," 227–48, especially 229 ff.

motivation to abstain in the face of contrary motivations, of sexual desire, appetite, or whatever. But let us look now at some others from these apparently nonmotivational virtues, and see how they may be construed, whether like compassion, or like self-control, or different from both.

Let us begin with courage, which Random House defines as "the quality of mind that enables one to encounter difficulties and dangers with firmness or without fear." Courage is obviously a quality one shows in situations that are thought to be dangerous. Is courage a matter of confidence? If confidence means confidence in one's own skills, it would seem not; for if one is a skilled boxer he knows there is no real danger if he gets involved in a street fight; so courage is not called for. It is, however, clear that we all have an aversion to death, being wounded, loss of status to a significant degree, or a significant risk of these. In the case of some persons, this aversion is so strong that it overcomes any desire for a course of action that risks the danger, however important doing so is for personal or social well-being. Such persons are cowards. This is not to say that a person is courageous if he sets *no* store at all by the safety of his person or status; a person who sets no store by safety is simply foolhardy or insensitive. How much store can a courageous person set by safety? The answer seems to be that the coward sets more store by personal safety than we think proper, although one person might identify a "satisfactory" level of concern for safety differently from another. A courageous man is one whose aversion to danger and risk of disaster is not all consuming; at least his concern for important things, such as principles, duty, the protection of his family, his own long-term goals, and so on, are sufficiently strong, and his aversion to danger relatively sufficiently weak, that he faces the danger and risk nevertheless (when it is worth it).

But perhaps this sketch is too unspecific, and there is no *one* trait (or motivation) that distinguishes the courageous from the cowardly. Perhaps courage is a trait only in the sense in which there is a (plural) trait of self-control, and which we acquire in much the way depicted above for self-control, and courage might be viewed as a *form* of self-control. I speculate that in fact this is the case, and that many of the phenomena we noted about self-control and learning it have parallels for the case of courage, although there are differences, because fear is not an appetite like desire for chocolate, but an emotionally qualified aversion to danger.

We know that some people fear high places, being in a crowd, giving a talk in public. How do people get to overcome these fears, when they do? Work done by psychologists to overcome fear seems restricted to situations that, in fact, are not dangerous, whatever the patient may think. Such persons are motivated to go to psychologists, either because they dislike fear or because it is disabling, for instance if a person is unable to go to his job because of agoraphobia. So there is motivation to overcome fear all right. Now the therapist does not simply give stern injunctions to behave properly. He proceeds by stages. If the person is, say, afraid of snakes, he may be encouraged to watch someone else fearlessly handle snakes, from a safe distance. Then, maybe next day, he is brought closer. Until finally he himself picks up a large snake, and has the exhilaration of feeling the movement of its muscles and looking it in the eye at close range. This regimen convinces a person that snakes are not dangerous, in a way no lecture could. So his fear has been reduced, and his approach has been strongly rewarded. The individual has overcome his disabling fear of snakes. Much the same for agoraphobics. They are currently treated in groups, and may board a bus as a group and ride around London. While free to leave, they remain aboard through the dynamics of group interaction. As in the case of snake fear, they learn that being in a crowd is not harmful and can reward themselves for surviving in a crowd. There is also mutual support among members of the group. The agoraphobia gradually becomes manageable. Or, if a person is terrified at the thought of making a speech in public, again there is training by stages. First the person is trained to relax his body. When he has learned to do this, he is then instructed to imagine himself preparing to make a speech, going on the platform, and so on. The thought is that the relaxation will associate with the image of speech-making conditions, and that this will carry over – as it seems to – to the real-life situation. These people have gradually come to be more relaxed in these formerly disturbing situations, having learned through rewards, support from other persons, association with a relaxed bodily state, and finding that, with this training, it is possible to "cope." These methods, then, have succeeded in dissociating fear from these situations, and the person is no longer disabled by it. Obviously, however, such persons hardly qualify to be called "courageous" in general.

Suppose there is real danger, say to a soldier who is exposed to mortar fire. How does he overcome his natural fear? (I know of no psychological literature on this.) I speculate that, as in the foregoing examples, the soldier may notice that relatively few individuals are hurt by mortar fire, and will reflect that if he is hurt he will be given good care and a vacation behind the lines. He may say to himself that he will be unharmed unless "his number comes up." This somewhat less worried attitude will be strengthened by the behavior of those around him, going about their business apparently without much concern (except to take cover if the fire comes too close), and by their giving him moral support. He will discover that he can "cope" – do his work despite the threat of harm. If he is given the responsibility of being a leader, this will strengthen his attitudes – the feeling he is being depended on. So he may become able eventually to lead an infantry charge effectively. Then is he courageous?

Unfortunately, the fears he has mastered may be specific. He may be terrified if confronted by a bayonet charge – or if not at that, too terrified to phone the attractive woman he met last night and ask her out, or to report someone's dereliction of duty to a commanding officer, or to ask for a promotion. So, just as a person may have overcome his appetite for chocolates, but not for drink or sex or self-glorification, so his "training" may enable him to carry on in the face of mortar fire, but not to do what he thinks is best for him in confronting a young lady on the telephone. How much *generalization* will there be from such learning to overcome fears of various dangers? Can a person come to a stage where, despite risks, he effectively does *whatever* he thinks is his duty, or is best for him to do? Perhaps we do not know.

Thus courage may be a "plural" virtue, like self-control. Perhaps no one is courageous in all areas, but we might say one person is more courageous than others if he faces, with firmness, more situations normally fear-arousing, than most. His motivation is strong enough to overcome his fears, as they are after treatment or experience. We do not call a person a coward if there are only some situations in which he is fearful and performs poorly, especially if they are unimportant. For all this, need we introduce some nonmotivational concept of "character trait"?

Some of the other virtues do not obviously yield to even the foregoing kind of complex motivational analysis, possibly because it is far from clear what kind of motivation is typical of a person with the virtue: for example, patience, perseverance, reliability. The *Oxford English Dictionary* defines "patience" as "the quality or capacity of suffering or enduring of pain, trouble, or evil with calmness and composure." For those of us for whom patience is called for in nothing more than being caught in a traffic jam, it is hard to imagine what it is like to suffer pain "with composure." Perhaps what is behind this "composure" is the awareness of the disutility of crying out or complaining – reactions one knows are only annoying or disturbing to others, or looked upon by them as a sign of weakness. One could also develop a kind of stoic ideal, be motivated to avoid what disconforms with that ideal, or to do what will be disturbing to others or what will be viewed by them as weaknesses. In either case, the "composure" behavior seems motivated either by positive desire for an ideal or by aversion to the results of noncomposed behavior. At least the suggestion is sensible.

What is it to be reliable? The *Oxford English Dictionary* defines this as that in which "reliance or confidence may be put." Of course, this is only the case if one is talking of a general trait of character. If someone says I am not a reliable guide to the geography of the State of Michigan, he may have nothing at all in mind beyond the fact that I frequently give mistaken advice when asked questions. Matters seem different if we are speaking of someone as a reliable (or responsible) person. Here it seems not improper to think of motivation to do what others properly expect of one: that one do one's job. Or, we might say it is aversive motivation toward failing to do one's job, or what others properly expect.

IV MORAL AND NONMORAL VIRTUES

When should we call one of these intentional-action-explaining traits a "virtue"? I suggest that the answer is *roughly* that the trait must be one *normally and importantly favorable* either for the well-being of society (or some group thereof) or for the flourishing of the agent (or those dear to him, for instance, his family).

Of course, the term "virtue" is sometimes used very broadly, to apply to nonactional traits or even to characteristics of nonpersons: for instance, we might say that it is a virtue of a certain make of automobile that it starts easily in winter, or that it is a virtue of a certain drug that it gives fast relief. And we might say of a teacher that one of her virtues is that she is an extremely lucid lecturer. What is correctly or incorrectly called a "virtue" is a subtle question of linguistic sense; but we do well in the present context to follow Aristotle and view virtue as a disposition having to do with intentional action. Only thus would we be able to regard a virtue as a trait of *character*.[43]

But what counts as a *moral* virtue? The *Oxford English Dictionary* takes as the primary use of "virtue" the moral use: a disposition to conform one's conduct with principles of morality, or of recognized standards of morality such as chastity. I think we might approach the notion better by utilizing a concept of J. S. Mill. He said that when we call anything "wrong" we mean to imply "that a person ought to be punished in some way or other for doing it – if not by law, by the opinion of his fellow creatures; if not by opinion, by the reproaches of his own

43 E. L. Pincoffs (*Quandaries and Virtues* [Lawrence, KS, 1986]) explains "virtue" more broadly than I have done. He says virtues and vices are "dispositional properties that provide grounds for preference or avoidance of persons" (82). So he includes carefulness, cheerfulness, cleverness, civility, courtesy, dignity, serenity, nobility, grace, wit, and liveliness. This is certainly different from motivations to intentional action. However, he distinguishes various types of virtue, and could distinguish sets like the one I recognize, as sub-classes. Perhaps the disagreement is largely semantic; but his "virtues" turn out to be a very heterogeneous collection.

conscience."[44] We can drop the part about law, and say that a moral virtue is some level of some kind of desire/aversion, having to do with intentional action, manifestation of the absence of which ought to be (Mill means, it is *desirable* that it be) punished [on utilitarian grounds], either by the disapproval of others, or by the reproaches of the agent's own conscience. I should prefer to say a virtue is moral if manifestation of its absence would be punished, in this way, by a moral system a rational person would support for a society in which he expected to live. This definition, however, is a bit restrictive in explaining "moral virtue" only as motivation to produce *required* behavior. We should loosen it, I think, by adding desires/aversions the manifestation of which a rationally preferable moral system would *reward* by admiration/praise, and *encourage* self-reward by the agent in feeling pride.[45]

Normative theories, for instance, rule utilitarianism, purport to show us which motivations are moral virtues, and how relatively strong they should be, perhaps by showing that a justified moral system would require certain motivations, and admire/praise others, with an ordering of strength, because of the utility of such a system.

It is possible that different moral virtues will motivate conflicting forms of behavior, in response to a particular situation. In that case the "strongest" one will dominate action. McDowell has suggested that what happens is that one virtue "silences" the others,[46] although he should concede that the virtues that are "silenced" may well reappear in feelings of compunction (to use a term employed by Ross).[47] Such a conflict may also motivate a good deal of reflection about the situation, partly about just what its features are, but also including reflection on what the relative weight of the different virtues (desires/aversions) should be.[48]

How are the moral virtues – at least those of them that can be analyzed in motivational terms, like sympathy and honesty – related to the agent's moral commitments or principles? Lester Hunt has proposed that traits of character are dispositions to act "on principle," because of beliefs "about what is in some sense right or good" (not good only as a means). Hence, someone has a trait of character "insofar as he holds the corresponding belief and holds it on principle; insofar, that is, as he believes

---

44 J. S. Mill, *Utilitarianism*, chap. 5, Library of Liberal Arts edition (Indianapolis, 1957), 60.
45 See Aristotle, *NE* 1103a10 and 1129b15–20.
46 John McDowell, "Are Moral Requirements Hypothetical Imperatives?" *Proceedings*, The Aristotelian Society (supplementary volume, 1978).
47 This point was called to my attention by Allan Gibbard.
48 This might be what Aristotle had in mind in *NE* 1103b29–1104a9.

it and acts on it consistently."⁴⁹ For instance, he holds that a courageous action is one that is done "from the principle that one's own safety, in general, has no more than a certain level of importance."⁵⁰ A great deal depends, of course, on what is meant by a "belief about what is good or right," a concept Hunt does not explain. Now suppose someone, in saying that something is morally obligatory, is expressing some degree of motivation to do that thing for itself and not from some personal interest, plus a disposition to feel guilty if he does not and to disapprove of others if they are not so motivated, and a belief that these attitudes are justified. Then, if to have a moral belief is to have such an attitude/belief complex, one will be motivated accordingly. If one is not motivated accordingly, one does not have the "principle." So construed, we can agree with Hunt that a virtue is a disposition to act consistently in accordance with a certain principle.

But shall we say, then, that for a person to have the *virtue* of compassion is *identical* with his being motivated (etc.) with respect to the principle of aiding those in need? I think not, for two reasons. In the first place, I suggest that a virtue is *purely* motivational; one can have the virtue of sympathy without necessarily having a disposition to feel guilty if one is not motivated in a sympathetic way, or to disapprove of others who are not, or to think one's attitude is justified. (But some psychologists think there is a *causal* connection.⁵¹) So to say someone has a certain virtue is to say less than that the corresponding principle is part of his moral code. But second, a person can have a principle in his moral code, but only weakly. He is somewhat disposed to give aid to those who need it, but not very strongly – not enough really to put himself out. I suggest that for a person to have a certain virtue is for him, in a *normal* frame of mind, to show corresponding moral motivation up to an acceptable level. ("Acceptable" does not mean "average.") A judgment about whether a person has a given trait to an acceptable degree must take into account how the individual perceives a situation, for example, as dangerous to him. With this, and doubtless other adjustments, we judge whether a person's trait is in the acceptable class by considering whether his behavior is acceptable in standard situations. So having a virtue is more demanding than simply to have a moral principle in the suggested sense. Of course, what is judged acceptable may differ from one person to another, and

49 Lester Hunt, "Character and Thought," *American Philosophical Quarterly* 15 (1978): 183.
50 Lester Hunt, "Courage and Principle," *Canadian Journal of Philosophy* 10 (1980): 289.
51 Martin L. Hoffman, "Development of Prosocial Motivation: Empathy and Guilt," in N. Eisenberg, ed., *The Development of Prosocial Behavior* (New York, 1982) and "Empathy, Justice and Moral Development," in N. Eisenberg and Janet Strayer, eds., *Empathy and Its Development* (Cambridge, 1987).

exactly what people mean by, for instance, "sympathetic," will differ accordingly. I have discussed this more in detail elsewhere.[52]

The question may be raised whether it is possible to have too much of any virtue, for instance, to be generous "to a fault"? One might say that a virtue like generosity is not to count as a virtue when it goes beyond a certain point, perhaps because there are other virtues, say justice and prudence, and too much generosity might conflict with one of these. The same with veracity, which can conflict with sympathy – unnecessarily telling someone hurtful truths. Can even conscientiousness – concern to do one's duty – go too far? It would seem that one can at least be too much concerned with it, say, always wondering what is one's duty in rather trivial situations. Or, one could let one's spontaneous following of desirable motivations be swallowed in concern to do exactly what is one's duty. In that sense there could be too much.

So much for the moral virtues. How about the nonmoral ones, such as industry? I propose we use the term "nonmoral virtue" for a relatively permanent desire or aversion that is normally beneficial for any agent (or those dear to him – or for some special group, or in his job) for him to have, that adds to his (their) "flourishing."[53] Thus a given desire/aversion (virtue) might qualify as both moral and nonmoral. If one held that it is always best for any agent to act morally, the moral virtues would seem to qualify also as nonmoral, in my sense. And, if one held that industry – and, in general, features that contribute to the well-being of the agent – is itself morally obligatory, at least some nonmoral virtues would qualify as moral. (It is also true that a rational person would *regret* the absence of one of the nonmoral virtues, perhaps feel ashamed because of a defect in one, and feel some pity for others who lack them.) But a more standard (and more acceptable) view is that the classes of moral and nonmoral virtues are not extensionally equivalent. Ambition, enviousness, patience, persistence, and industry are normally good (or bad) qualities for an agent to have, and often it is desirable that one (not) have them, from the point of view of society; but it is not clear that a rationally chosen moral system would *require* their presence or absence, or praise (admire) them.[54]

52 R. B. Brandt, "Traits of Character: A Conceptual Analysis," *American Philosophical Quarterly* 7 (1970): 36–37.

53 This is a distinction different from that drawn by G. Taylor and S. Wolfram, in "The Self-regarding and Other-regarding Virtues," *Philosophical Quarterly* 18 (1968): 238–48, especially 244 ff. Their view is that what distinguishes courage, temperance, etc., is the nature of the temptation not to do something that the agent thinks there is overriding reason to do. The temptation may be fear or danger or indulgence in pleasures. I am drawing a different distinction, between motivations it is desirable for society to require or praise and beneficial ones outside of this category.

54 Professor E. L. Pincoffs has a somewhat different way of classifying virtues and a different way of defining "virtue." See his *Quandaries and Virtues*, 78–92.

The relation between a person's moral code and his nonmoral virtues is not very close. A moral commitment need not put one at all on the way to having a nonmoral virtue; there just may be no nonmoral virtue corresponding to a given moral commitment. Take a commitment not to be deceptive. Is there a nonmoral virtue corresponding – a disposition of advantage to the flourishing of the agent? Perhaps not. Moreover, a person might have a nonmoral virtue like ambition or curiosity, and have no disposition to feel guilty for behavior not manifesting it, or to feel resentment or indignation at others whose behavior does not manifest it.[55] Shame or pity, perhaps, but not remorse or indignation. So much for the nonmoral virtues.[56]

I suggest that we so use the term "character" (as contrasted with "personality") so that all the virtues/vices (in the foregoing senses), both moral and nonmoral, count as traits of *character*.

What should we say about wisdom? Is it a virtue at all, and if so, is it moral or nonmoral? I suppose there is no agreed conception of what it is. It seems to be at least in part a cognitive achievement: of what one would want if one were fully and vividly informed about relevant facts, and of what kind of morality one would choose if one were so informed. I believe it would be thought that one is not really wise if there is not a favorable concern for what one would so want, or for the so identified morality. So, if all virtues are *purely* motivational, wisdom is not a virtue. Furthermore, if condemnation or praise will hardly change it,[57] it is not a property that there would be a point in society trying to bring about, fully, by teaching, or by criticism or praise. So, what is its status? Why not say, with Aristotle, that it is an intellectual *excellence*, a quality of mind it is a good thing for people to have, for action, both from their own point of view and from that of society?

55 For a fuller discussion, see my "W. K. Frankena and Ethics of Virtue," *The Monist* 64 (1981): 271–92 *passim*.
56 Lester Hunt, in "Character and Thought," lists various traits which he says are "all examples of traits of character." Among them he includes obedience, gentleness, and impulsiveness. The first two seem neither to be required by an optimal moral system, nor to be normally important for the agent's flourishing. (Do we even want a general trait of obedience among adults?) As for gentleness, it would seem that as a disposition for intentional action, traits like kindness and consideration cover the same ground. Gentleness strikes me as a stylistic trait of personality. My intuition is to exclude these. Impulsiveness is a harder case. I would think it implies action without awareness of options, consequences, etc. "Think first!" may be a disposition that is usually both socially and personally beneficial.
57 See Burnyeat, "Aristotle on Learning to Be Good," and Sorabji, "Aristotle on the Role of Intellect in Virtue."

V VIRTUES AND ACTION

What will a virtuous person do in a particular situation? The answer is that, if only one virtue is relevant to the situation, he will do what that virtue motivates him to do (provided temptations are not too strong). But in a great many cases more than one virtue will be involved, and they will motivate in contrary directions. What then does one do? The answer: whatever the strongest virtue – or the combined force of several virtues all motivating in the same direction – motivates one to do. This fact makes it necessary to emphasize that different virtues have different degrees of strength. But reflection on this situation also indicates a need to make our conception of a virtue more subtle. Take for instance a conflict between the virtues of fidelity to promise and that of compassion, for helping or at least not injuring. Evidently it makes a difference what kind of promise it is: how much failure to perform will damage or inconvenience others, whether the promise was casual and impulsive, or deliberated and made before a "cloud of witnesses," whether it was made long ago in circumstances different from those now obtaining. Similarly, there is the question of what kind of benefit, and to whom. Is the benefit to one's self? Is it a matter of giving emergency aid, or at any rate aid essential to saving a person from a disastrous situation? Evidently for guidance in real life situations we need something more specific than abstract properties like those called "fidelity" and "benevolence/compassion," but rather a complex set of motivations, of differing strengths, pertinent to the particular problems which may arise. In this sense having a virtue like honesty or veracity, just as such, abstractly, can hardly be a guide to life except in very simple situations.

If a person already has the "right" set of complex virtues built in, we might say that what he ought to do is simply what these relevant virtues motivate him to do. But suppose one comes to doubt whether one's built-in set of virtues is "right." Then what is one to do? A conscientious person will want to perform the act that is morally right – he has an overriding motive to do that. In this case he needs to reflect on what the relative weights of his motives *ought to be,* and it is not clear just how to discover this. It is here that a person's normative moral theory will come into play. For instance, one may hold that the (moral) virtues one ought to have are those it would be most beneficial for everyone to have, everything taken into account (including the social cost of teaching them) and with just the strength it is optimal for them to have. One may reflect on which these are, and one's conclusions may activate the motive of conscientiousness.

E

Implications of utilitarian theory

16

The morality and rationality of suicide

"Suicide" is conveniently defined, for our purposes, as doing something that results in one's death, from the intention either of ending one's life or to bring about some other state of affairs (such as relief from pain) that one thinks it certain or highly probable can be achieved only by means of death or that will produce death. It may seem odd to classify an act of heroic self-sacrifice on the part of a soldier as suicide. It is simpler, however, not to try to define "suicide" so that an act of suicide is always irrational or immoral in some way; if we adopt a neutral definition like the above we can still proceed to ask when an act of suicide in that sense is rational, morally justifiable, and so on, so that all evaluations anyone might wish to make can still be made.

The literature in anthropology makes clear that suicide has been evaluated very differently in different societies, and philosophers in the Western tradition have been nearly as divergent in their evaluative views of it. I shall not attempt to review these evaluations but rather to analyze the problem and appraise some conclusions from the viewpoint of contemporary philosophy.

I wish to discuss three questions, of which the first is in my opinion of least importance and the last of most importance. First, if an agent takes his own life when it is objectively morally wrong for him to do so, was his action necessarily morally blameworthy, or, to use a theological term, sinful? Second, when is it objectively morally right or wrong for an agent to take his own life? Third, when is it rational, from the point of view of an agent's own welfare, for him to commit suicide? What these questions mean, and how they differ, will be explained.

THE MORAL BLAMEWORTHINESS OF SUICIDE

In former times the question whether suicide is sinful was of great interest because the answer to it was considered relevant to how the agent would

This paper was written while the author was a Fellow at the Center for Advanced Study in the Behavioral Sciences and also a Special Fellow in the Department of Health, Education, and Welfare. Parts of it appear in S. Perlin, ed., *Handbook for the Study of Suicide* (Oxford University Press, 1975) and are reprinted with the permission of the editor and publisher.

spend eternity. At present the practical issue is not great, although a normal funeral service may be denied a person judged to have sinned by committing suicide. At present the chief practical issue seems to be that persons may disapprove morally of a decedent for having committed suicide and his friends or relatives may wish to defend his memory against moral charges. The practical issue does not seem large, but justifies some analysis of the problem.

The question whether an act of suicide was sinful or morally blameworthy is not apt to arise unless it is already believed that morally the agent should not have done it; this question will be examined in the following section. But sometimes we do believe this, for instance, if he really had very poor reason for doing so and his act foreseeably had catastrophic consequences for his wife and children. At least, let us suppose that we do so believe. In that case we might still think that the act was hardly morally blameworthy or sinful if, say, the agent was in a state of great emotional turmoil at the time. We might then say that, although what he did was wrong, his action is excusable, just as in criminal law it may be decided that, although a person broke the law, he should not be punished because he was temporarily insane, or did what he did inadvertently, and so on.

These remarks assume that to be morally blameworthy or sinful for an act is one thing, and for the act to be wrong is another. But what after all does it mean to say that a person is morally blameworthy because of an action? We cannot say there is agreement among philosophers on this matter, but I suggest the following account as being safe from serious objection: X is morally blameworthy because of an action A may be taken to mean that X did A, and X would not have done A had not his character been in some respect below standard, and in view of this it is fitting or justified for X to have some disapproving attitudes including remorse toward himself and for some other persons Y to have some disapproving attitudes toward X and to express them in behavior.

In case the above definition does not seem obviously correct, it is worthwhile pointing out that it is usually thought that an agent is not blameworthy or sinful for an action unless it is a reflection on him; the definition illustrates this fact and makes clear why this act did not manifest any defect of character. It may be thought that the definition introduces terms as obscure as the one we are defining, for instance, "character" and "below standard," and it is true these need explanation that cannot be provided here. But I think we are able to proceed more easily with them than with the original term; the definition is really clarifying. For instance, if someone charges that a suicide was sinful, we now properly ask, What defect of character did it show? Some writers have claimed

316

that suicide is blameworthy because it is cowardly, and since being cowardly is generally conceded to be a character defect, if an act of suicide is admitted to be both objectively wrong and also cowardly, the claim to blameworthiness is supported, if the above definition is correct. But most people would hesitate to call taking one's own life a cowardly act, and there will certainly be controversy about which acts are cowardly and which are not. But at least we can see part of what has to be done to make a charge of blameworthiness plausible.

The most interesting question is which types of suicide in general are ones that, even if objectively wrong, are not sinful or blameworthy? Or, in other words, when is a suicide morally excused even if it is objectively wrong? We can at least identify some types of cases: (1) Suppose I think I am morally bound to commit suicide because I have a terminal illness and continued medical care will financially ruin my family. Suppose, however, that I am mistaken in this belief, and that suicide in such circumstances is not right. Surely I am not morally blameworthy, for I may be doing, out of a sense of duty to my family, what I would personally prefer not to do and is hard for me to do. What character defect might my action show? Suicide from a genuine sense of duty is not blameworthy, even when the moral conviction in question is mistaken. (2) Suppose that I commit suicide when I am temporarily of unsound mind, either in the sense of the M'Naghten rule that I do not know that what I am doing is wrong, or of the Durham rule that, owing to a mental defect, I am substantially unable to do what is right. Surely any suicide in an unsound state of mind is morally excused. (3) Suppose I commit suicide when I could not be said to be temporarily of unsound mind, but simply because I am not myself. For instance, I may be in an extremely depressed mood. Now a person may be in a highly depressed mood and commit suicide because of being in that mood when there is nothing the matter with his character or, in other words, his character is not in any relevant way below standard. What are other examples of being "not myself," that might be states of a person responsible for his committing suicide, and that would or might render the suicide excusable even if wrong? Being frightened, distraught, or in almost any highly emotional frame of mind – anger, frustration, disappointment in love, or perhaps just being terribly fatigued. So there are at least three types of suicide that are morally excused even if objectively wrong.

The main point is this. Mr. X may commit suicide and it may be conceded that he should not have done so. But it is another step to show that he is sinful, or morally blameworthy, for having done so. To support this further charge, it must be shown that his act is attributable to some substandard character trait; so, after the suicide Mrs. X can concede that her husband should not have done what he did, but point out that it is no reflection on him.

WHEN SUICIDE IS MORALLY JUSTIFIED OR OBJECTIVELY RIGHT

Let us now consider our second topic, when a suicide is objectively right or morally justified. It may help the reader if I say at the outset that what I mean by "is objectively wrong" or "is morally unjustified" is "would be prohibited by the set of moral rules the currency of which in the consciences of persons in his society a rational person would choose to support and encourage, as compared with any other set of moral rules or none at all."

First, I wish to eliminate some confusions that have plagued discussions of this topic. The distinctions I am about to make are no longer controversial, and can be accepted by skeptics on the fundamental issues as well as by anyone else.

Persons who say suicide is morally wrong must be asked which of two positions they are affirming. Are they saying that every act of suicide is wrong, *everything considered?* Or are they merely saying that there is always *some* moral obligation, doubtless of serious weight, not to commit suicide, so that very often suicide is wrong, although it is possible that there are countervailing considerations which in particular situations make it right or even a moral duty? It is quite evident that the first position is absurd; only the second has a chance of being defended.

In order to illustrate what is wrong with the first view, we may begin with an example. Suppose an army pilot's single-seater airplane goes out of control over a heavily populated area; he has the choice of either staying in the plane and bringing it down where it will do little damage but at the cost of certain death for himself, or of bailing out and letting the plane fall where it will, very possibly killing a good many civilians. Suppose he chooses to do the former, and so, by our definition, commits suicide. Can anyone say that his action was morally wrong? It is improbable that even Immanuel Kant, who opposed suicide in all circumstances, would say that it is but rather would claim that this act is not one of suicide, "It is no suicide to risk one's life against one's enemies, and even to sacrifice it, in order to preserve one's duties toward oneself." [1] St. Thomas Aquinas [2] may claim it would be wrong, for he says, "It is altogether unlawful to kill oneself," admitting as an exception only the case of being under special command of God. But most likely St. Thomas would say that the act is right because the basic intention of the pilot was to save the lives of civilians, and whether an act is right or wrong is a matter of the basic intention.[1] I think a good reformulation of St. Thomas' view, consistent with his basic intentions, would be to assert that he recognizes that in this case there are two obligations, one to spare the lives of innocent civilians and the other not to destroy one's own life, and that of the two obligations the former is the stronger, and therefore the action is right.

In general, we have to admit that there are things there is some moral obligation to avoid that, because of other morally relevant considerations, it is sometimes right or even morally obligatory to do. There may be some obligation to tell the truth on every occasion, but there are surely many cases in which the consequences of telling the truth would be so catastrophic that one is obligated to lie. To take simple cases: Should one always tell an author truthfully how one evaluates his book, or tell one's wife truthfully whether she looks attractive today? The same applies to promises. There seems to be some moral obligation to do what one has promised (with some exceptions), but if one can keep a trivial promise only at serious cost to another (for example, keep an appointment only by failing to give aid to someone injured in an accident), it is surely obligatory to break the promise.

The most that the moral critic of suicide could say, then, is that there is *some* moral obligation not to do what a person knows will cause his death, but he surely cannot say there are *no* circumstances in which there are obligations to do things that in fact will result in one's death – obligations so strong that it is at least right, and possibly morally obligatory, to do something that will certainly result in one's own death. Possibly those who argue that suicide is immoral do not intend to contest this point, although if so they have not expressed themselves very clearly.

---

1 He says[2], "Nothing hinders one act from having two effects, only one of which is intended, while the other is beside the intention. Now moral acts take their species according to what is intended, and not according to what is beside the intention, since this is accidental as explained above" [Q. 43, Art. 3: I.-II., Q. 1, Art. 3, ad 3]. Mr. Norman St. John-Stevas, the most articulate contemporary defender of the Catholic view, writes as follows, "Christian thought allows certain exceptions to its general condemnation of suicide. That covered by a particular divine inspiration has already been noted. Another exception arises where suicide is the method imposed by the State for the execution of a just death penalty. A third exception is *altruistic* suicide, of which the best known example is Captain Oates. Such suicides are justified by invoking the principle of double effect. The act from which death results must be good or at least morally indifferent; some other good effect must result: the death must not be directly intended or the real means to the good effect: and a grave reason must exist for adopting the course of action"[3]. Presumably the Catholic doctrine is intended to allow suicide when this is required for meeting strong moral obligations; whether it can do so consistently depends partly on the interpretation given to "real means to the good effect." Readers interested in pursuing further the Catholic doctrine of double effect and its implications for our problem should read Philippa Foot[4].

If this interpretation is correct, then in principle it would be possible to argue that in order to meet my obligation to my family, I might take my own life as the only course of action that could avoid catastrophic hospital expenses in a terminal illness. I suspect critics may not concede this point, but in principle it would seem they must admit arguments of this type; the real problem is comparing the gravity of the obligation to extend my own life and of the obligation to see to the future welfare of my family.

The charitable interpretation of suicide critics on moral grounds, then, is to attribute to them the view that there is a strong moral obligation not to take one's own life, although this obligation may be superseded by some other obligations, say to avoid causing the death of others. Possibly the main point they would wish to make is that it is never right to take one's own life for reasons of one's own personal welfare, of any kind whatsoever.

What reasons have been offered for believing that there is a strong moral obligation to avoid suicide, that cannot be superseded by any consideration of personal welfare? The first arguments may be classified as theological. St. Augustine and others urged that the fifth commandment (Thou shalt not kill) prohibits suicide, and that we are bound to obey a divine commandment. To this reasoning one might reply that it is arbitrary exegesis of the fifth commandment to assert that it was ever intended to prohibit suicide. A second type of theological argument with wide support was accepted by John Locke, who wrote, "[M]en being all the workmanship of one omnipotent and infinitely wise Maker; all the servants of one sovereign Master, sent into the world by His order and about His business; they are His property, whose workmanship they are made to last during His, not one another's pleasure. . . . Every one . . . is bound to preserve himself, and not to quit his station wilfully"[5] Kant wrote, "We have been placed in this world under certain conditions and for specific purposes. But a suicide opposes the purpose of his Creator; he arrives in the other world as one who has deserted his post; he must be looked upon as a rebel against God. So long as we remember the truth that it is God's intention to preserve life, we are bound to regulate our activities in conformity with it. . . . This duty is upon us until the time comes when God expressly commands us to leave this life. Human beings are sentinels on earth and may not leave their posts until relieved by another beneficent hand."[6] Unfortunately, however, even if it were granted that it is the duty of human beings to do what God commands or intends them to do, more argument is required to show that God does *not* permit human beings to quit this life when their own personal welfare would be maximized by so doing. How does one draw the requisite inference about the intentions of God? The difficulties and contradictions in arguments to reach such a conclusion are discussed at length and perspicaciously by David Hume in his essay "On Suicide."[2]

A second group of arguments may be classed as arguments from natural law. St. Thomas says, "It is altogether unlawful to kill oneself, for three reasons. First, because everything naturally loves itself, the result being that everything naturally keeps itself in being, and resists corruptions so far as it can. Wherefore suicide is contrary to the inclination of nature, and to charity whereby every man should love himself. Hence suicide is always a mortal sin, as being contrary to the natural law and to charity."[2] Here St. Thomas ignores two obvious points. First, it is not obvious why a human being is morally bound to do what he has some inclination to do. (St. Thomas did not criticize chastity.) Second, while it is true that most human beings do feel a strong urge to live, the human being who commits suicide obviously feels a stronger inclination to do something else. The inclination of the deliberate suicide is not to cling to life, but to do something else instead. It is as natural for a human being to dislike and to take steps to avoid, say, great pain, as it is to cling to life. A somewhat similar argument by Kant may seem better. In a famous passage Kant writes, "[The maxim of a person who commits suicide] is 'From self-love I make it my principle to shorten my life if its continuance threatens more evil than it promises pleasure.' The only further question to ask is whether this principle of self-love can become a universal law of nature. It is then seen at once that a system of nature by whose law the very same feeling whose function is to stimulate the furtherance of life should actually destroy life would contradict itself and consequently could not subsist as a system of nature. Hence his maxim cannot possibly hold as a universal law of nature and is therefore entirely opposed to the supreme principle of all duty."[7] What Kant finds contradictory is that the motive of self-love (interest in one's own long-range welfare) should sometimes lead one to struggle to preserve one's life, but at other times to end it. But where is the contradiction? One's circumstances change, and, if the argument of the following section is correct, one sometimes maximizes one's own long-range welfare by trying to stay alive, but at other times by bringing about one's demise. So, if one's consistent motive is to maximize one's long-term welfare, sometimes (usually) one will do one thing, but sometimes another.

A third group of arguments, a form of which dates at least to Aristotle, has a more modern and convincing ring. These arguments purport to

2 This essay was first published in 1777, and appears in collections of Hume's works. For an argument similar to Kant's, see also St. Thomas Aquinas [2] (II, II, Q. 64, Art. 5).

show that, in one way or another, a suicide necessarily does harm to other persons, or to society at large. Aristotle says that the suicide treats the *state* unjustly.[8] Partly following Aristotle, St. Thomas says, "Every man is part of the community, and so, as such, he belongs to the community. Hence by killing himself he injures the community."[2] Blackstone held that a suicide is an offense against the king "who hath an interest in the preservation of all his subjects," perhaps following Judge Brown in 1563, who argued that suicide cost the king a subject, "he being the head has lost one of his mystical members."[9] The premise of such arguments is, as Hume pointed out, obviously mistaken in many instances. It is true that Freud would perhaps have injured society had he not finished his last book (as he did), instead of committing suicide to escape the pain of throat cancer. But surely there have been many suicides whose demise was not a noticeable loss to society; an honest man could only say that in many instances society was better off without them.

It need not be denied that suicide is often injurious to other persons, especially the family of a suicide; clearly it sometimes is. But we should notice what this fact establishes. Suppose we admit that there is some obligation not to perform any action that will probably or certainly be injurious to other people, the strength of the obligation being dependent on various factors, notably the seriousness of the expected injury. Then there is some obligation not to commit suicide, when that act would probably or certainly be injurious to other people – a conclusion that will probably not be disputed. But the fact that there is some obligation not to commit suicide when it will probably injure others does not show that suicide as such is something there is some obligation to avoid. There is an obligation to avoid injuring others, and to avoid suicide when it will probably injure others, but this is very different from showing that suicide as such is something there is some obligation to avoid in all instances.

Is there any way in which we could give convincing argument, establishing that there is or is not some moral obligation to avoid suicide as such, an obligation, of course, which might be overridden by other obligations in some or many cases?

To give all the argument that would provide a convincing answer to this question would take a great deal of space. I shall therefore present one answer to it that seems plausible to some contemporary philosophers and, I suspect, will seem plausible to the reader. Suppose it could be shown that it would maximize the long-run welfare of everybody affected if people were taught that there is a moral obligation to avoid suicide, so that people would be motivated to avoid suicide just because they thought it wrong, and so that other people would be inclined to disapprove of persons who commit suicide unless there were some excuse (such as those mentioned in the first section). One might ask, How could it maximize utility to mold the conceptual and motivational structure of persons in this way? To which the answer might be, Feeling this way might make persons who are impulsively inclined to commit suicide in a bad mood or a fit of anger or jealousy, take more time to deliberate; hence some suicides that have bad effects might be prevented. In other words, it might be a good thing for people to feel about suicide in the way they feel about breach of promise or injuring others, just as it might be a good thing for people to feel a moral obligation not to smoke or to wear seatbelts. I do not say this would be a good thing; all I am saying is that *if* it were welfare-maximizing for people's consciences to trouble them at the very thought of suicide, then there would be some moral obligation not to commit this act. I am not at all sure whether it *would* be welfare-maximizing for people to have negative moral feelings about suicide as such; maybe what is needed is just for them to have negative moral feelings about injuring others in some way, and perhaps negative moral feelings about failing to deliberate adequately about their own welfare before taking any serious and irrevocable course of action. It might be that negative moral feelings about suicide as such would stand in the way of courageous action by those persons whose welfare really is best served by suicide, and whose suicide is, in fact, the best thing for everybody concerned. One highly relevant piece of information concerning what should be instilled into people's consciences in this regard is why people do commit suicide and how often the general welfare (and especially their own welfare) is served by so doing. If among those people who commit suicide and are intellectually able to weigh pros and cons are many who commit suicide in a depression and do not serve anybody's welfare by so doing, then it could be beneficial to teach people that suicide as such is wrong.

WHETHER AND WHEN SUICIDE IS BEST OR RATIONAL FOR THE AGENT

We come now to a topic which, for better or worse, strikes me as of considerable practical interest: whether and when suicide is the rational or best thing for a person from the viewpoint of his own welfare. If I were asked for advice by someone contemplating suicide, it is to this topic that I would be inclined primarily to address myself. Some of the writers who are most inclined to affirm that suicide is morally wrong are quite ready to believe that from the agent's own selfish viewpoint suicide would sometimes be the best thing for him, but they do not discuss the point in any detail. I should like to clarify when it is and is not. What I hope to do is produce a way of looking at the matter that will help an individual see whether suicide is the best thing for him from the viewpoint of his own welfare – or whether it is the best thing for someone being advised, from the viewpoint of that person's welfare.

It is reasonable to discuss this topic under the restriction of two assumptions. First, I assume we are trying to appraise a successful suicide attempt disregarding unsuccessful attempts. The second assumption is that when a person commits suicide, he is dead, that is, we do not consider that killing himself is only a way of expediting his departure to an afterlife. I shall assume there is no afterlife. I believe that at the present time potential suicides deliberate on the basis of both these assumptions, so that in making them I am addressing myself to the real problem as prospective suicides see it. What I want to produce is a fresh and helpful way of looking at their problem.

The problem is a choice between future world courses – the world course which includes my demise, say, an hour from now, and several possible ones that contain my demise at a later point. We cannot have precise knowledge about many features of the latter group. One thing we usually cannot have precise knowledge about is how or when I shall die if I do not commit suicide now. One thing is certain: it will be sometime, and it is almost certain that it will be before my one-hundredth birthday. So, to go on the rational probabilities, let us look up my life expectancy at my present age from the insurance tables, making any corrections that are called for in the light of full medical information about my recent state of health. If I do not already have a terminal illness, then the choice is between a world course with my death an hour from now and several world courses with my death, say, twenty years from now. The problem is to decide whether the expectable utility to me of some possible world course in which I live for another twenty years is greater than or less than the expectable utility to me of the one in which my life stops in an hour.

Why say the choice is between world courses and not just a choice between future life courses of the prospective suicide, the one shorter than the others? The reason is that one's suicide has some impact on the world (and one's continued life has some impact on the world), and that how the rest of the world is will often make a difference to one's evaluation of the possibilities. We are interested in things in the world other than just ourselves and our own happiness. For instance, we may be interested in our children and their welfare, our future reputation, the contribution we might make to the solution of some problems, or possible effects of the publication of a book we are completing.

What is the basic problem for evaluation? It is the choice of the expectably best world course from my viewpoint. One way of looking at the evaluation, although in practice we cannot assign the specific numbers it is suggested we assign, is that we compare the suicide world course with the continued life world course (or several of them) and note the features in which they differ. We then assign numbers to these features, representing their utility to us if they occur, and then multiply this utility by a number that represents the probability that this feature will occur. (Suppose I live and am certain that either P or Q will occur, and that there is an equal chance that each could occur. I then represent this biography as containing the sum of the utility of P multiplied by one-half and the utility of Q multiplied by one-half.) We then sum these numbers, which will represent the combined expectable utility of that world course to us. The world course with the highest sum is the one that is rationally chosen. But of course it is absurd to suppose that we can assign these numbers in actual fact; what we can actually do is something in a sense simpler but less decisive.

If we look at the matter in this way, we can see that there is a close analogy between an analysis of the rationality of suicide and a firm's analysis of the rationality of declaring bankruptcy and going out of business. In the case of the firm, the objectives may be few and simple, and indeed for some boards of directors the only relevant question is will the stockholders probably be better off or worse off financially if we continue or if we declare insolvency? More likely the question considered will be a bit more complex, since an enlightened firm will at least wonder what will happen to its officers and employees and customers and even possibly the general public if it goes out of business, and how their utilities will be affected.

Perhaps a closer analogy to this choice between world courses is the choice between a life course in which I get twelve hours of sleep tonight and one in which I live through one (the best) of the various possible experiences open to me.

Since, as I have suggested, we cannot actually perform the operation of assigning personal utility numbers to anticipated distinctive outcomes, reduce these by a fraction representing their probability, and then sum in order to find which course of action will maximize expectable utility of a world course, what then can we do to determine which world course is best, from the viewpoint of our own welfare? I think the answer is – that the prospective suicide has to determine whether he wants the world course as it will be with his death occurring now or shortly or the best option open to him with his life continuing; whether he would want one or the other if he had these alternatives, envisaged correctly, clearly,

325

vividly, and in a normal, not emotional or depressed, frame of mind. I agree at once that it is a large order to get anything as complex as even the outlines of your prospective best life option before you vividly, but anyone can do what we all do from time to time – take pencil and paper and set down features of the prospective best life that one would want and features of it one would not want, do some matching of the good ones and the bad ones, and see where one comes out. The frame of mind of a prospective suicide is not apt to be one ideal for calm deliberation of this sort, and for this reason it will usually be helpful to have some discussions. But I want to explain why the particular sort of preferential comparison I have described is basic, and how in particular, failure to come to it will lead to wrong decisions in the emotional situation of the prospective suicide.

However, first let me say that I do not for a moment suggest that a person who takes this view of alternative world courses is necessarily going to prefer to continue living. On the contrary, when a person is seriously ill the probability is that he is going to feel worse and worse until sedations are so extensive that he is incapable of clear thought or emotional reaction toward anything and his physical condition is such that he cannot act to end his life even if he prefers to do so. If a person knows that this situation exists and has the prospect of his life being more and more undesirable, as each day passes, he may fulfill all my conditions of normal and fully informed wanting and elect quite rationally (at least in the absence of unusual situations such as Freud's) to choose the world course which contains as short a life span for himself as possible.

There are two other misconceptions I wish to eliminate. It is often argued that one can never be certain what is going to happen, and so one is never rationally justified in doing anything as final, drastic, and irreversible as taking one's life. And it is true that certainties are hard to find; strictly speaking they do not exist even in the sciences. Unfortunately for the critic who makes use of this line of argument, it works both ways. I might say, when I am very depressed about my life, that the one thing I am certain of is that I am now very depressed and prefer death to life, and there is only some probability that tomorrow I shall feel differently. So, one might argue if one is to go only by certainties, I had better end it now. No one would take this seriously; we always have to live by probabilities, and make our estimates as best we can. People sometimes argue that one should not commit suicide in order to escape excruciating pain because they are not certain that a miraculous cure for terminal illness will not be found tomorrow – a logical possibility. But if everyone had argued in this way in the past hundred years, many persons would have waited until the bitter end and suffered excruciating pain; the line of argument that ignores probabilities and demands certainty would not have paid off in the past, and there is no good reason to think it will pay off any better in the future. Indeed, if the policy were generally adopted that probabilities in practical decisions should be ignored when they are short of certainty, it can be demonstrated that the policy for action *cannot* pay off. The second misconception is reliance on the argument that if you are alive tomorrow you can always decide to end it all then, whereas if you are dead tomorrow you cannot then decide that it is better to live. The factual point is correct, of course. But the argument has practical bearing only if there is reason to think that tomorrow you might find life good and want to live; sometimes it is as nearly certain as matters of this sort can be, that you will not. It is true that one can always bear another day, so why not delay? But this argument can be used for every succeeding day, with the result that one never takes action. One would think that, as soon as it is clear beyond reasonable doubt not only that death is preferable to life today, but that life is going to be so bad that one would prefer to be dead every day from here on out, the rational thing to do is to act promptly.

Let us not pursue the question whether it is rational for a person with a painful terminal illness to commit suicide; obviously it is, unless there are some special activities or responsibilities that are more important to the patient than his pain. However, the issue seldom arises, because patients of this sort seldom take suicide seriously, perhaps because matters get worse so slowly that no particular time seems to be the one calling for action, or because sedation makes it impossible for complex decisions to be made. Let us rather turn to the practically much more important problem, whether it is rational for persons to commit suicide for reasons other than painful physical illness. Most persons who commit suicide do so, apparently, because they face some nonphysical problem which depresses them. It is to them that the conception mentioned a few moments ago is addressed – that a rational decision is the one in favor of the life course one would prefer, comparing death with the best option open to one if he had the alternatives correctly and vividly before him in a normal frame of mind. Let me mention some problems that bother people, and that apparently are among the most important reasons for suicide. For example, some event that has made one feel ashamed or involved loss of prestige and status, such as reduction from affluence to poverty, the loss of limb or of physical beauty, the loss of sexual capacity, the occurrence of some event that makes it impossible to achieve something important, loss of a loved one, disappointment in love, loneliness and the prospect of increasing loneliness, or the infirmities of increasing age. One cannot deny that such things can be sources of serious unhappiness.

327

I am assuming that a rational choice is one that a person makes with full and vivid awareness of the facts, so that he avoids making a choice he would not have made but for a factual misconception. (There are other requirements that would be mentioned in a second approximation.) These first simple requirements for a rational choice are exceedingly important in the case of a prospective suicide for the reason that most suicides take place at a time of severe depression; that often or always means that these requirements are very hard for the person to meet. Let me pursue several points the prospective suicide should bear in mind in deciding whether it is rational for him to take his life.

First, the prospective suicide should be aware of the fact that depression, like any severe emotional experience, tends to primitivize intellectual processes. It restricts the range of one's survey of the possibilities. The reason for reflection is to compare the world course of suicide with that of the best alternative. But the best alternative is precisely what will not come to mind if, as so often happens in a depressed mood, one's mind is obsessed only with thoughts of how badly off he is. You cannot both occupy yourself exclusively with thoughts of your present painful state of affairs and of how nice it would be to get out of the discomfort easily, and also reflect on your alternatives. If you are disappointed in love, you are apt to give your mind wholly to speeches you might make to your beloved, reflection on where you made mistakes in the past, or to how empty life is going to be without her; you are not going to consider vigorous courses of action you might take to replace this person with activities or other persons you will in time like just as well. The prospective suicide should not delude himself that he is acting rationally when he has not taken the trouble to give serious thought to his full range of options.

There is a second insidious influence of a state of depression. It seriously affects one's judgment on probabilities. A person disappointed in love is likely to take a dim view of himself, his prospects, and his attractiveness; he thinks that, because he has been rejected by one person, he will probably be rejected by anyone who looks desirable to him. Probably in a less gloomy frame of mind he would make different estimates. Part of the reason for such gloomy probability estimates is that depression tends to repress one's memory evidence that supports an optimistic prediction. Thus a rejected lover tends to forget all the cases in which he has elicited enthusiastic response from members of the opposite sex, and of the cases in which he was the rejector. Thus his pessimistic self-image is based on a highly pessimistically selected set of data. Even when he is reminded of the data, however, he is apt to resist an optimistic inference. He resembles students who have come to think that nothing but failure is in

328

store for them, even when it is pointed out that they often succeeded academically in the past. In a depressed mood one is apt to refuse to do the rational thing of projecting past successes and expecting probable future successes, but rather argue that past successes were lucky flukes and cannot be relied on for a prognosis of the future. Obviously, however, there is such a thing as a reasonable and correct prognosis on the basis of an accurate account of past experience, and it is the height of irrationality not to estimate the future on that basis.

What a person must do, then, is make herself vividly aware of the alternatives that are really open to her, and consider what they will be like, including whether she will be happy with them. Of course, a person cannot have as precise a picture of what she can have a year from now as of what she cannot have now, how-well off she is, and how she feels right now. But if she makes proper use of past experience she can have a fairly accurate knowledge of what is probably in store for her. If she uses knowledge of herself, she can know whether she will like it.

Suppose she envisages a probable future life and honestly admits that in all probability she will like it. How will this affect whether she will now want this alternative future or to commit suicide?

One effect should be guarded against as far as possible – one that is pervasive and not distinctive of depressed states. Future events seem quite distant just as objects distant in space look small. That is, the prospect of a distant event does not have the effect on motivational processes that it would have if it were expected in the immediate future. In that sense, all animals are impatient. Rat psychologists call essentially this fact the *goal-gradient* phenomenon; a rat will run faster toward a food box when it is close enough so that he can actually see it and does not do as well when he can only represent it in some nonperceptual way, as presumably he does in the early stages of a maze. In the same way, the commuter anxious to return home finds his footsteps quicken when he turns a corner and can actually see his home. Things in the future seem less important; it is always difficult for a weight reducer to decline a tempting chocolate even while visualizing the future benefits of being slender unless he remembers he has to make a confession before a weight-watchers group tomorrow night. When comparing present unpleasant states with probable pleasant future ones, this phenomenon of the reduction of the motivational size of distant events is like looking at the future through the wrong end of binoculars. This effect probably is the result of deficiency in vividness of the imagination or representation of the future event. Thus there is a cognitive defect if one makes one choice rather than another merely because of unequal awareness of the two events. A rational person will take precautions to see the future in its proper perspective and com-

329

pensate for this unfortunate phenomenon of human nature. How to accomplish this is no small problem; apparently appropriate verbalizing can be successful.

There is a final and very important effect of depression in decision-making – that of the emotional state on the motivational machinery. For instance, when we are hungry and think of bacon and eggs for breakfast, our mouths water and the idea seems attractive; we find ourselves tending to move toward the refrigerator. Similarly, when we have had many weeks of books and papers, the thought of vegetating in a deckchair seems most appealing. The grass looks green, as it were, in many directions. And, when we think of something like suicide, there are all sorts of things we might do or bring about that seem attractive in this way; the idea of suicide, at the cost of not looking at tomorrow's *Times* or football game, forgoing tomorrow's evening out, or not reading some books long unread, seems a very repellent idea. The trouble with a state of depression is that it simply shuts off all this motivational machinery. The only thought that moves one is about the source of the depression. When we are depressed about something, nothing else is attractive and the normally unattractive features of the things we have lost either fail to strike our attention or lose their repulsive force. We tend to emphasize, out of proportion, the unpleasant aspects of the situation. Why this is so is not so obvious; but in general, just as the thought of bacon and eggs, when we have just finished breakfast, leaves us cold, so the idea of anything we would normally want leaves us cold in a depressed frame of mind.

We know that this effect is temporary and should be allowed for, just as we know that when we have finished a good meal our satiety is temporary and we should make provision for another meal a few hours later. So, a rational person will want to take into account this temporary infirmity of his sensory machinery. To say this does not tell us how to do it, since to know that the machinery is out of order is not to tell us what results it would give us if it were working. One maxim is to refrain from making important decisions in a depressed frame of mind, and one of the important decisions is surely suicide. If decisions have to be made, at least one should use inductive inference from recollection of how certain sorts of outcomes were wanted in the past when in a normal frame of mind.

Most irrational suicides seem to be due to temporary despair. When a person is contemplating suicide in a moment of despair, he must be aware of all the factors that tend to make suicide temporarily attractive. He must see that if he is to be rational he must avoid impulsive acts that are contrary to the way he would normally act. He should see that the probability is very high that it is irrational for him to end his life. Rather in a moment of despair when one is seriously contemplating suicide, he should realize that a reassessment of goals and values is in order – one it is difficult to make objectively because of his very state of mind.

Let us consider in an example what form such a reassessment might take, based on a consideration of the "errors" we have been considering.

Suppose the president of a company is ousted in a reorganization and, to make matters as bad as possible, let us suppose he has made unwise investments so that his income from investments is small and, to cap it off, his wife has left him for another man. His children are already grown, and he is too old for appointment to a comparable position in another business. So his career and home life are gone. Here we have the makings of a suicide. Let us suppose he is right about the main outlines of his prospects: that there is no comparable future open to him in business, and that his wife is really gone. He must move from a luxurious home into a modest apartment; he will be unable to entertain his friends in the manner to which he has been accustomed; he is not going to have the affection of his wife and is going to be lonely at least for a time. Is all this bearable?

What sort of reflection is in order? First he has to deal with his personal life. If he does not fall victim to pessimistic deflation of his self-image, he will know that he is an interesting man and can find women with whom he can be close and who can mean as much to him as his wife did, or he may find several with whom he can find a life style he can enjoy more than the traditional married life. All this, however, will take some time and he will know that he has to be patient. He will also look at a textbook on behavior therapy and will find how he can remove the pain of his wife's departure in a very brief space of time. The matter of career is more serious. Even Kant, who condemned suicide in all cases, says, inconsistently, that a man unjustly convicted of a crime who was offered a choice between death and penal servitude, would certainly, if honorable, choose death rather than the galleys. "A man of inner worth does not shrink from death; he would die rather than live as an object of contempt, a member of a gang of scoundrels in the galleys." Kant may have been right about what it is rational to do in this extreme instance. Would death be better for the ex-president of a company than accepting a job, say, as a shoe salesman? (An older man might not find employment even here, but with a bit of imagination, entrepreneurial opportunities are open to any talented man in a capitalist society!) This might at first seem repellent, but on reflection one will see there are some good points. He may be able to remember how he enjoyed doing somewhat similar things as a boy. An intelligent man might find it interesting to engage in conversation with a variety of customers from all walks of life. He could try out his

331

psychological knowledge by using devices to play on the vanity of women (or men!) as a motivation for buying expensive shoes. Further, he will not require sleeping pills in this new job, pills he has been taking because he could not get company problems off his mind. He may see that after a time he could enjoy the new job, perhaps not so much as the old one, at least after he gets over contrasting it with a past career no longer open to him. One thing he will surely bear strongly in mind: that his real friends are not going to change their attitudes toward him because of his new career, his less ostentatious circumstances, or the loss of his wife. On the contrary, these new circumstances are apt to make them like him better. Of course, all these considerations may not seem attractive to him at first, but he will know that they *will* be attractive to him after some little time has passed, and he has thought through a realistic comparison of his new life with his old life situation.

At this point David Hume was not his usual perspicuous self – nor Plato before him.[10] In "On Suicide," Hume speaks of the propriety of suicide for one who leads a hated life, "loaded with pain and sickness, with shame and poverty." Pain and sickness are one thing; they cannot be enjoyed and cannot be escaped. But shame and poverty are another matter. For some situations Hume might be right. But Hume, accustomed as he was to the good things of life, was too short with shame and poverty; a life that he would classify as one of shame and poverty might be a tolerable life, inferior to Hume's life style, but still preferable to nothing.

A decision to commit suicide for reasons other than terminal illness may in certain circumstances be a rational one. But a person who wants to act rationally must take into account at least the various possible "errors" mentioned above, and make appropriate rectifications in his initial evaluations.

THE ROLE OF OTHER PERSONS

We have not been concerned with the law, or its justifiability, on the matter of suicide, but we may note in passing that for a long time in the Western world suicide was a felony and in many states attempted suicide is still a crime. It is also a crime to aid or encourage a suicide in most states; one who makes a lethal device available for a suicidal attempt may be subject to a prison sentence – including physicians, if they provide a lethal dose of sedatives.[3]

The last mentioned class of statutes raises a question worth our con-

3 For a proposal for American law on this point see the *Model Penal Code*, Proposed Official Draft, The American Law Institute, 1962, pp. 127–8; also Tentative Draft No. 9, p. 56.

sideration, What are the moral obligations of other persons toward those who are contemplating suicide? I ignore questions of their moral blame-worthiness, and of what it is rational for them to do from the viewpoint of personal welfare as being of secondary concern. I have no doubt that the question of personal interest is important particularly to physicians who may not wish to risk running afoul of the law, but this risk is, after all, something that partly determines what their moral obligation is, since moral obligation to do something may be reduced by the fact that it is personally dangerous to do it.[4]

The moral obligation of other persons toward one who is contemplating suicide is an instance of a general obligation to render aid to those in serious distress, at least when this can be done at no great cost to one's self. I do not think this general principle is seriously questioned by any-one, whatever his moral theory, so I feel free to assume it as a premise. Obviously the person contemplating suicide is in great distress of some sort; if he were not, he would not be seriously considering terminating his life.

How great a person's obligation is to one in distress depends on a number of factors. Obviously a person's wife, daughter, and close friend have special obligations to devote time to helping this sort of person – to going over her problem with her, to think it through with her, etc. – that others do not have. But that anyone in this kind of distress has a moral claim on the time of anyone who knows the situation (unless there are others more responsible who are already doing what should be done) is obvious.

What is there an obligation to do? It depends, of course, on the situation and how much the second person knows about the situation. If the individual has decided to terminate his life if he can, and it is clear that he is right in this decision, then, if he needs help in executing the decision, there is a moral obligation to give him help. If it is sleeping pills he needs, then they should be obtained for him. On this matter a patient's physician has a special obligation.

On the other hand, if it is clear that the individual should not commit suicide, from the point of view of his own welfare, or if there is a pre-sumption that he should not, when the only evidence is that a person is discovered unconscious with the gas turned on, it would seem to be the individual's obligation to intervene and prevent the successful execution

4 The law can be changed, and one of the ways in which it gets changed is by responsible people refusing to obey it and pointing out how objectionable it is on moral grounds. Some physicians have shown leadership in this respect, for example, on the matter of dispensing birth control information and abortion laws. One wishes there were more of this.

of the decision, see to the availability of competent psychiatric advice and temporary hospitalization, if necessary. Whether one has a right to take such steps when a clearly sane person, after careful reflection over a period of time, comes to the conclusion that an end to his life is what is best for him and what he wants, is very doubtful, even when one thinks his conclusion a mistaken one. It would seem that a man's own considered decision about whether he wants to live must command respect, although one must concede that this could be debated.

The more interesting role in which a person may be cast, however, is that of adviser. It is often important to one who is contemplating suicide to go over his thoughts with another and to feel that a conclusion, one way or the other, has the support of a respected mind. One thing one can obviously do, in rendering the service of advice, is to discuss with the person the various types of issues discussed above, made more specific by the concrete circumstances of his case, and help him find whether, in view, say, of the damage his suicide would do to others, he has a moral obligation to refrain and whether it is rational or best for him, from the viewpoint of his own welfare, to take this step or adopt some other plan instead.

To get a person to see what is the rational thing to do is no small task. Even to get a person in a frame of mind when he is seriously contemplating or perhaps has already unsuccessfully attempted suicide, to recognize a plain truth of fact may be a major operation. If a man insists, "I am a complete failure," when it is obvious that by any reasonable standard he is far from that, it may be tremendously difficult to get him to see the fact. The relaxing quiet of a hospital room may be a prerequisite of ability to think clearly and weigh facts with some perspective.

But there is another job beyond that of getting a person to see what is the rational thing to do, and that is to help him *act* rationally or *be* rational after he has determined what course of action is rational.

How either of these tasks may be accomplished effectively may be discussed more competently by an experienced psychiatrist than by a philosopher. But it may not be inappropriate to point out that sometimes an adviser can cure a man's problem in the course of advising. Loneliness and the absence of human affection are states that exacerbate any other problems; disappointment, reduction to poverty, etc., seem less impossible to bear in the presence of the affection of another. Hence, simply to be a friend, or to find someone a friend, may be the largest contribution one can make to helping a person either be rational or see clearly what is rational for him to do; this service may make one who was contemplating suicide feel that there is now a future for him which is possible to face.

334

THE MORALITY AND RATIONALITY OF SUICIDE

REFERENCES

[1] Immanuel Kant I, *Lectures on Ethics* (New York: Harper Torchbook, 1963) p. 150.

[2] St. Thomas Aquinas, *Summa Theologica*, Second Part of the Second Part, Q. 64; see also art. 5.

[3] N. St. John-Stevas, *Life, Death and the Law* (Bloomington, IN: Indiana Univ. Press, 1961) pp. 250–1.

[4] Philippa Foot, "The problem of abortion and doctrine of double effect," *Oxford Rev.* 5(1967), 5–15.

[5] John Locke, *Two Treatises of Government*, chap. 2.

[6] Kant, *Lectures on Ethics*. p. 154.

[7] Immanuel Kant, *The Fundamental Principles of the Metaphysic of Morals*, trans. H. J. Paton (London: The Hutchinson Group, 1948) chap. 2. (First German edition, 1885.)

[8] Aristotle, *Nicomachaean Ethics*, bk. 5, chap 10, p. 1138a.

[9] Sir William Blackstone, *Commentaries*, IV: 189; Brown in *Hales* v. *Petit*, I Plow. 253, 75 ER 387 (CB 1563).

[10] Plato, *The Laws*, bk. IX.

17

Utilitarianism and the rules of war

The topic of this paper is roughly the moral proscriptions and prescriptions that should govern the treatment by a belligerent, and in particular by its armed forces, of the nationals of an enemy, both combatants and noncombatants. In addressing myself to it, the central question I shall try to answer is: What, from a moral point of view, ought to be the rules of war? But this question, taken as an indication of what I shall be discussing, is both too broad and too narrow. Too broad because the rules of war include many topics like the rights and duties of neutral countries and the proprieties pertaining to an armistice. And too narrow because a full view of the topic requires me to consider, as I shall, such questions as: Is it ever morally right for a person to infringe "ideal" rules of war?

I shall aim to illuminate the topic by discussing it from the point of view of a rule-utilitarianism of the "contractual" variety (to use a term employed by John Rawls in his book *A Theory of Justice*).[1] This point of view has to be explained, as do the special problems raised by the fact that the rules are to apply to nations at war. I believe it will become clear that the rule-utilitarian viewpoint is a very helpful one for thinking of rules of warfare, and I believe reflection on its implications will confirm us in both conclusions about certain normative rules and a conviction that a contractual utilitarian view of such matters is essentially sound. Needless to say, I shall be led to express some disagreement with Professor Nagel.

I NAGEL'S ABSOLUTISM

I shall take Nagel to be defending, first, the general view that certain kinds of actions are, from a moral point of view, absolutely out of bounds,

This paper was read in a symposium on the morality of the conduct of war at the meetings of the American Philosophical Association, Pacific Division, on March 27, 1971, first published in *Philosophy and Public Affairs*, I (1972), no. 2. The other symposiast was Professor Thomas Nagel, of New York University, who read a paper entitled "War and Massacre."
1 (Cambridge, MA, 1971.)

no matter what the circumstances; and second, a specific prohibition that applies this principle to the area of our interest. (His first thesis makes it proper to call his view "absolutist," in the sense that some general moral prohibitions do not have *prima facie* force only but are binding without exception, indefeasible.) Nagel is tentative in his espousal of these two theses, and sometimes contends only that we have some moral intuitions of this sort and that a study of these will show "the complexity, and perhaps the incoherence" of our moral ideas. Indeed, he says he is offering only a "somewhat qualified defense of absolutism," and concedes that in extreme circumstances there may be exceptions to his absolutist principles after all. Where Nagel is committed definitely is to a criticism of utilitarianism; he speaks scathingly of "the abyss of utilitarian apologetics for large-scale murder." In view of Nagel's tentativeness, I think it fair to dissociate him from the positive view I wish to criticize, although I am *calling* it Nagel's "absolutism." This positive view is, however, the only definite proposal he puts forward, and if I am to consider critically any positive antiutilitarian view in connection with Nagel's essay, it has to be this one. At any rate, this view is one that somebody *might* hold, and is well worth discussing.

The first point I wish to make is that a rule-utilitarian may quite well agree with Nagel that certain kinds of actions are morally out of bounds absolutely no matter what the circumstances. Take, for instance, some of the rules of warfare recognized by the United States Army:

It is especially forbidden . . . to declare that no quarter will be given. . . . It is especially forbidden . . . to kill or wound an enemy who, having laid down his arms, or having no longer means of defense, has surrendered at discretion. . . .

It is especially forbidden . . . to employ arms, projectiles, or material calculated to cause unnecessary suffering. . . .

The pillage of a town or place, even when taken by assault, is prohibited. . . .

A commander may not put his prisoners to death because their presence retards his movements or diminishes his power of resistance by necessitating a large guard, or by reason of their consuming supplies, or because it appears certain that they will regain their liberty through the impending success of their forces. It is likewise unlawful for a commander to kill his prisoners on grounds of self-preservation, even in the case of airborne or commando operations, although the circumstances of the operation may make necessary rigorous supervision of and restraint upon the movement of prisoners of war.[2]

2 Department of the Army Field Manual PM 27–10, *The Law of Land Warfare* (Department of the Army, July 1956), pp. 17, 18, 21, 35. The Manual specifically states that the rules of war may not be disregarded on grounds of "military necessity" (p. 4), since considerations of military necessity were fully taken into account in framing the rules. (All page numbers in the text refer to this publication, hereafter called the Army Manual.)

Other valuable discussions of contemporary rules of warfare are to be found in L.

A rule-utilitarian is certainly in a position to say that utilitarian considerations cannot morally justify a departure from these rules; in that sense they are absolute. But he will also say that the moral justification of these rules lies in the fact that their acceptance and enforcement will make an important contribution to long-range utility. The rule-utilitarian, then, may take a two-level view: that in justifying the rules, utilitarian considerations are in order and nothing else is; whereas in making decisions about what to do in concrete circumstances, the rules are absolutely binding. In the rule-utilitarian view, immediate expediency is not a moral justification for infringing the rules.[3]

It is not clear that Nagel recognizes this sort of absolutism about "ideal" rules of war as a possible utilitarian view, but he seems to disagree with it when he claims that some moral prohibitions are entirely independent of utilitarian considerations.

What absolute rule does Nagel propose? I shall formulate and criticize his proposal in a moment. But first we should note that his rule is intended to be restricted in scope; it applies only to what "we deliberately do to people." This is an important restriction. Suppose bombers are dispatched to destroy a munitions factory – surely a legitimate military target in a night raid; in fact and predictably, and from a military point of view incidentally, the bombs kill five thousand people. Is this a case of "deliberately doing" something to these people? Nagel's view here seems obscure. He rejects the law of double effect and says he prefers to "stay with the original, unanalyzed distinction between what one does to people and what merely happens to them as a result of what one does." He concedes that this distinction "needs clarification." Indeed it does. Without more clarification, Nagel is hardly giving an explicit theory. I note that the U.S. Army Manual appears to reject this distinction, and in a paragraph declaring the limitations on strategic bombing states that "loss of life and damage to property must not be out of proportion to the military advantage to be gained" (p. 19).

The absolutist principle that Nagel espouses as the basic restriction on legitimate targets and weapons is this: "hostility or aggression should be directed at its true object. This means both that it should be directed at the person or persons who provoke it and that it should aim more spe-

---

Oppenheim, *International Law*, ed. H. Lauterpacht, 7th ed. (New York, 1952), and in Marjorie M. Whiteman, *Digest of International Law*, esp. vol. X (U.S. Department of State, 1963).

3 It is conceivable that ideal rules of war would include one rule to the effect that anything is allowable, if necessary to prevent absolute catastrophe. As Oppenheim remarks, it may be that if the basic values of society are threatened nations are possibly released from all the restrictions in order to do what "they deem to be decisive for the ultimate vindication of the law of nations" (*International Law*, p. 351).

cifically at what is provocative about them. The second condition will determine what form the hostility may appropriately take." I find this principle reasonably clear in its application to simple two-person cases discussed by him, but I find it difficult to apply in the identification of morally acceptable military operations. With some trepidation I suggest that Nagel intends it to be construed to assert something like the following for the case of military operations: "Persons may be attacked 'deliberately' only if their presence or their position prevents overpowering the military forces of the enemy in some way; and they may be attacked only in a manner that is reasonably related to the objective of disarming or disabling them." If this is what he has in mind it is still rather vague, since it does not make clear whether attacks on munitions factories are legitimate, or whether attacks on persons involved in supporting services, say, the provisioning of the army, are acceptable.

It is worth noting that a principle resembling this one might have a utilitarian justification of the kind alluded to above. But the principle standing by itself does not seem to me self-evident; nor does another principle Nagel asserts, that "the maintenance of a direct interpersonal response to the people one deals with is a requirement which no advantages can justify one in abandoning."

II MORALLY JUSTIFIABLE RULES AS RULES IMPARTIALLY PREFERABLE

I shall now proceed to a positive account of the rules of war and of their justification. We shall have to consider several distinct questions, but the central question will be: Which of the possible rules of war are morally justifiable?

But first, what do I mean by "rules of war" or by talk of the "authoritative status" of rules of war? What I have in mind is, roughly, rules with the status that the articles of the Hague and Geneva Conventions have or have had. That is, certain rules pertaining to war are stated in formal treaties. These rules are seriously taught, as being legally binding, to officers and to some extent to enlisted men; they are recognized as legally binding restrictions on the decisions of the general staff; members of the army know that actions forbidden by these rules are contrary both to international law and to their own army's manual of rules for proper conduct; these rules are enforced seriously by the courts, either military or international; and so on. Proscriptions or prescriptions with this status I call "rules of war"; and in speaking of a rule having "authoritative status" I have this kind of force in mind. The U.S. Army Manual lists such rules; and digests of international law such as those by Whiteman and Oppenheim contain information on what such rules are and have been.

I have said that I shall offer a utilitarian answer to the question which rules of war (in the above sense) are morally justifiable. But I have also said that I shall be offering what I (following Rawls) call a *contractual* utilitarian answer. What I mean by that (the term "contractual" may be a bit misleading) is this. I accept the utilitarian answer to the question which rules of war are morally justifiable because utilitarian rules of war are the ones *rational, impartial persons would choose* (the ones they would be willing to put themselves under a contract to obey). The more basic question is: Which rules of war would people universally prefer to have accorded authoritative status among nations if the people deciding were rational, believed they might be involved in a war at some time, and were impartial in the sense that they were choosing behind a veil of ignorance? (It is understood that their ignorance is to be such as to prevent them from making a choice that would give them or their nation a special advantage; it would, for instance, prevent them from knowing what weaponry their country would possess were it to be at war, and from knowing whether, were war to occur, they would be on the front lines, in a factory, or in the general staff office.) In other words, the more fundamental question is: What rules would rational, impartial people, who expected their country at some time to be at war, want to have as the authoritative rules of war – particularly with respect to the permitted targets and method of attack? I suggest that the rules of war that rational, impartial persons would choose are the rules that would maximize long-range expectable utility for nations at war. In saying this I am offering a contractual utilitarian answer to the question what rules of war are morally justifiable. I am saying: (1) that rational, impartial persons would choose certain rules of war; (2) that I take as a basic premise ("analytic" in some sense, if you like) that a rule of war is morally justified if and only if it would be chosen by rational, impartial persons; and (3) that the rules rational, impartial persons would choose are ones that will maximize expectable long-range utility for nations at war.[4]

Nagel objects to utilitarianism and hence presumably would object to (3), but he might be agreeable to both (1) and (2). At least he seems close to these principles, since he seems to hold that an action is justified if one can justify to its victim what is being done to him. For instance, he implies that if you were to say to a prisoner, "You understand, I have

4 This summary statement needs much explanation, for example, regarding the meaning of "rational." It is only a close approximation to the view I would defend, since I think it is better to substitute a more complex notion for that of impartiality or a veil of ignorance.

to pull out your fingernails because it is absolutely essential that we have the name of your confederates" and the prisoner agreed to this as following from principles he accepts, then the torture would be justified. Nagel rather assumes that the prisoner would not agree, in an appropriate sense. In this connection we must be clearly aware of an important distinction. A judge who sentences a criminal might also be unable to persuade the criminal to want the sentence to be carried out; and if persuading him to want this were necessary for a moral justification of the criminal law, then the system of criminal justice would also be morally objectionable. We must distinguish between persuading a person to whom something horrible is about to be done to want that thing to happen or to consent to its happening at that very time and something quite different – getting him to accept, when he is rational and choosing in ignorance of his own future prospects, some general principles from which it would follow that this horrible thing should or might be done to a person in his present circumstances. I think Nagel must mean, or ought to mean, that a set of rules of war must be such as to command the assent of rational people choosing behind a veil of ignorance, *not* that a person must be got to assent at the time to his fingernails being pulled out in order to get information, if that act is to be justified. It may be, however, that Nagel does not agree with this distinction, since he hints at the end of his paper that something more may be required for moral justification than I have suggested, without indicating what the addition might be.

We should notice that the question which rules of war would be preferred by rational persons choosing behind a veil of ignorance is roughly the question that bodies like the Hague Conventions tried to answer. The representatives of various nations gathered together, say in 1907, many or all of them making the assumption that their nations would at some time be at war. Presumably in the light of calculated national self-interest and the principles of common humanity, they decided which rules they were prepared to commit themselves to follow, in advance of knowing how the fortunes of war might strike them in particular. The questions the signatories to the Hague Conventions actually did ask themselves are at least very close to the questions I think we must answer in order to know which rules of war are morally justified.

III THE RATIONAL, IMPARTIAL CHOICE: UTILITARIAN RULES

I wish now to explain why I think rational, impartial persons would choose rules of war that would maximize expectable utility. I shall then classify the rules of war into several types, and try to show that representative rules of each type would be utility-maximizing and therefore chosen. I shall hope (although I shall not say anything explicitly about this) that the ideal rules of war, identified in this way, will coincide with the reflective intuitions of the reader. If so, I assume that this fact will commend to him the whole of what I am arguing.

I have suggested that rational persons, choosing behind a veil of ignorance but believing that their country may well be involved in a war at some time, would prefer rules of war that would maximize expectable utility, *in the circumstance that two nations are at war.* Why would they prefer such rules? About this I shall say only that if they are self-interested they will choose rules that will maximize expectable utility generally, for then their chance of coming out best will be greatest (and they do not know how especially to favor themselves); and that if they are altruistic they will again choose that set of rules, for they will want to choose rules that will maximize expectable utility generally. The rules of war, subject to the restriction that the rules of war may not prevent a belligerent from using all the power necessary to overcome the enemy, will be ones whose authorization will serve to maximize welfare.

It is worth noting that a preamble to the U.S. Army Manual offers an at least partially utilitarian theory of the rules of war (I say "at least partially" because of doubts about the interpretation of clause *b*). This preamble states that the law of land warfare "is inspired by the desire to diminish the evils of war by: *a.* Protecting both combatants and non-combatants from unnecessary suffering; *b.* Safeguarding certain fundamental human rights of persons who fall into the hands of the enemy, particularly prisoners of war, the wounded and sick, and civilians; and *c.* Facilitating the restoration of peace" (p. 3).

Which rules, then, would maximize expectable utility for nations at war? (I shall later discuss briefly whether the ideal rules would altogether forbid war as an instrument of national policy.)

First, however, we must understand why the above-mentioned restriction, guaranteeing that the rules of war will not prevent a belligerent from using all the force necessary to overcome the enemy, must be placed on the utility-maximizing rules of war. The reason for this restriction is to be found in the nature of a serious war. There are many different kinds of wars. Wars differ in magnitude, in the technologies they employ, in the degree to which they mobilize resources, in the type of issue the belligerents believe to be at stake, and in many other ways as well. The difference between the Trojan War and World War II is obviously enormous. The former was a simple, small-scale affair, and the issues at stake might well have been settled by a duel between Paris and Menelaus, or Hector and Achilles, and the belligerents might not have been seriously dissatisfied with the outcome. In the case of World War II, the British thought that Hitler's Germany and its policies threatened the very basis of civilized society. The destruction of Hitler's power seemed so important to the British that they were willing to stake their existence as a nation on bringing it about. Wars have been fought for many lesser reasons: to spread a political or religious creed, to acquire territory or wealth, to obtain an outlet to the sea, or to become established as a world power. Wars may be fought with mercenaries, or primarily by the contribution of equipment and munitions; such wars make relatively little difference to the domestic life of a belligerent.

It is possible that the rules that would maximize expectable utility might vary from one type of war to another. I shall ignore this possibility for the most part, and merely note that practical difficulties are involved in equipping military handbooks with different sets of rules and establishing judicial bodies to identify the proper classification of a given war. I shall take the position of Britain in World War II as typical of that of a belligerent in a serious war.

The position of a nation in a serious war is such that it considers overpowering the enemy to be absolutely vital to its interests (and possibly to those of civilized society generally) – so vital, indeed, that it is willing to risk its very existence to that end. It is doubtful that both sides can be well justified in such an appraisal of the state of affairs. But we may assume that in fact they do make this appraisal. In this situation, we must simply take as a fact that neither side will consent to or follow rules of war that seriously impair the possibility of bringing the war to a victorious conclusion. This fact accounts for the restriction within which I suggested a choice of the rules of war must take place. We may notice that the recognized rules of war do observe this limitation: They are framed in such a way as not to place any serious obstacle in the way of a nation's using any available force, if necessary, to destroy the ability of another to resist. As Oppenheim has observed, one of the assumptions underlying the recognized rules of war is that "a belligerent is justified in applying any amount and any kind of force which is necessary for . . . the overpowering of the opponent."[5] This limitation, however, leaves a good deal of room for rules of war that will maximize expectable long-range utility for all parties.

This restriction, incidentally, itself manifests utilitarian considerations, for a nation is limited to the use of means *necessary* to overcome an opponent. Clearly it is contrary to the general utility that any amount or manner of force be employed when it is *not* necessary for victory.

5 *International Law*, p. 226.

It will be convenient to divide the rules restricting military operation, especially the targets and weapons of attack, into three types. (I do not claim that these are exhaustive.)

1. Humanitarian restrictions of no cost to military operation. There are some things that troops may be tempted to do that are at best of negligible utility to their nation but that cause serious loss to enemy civilians, although not affecting the enemy's power to win the war. Such behavior will naturally be forbidden by rules designed to maximize expectable utility within the understood restriction. Consider, for example, rules against the murder or ill-treatment of prisoners of war. A rule forbidding wanton murder of prisoners hardly needs discussion. Such murder does not advance the war effort of the captors; indeed, news of its occurrence only stiffens resistance and invites retaliation. Moreover, there is an advantage in returning troops having been encouraged to respect the lives of others. A strict prohibition of wanton murder of prisoners therefore has the clear support of utilitarian considerations. Much the same may be said for a rule forbidding ill-treatment of prisoners. There can, of course, be disagreement about what constitutes ill-treatment – for instance, whether a prisoner is entitled to a diet of the quality to which he is accustomed if it is more expensive than that available to troops of the captor army. It is clear, however, that in a war between affluent nations prisoners can generally be well housed and well fed and receive adequate medical care without cost to the war effort of the captors. And if they receive such treatment, of course the captives gain. Thus a policy of good treatment of prisoners may be expected to make many nationals of both sides better off, and at a cost that in no way impairs the ability of either to wage the war.

Again, much the same may be said of the treatment of civilians and of civilian property in occupied territories. There is no military advantage, at least for an affluent nation, in the plunder of private or public property. And the rape of women or the ill-treatment of populations of occupied countries serves no military purpose. On the contrary, such behavior arouses hatred and resentment and constitutes a military liability. So utility is maximized, within our indicated basic limitations, by a strict rule calling for good treatment of the civilian population of an occupied territory. And the same can be said more generally for the condemnation of the wanton destruction of cities, towns, or villages, or devastation not justified by military necessity, set forth in the Charter of the Nuremberg Tribunal.

Obviously these rules, which the maximization of expectable utility calls for, are rules that command our intuitive assent.

2. Humanitarian restrictions possibly costly to military victory. Let us turn now to rules pertaining to actions in somewhat more complex situations. There are some actions that fall into neither of the classes so far discussed. They are not actions that must be permitted because they are judged necessary or sufficient for victory, and hence actions on which no party to a major war would accept restrictions. Nor are they actions that morally justified rules of war definitely prohibit, as being actions that cause injury to enemy nationals but serve no military purpose. It is this large class of actions neither clearly permitted nor definitely prohibited, for reasons already discussed, that I wish now to consider. I want to ask which rules of war are morally justified, because utility-maximizing, for actions of this kind. In what follows I shall be distinguishing several kinds of actions and suggesting appropriate rules for them. The first type is this: doing something that will result in widespread destruction of civilian life and property and at the same time will add (possibly by that very destruction) to the *probability* of victory but will not definitely decide the war. Some uses of atomic weapons, and area bombing of the kind practiced at Hamburg, illustrate this sort of case.

A proper (not ideally precise) rule for such operations might be: Substantial destruction of lives and property of enemy civilians is permissible only when there is good evidence that it will significantly enhance the prospect of victory. Application of the terms "good evidence" and "significantly enhance" requires judgment, but the rule could be a useful guideline all the same. For instance, we now know that the destruction of Hamburg did not significantly enhance the prospect of victory; in fact, it worked in the wrong direction, since it both outraged the population and freed workers formerly in non-war-supporting industries to be moved into industry directly contributing to the German war effort. The generals surely did not have good evidence that this bombing would significantly enhance the prospect of victory.

This rule is one parties to a war might be expected to accept in advance, since following it could be expected to minimize the human cost of war on both sides, and since it does not involve a significant compromise of the goal of victory. The proposed rule, incidentally, has some similarities to the accepted rule cited above from the U.S. Army Manual, that "loss of life and damage to property must not be out of proportion to the military advantage to be gained."

This rule, which I am suggesting only for wars like World War II, where the stakes are very high, may become clearer if seen in the perspective of a more general rule that would also be suitable for wars in which the stakes are much lower. I pointed out above that what is at stake in a war may be no more than a tiny strip of land or national prestige. (The utility of these, may, however, be considered very great

345

by a nation.) Now, it is clear that a risk of defeat that may properly be taken when the stakes are small may not be a proper risk when the stakes are virtually infinite; and a risk that could not properly be run when the stakes are enormous might quite properly be run when the stakes are small. So if the above-suggested rule is plausible for serious wars, in which the stakes are great, a somewhat different rule will be plausible in the case of wars of lesser importance – one that will require more in the way of "good evidence" and will require that the actions more "significantly enhance" the prospect of victory than is necessary when the stakes are much higher. These thoughts suggest the following general principle, applicable to all types of wars: A military action (for example, a bombing raid) is permissible only if the utility (broadly conceived, so that the maintenance of treaty obligations of international law could count as a utility) of victory to all concerned, multiplied by the increase in its probability if the action is executed, on the evidence (when the evidence is reasonably solid, considering the stakes), is greater than the possible disutility of the action to both sides multiplied by its probability. The rule for serious wars suggested above could then be regarded as a special case, one in which the utility of victory is virtually set at infinity – so that the only question is whether there is reasonably solid evidence that the action will increase the probability of victory. The more general rule obviously involves difficult judgments; there is a question, therefore, as to how it could be applied. It is conceivable that tough-minded civilian review boards would be beneficial, but we can hardly expect very reliable judgments even from them.[6]

These rules are at least very different from a blanket permission for anything the military thinks might conceivably improve the chances of victory, irrespective of any human cost to the enemy. In practice, it must be expected that each party to a war is likely to estimate the stakes of victory quite high, so that the rule that has the best chance of being

6 If we assume that both sides in a major struggle somehow manage to be persuaded that their cause is just, we shall have to expect that each will assign a net positive utility to its being the victor. For this reason it makes very little difference whether the more general principle uses the concept of the utility of victory by one side for everyone concerned, or the utility for that side only.

One might propose that the general restriction on rules of war, to the effect that in a serious war the use of any force necessary or sufficient for victory must be permitted, might be derived from the above principle if the utility of victory is set virtually at infinity and the probability of a certain action affecting the outcome is set near one. I believe this is correct, if we assume, as just suggested, that each side in a serious war will set a very high positive utility on *its* being the victor, despite the fact that both sides cannot possibly be correct in such an assessment. The reason for this principle as stated in the text, however, seems to me more realistic and simple. There is no reason, as far as I can see, why *both* lines of reasoning may not be used in support of the claim that the principle (or restriction) in question is a part of a morally justifiable system of rules of war.

respected is probably the first one mentioned, and not any modification of it that would be suggested to an impartial observer by the second, more general principle.

The reader may have been struck by the fact that these suggested rules are essentially institutionalized applications of a kind of act-utilitarian principle for certain contexts. This may seem inconsistent with the notion of a system of absolute rules themselves justified by long-range utilitarian considerations. But there is nothing inconsistent in the suggestion that some of the "absolute" rules should require that in certain situations an action be undertaken if and only if it will maximize expectable utility.

It may be objected that the rules suggested are far too imprecise to be of practical utility. To this I would reply that there is no reason why judgment may not be required in staff decisions about major operations. Furthermore, the U.S. Army Manual already contains several rules the application of which requires judgment. For example:

Absolute good faith with the enemy must be observed as a rule of conduct. . . . In general, a belligerent may resort to those measures for mystifying or misleading the enemy against which the enemy ought to take measures to protect himself.

The measure of permissible devastation is found in the strict necessities of war. Devastation as an end in itself or as a separate measure of war is not sanctioned by the law of war. There must be some reasonably close connection between the destruction of property and the overcoming of the enemy's army. . . .

The punishment imposed for a violation of the law of war must be proportionate to the gravity of the offense. The death penalty may be imposed for grave breaches of the law. . . . Punishments should be deterrent. (pp. 22, 23-4, 182)

It has sometimes been argued, for instance by Winston Churchill, that obliteration bombing is justified as retaliation. It has been said that since the Germans destroyed Amsterdam and Coventry, the British had a right to destroy Hamburg. And it is true that the Hague Conventions are sometimes regarded as a contract, breach of which by one side releases the other from its obligations. It is also true that a government that has itself ordered obliteration bombing is hardly in a position to complain if the same tactic is employed by the enemy. But maximizing utility permits obliteration bombing only as a measure of deterrence or deterrent reprisal. This rule, incidentally, is recognized by the Army Manual as a principle governing all reprisals: "Reprisals are acts of retaliation . . . for the purpose of enforcing future compliance with the recognized rules of civilized warfare. . . . Other means of securing compliance with the law of war should normally be exhausted before resort is had to reprisals. . . . Even when appeal to the enemy for redress has failed, it may be a matter of policy to consider, before resorting to reprisals, whether the opposing forces are not more likely to be influenced by a steady adherence to the law of war on the part of the adversary" (p. 177). Purposes of retaliation do not permit bombing in contravention of the suggested general principles.

Special notice should be taken that widespread civilian bombing might be defended by arguing that a significant deterioration in civilian morale could bring an end to a war by producing internal revolution. Our principle does not exclude the possibility of such reasoning, in the presence of serious evidence about civilian morale, when the stakes of victory are high. But we know enough about how bombing affects civilian morale to know that such bombing could be justified only rarely, if at all. The U.S. Army seems to go further than this; its rule asserts that any attack on civilians "for the sole purpose of terrorizing the civilian population is also forbidden."[7] It may be, however, that in actual practice this rule is interpreted in such a way that it is identical with the less stringent rule that is as much as utilitarian considerations can justify; if not, I fear we have to say that at this point the Army's theory has gone somewhat too far.

3. Acceptance of military losses for humanitarian reasons. Let us now turn to some rules that have to do with what we might call the *economics* of warfare, when the ultimate outcome is not involved, either because the outcome is already clear or because the action is fairly local and its outcome will not have significant repercussions. What damage may one inflict on the enemy in order to cut one's own losses? For instance, may one destroy a city in order to relieve a besieged platoon, or in order to avoid prolonging a war with consequent casualties? (The use of atom bombs in Japan may be an instance of this type of situation.) It is convenient to deal with two types of cases separately.

First, when may one inflict large losses on the enemy in order to avoid smaller losses for oneself, given that the issue of the war is not in doubt? A complicating fact is that when the issue is no longer in doubt it would seem that the enemy ought to concede, thereby avoiding losses to both sides. Why fight on when victory is impossible? (Perhaps to get better terms of peace.) But suppose the prospective loser is recalcitrant. May the prospective victor then unleash any horrors whatever in order to terminate the war quickly or reduce his losses? It is clear that the superior power should show utmost patience and not make the terms of peace so severe as to encourage further resistance. On the other hand, long-range utility is not served if the rules of war are framed in such a way as to provide an umbrella for the indefinite continuation of a struggle by an inferior power. So it must be possible to inflict losses heavy enough to

7 Whiteman, *Digest of International Law*, X, p. 135.

produce capitulation but not so heavy as to be out of proportion to the estimated cost of further struggle to both sides. This condition is especially important in view of the fact that in practice there will almost always be other pressures that can be brought to bear. The application of such a rule requires difficult judgments, but some such rule appears called for by long-range utilitarian considerations.

The second question is: Should there be restrictions on the treatment of an enemy in the case of local actions that could hardly affect the outcome of the war, when these may cause significant losses? Rules of this sort are in fact already in force. For instance, as mentioned above, the Army Manual forbids killing of prisoners when their presence retards one's movements, reduces the number of men available for combat, uses up the food supply, and in general is inimical to the integrity of one's troops. Again, the Second Hague Convention forbids forcing civilians in occupied territory to give information about the enemy, and it forbids reprisals against the general civilian population "on account of the acts of individuals for which they cannot be regarded as jointly and severally responsible."[8] The taking of hostages is prohibited (Army Manual, p. 107).

All these rules prescribe that a belligerent be prepared to accept certain military disadvantages for the sake of the lives and welfare of civilians and prisoners. The disadvantages in question are not, however, losses that could be so serious as to affect the outcome of a war. Furthermore, the military gains and losses are ones likely to be evenly distributed, so that neither side stands to gain a long-term advantage if the rules are observed by both. Without affecting the outcome of the war and without giving either side an unfair advantage, a considerable benefit can come to both belligerents in the form of the welfare of their imprisoned and occupied populations. Thus the long-run advantage of both parties is most probably served if they accept forms of self-restraint that can work out to be costly in occasional instances. Such rules will naturally be accepted by rational, impartial people in view of their long-range benefits.

IV RULES OF WAR AND MORALITY

I have been arguing that there is a set of rules governing the conduct of warfare that rational, impartial persons who believed that their country might from time to time be engaged in a war would prefer to any alternative sets of rules and to the absence of rules. I have also suggested, although without argument, that it is proper to say of such a set of

8 Article L.

rules that it is morally justified (and of course I think that such a set ought to be formally recognized and given authoritative status). There is thus a fairly close parallel with the prohibitions (and justifications and recognized excuses) of the criminal law: Certain of these would be preferred to alternative sets and to an absence of legal prohibitions by rational, impartial persons; the prohibitions that would be so preferred may (I think) be said to be morally justified; and such rules ought to be adopted as the law of the land. I do not say the parallel is exact.

It may be suggested that there will be a considerable discrepancy between what is permitted by such "morally justifiable" rules of war and what it is morally permissible for a person to do in time of war. (Nagel mentions dropping the bomb on Hiroshima, attacks on trucks bringing up food, and the use of flamethrowers in any situation whatever as examples of actions not morally permissible; but it is not clear that he would say these would be permitted by morally justifiable rules of war, or even that he recognizes a distinction between what is morally permissible and what is permitted by morally justifiable rules of war.) Moreover, it might be thought that such "morally justifiable" rules of war could not be derived from justified moral principles. It might be asked, too, what the moral standing of these "morally justified" rules of war is, in view of the fact that the rules of war actually accepted and in force may, at least in some particulars, be rather different. These are difficult questions, about which I wish to say something.

It is obvious that there may well be discrepancies between what a person morally may do in wartime and what is permitted by morally justified rules of war, just as there are discrepancies between what is morally permitted and what is permitted by morally justifiable rules of the criminal law. For one thing, the rules of war, like the criminal law, must be formulated in such a way that it is decidable whether a person has violated them; it must be possible to produce evidence that determines the question and removes it from the realm of speculation. More important, just as there are subtle interpersonal relations – such as justice and self-restraint in a family – which it is undesirable for the criminal law to attempt to regulate but which may be matters of moral obligation, so there may well be moral obligations controlling relations between members of belligerent armies the rules of war cannot reach. For instance, one might be morally obligated to go to some trouble or even take a certain risk in order to give aid to a wounded enemy, but the rules of war could hardly prescribe doing so. I am unable to think of a case in which moral principles require a person to do what is forbidden by morally justifiable rules of war; I suppose this is possible.

350

But it is easy to think of cases in which moral principles forbid a person to injure an enemy, or require him to aid an enemy, when morally justifiable rules of war do not prescribe accordingly and when the military law even forbids the morally required behavior. (Consider, for instance, the fact that, according to the Manual, the U.S. Army permits severe punishment for anyone who "without proper authority, knowingly harbors or protects or gives intelligence to, or communicates or corresponds with or holds any intercourse with the enemy, either directly or indirectly." [p. 33].)

The possible contrast between morally justifiable rules of war and what is morally permitted will seem quite clear to persons with firm moral intuitions. It may be helpful, however, to draw the contrast by indicating what it would be, at least for one kind of rule-utilitarian theory of moral principles. A rule-utilitarian theory of morality might say that what is morally permissible is any action that would not be forbidden by the kind of conscience that would maximize long-range expectable utility were it built into people as an internal regulator of their relations with other sentient beings, as contrasted with other kinds of conscience or not having a conscience at all. Then justifiable rules of war (with the standing described above) would be one thing; what is morally permissible, in view of ideal rules of conscience, might be another. Rational, impartial persons, understanding that their country may be involved in a war, might want one set of rules as rules of war, whereas rational, impartial persons choosing among types of conscience might want a different and discrepant set of rules as rules of conscience. In the same way there may be a discrepancy between a morally justified system of criminal law and morally justified rules of conscience. And just as, consequently, there may occasionally be a situation in which it is one's moral duty to violate the criminal law, so there may occasionally be a situation in which it is one's moral duty to violate morally justifiable rules of war.

It might be asked whether a person who subscribed to sound moral principles would, if given the choice, opt for a system of rules of war; and if so, whether he would opt for a set that would maximize expectable utility for the situation of nations at war. I suggest that he would do so; that such a person would realize that international law, like the criminal law, has its place in human society, that not all decisions can simply be left to the moral intuitions of the agent, and that the rules of war and military justice are bound to be somewhat crude. He would opt for that type of system that will do the most good, given that nations will sometimes go to war. I am, however, only *suggesting* that he would; in order to show that he would, one would have to identify the sound moral principles that would be relevant to such a decision.

351

Another question that might be raised is whether a person should follow the actual military rules of his country or the morally justifiable ones (in the sense explained above). This question can obviously be taken in either of two ways. If the question is which rules are legally binding, of course the actual rules of war recognized at present are legally binding on him. But the question might be: Is a person morally bound to follow the "ideal" rules of war, as compared with the actual ones (or the legal orders of his officer), if they come into conflict? Here two possible situations must be distinguished. It is logically possible that a morally justifiable set of rules of war would permit damage to the enemy more severe than would the actual rules of war; in that case, assuming the actual rules of war have the status of an obligation fixed by a treaty, the moral obligation would seem to be to follow the provisions of the treaty (subject to the usual difficulties about older treaties not contemplating contemporary situations). Suppose, however, that a superior officer commands one to do something that is permitted by the actual rules of war (that is, not explicitly forbidden) but which clearly would be forbidden by morally justifiable rules of war. The question is then whether a moral person would refuse to do what is permitted by an unjust institution but would be forbidden by a just one. It would have to be argued in detail that sound moral principles would not permit a person to do what would be permitted only by an unjust institution. I shall not attempt to argue the matter, but only suggest that sound moral principles would *not* permit obedience to an order forbidden by morally justifiable rules of war. It is quite possible, incidentally, contrary to what I have just said about the legal issues, that a court-martial would not succeed in convicting a person who refused an order of this sort and defended his action along these lines.

There is space only to advert to the larger issue of the moral justification for nations being belligerents at all. Presumably, just as there are morally justified rules of war, in the sense of rules that rational, impartial persons would choose on the assumption their country might be involved in a war, so there are morally justified rules about engaging in a war at all, in the sense of rules governing the behavior of nations that rational, impartial persons would subscribe to if they believed that they would live in a world in which the chosen rules might obtain. Not only are there such morally justified rules regarding belligerency, but almost every nation is in fact signatory to a treaty abjuring war as an instrument of policy. Moreover, it has been declared criminal by the Treaty of London for a person to plan, prepare, initiate, or wage a war of aggression or a war in violation of international treaties, agreements, or assurances. So there is basis both in morally justified principles of international law and

352

in actual international law for questioning the position of a belligerent. Presumably the relation between these and the moral obligations of citizens and government officials is complex, rather parallel to that just described for the case of rules of war.

18

Public policy and life and death decisions regarding defective newborns

Decisions about the use of surgery and/or life-support systems for prolonging or improving the lives of defective newborns are normally made by the parents in consultation with the attending physicians, sometimes after consultation with a hospital ethics committee. Decisions, however, are subject to certain legal restrictions, partly embodied in criminal law, partly by court power to appoint a guardian *ad litem* to make a decision in the place of the parents, and partly by regulations of the Department of Health and Human Services laying down requirements for hospitals receiving federal funds. Juvenile courts and child protection agencies directly or indirectly play a role. In what follows I wish to consider what, from a moral point of view, such laws and policies should be.

When I say I wish to consider what these policies should be, from a moral point of view, you will at once want to know on which general moral principles I am going to rely and why. I shall respond to this query at once, but shall not attempt to defend my answer here, except for brief remarks near the end of this paper. First, then, I affirm that a policy is justified from a moral point of view if and only if it is one that factually informed, rational, and otherwise normal persons would *want* for a society in which they expected to live a lifetime. This statement does not tell us anything about which policies such persons might want, however. So I shall affirm, second, that the policies such persons would want are those that, when adopted by the appropriate agencies of society, would be most beneficial for society in the long run. This second statement is somewhat vague as formulated. For instance, what counts as being "beneficial"? I shall spell this concept out more fully as we go along.

First of all, I want to state what is a legal fact, at least in most states, that bears on the issue we are concerned with, and I shall explain why I think it is right that this legal fact exists. This legal fact is that in many states, certainly in the states of Michigan, Wisconsin, and Minnesota, parents, at the time they would normally take their infant home from the hospital, *or later,* can go into juvenile court and sign papers waiving their parental rights, turning the child over to the state. Child protection agencies are then given custody of the child, and arrange for adoption or placement in a foster or group home, or institution. In some states parents are liable for the costs of their infant unless or until an adoption is arranged for, or unless the court finds them incapable of financial support. But in Michigan and Minnesota, for example, in practice no attempt is made to collect costs from the parents. Parents, at least in Michigan, are not required to give a *reason* for the state to take over if the parents declare that they do not want their child.

Is it good to have this legal "out" for the parent? I believe it is. The state can mandate provision of food, shelter, and medical care, or the cost thereof, but it cannot mandate love or psychological support. The state cannot even manage to collect for support in many cases – for example, if the mother is an unwed teenager. So, from the point of view of the welfare of children, it seems best for the state to stand ready to take over and it ought to do so.

This conclusion may be questioned. The immediate response of many to the question whether parents must be responsible for (and also have decision rights over) the care of their child is: "Of course, the parents have the responsibility for the infant. It's theirs, isn't it? Didn't they produce it?"[1]

This response may reflect the influence of traditional tort law on our thinking. In tort law, the cost of an accident falls on the victim. If I fall downstairs and am confined to a wheelchair thereafter, that is my problem (unless I have accident insurance). Certainly it is not anyone else's problem, unless the loss was caused by the negligence of someone else. The same with the defective baby: The loss is on the parents, unless the defect was a result of, say, the fault of the manufacturer of some food or medicine. So we tend to think. But there is another way of looking at the matter. Workmen's compensation laws call for payment for injury on the job, irrespective of fault. The same is true for no-fault automobile insurance. In New Zealand there is social insurance for all accidents. So, in view of the fact that a defective child may result from an activity of which society approves – that of having a family and rearing the next generation – and in view of the fact that there was no negligence on the parents' part, it would be in accord with present trends that the *state* provide for the care of a defective infant. This would certainly be true if it *mandated* that the infant be given aggressive hospital treatment so that its life be saved.

AN APPRAISAL OF REGULATIONS ON LIFE-SUSTAINING TREATMENT

Let us now consider the main question: What should public policy mandate about life-sustaining treatment for defective newborns, in which

1 This seems to be the view of Professor J. M. Gustafson [5].

types of cases should there be discretion about treatment, and in whom should the discretion be vested? We are not interested in what the present public policy is, but what it should be, from the point of view of morality.

Some think the issue is settled by the alleged fact that every infant has a *right* to life. Some may think there is a legal right to life, which requires life-sustaining treatment in all cases. And there is if legislatures mandate it. There is, however, no such *constitutional* right; the Fourteenth Amendment says that a state may not deny equal protection of the laws. Hence you might say the Constitution demands that states that prohibit killing adults must also prohibit killing defective infants. True, but the Constitution does not demand the provision of all possible medical technology for saving anybody's life. In any case, we are concerned with whether infants have a *moral* right to life. Do all infants, defective to whatever degree, have a *moral* right to life-sustaining treatment? One writer answers by saying, "Simply because of his or her humanity, every human being is a person possessing rights. The right to life is the most basic and paramount of all" ([13], p. 248). But here we should be careful not to make what I think is a philosophical mistake. For when someone says that something should be done for an infant because the infant has a moral right, he seems to overlook the fact that what it *means* to say that someone has a certain moral right is to say, no more and no less, that some or all people have certain moral obligations with respect to the person said to have the right. In other words, to say that a person has a certain right is the same thing as to say that it is wrong to treat him, or fail to treat him, in certain ways. So, if there is doubt whether a person can morally be treated in a certain way, it is no answer to say that he has a certain corresponding right; for insofar as there is doubt whether he ought to be treated in a certain way, there is equal doubt about whether he has a right, or what is the scope of the right. So an attempt to resolve the question how infants or fetuses should be treated by discussing the question whether infants and fetuses have a right to life is essentially confused.

Some philosophers say that a fetus has a moral right to life if it is a *human being*, others that it has such a right only if it is a *person*, and give explanations of what it is to be a person: A person must have a self-consciousness, a sense of past and future, a capacity for making plans and having desires, and so on. All this discussion is irrelevant. The basic question is whether it is wrong to kill, or withhold life-supporting treatment from, a fetus or newborn whose mental state, or prospective mental state, is such and such, and all the discussion about who has rights and what exactly they are is only a detour that brings us around to the very same questions with which we started, none the wiser for the detour.

So let us directly approach the question whether, from a moral point of view, regulations should mandate life-sustaining treatment for defective newborns. It will be helpful to approach the question by examining the conclusions of the President's Commission. Three points are made: First, the decision must ignore "negative effects of an impaired child's life on other persons, including parents, siblings, and society" ([14], p. 218). Second, prospective handicaps should lead to a negative decision

> only when they are so severe that continued existence would not be a net benefit to the infant. . . . Net benefit is absent only if the burdens imposed on the patient by the disability or its treatment would lead a competent decision maker to choose to forgo the treatment. . . . For many adults, life with severe physical or mental handicap would seem so burdensome as to offer no benefits. . . . From the perspective of an infant, who can be helped to develop realistic goals and satisfactions, such frustrations need not occur. ([14] pp. 218–19)

Third, within these restrictions a decision about life-sustaining supports is to be made by the parents and physicians if they agree, and by a hospital board or court if they do not.

Let us begin with the first proposal: that the prospective costs, however great, to the family and society should be *altogether* ignored. Taken literally, this proposal cannot be right. We do not use such standards elsewhere. One estimate of U.S. Army Policy in saving lives by providing artillery and other support concludes that the policy implies that the Army regards the life of an average private to be worth about $250,000. In a suit for negligent killing, courts gauge the worth of a life in terms of the lifetime earning power of the decedent. Extra wages demanded by workers in high-risk occupations work out to a much smaller estimate of the value of a life. Moreover, we could build ships that are virtually unsinkable in a storm, but it would be uneconomical to do so. We could build only homes that provide some protection in case of a tornado, but we do not do so because of the added expense. So we normally do take into account the impact on others in deciding whether to take steps to save lives. Why should the President's Commission think not in the treatment of defective newborns? It offers no argument.

People who agree with the Commission may think of human life as being something different from what, in fact, it is. As far as I can see, human life, or what is worthwhile about human life, is a succession of *experiences* (associated with the body), many of which can be remembered later, and some of which are anticipated, planned, and desired in advance. Let us say, then, that life is essentially a connected stream of experiences. When we sustain a life, we prolong that stream of experiences. When we fail to sustain it, the result is an earlier termination of the stream. It is not as if we destroy an immortal soul; if we have an immortal soul it cannot be destroyed. Some writers speak of human life as being "sacred." But we ourselves – and we cannot be accused of selfishness in our own case – set a *finite value* on the worth of continuing *our own* stream of experiences; we would not want to prolong our own experiences at the cost of bankrupting our children, especially if we thought the stream would not be very good (for instance, if we anticipated having to spend the final year of life in bed, unable to do any creative work).

But, if the President's Commission is wrong in thinking the unfavorable impact on others should be ignored, what kind of trade-off should we acknowledge? The utilitarian would want a plan maximizing the welfare of human beings whoever they are, and at whatever stage of life. So he would say that if the lifelong care of a defective newborn would cost $1,000,000, we should proceed to spend the money that way, if we had to choose, only if the money could not be spent to produce a better life stream of experiences elsewhere (for example, by providing better education for children who could benefit). We must be careful here, for one of the values we do not want to lose is that of general caring for others, and especially for children; we want to avoid thinking of their lives in monetary terms. Perhaps it is therefore better, if we are thinking how to compare the benefits of life-sustaining treatment for defective newborns with costs elsewhere, to think of the impact on the infant's family. What is the impact? If the family is not well insured, the costs of surgery and continuing care may mean that the life of the family is lived at a spartan level for many years. The siblings of the defective child may have to be deprived of a college education. There are, moreover, serious disruptions in the family. The life of the parents may come to revolve in a small circle around the child. The family may feel unable to have a social life because it is uncomfortable to have guests at a meal, given the unpredictable behavior of the defective family member. One could go on, but surely the continued presence of the child may well reduce dramatically the quality of life of the family. Of course, sometimes the opposite will be the case: The needs of the defective child may serve to unify the family. What I propose is that a satisfactory policy will take into account *both* the total prospective benefit to the infant and the total loss to the family, and will maximize net benefit, doubtless giving the benefit of aggressive treatment to the child if the divergence is not large.

There is another way of thinking of matters, which I owe to Derek Parfit (that he presented at a lecture at Oxford); it highlights the fact that if the life of a defective infant is not sustained, the parents may feel able to replace it by a normal child. The reasoning follows.

Suppose a woman wants a child, but is told that if she conceives a child now it will be defective, whereas if she waits three months she will produce a normal child. Obviously we think she should delay. Of course, if she delays, she will not have the *same* child as the one she would have had if she had not delayed, but we do not think we need worry about any rights of the child she might have had.

Suppose, however, a woman conceives but discovers, five months later after amniocentesis, that the fetus will develop into a defective child. Furthermore, the probability is good that she can have a normal child later if she has an abortion and tries again. Now this time there is still the same reason for having the abortion that there was formerly for the delay: that she will produce another child with a better life. Ought she not have the abortion? If the quality of the child's life is poor, he could well complain that he was injured by being brought to term, and in fact, some court suits along this line have actually been filed. I believe that the vast majority of persons would think this woman should have an abortion. The reason amniocentesis is becoming so frequent is that many women fear there may be congenital defects.

Now suppose a woman cannot discover until after birth that her child is seriously defective. She learns then that, were she to conceive again, it is highly probable that she would have a normal child. Are things really different from the previous cases during the first few days? One might think that a rational person would want, in each of these cases, the substitution of a normal child for a defective one, of a better life for a worse one.

So it seems, in deciding what should be done about sustaining the life of a defective newborn, we have to compare the good of its life not only with the possible harm done to other family members (and society), but also with the better life that could be lived by a child that might be born to take its place. Why is not all of this relevant?

So much for the Commission's first contention that costs be wholly ignored. That brings us to the second one: that a life should be sustained if there will (probably) be net benefit to the infant over its lifetime, taking the point of view of the aspirations, etc., of the infant.

How is one to decide whether a life is worthwhile from the individual's point of view? The Commission mentions pain and frustration as negative weights; if a life were nothing but these, with no countervailing benefits, it would overall be bad. How might we decide whether it is good or bad *for* the infant? One way of deciding is this (and possibly this is what the Commission had in mind): Suppose we draw a curve corresponding to a person's lifetime, points below the curve representing experiences *disliked* at the time, the distance below the x-axis being fixed by how strongly the person disliked the experience at the time.[2] (Positions on the x-axis

2 Identifying where these points should go is not theoretically easy, and involves the

359

represent successive moments of experience during the individual's life.) Then we could also draw points above the line, representing how strongly the individual liked the experience he was having at the moment, the distance from the x-axis representing how strongly the individual liked his experience at the time. Now we can draw a curve connecting these sets of points and ideally compute the area between the curves and the x-axis. If the area above the line exceeds that below the line, then life has a net benefit for that person, the amount corresponding to the size of the area.

There is another way of estimating whether a life is good or bad for a person overall. We might say that a person's life is good overall if the individual, toward the end of it, could recall all of it vividly, and be glad that she had lived that life. *How* glad she is would presumably determine how worthwhile her life has been to her. One trouble with this proposal is that it seems impossible to recall a whole life vividly at one moment (not to mention the practical problem of predicting in advance how a person then would feel). And, even if a person does recall it to some extent, whether the picture attracts or repels may very well be subject to the mood of the moment: If she is happy the picture looks rosy, whereas if she is depressed the picture looks gray. Still, you might prefer this criterion for whether a life is worthwhile for a person since it is less hedonistic; it does not rate a life just by noting how enjoyable its successive moments were to the individual at the time.

Now if one of the foregoing is accepted as the criterion for a life that is better for a person than not, how do we apply it to the case of defective newborns? How do we decide whether a given newborn should be given treatment, in view of the prospective value of his life to him? If Dr. John Lorber's statistics [7, 8, 9] about spina bifida are right, we have some useful information to consider.[3] For then we know that probably, if the newborn has some observable symptoms, which Lorber enumerates, even if treated aggressively it has a 60 percent chance of being dead within seven years and will probably have gross paralysis, some leg deformity, frequent bone fractures, incontinence of urine and feces, a marginally normal intelligence, and be repeatedly subject to further surgery if a shunt is required to relieve hydrocephaly. On this basis Lorber recommends selective treatment only for those infants without the symptoms he enumerates.

But the objective physical results likely for the infant are only part of what we should know to make decisions about treatment. What do they

traditional philosophical problem of the measurement and interpersonal comparison of utilities. For recent discussions of this problem see [1], [2], [6], and [15].
3 For some criticism, see [4].

tell us about the worth of an individual's future life to him? Fractures, incontinence, and operations are misfortunes to which nearly everyone is subject at one time or another, and they are not devastating. If there is relatively continuous severe pain or frequent worry about early death, that is another matter. We must remember, however, what writers often seem to overlook: that we are talking of a whole life, during part of which a person will likely not have the psychological support of parents.

What strikes me as a very serious problem for the value of a life is the possibility of long stretches of unrelieved boredom or tedium when, during the day, one looks forward to nothing but going to sleep. It is true that low I.Q. and handicaps do not necessarily mean poor quality of life in adult years, at least not directly. But they do limit opportunities, and these opportunities may be important for making life worthwhile. What is needed in life to prevent unrelieved tedium? A. H. Maslow [10] has devised a list of human "needs," which we might look at to assess a defective newborn's prospects for a good life. Among the needs a defective child will likely have difficulty with are activity, sex, love and belongingness, esteem by others and self-esteem, understanding, and what Maslow calls "self-actualization" (development of one's own special abilities). (It is interesting to note that apparently an animal does not need much of some of these in order to feel cheerful.) J. Griffin, in *Wellbeing*, lists the making of autonomous choices, a sense of accomplishment, enjoyments, and deep personal relations as important to a good quality of life. For a relatively satisfying life, a human being seems to require, on the basis of my own experience, interpersonal relations including friendly conversations, projects of interest such as collecting stamps or solving complex problems, responsibilities with social pressure to discharge them, probably some love relationships, and the ability to look forward to a few exciting activities and experiences involving others. A report of the University of Michigan Institute for Social Research roughly supports the foregoing judgments. It concludes that

Those people whose feelings of well-being are distinctly negative are all deprived of some critical element of their lives – social support, good health, employment, or status. ... There are obviously many things people learn to do without, but for most people marriage, health, and work ... are major contributors to a positive outlook on life. ([3], p. 232)

Dr. Lorber tells us that among the total group of spina bifida patients aggressively treated, only 10 percent can hold a job. (I do not know if "sheltered shops" are available in England. Many Down's syndrome children in the United States of America are able to find life-long employment there.) Most mentally defective children can watch television

361

with enjoyment, but it seems doubtful that a person can make much of a life out of this. So for many defective newborns – we must remember that Lorber is talking only of spina bifida children, not Down's syndrome, or any of the myriad children who have suffered severe brain damage before or after birth or had seriously premature births – there will probably be no interesting job available to them, and hence no pressure to perform tasks responsibly (but Down's children do seem intent on performing simple manual tasks), very little activity, no sexual relations, relatively low esteem by others and little basis for self-esteem, little prospect for "understanding" if the person has a low level of intelligence, and little that can be called "self-actualization." A seriously defective newborn may enjoy plenty of love and support in his family during his early years, but as he and his parents grow older (and particularly after the death of his parents), he is apt to have little of this. It seems he will be able to have his physical needs satisfied, but will miss the major distinctively human goods.

There are qualifications to be added to this somewhat gloomy prognosis. First, there have been improvements in treatment and many of the children Lorber classified as hopeless would probably do much better at the present time. Second, many children who would have been regarded as hopeless cases now can be given training – say, with behavior-learning techniques – and learn to perform socially useful tasks and live in groups where there is some peer support. Third, the elimination of institutional care in favor of small foster or group homes is psychologically stimulating and provides social interaction. (Indeed, this may be much better than life in the child's own family where, despite professions of love and seeming concern, the child may be resented or even hated, and live an essentially isolated life.)

It seems to me that, as matters stand today, defective newborns fall into three main classes. First, some are so seriously defective that at best they will have a short and unpleasant life, despite anything medicine can do for them. It is a favor to them to allow an early death. Second, there are some whose lives will be only marginally beneficial to them, but at a high economic and/or psychological cost to others. The family should not be expected to bear the burden of providing this marginally valuable existence at great cost, and the infant should be aggressively treated only if society is prepared to pay what is necessary to provide a life that is reasonably worthwhile, given the child's potentialities. Third, there are those who have the capacity to survive and over the long term make a reasonably decent life for themselves, or even a normal life. These should, of course, be aggressively treated, and someone – family or society – should provide the necessities for them to develop their capacities and live good lives. Such children will presumably be acceptable for adoption if their parents do not wish to undertake care for them. There is, of course, a fourth class, that of children whose lives will be only marginally beneficial to them, but whose parents are willing to accept them as part of the family and whose condition is such that their presence will not be a significant burden to the family. Then, of course, aggressive treatment is indicated.

Unfortunately, while there will be many infants that clearly, on the day of birth, can be identified as belonging squarely in one of these classes, there will be many borderline cases. A decision need not be made on the day of birth; it can be delayed for months until the diagnosis and prognosis become clear (so long as it is not so delayed that the infant becomes aware of the situation and can begin to suffer from anxiety about what is going to happen, or that attachments with parents form, which are painful to break). It is manifest that it is psychologically important for all concerned that a decision whether to continue aggressive treatment be made as early as possible.

This brings us to our third problem: *Who* is to make the decision about continuation of aggressive treatment? What is needed is an individual or group acquainted with the exact symptoms of the child and prognosis for the child's future, indeed long-term future if the prognosis does not rule out the possibility of this. The chooser should also know the circumstances of the family, whether the presence of the infant will be a severe burden to them. The chooser should also know what kind of life the individual will have if he becomes a ward of the state – what kinds of care and education are available, whether all assistance will cease at age twenty-six, and so on. Some writers have urged that society has a *duty* to provide care good enough to make life worthwhile for wards of the state, but unless and until that is done the chooser should bear in mind what kind of care will actually be furnished and what life will probably be like in that situation. The decision will be an especially difficult one if the infant can count on a marginally acceptable life if he is cared for in a family, where such care would be a heavy burden for the family, but a life on the whole not acceptable if he has to be a ward of the state.

Traditionally, the parents of the child have been recognized as having a decisive voice in such decisions, but unless the parents stand ready to accept the child into their family, it is far from obvious why they should have this traditional prerogative. On the other hand, it may be said that the parents, at least in consultation with the attending physician, are in a position to make the best decision from the point of view of the child; they may know more of the facts and will have the interest necessary for

363

giving careful thought to the issue. But it is clear that the scope of their right to decide should be limited. On the one hand, they should not be free to sentence an infant to further suffering if the medical prognosis is such that further treatment would only prolong life briefly and be painful for the patient. On the other hand, they should not be free to mandate no aggressive treatment for a child whose defects are relatively minor and who, in the judgment of child care agencies, can be adopted.

Even with these restrictions, however, there is a question whether the parents and the physician are very well qualified to make decisions about continuing aggressive treatment. The physician may be a very busy person who has given relatively little thought to the issues involved – he may never have visited the state-provided foster homes or schools, and have no idea what is in store for a defective child who becomes a ward of the state. And, unless the parents are intelligent and well educated, they will not be able to think through clearly what prolonged life would be like for their child, or what their own life would be like with such a child in their midst. Nor will they, normally, be familiar with the quality of state-provided facilities. They may be emotionally unsettled, subject to social pressures from friends or self-appointed advisers, and all too ready to rely on the advice of their physician.

What should be available for the decider to use is systematic statistical information along the lines Dr. Lorber provides, but brought up to date, improved and expanded to cover a wider range of defects. Ideally, the physician ought to be able to refer to the results of such statistical studies and say, "The medical profession, in view of the statistics about past cases, would recommend in this case that such-and-such be done." However, this kind of ideal situation does not yet obtain. If the child does not clearly fall in the first class identified above – of infants in effect already destined to an early death – and the parents wish to take the responsibility for the child themselves, there appears to be no real problem; the parents may decide they want to opt out later, but that seems to be a risk worth taking, everything considered.

But if this is not the case, it appears we shall have to look to a hospital ethics committee for the decision for problematic cases. Such a committee would presumably include the attending pediatrician and perhaps a second pediatrician, a neurologist, preferably a psychoneurologist, at least one social worker (who will be familiar with what is in store for the child if it becomes a ward of the state), a specialist in ethical decisions (preferably a philosopher attached to the medical staff, but possibly a specially trained clergyman provided his theological views do not commit him to advocating aggressive treatment for absolutely all infants because they are God's property, etc.) and perhaps a sensible layman. The members of such a committee must be sufficiently public-spirited to be willing to give thought to the problems. Such a committee seems to be the best solution for the decision problem at present and, incidentally, would provide a legal shield for the physician. It is not easy to see how it can be helpful to involve the courts; a judge would seem to be far worse qualified than a hospital ethics committee to make such decisions. If there is no standing ethics committee in a hospital, presumably it will always be possible to assemble an ad hoc committee that is willing to listen to the details of a single case.

How do the foregoing remarks differ from the recommendations of the President's Commission? (1) Most important, they permit taking into account not only the future "net benefit" for the child, but also the total impact on everyone affected, including the family and society, bearing in mind the possibility of the parents' having a normal child in the future, if treatment of the present child is discontinued or the child is made a ward of the state. (2) They attempt to make a start at filling in the concept of "net benefit" for the infant, conceived as stretching over a lifetime (consistently, I think, with what the Commission says), but developed along lines of widespread (but far from universal) thinking among moral philosophers. (3) They are somewhat more restrictive than the Commission about leaving decisions about treatment in the hands of the parents in consultation with the physician. The parents are not free to mandate continued aggressive treatment where this is medically contraindicated, or to forbid such treatment when the defects of an infant are relatively minor, and their authority lapses unless they are prepared to accept their infant at the end of the aggressive treatment. In problematic cases, unless the parents want aggressive treatment and are prepared to accept the child when it is ready to leave the hospital, the decision should be made by the hospital's ethics committee – ideally supported by generally accepted professional standards, somewhat along the lines of Dr. Lorber, but expanded to other types of problems and based on up-to-date statistics representing modern modes of treatment. The ethics committee would be free to mandate no further treatment in light of its judgment about the benefits to everyone concerned.

THE MORAL STATUS OF THE PROPOSAL

Since the foregoing proposal implies nontreatment for some infants, and is therefore a virtual sentence of death for them, it is sure to be questioned by some. Not, perhaps, for those infants whose prognosis is so poor that they are in effect already irremediably dying, or whose future contains so much pain and is in any case almost certainly so short that it would clearly be doing them no favor to prolong their existence. But there will be a sizable group that parents and physician, or hospital committee, will assign to the nontreatment group, either because of a somewhat negative prospect for an acceptable life from the infant's own point of view over the long term, or else a somewhat positive prospect for the longer term conjoined with the near certainty of very heavy costs to family or society.

This problem naturally leads us to look at general theories in normative ethics to see if there is any one with plausibility and that would forbid this conclusion I have suggested. The conclusion suggested has been selected to conform to what has historically been the most influential theory: a variant of a utilitarian test of public policies.[4] According to the utilitarian thesis, a policy is morally justified if the total net benefit of its adoption, direct or indirect, is greater than the total net benefit of adoption of any other possible policy. The theory thus affirms that the moral test of a policy is its maximizing the net long-term benefit over *everyone* involved. Thus the theory directs that criminals should be treated in a way not necessarily best just for *their* welfare, but in a way best for the long-range benefit of everyone, criminals included. In our case, the test is the maximal benefit of the whole society, not necessarily the maximum benefit of the infant, although in most cases a policy mandating the maximal net benefit for the infant will not diverge from one aiming at the maximal net benefit of society.

Now suppose that my recommendation of a policy for not treating some defective newborns is implied by this utilitarian theory. Would that count as a serious recommendation? The present is not the place for discussing the merits of the currently much maligned utilitarian theory, but I think this view is the one rational, informed people would prefer to support as a morality for their society, as contrasted with other normative theories or with no theory at all. If so, the fact that utilitarianism calls for this policy is no mean point in its favor.

At the present time the chief *systematic* normative theory contrasting with utilitarianism is that of John Rawls. This is not in respect of his background theory – that an act is right if the principle involved is one that would be chosen by rational persons behind a veil of ignorance – for a defendant of utilitarianism might say that his principles, too, would be so chosen.[5] But it is in respect of his positive normative principles, especially the so-called Difference Principle, that economic institutions should be arranged so as to favor the worst-off group (say by tax or welfare benefits) up to the point where further favoring would result, in

---

4 The utilitarian theory is accepted in the Report by a Working Party [11].
5 John Harsanyi does, for example; see [6].

the long run, in making them still worse off than they would otherwise be. This principle might seem to apply to our problem, since a handicapped child is very badly off. Should such children be given favored treatment up to the point where more benefits to them would in the long run be self-defeating? About this suggestion one can say that Rawls's theory is addressed to a very important but somewhat narrower range of problems having to do with the social and economic system and with people who are more or less normal and expected to live a full life. We can be sure that Rawls himself did not have this application in mind, and the difference between our problem and the problems he addresses is likely so great that difficulties would arise in an attempt to transpose his arguments, used to support his view for its intended domain, in support of some view for the problem we are considering.

Some critics of Kantian inclinations might assert that failing to treat defective newborns because of great psychological or economic costs to others is failing to treat them as ends in themselves. And it is true that the utilitarian proposes, if he advocates nontreatment in this situation, to make a newborn worse off than he otherwise could have been because of costs to others. But there is another side to matters. A newborn's family also consists of people, and if society imposes severe burdens on them for the sake of the newborn, is it not using *them* as means to *his* ends? It is not very clear to me what the Kantian principle implies to be done when the interests of parties are conflicting.

There are various philosophers who think we know that no one ought to kill innocent human beings, no matter what their life prospects are or what the cost to others will be, without their consent. This view derives mostly from the Christian tradition, but, when shaken loose from speculative theological underpinnings, its logical status appears to be no more than a basic intuition.

NONTREATMENT VERSUS ACTIVE TERMINATION

Suppose it has been decided that the condition of a given newborn is such that it ought not to be treated, either for its own sake in that the quality of its life will be negative, or because of the very great cost, psychological or economic, to others, with only a very marginally desirable existence for the infant. There is then a troubling problem: The infant may survive for a long time, gradually deteriorating to death, and its condition while alive will be worse if it is not aggressively treated, rather than if it is. Some, on this account, favor aggressive treatment of virtually all infants, even though they think it would be better if they would die quickly.

There is an alternative: what has been done with severely defective infants from earliest times – that they not be allowed to survive at all. The infant could be given a terminating anesthetic. Call it "delayed abortion" or "legal miscarriage" if you will. Such an idea seems hardhearted, but it is surely kinder than allowing slow deterioration until death arrives, with or without medication. It could be no worse for the infant than undergoing a general anesthetic, and it is better than a late abortion, which can be painful to the fetus. I concede that the idea of actively giving an infant a lethal anesthetic is somewhat horrifying, although, strangely, the idea of just letting it die miserably does not seem to bother people so much. What is done quietly and *sub rosa* we find easy to accept; it is a "medical" decision.

Active termination by anesthetic is currently contrary to law. But the law about neonates, when compared with the law about abortions, seems very strange. For example, if a woman learns during the sixth month of pregnancy that the fetus will probably be born with defects, she is free to have an abortion. (Indeed, she is free to have an abortion for no reason at all.) Consider a woman who is a carrier of hemophilia. If she discovers by amniocentesis that her child will be male, then, although there is a 50 percent chance a male child will be normal, and given the fact that hemophiliacs sometimes have good lives anyway, she is not only free to have an abortion, but many people think it is her moral obligation to do so. As Peter Singer points out [12], it would be more rational to wait until after birth, when it can be definitely determined whether the infant is a hemophiliac, and then permit nontreatment or termination at that point. The mere timing of the termination of a life seems morally trivial, unless there were serious reasons to think that delayed decisions would undermine our social moral fabric and lead to the erection of gas chambers, as obviously it would not. There is nothing sacrosanct about birth as the time at which a child's legal right to life begins. The Supreme Court decided that "state interest" in a child begins at the point at which it is viable – a decision that was largely arbitrary. There is no reason why the Court might not decide that the date of one month after birth is the time at which seriously defective infants acquire a legal right to life. This would be a more coherent policy than one vesting decision about abortion in the hands of the parents up until nearly the end of pregnancy, and vesting no power in the hands of parents, or parents in consultation with physicians and a hospital ethics board, to make the same terminating decision soon after birth, when there is much better evidence on which to base a decision.

Fortunately, there is hope that these problems may be partially resolved within the next few years, when better methods of prognosis through prenatal testing will enable physicians to identify fetuses with prospectively serious defects so that they can be aborted during early pregnancy. Such abortions, barring changes in the views of the Supreme Court, will be legal and accepted by the general public.

REFERENCES

[1] L. Bergstrom, "Interpersonal Utility Comparisons," read at a conference in Vienna, 1982, and available from the Department of Philosophy, University of Uppsala, Uppsala, Sweden.

[2] R. B. Brandt, *A Theory of the Good and the Right* (Oxford: Clarendon Press, 1979), chap. 13.

[3] A. Campbell, *The Sense of Well-Being in America* (New York: McGraw-Hill, 1981).

[4] J. M. Freeman, "The Shortsighted Treatment of Myelomeningocele: A Long-Term Case Report," *Pediatrics* 1981 **53**, 311–13.

[5] J. M. Gustafson, "Mongolism, Parental Desires, and the Right to Life," *Perspectives in Biology and Medicine* 1973 **16**, 529–57.

[6] J. Harsanyi, "Morality and the Theory of Rational Behavior," *Social Research* 1977 **44**, 623–56.

[7] J. Lorber, "Results of Treatment of Myelomeningocele," *Developmental Medicine and Child Neurology* 1971 **13**, 279–303.

[8] J. Lorber, "Early Results of Selective Treatment of Spina Bifida Cystica," *British Medical Journal* 1973 **4**, 201–4.

[9] J. Lorber, "Selective Treatment of Myelomeningocele," *Pediatrics* 1974 **53**, 307–8.

[10] A. H. Maslow, *Motivation and Personality*, 2d ed. (New York: Harper & Row, 1970).

[11] Report by a Working Party: vol. I "Ethics of Selective Treatment of Spina Bifida," *The Lancet*, January 11, 1975, 85–8.

[12] P. Singer, *Practical Ethics* (New York: Cambridge University Press, 1979), pp. 136–8.

[13] W. R. Trinkaus, "Decision Making for Newborns," in A. E. Doudera and J. D. Peters, eds., *Legal and Ethical Aspects of Treating Critically and Terminally Ill Patients* (Ann Arbor, Mich.: AUPHA Press, 1982) (AUPHA Press, now Health Administration Press, Washington, D.C.)

[14] U.S. President's Commission for the Study of Ethical Problems in Medicine and Biomedical and Behavioral Research, *Deciding to Forgo Life-Sustaining Treatment* (Washington, D.C.: U.S. Government Printing Office, 1983).

[15] J. Waldner, "The Empirical Meaningfulness of Interpersonal Utility Comparisons," *Journal of Philosophy* 1972 **69**, 87–103.

19

Utilitarianism and welfare legislation

Utilitarianism is a theory about what people morally ought to do and, hence, is at least indirectly about which laws and institutions (since people can affect them) are morally acceptable. I wish to focus on the implications of this theory for legislation on income distribution, primarily with respect to legislation to improve the lot of the economically deprived segments of society.

It may seem quixotic to suppose that reflection on utilitarianism can throw any light on how to resolve the baffling practical dilemmas that legislators and administrators face in trying to devise welfare programs to meet diverse and seemingly conflicting objectives. But there is some theoretical interest in seeing how tax-welfare legislation fits into a utilitarian philosophy of government and society. And taking a broad view could have the practical effect of suggesting options that otherwise would not have been thought of, or of making the dilemmas seem less serious by placing them in perspective.

WHAT IS UTILITARIANISM?

The heart of utilitarianism has been its thesis about which acts are morally right: that the moral rightness of actions is fixed, somehow or other, by optimality of consequences. It has also been a theory about the conditions under which institutions are morally acceptable: Epicurus considered a law just if and only if it is a beneficial law; Jeremy Bentham made optimal consequences the standard for an acceptable system of criminal justice; and recent proposals of the American Law Institute are, similarly, very utilitarian in spirit. (The utilitarian need not say that an institution is morally unacceptable just because it is short of optimal; but he must say that it is morally unacceptable if, by utilitarian standards, it can be improved and if there is an unsatisfied moral obligation on those who can improve it to do so.)

Utilitarianism as a theory of right *action* – which seems to have appeared first in the work of Richard Cumberland around 1672 – must be divided into two types. Some utilitarians, now called "act-utilitarians," think an act is right only if its net actual benefit or its expectable benefit,[1] is as great as that of any other act the agent might perform. Other, historically earlier utilitarians, now called "rule-utilitarians," have argued that an act is right roughly if and only if it is of a kind that would have the best or best expectable consequences for a moral code to permit. For instance, rule-utilitarians think that is right to keep a certain kind of promise, even when it does more harm than good in the case at hand, because that would be required by the moral code it would have best consequences to have in force in the society. Some utilitarians saw the Ten Commandments or the requirements of conscience in this light, as laws laid down by God because he wanted the happiness of mankind and saw that promulgation of these laws would best achieve it.

But what is to count as the "benefit" or "good" that is to be maximized? Utilitarians disagree on this point. Until the present century, there was virtual unanimity among utilitarians that only one kind of consequence is a benefit or good in itself (further consequences aside), and that is happiness, enjoyment, or an experience that makes the subject want to continue or repeat it, for itself, at the time. There is frequent complaint that this conception of "good" or "benefit" is much too narrow; but many experiences are enjoyable in the stated sense – not only eating and sex, but running, playing chess, reading books, and solving problems. What do utilitarians who object to the happiness conception want to add? Some of them, occasionally called "ideal utilitarians," want to count as goods to be maximized just for themselves such benefits as knowledge, good character, and the distribution of happiness according to merit. One trouble with this is that each person must determine by his or her own intuition how much pleasure is just as good as how much knowledge or virtue. It has been seriously debated whether the benefits in enjoyment (etc.) that might result from successfully bribing a guard in a war-time prison camp could equal the loss in debasing the character of the guard by exposing him to temptation. In contrast, the happiness theory asserts that only one sort of thing is to be maximized, so that determining which course of action is optimal becomes a purely factual question, however great the problems of measurement and interpersonal comparisons may be. There is also the currently popular *desire* or *preference* theory which holds that some state of affairs is a good, or a benefit, in itself, just to the extent that someone *wants* it to obtain. This theory permits many things to be intrinsically good – pleasure, knowledge, art galleries, social and economic equality – but only in that someone wants them. Sometimes

1 The expectable net benefit is the sum of products of the utility of each consequence multiplied by its probability if the act is performed.

the following qualification is added: Something is good in itself only if somebody *would* want it to obtain *if* he had full information, clearly in mind, on what it would be like for that state of affairs to obtain. As with the happiness theory, this theory avoids reliance on intuitions and makes the determination of the optimal course of action a factual matter because, although there are serious problems in measuring and comparing intensity of desire, it is supposed that observation will determine the course of action that will maximize desire satisfaction.

The happiness and the desire theories are not very far apart, since human psychology is such that we tend to want the recurrence of conditions we have enjoyed in the past, but they do differ to some extent. For simplicity I shall view the dispute as an in-house controversy, and view both as possible forms of utilitarian theory. I happen to prefer the currently unpopular happiness theory, and I shall think in terms of that theory rather than the desire or "ideal utilitarian" theory. For our purposes it makes little difference if I do that.

To understand utilitarianism as a general theory, it is important to identify the competing theories it denies. When we look at these theories we begin to see that different general theories may well have different implications for tax-welfare legislation.

A feature the competing theories have in common is that they assume there are factors, other than consequences for good or ill, that are relevant to the moral rightness of an action or institution. Some influential philosophers have thought that promises ought to be kept, the truth told, injuries recompensed by the responsible party, generous deeds gratefully recognized in some manner, and moral worth rewarded by a corresponding degree of happiness (by God if not by man), for no further reason whatsoever – and especially not because it would maximize welfare if these rules were followed. This view strikes a responsive chord in many people who think these things simply should be done, and do not think good consequences are the reason. More important for our interests are some similar principles that have been asserted with respect to property and income. John Locke, for instance, asserted that "every man has a 'property' in his own 'person.' This nobody has any right to but himself. The 'labor' of his body and the 'work' of his hands, we may say, are properly his. Whatsoever, then, he removes out of the state that Nature hath provided and left it in, he hath mixed his labor with it, and joined to it something that is his own, and thereby makes it his property . . . at least where there is enough, and as good left in common for others."[2] The exegesis and conceptual background of this affirmation are doubtless

2 *Two Treatises of Government*, first published 1690. Second treatise, chap. 5, sect. 26.

controversial, but it seems clear that Locke says one has an absolute right over one's own body (except that one may not contravene the natural law which, for example, prohibits suicide) and over one's labor. Probably he thought that if one invents something, one is free to keep it for one's self, regardless of how important it is to others that it be shared. This conception is doubtless widely held. Would the utilitarian agree with such an absolute moral right? He might, depending on his appraisal of the benefits of having such a rule in force. But he might not.

Another principle that reputable persons, including William Frankena and Nicholas Rescher, find persuasive is a requirement – distinct from *maximizing* welfare – to ensure some *equality* of welfare. In similar vein, A. K. Sen has criticized utilitarianism because that theory, as he sees it, provides that handicapped persons should receive less income than the normal person because income to a handicapped person will buy less happiness than it will for the normal person. Sen's intuitions are that a person who is handicapped at least should not be disadvantaged in income.[3]

Still others think that an industrious person's money income should be greater in order to reward his greater effort or industry (loafers should have less than those who work). Others have thought that superior talent or skill should have an economic reward (so the more intelligent should be more highly paid – if not college professors, at least intelligent persons in industry). Or some may think that a person's income should be greater if his output or contribution is greater for whatever reason; thus the rapid typist obviously deserves more income than the slowpoke. Most of these principles are not just darlings of philosophers but enjoy wide acceptance among people generally.

This is not the place to assess the merits of these alternative principles, although when we spell them out in detail and inquire exactly how they should be applied, it appears that there are problems for all of them, and the claim that these are obviously acceptable principles loses its appeal. The purpose of introducing these principles here is to illustrate what utilitarianism rejects as *basic* principles. Introducing them also serves to make clear the standing these principles can have as secondary rules in a utilitarian conception of the ideal social and economic order. We should emphasize that the utilitarian can accept these principles either as ones that should usually be followed or as principles that should be incorporated into the moral or legal code without qualification, since welfare would be maximized if they were. However this may be, if we accept utilitarianism as the *basic* theory from which these secondary principles

3 A. K. Sen, *On Economic Inequality*, 1973.

can be derived, a major consequence follows: If one should question precisely how one of these rules is to be formulated or what its relative *weight* will be, the utilitarian has at hand a procedure that will provide an answer. The procedure is to determine exactly which principle or priority schedule would maximize social welfare, and then adopt that principle or priority schedule. Not that doing this is an easy matter, but at least the principle is clear: The rule and its relative force are fixed by the prospective benefits for all, provided the rule is recognized or in force.

This feature of utilitarianism is of special interest to some persons concerned with welfare legislation, because in their view, certain principles of "vertical" and "horizontal" equity are at least as weighty as are the principles mentioned above, in devising an acceptable welfare system. That is, it is felt that persons with the same need should receive the same degree of relief (horizontal equity), and that a person initially worse off should not receive so much relief that he is better off than the person who receives little or no help because he has a job and is working (vertical equity). These equity principles express intuitive moral preferences on the part of those concerned with welfare legislation.

But while both principles seem plausible, each has its drawback. With the first, it is complexity (should welfare allocations vary with the cost of living in different areas of the country, or in rural versus urban areas?). The drawback of the second is cost (to provide adequate help at the lower level while preserving vertical equity would require considerably increased payments at the upper levels, where it may not really be needed, and it would conflict with the principle of horizontal equity). I shall return later to this and related problems of conflicting priorities for the welfare system.

However, it is clear at once that, in principle, the utilitarian theory gives advice on how the weight of these principles is to be assessed. The first step is to inquire into the utility gain (and utility cost) of incorporating each of these principles into the system, *or* some specific compromise between them.[4] When that has been done, and we have estimates of the relative optimality of various systems, in terms of their probable degree of utility, we must ask a second question: whether some of these systems are morally required or are morally unacceptable. From the utilitarian point of view, this question is whether utility would be maximized by introducing and keeping in place a *moral* code that permitted, required,

---

4 Variations in the degree to which these principles are incorporated into the system will have an impact on other objectives, such as administrative simplicity and maintenance of work incentives; thus the total impact of possible systems on the general utility will require comparing all these associated costs and benefits, but the procedure is at least clear in principle and does not rely on subjective intuitions about moral principles.

or prohibited some particular action on the part of persons in a position to influence the welfare system. Answering this second question is again not a simple matter, but it seems very unlikely that the *optimal* (utility-maximizing) welfare system would turn out to be morally objectionable, although it is just possible that the optimal moral code would place such weight on equity that the utility-maximizing *moral code* might not favor a *welfare system* that promised to be utility-maximizing. This sounds complicated, but so are the problems. At a later stage I shall suggest that these matters are in fact not overwhelmingly complex.

UTILITARIANISM AND RIGHTS

If utilitarianism is the thesis that maximally beneficial consequences are what directly or indirectly determine what conduct is morally right and what institutions are morally justified, one might still ask whether it is a thesis about moral *rights*, and if so, what the thesis is. This should be of interest to persons concerned about tax-welfare programs, since many people (and articles 22–27 of the United Nations *Universal Declaration of Human Rights*) affirm that all adults have a right to economic security, to equal pay for equal work, to remuneration sufficient to provide an existence worthy of human dignity, including a standard of living adequate to provide food, clothing, housing, and medical care, and so on.

The first thing to notice is that utilitarianism is not a metaethical theory about what it *is* for a person to have a right (what the term "moral right" means or should mean in clarified discourse); it is a normative theory about *which* rights people have. Utilitarians often say nothing at all about what it is to have a right; they take the concept of a "right" as something agreed on or argued over among philosophers whether or not they are utilitarians. The normative thesis of utilitarianism on rights is that the moral rights people have are roughly the ones whose incorporation into the moral code is maximally beneficial to society.

To see the relationship between the utilitarian thesis about rights and their general thesis, it is necessary to consider some metaethical theory about what it is to have a right. What I propose to do is outline the view of rights proposed by J. S. Mill in *Utilitarianism* – not exactly, but only roughly, since he confused some things, such as the concept of justice with the concept of a right. As modified, I think his view is substantially correct.

Consider the claim that X has a right to Y (for example, to *do* something, enjoy something, be protected in having something). Mill does not mean that X has a right to Y merely because it would be *nice* or *beneficial* for X to do Y or enjoy Y. Rather, it is his view (widely held) that what it is for X to have a right to Y is for some person or persons to be *morally bound* or *obligated* not to interfere with his doing Y, but rather to make it possible for him to enjoy Y or be secure in having Y. One person's right thus coincides with a moral obligation on the part of others. And for Mill, what makes a person *morally bound* to do something is that this action is *required* in the sense that it is morally justified that he be punished either by law or by public opinion, or, at least, by his conscience, if the action is not forthcoming. But this is not yet quite enough to establish a moral right, because people can sometimes be morally obligated to do something when there is no corresponding right. For example, a contribution to charity may be a moral obligation, but a potential recipient may not have a right to it – if the donor's obligation is only to do *something* charitable. When a person has a right, there is a moral obligation to do something specifically for *him*. So, for X to have a moral right to Y is for other people to be morally bound to do, or refrain from doing, something specifically for X. But, according to Mill, we do not say that a person has a right to something unless that person will be hurt or deprived – in an important way[5] – if the corresponding obligatory behavior is not forthcoming.[6] So Mill says that "rights" (or he should say this – in fact he says "justice") concern "certain classes of moral rules, which concern the essentials of human well-being more nearly, and are therefore of more absolute obligation, than any other rule for the guidance of life." To which he adds: "To have a right, then, is, I conceive, to have something which society[7] ought to defend me in possession of. If the objector goes on to ask, why it ought? I can give him no other reason than general utility." The last words of this sentence, of course, express his utilitarianism.

One might add or subtract a bit. One might suggest as an addition that when a person has a right, he essentially has the capacity to waive it (and hence to that degree can *control* how others treat him). That is, the right-

5 The requirement of importance may hold for all rights in society, civil or political; it is not so obvious that there are *no* rights which concern fairly trivial matters (for example, the right of the child to equal treatment from his parents) in some particular.
6 Suppose A has contracted with B to provide care for C, an elderly relative of B. Then we say that B has a right against A, that C be cared for. But, it might be asked, if C is the person who is harmed or deprived if the care is not forthcoming, ought we not to say that C is the right-holder? The correct answer for Mill to make, it would seem, is that B must be construed to be harmed by the failure to care for C; if it were not important to B that C be cared for, presumably he would not have paid A to provide care for C.
7 In some cases (such as the rights of a child in the family), there seem to be rights with which society should not concern itself, at least in the sense of providing legal protection. Perhaps Mill meant that society should concern itself with them only in seeing to it that sanctions are provided by public opinion or by conscience.

holder has the power to release others from the obligation toward him that they otherwise would have. (This addition might be contested for some rights on the ground, say, that another's duty not to take away the life – at least where that would be an injury – of a person cannot be nullified by the person's consent to his doing so.) Or, one might add that whenever X has a right to Y, he need not feel embarrassed or ashamed about making a claim to Y in his own behalf.

If this account of a "right" is substantially correct, then we shall have to admit that X's right to Y may sometimes conflict with Z's to W, and hence we must make another distinction. We can avoid admitting the possibility of such a clash by saying that there is only one right – a very abstract right, to whatever the justified system of morality or law would secure one. Once we mention more specific rights, though, we are in for conflict, because the right to a certain level of economic welfare may well conflict with the right to procreate – at least the U. N. *Declaration* speaks of such a right. Or one person's right to privacy may conflict with another person's right to get evidence helpful to him in a criminal trial. Then how can a person have a right in the sense explained, when it is incompatible with a conflicting right another person has? Most philosophers get around the difficulty by holding that most, or even all, rights are *prima facie* in the sense that they must sometimes give way to some more urgent moral claim or right. One could say that a person's right is absolute only in the specific situation where his right is *paramount*. Thus, when we say that a person has a right to freedom of speech, we ought not to claim that free speech must be secured to him unconditionally. What we may seriously claim is that securing it to him is a very high priority, but that there can be morally more weighty considerations that sometimes stand in the way. To have a right to Y is to enjoy very high moral priority on being secured in Y, but not necessarily to hold the highest priority in all situations. Mill did not make this distinction.

There are many such rights that society cannot sustain unconditionally. But what happens if a society cannot sustain a certain purported right at all? The U. N. *Declaration* says a person has a right "to a standard of living adequate for the health and well-being of himself and of his family, including food, clothing, housing, and medical care and necessary social services, and the right to security in the event of unemployment, . . . old age," and so on.

But what about India, which may be simply unable to provide these things, even with indefinite sacrifice on the part of the better-off? Then, if we agree with Kant that "ought" implies "can," where something is impossible it is not morally obligatory; and if it is not morally obligatory, then by our conception there is no right. This thinking may lead us to conclude that the U. N. *Declaration* was a bit profligate in its list of rights. But should we think this way? Maybe what is a right is not a matter of what the individual's own government can provide. Perhaps it is enough if a world government could provide it. Of course, there isn't a world government. So perhaps what is meant is that if all persons were to do what they perfectly well can do – namely, get together in a united effort – then it could be done. It appears that there is vagueness here and that to have a clear concept of "a right" we need to make up our minds what we want to say, what kind of claim we want to make.[8]

The implications of utilitarianism for rights should now be clear, for utilitarianism is a proposal about what people are morally bound to do, and what people are morally bound to do is *logically* tied to what people's rights are. So, for the utilitarian, a person's moral rights are roughly what would be secured for him by the justified moral code (or morally justified law) of his country (or the world, or whatever); and what is to be secured for him is fixed by the probable social benefits of getting and keeping that moral and legal code in place.

WELFARE RIGHTS, TAX RATES, AND UTILITARIANISM

One might suppose that on grounds of maximizing utility, a utilitarian would straightaway advocate a moral system requiring income transfers from the rich to the poor to the point where the marginal utility of the income of everyone would be the same, and that such transfers would be the *right,* or at least the *prima facie* right, of the less well off. Historically this has certainly not been the case – and, as we shall see, for good reason.

Mill took some steps in the direction of what might seem the thoroughgoing utilitarian stance, for he thought taxes should be levied on the principle of "least sacrifice."[9] Nevertheless, although he conceded that the marginal utility of income continues to decline no matter how large that income, he could not bring himself to support a graduated tax rate, since the marginal utility of income is not "capable of being decided with the degree of certainty on which a legislator or a financier ought to act."[10] Moreover, seeming to backslide to a nonutilitarian principle, he says that "to tax the larger incomes at a higher percentage than the smaller is to lay a tax on industry and economy; to impose a penalty on people for having worked harder and saved more than their neighbors."[11] He

8 The last five sentences of the above paragraph arose out of conversation with Allan Gibbard.
9 J. S. Mill, *Principles of Political Economy,* 1848, p. 807.
10 Ibid.
11 Ibid., p. 808.

agreed that some disparities of income derive from unequal initial opportunities, but thought that if the government does what it can to eliminate these, no one can take offense at large differences in earnings. (He did, however, favor steep inheritance taxes, since the beneficiary has not earned his advantage.) Mill's utilitarian concession to the declining marginal utility of income was to advocate a personal exemption from taxation, but a small one: "sufficient to provide the number of persons ordinarily supported from a single income with the requisites of life and health, and with protection against habitual bodily suffering, but not with any indulgence." Doubtless he would have approved the present exemption in the U. S. tax plan. As for actual welfare grants for the unemployed or unemployable, although Mill *wrote*[12] that "Since no one is responsible for having been born [hardly a utilitarian consideration!], no pecuniary sacrifice is too great to be made by those who have more than enough, for the purpose of securing enough to all persons already in existence," nevertheless he thought that such grants should be made unpleasant, lest there be a disastrous increase in the birthrate among the poor, with a consequent over-supply of labor and further reduction of wage rates. Indeed, Mill did not object to confining the poor to workhouses, where indeed he thought all sexual activity should be prohibited on the ground that it would only breed more paupers. Mill's view of population growth and the relation of wage rates to population size led him to think that grants to the poor, except when made unpleasant to the recipient, would in the long run do more harm than good. Mill evidently would have said that the poor have a right only to be kept uncomfortably alive, although free from pain. Henry Sidgwick, the most careful and systematic of the utilitarians, writing a quarter-century later, was not very different.[13]

Mill and Sidgwick read as if they are in the distant past, in an era with no labor unions and with a rather simple-minded economic theory, before the lesson of the 1930s that unemployment is not a function merely of lack of industry, and before a time when people began to live with a graduated income tax and became convinced it was at least a necessary evil. If we move them into the present, keeping their basic assumption that morality, law, and economic and political institutions are to be tested by their contribution to welfare, where will they come out?

The first question I want to raise is what level of income support, for the working poor, the unemployable, and the involuntarily unemployed, can be said to be a moral *right, prima facie* or otherwise? Mill and Sidgwick evidently set this level very low, Sidgwick wanting government to mitigate

12 Ibid., p. 363.
13 Henry Sidgwick, *Principles of Political Economy*, 1883; *The Elements of Politics*, 1891. Both books had later editions.

"the harshest inequalities in the present distribution of incomes,"[14] but evidently not to do more. What level of income, then, from a consistent utilitarian point of view, is a moral right at present?

It is convenient to make the simplifying assumption that there soon will no longer be serious dispute that this country should have universal medical service. Such service will incidentally remove one of the most inequitable "notch"[15] problems of the present welfare system. So, medical care aside, what about level of income?

It is widely agreed among economists that – *other things being equal,* which they are not – the most efficient (utility-productive) division of the national income would be one that made the marginal utility of all incomes equal. Equality of marginal utility is hardly an identifiable target, however, in view of the general unreliability of our comparative judgments about the utility curves of individuals. But it was shown some years ago by A. P. Lerner and others that, given *ignorance* of individual utility curves, the most utility-productive way to distribute money income is *probably* to distribute it equally, again *other things being equal.*

But other things are not equal: A system providing exactly equal money incomes would be counterproductive, not only because there are *some* persons (such as the ill and the handicapped) about whom we know (that much is known about some utility curves) that a more than equal income is required to bring their marginal utility up to that of the normal person, but also because, more important, we know that inequality of income is necessary both to provide work incentives and to channel the supply of labor into the places where it is needed.

The utilitarian thus has a complicated question for the economist, which he will want answered so a decision can be made about which income-welfare system is optimal. The question for an ideally omniscient economist is how income would be distributed in the total population on the basis of various tax and welfare schemes, or, more broadly if you like, on the basis of economic systems including tax and welfare schemes (with different proportions of total national income allocated for the welfare system, with different degrees of progressivity, different exemptions, different schemes of welfare allocation, and, especially, different levels of tax credits combined with work requirements). If the answer is provided, the utilitarian will then try to estimate what level of total social welfare would go along with these various schemes, given that he has been told how many will get how much, for each scheme. In making this judgment of welfare, he will be helped by information about the cost of

14 *Elements of Politics,* p. 160.
15 This is the problem of vertical equity; see below.

a modest but adequate diet (some clue to which is given by how much the average person spends on food), since the disutility of inadequate nutrition is so manifest that an income that secures a reasonable diet will be deemed the bread, which is more important than a great deal of cake for the better off. Having identified the scheme that will produce the greatest social welfare, he can declare that that scheme of distribution – with its proposals for the shares of the jobless, the handicapped, the unskilled worker, and so on – is, on the evidence, *optimal.*[16]

Is anything less than the optimal system of distribution *morally unacceptable?* To show that it is, the utilitarian must show that the utility-maximizing moral code would *require* the expectable-welfare-maximizing distribution system. One might ask whether an optimal moral code would contain *any* requirement about the *distribution* of goods. Obviously our actual moral code does, since it contains injunctions about treating members of one's family equally, and it contains (I think) an injunction that one relieve the distress of others when this can be done at little cost to one's self. I think myself that an optimal moral code would contain a general injunction to do what one can to bring about an optimal distribution,[17] but this could be debated. Let us assume, for the moment, that an optimal moral code would require effort to approximate to an optimal system of distribution of economic goods.

The question still remains whether everyone has a *moral right* to the share he would get according to the optimal scheme of distribution. For an answer, we can look back to the conception of a "moral right" that I sketched roughly along the lines of Mill's view. According to that theory, if we have shown that it is *morally required* to secure something for a person in a given society, we have already taken the first step in showing that the individual has a moral right to that thing. The second condition is that there must be an obligation to do something specific for a specific person. This second condition is obviously also met, since the welfare-maximizing system would identify all those individuals in a class to whom a certain income is due, and every one of them should be secured in it. So each specific person is identified, as a proper target for the distribution.

The third condition is that the recipient will be "hurt" or "deprived" if the donor has not done for him what ought to be done. Here again the condition appears to be met, for I suppose any loss of income – except to an already wealthy person – beyond what he might otherwise have had would count as a "deprivation." Finally, would the deprivation be

16 I have discussed how such estimates may be made more fully in *A Theory of the Good and the Right,* 1979, chap. 16.
17 I have argued for this in the chapter referred to in the previous footnote.

"important"? Or is it something one should not feel ashamed about making a claim to? Here the answer seems to be: It depends on the disparity between the ideal and what one is actually getting, and how poorly off one is. We can probably agree that how much income one gets, at the bottom end, is pretty important. So it looks as if, given that the optimal distribution of income is morally required, we should opt for the view that the income one would get by application of the optimal system is at least normally one's moral right.

Is such an income a right, everything considered, or only a *prima facie* right? There is no reason why it should not be said to be only *prima facie*, since to say this is only to say that it must stand aside if more morally urgent considerations require it. I have already suggested that following the economically optimal plan might not be morally required, all things considered, in view of possible unfavorable effects of the system on freedom. If there were an atomic war, it is believable that the right to the optimal distribution must stand aside. It is conceivable that there might be some conflict between this right and the means necessary to end racial discrimination. And so on. So let us conclude that the right to a utility-maximizing level of income is *prima facie* only.

UTILITARIANISM AND SOME DETAILS

At the outset I expressed some doubt whether reflection on utilitarianism would throw much light on the practical problems that baffle persons working on welfare legislation. But a clear, simple, conceptual framework like the utilitarian theory will have definite implications for these matters if any moral theory at all will do so. So let us look at some implications, encouraged by the thought that it is at least in the tradition of Plato for philosophers to make proposals about how practical affairs should be managed.

We shall use three simplifying assumptions as a framework within which to conduct our thinking. I shall not attempt to justify them (and the required justification would be different in each case), but I believe readers will be willing to grant them. The first is that we should think in terms of some program of universal medical service, since this would enable us to avoid some problems about who is to be entitled to "medicaid" and at what cost. Second, we must think in terms of a tax system in which "loopholes" have been removed. We do have a concept of income that is disposable for living, as distinct from expenses involved in obtaining that income. Deductions might be limited to legitimate business expenses, court-ordered child support, alimony, perhaps uninsured loss such as from fire or theft, and perhaps, in the public interest, charitable contributions. Third, I am supposing that somehow we can manage not to think about more than one tax-welfare system, specifically not about state-local taxes and welfare grants. I am supposing that, at least for our purposes, all this can be amalgamated.

There is also a further assumption, of a somewhat different kind, that we could make: Unless and until more scientific evidence to the contrary arrives, there is no reason grounded in utility for the tax-welfare system to treat males and females differently. Sex alone is not a reason for different treatment. If jobs outside the home are psychologically desirable for men, they are equally so for women; if a single male parent is expected, on grounds of public and personal benefit, to work as a condition for obtaining welfare assistance, a single female parent should equally be expected to work. It is conceivable that there are some physiological or psychological differences that make it utility-productive to treat the sexes differently, but as of the present no important differences are known (except that men cannot qualify for a pregnancy leave-of-absence). A tendency toward aggressiveness and superior ability at spatial visualization seem to be sex-linked, but these features are hardly relevant to the construction of a tax-welfare system.

Within the framework of these assumptions, what would be the main features of a tax-welfare system on which a utilitarian would insist?

(1) The first thing is a guaranteed job for every adult who wants to work and will perform diligently in it. (If this is economically infeasible, at least a guaranteed job for everyone who would otherwise qualify for welfare payments.) To each job, of course, will be attached the income the market provides, with whatever minimum wage restriction the optimal economic system (discussed above) would call for. It seems clear that in normal times a program of guaranteed jobs will involve some government-provided or government-subsidized jobs, and it is also clear that, in order to motivate persons to move to the private sector when possible, these jobs must pay less than the minimum wage in the private sector. A related desideratum is that, since it will optimize performance to have the best qualified persons in the more demanding jobs, discrimination of all sorts – and especially on the basis of race, age, and sex – should be removed from the labor market (and the unions), and information and assistance should be given to facilitate placing persons in jobs where they can be used most effectively. Furthermore, there should be a training program available, so that all individuals can be prepared to perform useful work.

(2) Before discussing the reasons for this requirement, let us look at its complement: a requirement that all able-bodied adults be *required* to work as a condition of receiving more than a subsistence income from welfare programs. Then the total income of members of an economic unit

could be considered in reckoning whether, and how much, welfare assistance the economic unit is entitled to.[18]

There are several reasons for these proposals. The first is the extreme importance of a job for the psychological health and optimal development of every man and woman. We may concede that some jobs do not contribute much to psychological health or development, and one aim should be to make all jobs as meaningful (that is, as challenging and interesting) as possible. It may be said that this is a good reason for making jobs available but not for making them a condition of qualifying for maximum support in a welfare program. It is true that there is a certain element of paternalism in the work requirement, in the thought that whereas a person might not take a job if he didn't need it for the income, he'd be better off if he did and later be glad that he had. But there is another reason, sufficient by itself: We cannot afford to provide modestly good incomes for the underprivileged without a work requirement (there are, probably, just too many who would elect to go fishing). The nation is economically able to provide a merely subsistence income for all who are prepared to live on that income in return for the privilege of leisure.

(3) Over and above the job program there should be provision for a subsistence level of support for persons able, but unwilling, to work; and for those who meet the work requirement or those who are unable to do so for reasons of health, disability, or age, there would be a supplemental assistance program, up to the level of the "optimal" income-distribution system discussed above. Such a program could be administered by the Internal Revenue Service through a negative income tax. The program would require some changes from the present arrangements, because, for instance, these supplemental assistance payments presumably would be made at least once a month, with only a final settlement at the end of the year. There would also have to be some job insurance program to provide temporary relief for unemployment. The negative income "tax" schedule would be so set as to make up the difference between the total work income of an economic unit and the level set by the optimal income system, whatever that might be. (The system, we should note, would

18 Given this requirement, the question of child care arises. One possible solution is to make child care universally available, like medical service. This solution appears to be the only one which fully avoids problems of "vertical equity" (see below). Another possibility is that, if the government is prepared to pay a certain per-child sum for care (for, say, forty hours per week), this sum might be paid to any parent who prefers to provide care for his or her own children in place of taking a full-time job. On the other hand, having children is a consumer good, and an expensive one for somebody, and hence the parents should be prepared to shoulder part of the cost of child care in return for the benefits. (If they do not think there are benefits, they do not need to have the children.) Nor should they expect welfare support for an indefinite number of children (see below).

provide work or assistance for single persons and childless married couples.) In this program, food stamps would disappear.

Since the above payments have to be covered by someone, income tax rates would go up, beginning at the point at which, on the optimal system, assistance payments would cease. But they would not go up in such a way as to remove incentive for performing well in one's job, for preparing one's self to move into more demanding jobs, or for moving into jobs where consumer demand calls for more personnel. We can hardly keep higher tax rates from having some effect on incentive – our present tax system already removes some incentive – but the tax would not remove incentives to a serious degree.

Let us look now at two problems of "equity" which currently concern persons working in the welfare program.

Horizontal equity

We have seen that a utilitarian is not concerned with matters of fairness or equity, as such, including horizontal equity in the sense of functionally equal support for similar situations. But he is interested in what comes to the same thing under a different description, in welfare-maximizing regulations, or "best buys." Thus he will advocate, as far as feasible, local variations in supplemental assistance payments based on the relative cost-of-living figures: Otherwise persons in low-cost communities will be funded for luxuries (less preferred items) that persons in high-cost communities cannot afford, so that the real benefit from the total expenditure would be less than it would otherwise be. (It might be argued, however, that it is a consumer good to live in a high-cost community, and that a system of equal payments leaves the individual the option of moving to a low-cost community if his preferences are to spend his income for other things than living in a certain place. Whether local variations in supplemental assistance payments will really optimize welfare, especially when administrative complexities are taken into account, is a matter for further research.)

Again, the utilitarian will advocate larger payments to the blind and handicapped, on the ground that enough is known of their utility curves (as compared with those of the average person) to make clear that an additional sum is needed for the marginal utility of their incomes to be equal to that of the average person receiving supplemental assistance. Further, the utilitarian will urge that payments be adjusted for the composition of the economic unit: say, a sizable basic amount for up to two adults in the unit; a smaller sum for other adults in the same unit (but not so small as to make it worth their while to move into a separate unit);

smaller sums for children, perhaps along the line of the Griffiths plan, declining after two (in the hope of discouraging persons from enlarging the family just to increase welfare payments – a practice that brings essentially unwanted children into the world). Obviously money is more efficiently expended in this way. If payments to economic units were equal, small families would be able to buy more luxury items whereas larger families would have to forgo necessities.

Vertical equity

The principle of vertical equity that appeals to persons concerned with welfare legislation is that welfare payments should not put a welfare family financially ahead of a nonwelfare family, and that they should not "unduly compress" the initial distance between the units. We need not here consider whether a utilitarian could or should support some utilitarian analogue of the principle of vertical equity, because, apparently, the principle can in any case not be infringed by the utilitarian system of tax-welfare described so far.

There are three main points at which the principle is infringed under the present system. First, a family that barely qualifies for welfare support receives full rights to Medicaid, whereas a family that barely fails to qualify receives no Medicaid at all. Second, a family that barely qualifies receives child-care assistance, where one that barely fails to qualify does not. Finally, the schedule of assistance for those who qualify for welfare payments may place them financially ahead of those who wholly depend on wage income and barely do not qualify for welfare support. It is obvious that with a plan for universal medical service and for universal child care (or a system approximating this), the first two inequities would not occur. Moreover, a work requirement would eliminate the third inequity; if a person does not work he will receive only a subsistence allotment, that will surely not place him ahead of those who do work. There will, of course, remain many inequalities; some people will be in interesting, high-paying jobs, for one reason or another. A utilitarian system will in effect reduce such disparities because of the high taxes on those who are well paid, but the utilitarian is not aiming to remove all inequalities in life. Perhaps he should; but if he should, then utilitarianism is to that extent a defective theory. The utilitarian will probably offer a practical defense of his position, against those sensitive to natural inequalities and other inequalities that arise out of them, by arguing that there is only so much a system of tax-welfare can be expected to do.

The principal question raised against such a system as I have sketched is whether it is not hopelessly expensive. The answer is no, since the welfare level at which negative income tax would begin is to be set at a point where the cost is not impossible. It is true that people in the upper income, even middle income, brackets would pay more taxes than they now do. They would not, however, pay so much tax that incentives would be significantly reduced. The level, as explained earlier, would be set at an optimal point, where the production of goods and services, taken with the distribution system, would leave total social *welfare* at a maximum. Those in higher income brackets may not rejoice at the prospect of higher taxes, but there are surely many who would happily give up something for the knowledge that no one in their society was in serious need. There is a question whether the provision of jobs on the scale suggested above is possible without significant changes in the economic organization of society; to the best of my knowledge, no one has yet proved that the provision of jobs would entail a revamped economy.

Changes in the welfare-support system in the United States in the past ten years, and the bills that have recently been presented to the Congress, suggest that the U.S. welfare system is moving slowly but steadily in the direction of the simple conception outlined above, although the system is certainly not there yet. The welfare support available varies greatly from one state to another; there is a complex system of different federal programs (Food Stamps, Medicaid, supplemental assistance to the disabled, etc.); there is a job program and the aim of encouraging work by training programs and by the schedule of welfare payments, but no work requirement; there are vertical inequities; and so on.

Is there anything the utilitarian can say about desirable changes in the system, and particularly about the assignment of priorities to the various objectives? He can say several things, although all of them are simply applications of the principle that the system should be changed in such a way as to maximize expectable welfare. The first is to increase the level of welfare benefits; welfare will be improved if the gap between the better off and the worse off is narrowed – and if this can be done without seriously disturbing incentives. Eligibility for assistance should be extended to all those who are willing to work but cannot find a job. It would be an obvious benefit to amalgamate state and federal programs and make the system uniform; but it is not obvious how to do so. It is not clear how to avoid the cost in utility of vertical inequities in the present system, which attempts to combine adequate support levels, incentive to work (by permitting supported individuals to keep most of their earnings even when so doing brings them above the poverty line), and no universal medical service. The cost is not vast, and the utilitarian will not worry about the inequity per se. But the problem is a good reason to change to a different system that does not have the problems.

Index

389